THE
BRITISH SUB AQUA CLUB
DIVING MANUAL

*A Comprehensive Guide
to the Techniques of
Underwater Swimming*

1st Edition 1959	*5th Edition 1966*
2nd Edition 1960	*6th Edition 1968*
2nd Impress 1961	*6th Revised 1970*
3rd Edition 1962	*7th Edition 1972*
4th Edition 1964	*8th Edition 1975*

Printed by Standard Press (Andover) Limited, South Street, Andover, Hants.

The retail price of this book is £3.75   SBN 902988 00 X

CONTENTS

Front Cover Photograph by G. Harwood

7.   Foreword   Alexander Flinder,
                          Chairman, BSAC
9.   Introduction   Leo Zanelli,
                          Editor.
                          National Diving Officer, BSAC

Chapter 1—**TRAINING**
13.   Training   Brian Booth,
       Organisation   *1st Class Diver, National Instructor*
25.   Rescue, Lifesaving G. T. Skuse,
       and Deep Water   *1st Class Diver, National Instructor,*
       E.A.R.   *RLSS/BSAC Liaison Officer*
35.   Artificial Respiration   Dr. M. Davis
45.   First Aid   G. T. Skuse

Chapter 2—**PSYCHOLOGY OF DIVING**
59.   Adaptation   Dr. Alan D. Baddeley,
                          Medical Research Council
64.   The Mental Attitude   Alan V. Broadhurst,
                          1st Class Diver,
                          Former National Diving Officer

Chapter 3—**PHYSICS**
73.   The Sea   Dr. J. Woods,
                          Scientific Officer, BSAC
84.   Effects of Pressure   M. K. Todd,
                          1st Class Diver, Club Instructor,
                          Regional Diving Coach (London)
87.   Buoyancy   Dr. J. Woods
97.   Vision Underwater Dr. J. N. Lythgoe,
                          MRC Vision Unit, University of
                          Sussex

Chapter 4—**MEDICAL**
107.   Fitness and Medical   Dr. John Betts,
       Certificates   *Medical Adviser, BSAC*
112.   Ears and Sinuses   Sgn. Lt.-Cdr. J. Murray Young,
                          Royal Naval Physiological
                          Laboratory
117.   Respiration and   Sgn. Lt.-Cdr. J. Murray Young
       Anoxia
128.   Exhaustion   Dr. John Betts

3

CONTENTS

131.	Burst Lung and Ascent Hazards	R. L. F. Darby, *1st Class Diver, National Instructor, Regional Diving Coach (Midlands)*
136.	Decompression Sickness	H. Val Hempleman, *Royal Naval Physiological Laboratory*
147.	Carbon Monoxide Poisoning	Leo Zanelli, *1st Class Diver, National Diving Officer, BSAC*
148.	Nitrogen Absorption	George F. Brookes, *1st Class Diver, Hon. Life Member, BSAC*
151.	Nitrogen Narcosis	P. B. Bennett, PhD, BSc, MIBiol, *Royal Naval Physiological Laboratory*
153.	Carbon Dioxide Poisoning	Sgn. Lt.-Cdr. D. H. Elliott, *Royal Naval Physiological Laboratory*
154.	Oxygen Poisoning	J. Bevan, *1st Class Diver, National Instructor, Royal Naval Physiological Laboratory*
162.	Air Analysis	P. Freeland, *Air Analysis Officer, BSAC*

Chapter 5—EQUIPMENT

167.	Basic Equipment	M. K. Todd
169.	Protective Clothing	Dr. John Betts
175.	The Weight Belt	Leo Zanelli
176.	Principles of the Aqualung	R. B. Campbell, *1st Class Diver, Club Instructor, National Equipment Officer BSAC*
189.	Air Cylinders and Recharging	Dr. P. Baker, *1st Class Diver, National Instructor,* and R. B. Campbell
206.	Diving Accessories	G. T. Skuse
219.	Lifejackets	Leo Zanelli
227.	Maintenance of Equipment	F. Lock, *Examining Instructor, BSAC/Scout Association Liaison Officer*

CONTENTS

Chapter 6—TECHNIQUES

233. Snorkel Diving — Kendall McDonald, *Publicity Officer, BSAC*

240. Aqualung Use and Buoyancy Control — R. B. Campbell

Surfacing Drill

249. 1. Ascent Procedure — Leo Zanelli

250. 2. Emergency Ascents — R. Vallintine, *1st Class Diver, National Instructor*

257. Signals — R. M. Bruce

266. Ropes and Roping Methods — Lt.-Cdr. Alan Bax, RN

275. Underwater Navigation — Brian Booth

284. Decompression in Practice — P. Garner, *National Instructor, Instructor National de Escafandrismo*

287. Low Visibility Diving — National Diving Committee

289. Deep Diving — Charles Ellis, *1st Class Diver, Former National Diving Officer*

295. Air Endurance — George F. Brookes

297. Diving Under Ice — Leo Zanelli

299. Night Diving — D. Robertson, *1st Class Diver, National Instructor*

304. Cave Diving — Dr. K. Pearce

310. Spearfishing — Philip T. Smith

Chapter 7—THE OPEN WATER

323. Open Water Diving — George F. Brookes

331. Diving Expeditions — D. M. F. Cockbill, *1st Class Diver, Vice-Chairman, BSAC*

335. Basic Seamanship — Lt.-Cdr. Alan Bax, RN

362. Basic Navigation — Lt.-Cdr. Alan Bax, RN

377. Charts and Tides — Vernon Knapper, *National Instructor*

381. Dive Reports and Log Books — George F. Brookes

385. Scientific Expeditions — Dr. N. C. Flemming

CONTENTS

392.   Exploration   George F. Brookes

398.   Wrecks and Salvage   D. M. F. Cockbill

412.   Safety   Brian Booth

Chapter 8—**UNDERWATER ACTIVITIES**—Edited by Kendall McDonald

423.   Archaeology   Joan du Plat Taylor, *Institute of Archaeology*

427.   Biology   Drs. Norman and Joanna Jones, *Marine Biological Station, I.o.M.*

430.   Geology   Major Hume Wallace, *1st Class Diver*

435.   Photography   Dr. H. E. Dobbs, *1st Class Diver*

Chapter 9—**PUBLIC RELATIONS**

445.   Public Relations and You   Michael Treloar, *1st Class Diver, Former National Diving Officer*

Chapter 10—**BSAC ENDORSEMENTS**

455.   The Sub Aqua Bronze Medallion of the RLSS   G. T. Skuse

460.   The Deep Rescue Test   National Diving Committee

465—**APPENDICES**

   1   BSAC—and how it works

   2   The Divers' Code

   3   Training and Diving Organisation

   4   Baths Discipline

   5   Diving Flags

   6   Weather

   7   Tidal Constants

   8   Recompression Chambers

   9   Distress Signals at Sea

  10   Coastguard Stations

  11   Fish Law

  12   Conversion Tables

  13   Bibliography

  14   Underwater Films

  15   Diving Operations, Special Operations

  16   Beaufort Wind Scale

  17   Decompression Tables

  18   Metrication

  19   BSAC Tests and Qualifications

FOREWORD

Since its birth in 1953 the British Sub Aqua Club has grown to be the largest single Diving Club in the world, with over 450 branches and over fourteen thousand members. It is the recognised governing body for the sport in the United Kingdom and a major member of the International Federation, the Confédération Mondiale des Activités Subaquatiques.

The Club has kept pace with the rapid developments in underwater exploration and research and its members have made significant contributions in these fields. Indeed a high proportion of the leaders in underwater science and technology in Britain, learnt their diving in the BSAC.

At this stage in the Club's expansion, it might be thought that the BSAC has outgrown its original concept and has become remote from the rank and file diver. Nothing could be further from the truth, for the most attractive characteristic of the Club is the strong feeling of comradeship held by its divers in the branches as far afield as Australia and the United States. The Branches are united by a mutual love of diving and above all, by the codes and training principles originally established by the Club in its early days and which have grown to be its backbone. It is these principles which are exemplified in the Diving Manual of the British Sub Aqua Club. The Manual is given to every new member and because of the Club's concern for good and safe diving everywhere, it has been made available to the general public for many years.

The Manual is written by members and close friends of the Club and in it will be found the most up-to-date training procedures and articles from the pens of experts on all aspects of diving and underwater exploration. Thousands of Manuals have been printed in its six editions, and it is the first and most essential item of every diver's equipment. I am sure that this 7th edition in its new layout will prove even more popular and as indispensable as its predecessors.

Alexander Flinder

Chairman, British Sub Aqua Club.

INTRODUCTION

This is a new style Diving Manual; the layout of the contents has been altered and the text has been metricated. Many members will want to know the reasons for these changes, therefore this is more in the nature of an Explanation than an Introduction.

The contents have been compiled using, as a basis, all the lectures comprising the BSAC training programme. To this has been added sections of related interest not included among BSAC lectures. And the whole book sectioned for easy reference.

Metrication was given a great deal of thought. It is a system eminently suitable for diving practice. As an example, one bar (or atmosphere) is virtually equal to 10 metres (or 33 feet). Thus we have a progression in depth, in terms of bars, of 10, 20, and 30 metres instead of the rather unwieldy 33, 66, and 99 feet.

Of greater importance is the fact that eventually everything will be metricated—Admiralty charts being printed have already changed over to the metric system—and a lack of knowledge in this direction could be disastrous for the diver. It was, then, really a question of whether we stumbled along for years, changing gradually and in a constant state of confusion; or virtually immediately, making the change quickly. The latter decision has been taken, and I think in the near future it will be seen that the decision was correct.

However, shortage of time has precluded complete metrication. Some of the Appendices—particularly the ones pertaining to BSAC tests—have retained the old measurements for varying reasons. The next edition will see this completed.

Leo Zanelli,
Editor,
National Diving Officer.

ACKNOWLEDGEMENTS

The British Sub Aqua Club gratefully acknowledges the ready participation of so many specialist authors, named throughout this volume, who have contributed. For this edition, thanks are also due to Hugh Singer, who handled production, and Editor Leo Zanelli.

We also take great pleasure in thanking those concerned with the previous editions, including Oscar Gugen, Club Vice-President and founder Chairman; Colin McLeod, Club Vice-President and founder Vice-Chairman; the late Alan V Broadhurst and George F Brookes who produced the 1960 edition; and A Baverstock, Dr J Beynon, A F Brooker, Dr R C Brookes, P A Browne, M Everard, W F Gannon, the late M Goldsmith, R Goodwin, B G Hewitt, S B Jones, R W Knell, R Larn, B Marshall, R B Matkin, D Moody, J Newby, J R Phoenix, Q Reynolds, L Zanelli, A H Ridout, Miss Annette Atkinson and the following officers of the Royal Navy; Sgn Lt-Cdr Peter Barnard, Sgn Lt-Cdr Rex Gray (RAN), Sgn Cdr Eric Mackay, Sgn Rear Admiral Stanley Miles, Capt A Checksfield RN.

Finally, a special acknowledgement is rightly due to the first Club Diving Officer, Jack Atkinson, upon whose original ideas the Club's training programme is based.

CHAPTER ONE

TRAINING

Training Organisation : Brian Booth

Rescue, Lifesaving and Deep
Water E.A.R. : G T Skuse

Artificial Respiration : Dr M Davis

First Aid : G T Skuse

TRAINING ORGANISATION

For convenience, this section is aimed more at the instructor than at the pupil, but it is designed to give both an insight into what is required for the acquisition of skill in this sport of diving. In this respect, the best standards are the ones that have been well tried, and those of the British Sub Aqua Club are second to none.

The general programme of training in the BSAC consists of a classification system, with members qualifying in Snorkel Diver, 3rd, 2nd and 1st Class Diver categories, and as Instructors.

While it is realised that British waters, with their unfavourable conditions of low visibilities and temperatures and rapid changes of stream, tide and current, make training difficult, it is just these very hazards that call for responsible adherence to the training programme, with a full realisation of its purpose and intention.

Many of the technical aspects of diving training, and most of the preparatory work, can be taught in the comfort of a swimming pool— indeed, it is advisable that they should. The only objection to pool training is that it gives pupils a false sense of security and over confidence. To offset this, diving sense and water safety can be gained by snorkel diving in open water, and one of the aspects of the training programme is the insistence on an apprenticeship in outdoor snorkel diving before a member qualifies for his rating as 3rd Class Diver.

It should be most strongly emphasised that the sole purpose of the tests is to develop knowledge through experience, safety through sound technique. The British Sub Aqua Club is recognised as a leading authority amongst serious underwater clubs and societies the world over, and its strength and reputation depend largely on the maintenance of its uniformly high standards of training.

The maintenance of these standards is the responsibility of the Club Diving Officer, and through him, of branch diving officers and their appointed assistants. Thus branch diving officers rightly hold wide discretionary powers to fail pupils, even though they may technically have passed the necessary tests, if, in the opinion of the branch diving officers, the requisite standards of ability, knowledge and experience have not been attained.

Once the pupil has completed his swimming and primary tests in the training pool, he may commence pool aqualung training, at the same time making every effort to broaden his practical experience by completing his outdoor Snorkel Diving Test. On completion of his pool training he may progress to open water aqualung training, but he is not qualified to dive except under the supervision of a branch instructor. Upon completion of these tests and training he may, at the discretion of his branch diving officer, be rated 3rd Class Diver.

After 20 further open water dives—of which five must be carried out in the open sea—during which the 3rd Class Diver must, under supervision, exercise the various emergency drills he has learned in the training pool, he may, again at the discretion of the branch diving officer, be re-classified as 2nd Class Diver. At this stage he is a fully qualified BSAC diver and is expected to be capable of leading expeditions.

Experience has shown that it requires numerous dives under varying conditions for divers to become thoroughly at home in the water with free diving equipment, and capable of dealing in a cool and calm manner with most emergencies, and of exercising discretion with regard to natural hazards.

The award of the 1st Class Diver's certificate will, therefore, only be made after at least 100 dives have been logged and duly witnessed. The candidate must also pass a written examination set by the Club Diving Officer.

As a member progresses through his training, the dives he does and the tests he passes are entered in his diving logbook, which is thus a reliable and clear indication of his diving proficiency. The member's diving logbook is a valuable document and an essential aid in keeping a universal standard throughout the Club.

In order to keep in 'diving trim' it is recommended that experienced and qualified divers should periodically re-take the training tests. The Club Diving Officer maintains an 'Active List' of 1st Class Divers who have completed at least ten dives under varying conditions during the preceding year.

The Club's aims are to encourage skin diving in all its forms, that is snorkel diving using basic equipment only and free diving with the use of compressed air types of underwater breathing apparatus. Oxygen and helmet diving equipment are considered dangerous and unnecessary for sports diving and, therefore, their use has not been included in the Club's training programme, nor has it been dealt with in this diving manual.

The need for training

It is not particularly difficult for the average person who is physically fit and of reasonable swimming ability to learn to dive, but due to the hazards of the underwater environment it is essential to have competent instruction according to a training programme. It may be possible in some sports to dispense with an instructor and by practice and experiment acquire some degree of proficiency, but this is not so with diving, for a mishap underwater can cost a person his life. Diving training under the close supervision of a competent instructor is therefore, necessary, and not until the novice has achieved a high degree of confidence and efficiency should he be allowed out of easy reach.

There are many aspects of diving which are still unknown quantities and even the most experienced diver may find himself in circumstances from which he must be rescued. It follows that all diving and training must be carried out with the fullest safety precautions and no diver should ever dive alone.

The swimming test

The purpose of the swimming test is to ensure that prospective divers are reasonably competent in the water. The test is not designed to find potential Olympic swimmers, but to establish that a candidate is at home in the water, and to check his ability to tolerate waves and choppy water, his physical fitness, and his resistance to panic. It is most important that the standards set are not too low, otherwise a pupil may be given a false sense of security and be rash when he subsequently uses fins. On the other hand, one must exercise discretion and not fail some obviously competent person on some minor point for the sake of rigidly applying the rules. If a person fails to come up to standard he should not be forgotten; some attempt to improve his swimming ability should be made. It should also not be overlooked that a person whose swimming ability is weak may benefit considerably by a period of practice with basic equipment.

A great deal of information can be obtained from close observation of the initial swimming test and often even at this early stage the experienced instructor can assess whether a person will become an efficient underwater swimmer, although there are always exceptions to the rule.

Instructors requiring further information on swimming tests should refer to the BSAC publication *Diving Officers' Handbook* and Appendix 20 in this manual.

On completion of the swimming test, the prospective diver should undergo the medical examination applicable to diving. If not already completed, the BSAC application and indemnity form should be completed.

Diving theory lectures

In all diving training there should obviously be a period of theoretical instruction before taking a test. Trainees should be briefed on what is ahead of them and it most important that lectures or informal instructional talks be given before they commence basic and aqualung training. Underwater swimming is not an activity that comes naturally, and a certain amount of knowledge and understanding of specialised subjects is required if a person is to take part in it. If a newcomer attempts snorkel diving let alone aqualung diving without instruction, he will not only fail to progress and enjoy the sport, he may also endanger his life.

It is important to gear the subject of the lecture to the requirements of the members concerned and not to 'blind them with science' by giving unessential details. The lecture should be given in layman's language where facts essential to safety and understanding are involved; the more technical and scientific details which may be of help and interest to the more advanced members can be brought in incidentally.

In putting a lecture over, it helps to draw deeply from personal diving experience. In this way the subject is brought to life and details are more easily remembered. The basic principles of teaching are contained in a pamphlet called ' Good Instruction ', which is produced below as follows :

Introduction. Teaching and instructing is a skill, and therefore improves with practise, but only by observance of rules and *constant self-criticism.*

Instructors should ask themselves : ' Could I have put that over better? ' ' Am I distracting the class? ' ' Is there a better way of explaining this? '

Essentials—The 3 ' P's. The 3 ' P's are (1) Planning; (2) Preparation and (3) Presentation.

1   Planning.

a   Be quite clear in your mind what you intend to teach in the lesson period, paying due regard to the time available, the speed of learning of the class, visual aids available, etc.

b   Make a rough plan of the development of the lesson period. Gradually build up logically to the final points to be remembered.

In this, you should have a good idea of when and where you are going to use visual aids, ie introduce models, show specimens, etc. You should also prepare a blackboard plan which will show the outline notes of the lesson to be learned.

2   Preparation. This breaks down into two main parts :

a   Preparation of detailed lesson notes, which you will use yourself, to ensure that no important facts are overlooked.

b   Preparation of any visual aids to assist with the teaching.

Lesson Notes. In the preparation of these, it is necessary to realise how we learn, ie 75% by sight; 15% by hearing and 10% by other senses. But retention of knowledge is greatly increased by doing. Too much listening is very little use unless accompanied by use of the other senses of sight, touch, or even smell.

Lesson Plan. This breaks down as follows :

Introduction. Briefly introduce subject, giving reasons for learning and an idea of how deeply you intend to go into the subject.

Main Body. Commence with knowledge already possessed by class and build logically on this knowledge, introducing new facts, if possible, by questioning the class.

Conclusion. Having got over the main body, summarise what you have taught so that the salient points are brought out.

Note.

a Rate of teaching will depend upon the slowest member of the class, particularly where DANGER is involved in the information being imparted, ie in teaching DIVING knowledge.

b Do not attempt to teach too much in the time allowed.

c It is impossible to concentrate on listening for more than about 40 minutes. Attention begins to wander after about 20 minutes. Therefore, introduce class Activity, ie demonstrate with models, pass round specimens, give notes, films, photographs, or other visual aids, to regain maximum concentration of class.

Use of Visual Aids. For reasons given above, always use as many as you can to make the point required. The ones to be used should have been decided (and prepared) in the planning stage.

Visual Aids. These include :

a Blackboard. Usually available, make full use of it. If not available, easy to improvise ; don't forget the pointer.

b Magnetic Boards.

c Wall Diagrams.

d Models and demonstrations, pieces or sections.

e Films and Film Strips.

f Photographs and Leaflets.

Visual Aids are, in fact, limited only by the imagination of the Instructor.

The more use one can make of the senses, other than the obvious one of hearing, the better will be the learning and retention of knowledge.

Note the following :

a Make certain that the visual aid is ready when it is required.

b Keep it out of sight until required, otherwise it may distract class attention.

c Make certain it works. Nothing is more irritating than to be shown a model or other device which is supposed to work but doesn't.

3 Presentation.

Personal points for the instructor to remember :

1 Personal mannerisms distract and irritate the class, ie chinking coins in the pocket, scratching ear, saying 'er' or 'OK', etc. Watch yourself on this ; even your best friends won't tell you.

2 Use a pleasant tone of voice ; don't shout or whisper but suit volume to size of class or audience.

3 Modulate the voice and keep it interesting. It is very easy to put a class to sleep by using a constant monotonous tone of voice.

4 Appear keen, interested, cheerful in front of the pupils—no matter what happened the night before.

5 Introduce humour if you can, and *if applicable,* but avoid sarcasm.

6 Finally, always be smartly dressed. An untidy appearance can put off the class. They lose confidence in you. It is essential that you retain the confidence of the class, otherwise they will doubt your ability.

The above principles apply to teaching any subject to any class and are based on long and sound experience.

The responsibility to see that the necessary lectures are correctly given rests with the Diving Officer. He may give them all himself or delegate this duty to another person who is suitable and qualified to do so, such as a qualified Instructor.

Normally, the necessary lectures should be given before commencing the training to which they apply. The lectures are given in the log book in a logical order for progression through a course of training, and it is preferable if this order can be followed.

Would-be instructors should see the *Diving Officers' Handbook* for further information on lectures.

Snorkel diver training

To train with mask, fins and snorkel in a pool or safe open water is the logical intermediate step between ordinary swimming and aqualung diving. It increases physical fitness, swimming ability, confidence and water discipline prior to aqualung diving. It also introduces the novice to some of the effects of water pressure and to some of the problems involved such as ear-clearing, the collapse of face-mask due to pressure, the difference in vision due to refraction, the use of signals, fins and snorkel tube.

However, although snorkel diving is an ideal lead-up to aqualung training, the programme should not be so drawn out that the trainee is frustrated in his desire to use an aqualung. If this happens he may lose interest in the training scheme and in diving generally. In the event that a club has so many trainees that there is a considerable wait before proceeding to aqualung training after passing the appropriate qualifying tests, it is prudent to give pupils the opportunity to use the aqualung in the safe confines of a swimming pool. The essential safety rules should be pointed out and the dive should be conducted under the close supervision of an instructor.

Aqualung training in swimming pool or safe open water

The trainee should have received the appropriate lectures before commencing aqualung training, be a qualified snorkel diver and be medically fit. It is most important to arrange the initial dive so that a simple, logical sequence of events is followed. This will prevent the natural anxieties developing into fear or panic. After numerous dives it may be difficult for the instructor to recollect his original misgivings on first diving but he must try to imagine the trainee's disposition even in the safe confines of a swimming pool.

A typical routine to be adopted for a first dive would be as follows.

1 The instructor demonstrates aqualung preparation and the pre-dive check with his own set, and the trainee then prepares his own set supervised by the instructor.

2 The instructor gives a short pre-dive brief to remind the pupil of the essential points made in the lecture room, such as the need to relax, the danger of holding breath on ascent, how to clear ears and counteract water-pressure on face-mask, the buoyancy check, and the signals required. An outline of the dive plan should also be given.

3 Both trainee and instructor fit equipment and the trainee should be allowed to breathe from the aqualung out of water until familiar with the breathing action.

4 The instructor or his assistant should check that the trainees' equipment is in order (face-mask de-misted and on properly etc) and then enter the water down the ladder followed by the trainee. Once again, the trainee should be allowed to familiarise himself with the equipment by being allowed to breathe just below the surface, by standing in shallow water or going a step underwater in the deep part of the pool.

5 On seeing that the trainee is all right, both should surface and the trainee should be asked if he has any questions or problems before proceeding further. The next part of the dive should then be explained.

6 If all is in order, they both descend slowly to the bottom, which should not be at too great a depth. The trainee may use the ladder to stop himself easily at any depth. If lack of confidence is apparent, the helping hand of the instructor holding the trainee will often supply the extra incentive needed.

7 At the bottom, the pupil should be allowed to remain stationary to familiarise himself with the new environment.

8 The buoyancy check may then be demonstrated by the instructor, followed by the pupil.

9 Once familiar with the aqualung and of the correct buoyancy, slow finning may be practised.

10 On completion of the dive, the instructor should comment on various points noted such as the more common fault of overbreathing or breathing too fast, finning too rapidly or incorrectly, mask overtight, etc. Questions should be encouraged, and air consumption differences between pupil and instructor should be shown, if necessary.

11 Aqualung after-use routine should be demonstrated by instructor, followed by pupil.

From this initial dive, the instructor should be able to assess the pupil and decide on future training, whether the pupil requires more familiarisation with the aqualung or if he is sufficiently confident to proceed.

Training courses

In a new large branch there will probably be quite a number of trainees requiring instruction. In such cases it is an ideal arrangement to run a prescribed course instead of using individual instruction. It is, however, the responsibility of the Diving Officer to decide whether he is to train his members by individual instruction or by course instruction.

One arrangement for such a course could be to give an hour's lecture or talk to be followed by pool training. Open water experience should be obtained at the appropriate stages of the course and further lectures and pool training would follow in the correct sequence until the Snorkel Diver and 3rd Class Diver standards had been reached.

If course training is undertaken, it is recommended that the pupils always work in pairs; this will instil in a practical way the need always to dive with a companion.

Class instructional technique

1 For success in any lesson there should be a good instructor/pupil relationship. The instructor's appearance should be clean and smart and he should present his work in a competent manner.

There should be complete control, particularly in a swimming bath, and although a firm attitude is required, the instructor should reveal patience and understanding. A self-imposed discipline based on mutual respect and confidence is one which the instructor should encourage. A sense of humour, enthusiasm, ability to demonstrate well and a thorough knowledge of the subject are attributes which serve well, but in addition the instructor must develop keen powers of observation and the ability to assess performance in terms of fundamental principles in order to correct faults effectively.

2 It is essential that explanations are heard clearly but as a general rule the acoustic properties of swimming baths are poor. The following should, therefore, be noted:

The position of the instructor is important; when detailed class instruction is necessary, pupils should be called to a pre-arranged demonstration position where they will be gathered into a compact group.

When speaking, a slow delivery is necessary for the complete instruction to be heard. Hand signs and body movements should be used to indicate the point to be stressed.

The value of a perfect demonstration cannot be over emphasised. Pupils will learn from visual impression and every possible care should be taken to ensure that the demonstration is accurate.

3   Having gained the attention of the pupils, there must follow instruction and stimulus to action. First there must be an *explanation* of what is required, and this should be clear and concise. This is followed by a *pause* sufficient to give time for the instruction to be absorbed and understood. Finally follows the signal to commence, which may be a formal ' go ' or an informal ' carry on '. The pupils are now in *action* whilst the instructor observes. As a result of his *observation* the instructor will *comment*. This comment will take the form of *praise* or *correction*. Then follows *repetition* of the action for the purpose of improvement by emphasising the point on which the comment was made.

4   In the teaching and the learning of skills, the following factors should be borne in mind.

a   It should be recognised that each person is unique. A class of pupils is composed of numerous individuals, each differing from the other in many ways, physically, intellectually and emotionally.

b   There are many ways of teaching a skill and no one way is right all the time. Methods must be varied to suit the conditions of the situation, the pupils and the instructor.

c   It is sound practice to allow opportunities for exploration before introducing specific skill practises, provided there are no inherent dangers. Such exploration gives the pupil an insight of the situation and the instructor an opportunity of assessing the pupil.

d   In learning a skill, it is generally recognised that the whole skill should be experienced as soon as possible.

e   Frequent attempts at the complete skill during a sequence of practises is essential if interest is to be maintained and to make sure that the real purpose of the practise is not forgotten. Interest can easily be lost if there is an excess of technique.

f   The use of visual aids in the form of demonstrations, photos, films, etc, is helpful in the process of learning, but to be fully effective such aids should be accompanied by verbal instruction and explanations.

g   Repetitive practises will rarely succeed unless the presentation by the instructor is such that interest is maintained and unless the pupils have an understanding of the principles involved in the skill.

h   Nothing succeeds like success and the pupil should be given the chance to be successful in some specific exercise to ensure his progress.

Swimming pools can be of great value for training underwater swimmers but care must be taken to ensure that the trainee does not develop into a confident pool diver only and is unsafe or frightened in open water through confining his activities to the swimming pool.

Progressive training in open water

In taking a trainee diver underwater, the instructor must accept the moral responsibility that this situation involves and that he is as responsible for the safety of his pupil as he is for his own. The dive should be conducted with this in mind.

Prior to entering the water the instructor must check not only his own diving equipment but also that of his pupil. He should ensure that maximum safety precautions compatible with the circumstances are arranged and that the pupil is competent to carry out any necessary safety exercise in an emergency.

The pre-dive brief should remind the trainee of the essential points covered in previous training. The methods of releasing weight belts, inflating lifejackets and checking the contents of air cylinders should be confirmed, and a briefing on the object of the dive and the route to be taken should be given at some juncture. It is prudent to give an opportunity for those who have misgivings about the dive to withdraw.

On entering the water, the dive should be carried out on the 'fail safe' principle—a guarantee that in some unforseen circumstance there is always some alternative method of ensuring safety. Example: the trainee gets into difficulties underwater, the instructor cannot release the trainee's weight belt due to the pin jamming, and the lifejacket fails to inflate due to a faulty mechanism. However, the instructor knows he can still take the trainee to the surface and support him at the safety cover boat overhead (or snorkel cover with large inflated inner-tube) and in any case he is not too far from shore to take him in without undue trouble. This is the 'fail safe' principle. The case illustrated may sound far fetched, but an emergency in the water usually derives from a chain reaction process rather than from any one thing and one must have a chain of alternative safety measures in reserve. To take another example: the pupil enters the water with mask not quite fitting correctly; as he descends water enters his mask; in trying to clear his mask he loses his mouthpiece; he panics and shoots to the surface in distress. Through not having taken the simple precaution of seeing the mask fitted correctly, the trainee finds himself in dire distress—an example of chain reaction.

Of course, the experienced diver would have stopped the process at any point through sufficient training, and an efficient instructor would not have allowed this to happen.

Another point worthy of consideration is the limitations of the partner, or buddy, system, which is often thought to be a 100% guarantee of safety. There will not be many divers who can honestly say they have not lost sight of their partner underwater at some time or another. Vision underwater is greatly reduced by many factors, not the least of which is that the diver's face mask is something akin to a horse's blinkers, enabling him only to see ahead. In anything but good underwater visibility something more positive than reliance on visual contact is required with trainee divers. To supplement visual contact the instructor can utilise the sense of touch by holding his trainee's wrist or hand. He can thus retain contact, give confidence, and guide him at the same time. The buddy line system and the use of lifelines are other methods of retaining contact which should be considered on their merits according to prevailing conditions. Any one instructor should not be responsible for more than two trainee divers, and the ideal arrangement is a one-to-one basis. This may not be practicable with many commercial organisations or diving schools, but in Club diving it should not prove difficult to arrange for one experienced diver to accompany each one or two trainees. With trainees about whom there is any doubt, the sole attention of an instructor is required.

Panic is a major hazard to divers, and this is often underestimated, especially with inexperienced divers. Even in the best planned dives, emergencies can and do occur, but the experienced diver will apply mental brakes to avoid panic and rectify the situation by taking the appropriate action for safety. This may not be the case with a trainee : even after much swimming pool training, a few drops of water in the face mask can cause him to dash to the surface, possibly holding his breath in an instinct of self-preservation, only to find he is then in even more trouble. The instructor should be prepared for such emergencies and it is often possible to pick out the types who may panic. The expression of the eyes underwater often gives a good indication.

It should never be forgotten that a small incident can develop into a major catastrophe with amazing rapidity in water, and it is the instructor's prime responsibility to see that every precaution is taken to ensure the safety of his trainee.

Training considerations

1   The choice of diving site is very important for training; a good safe site with easy access and exit is required.
2   The dive should be carried out with the maximum safety according to prevailing conditions.
3   Equipment should be checked thoroughly prior to diving.
4   Pre-dive briefs should be given to remind trainees of essential points.
5   The instructor should be first to enter water and the last to leave it.
6   The trainee should not be at a lower depth than the instructor.
7   Orders and signals should be rigidly observed, but the dive should not be carried out as though on a regimental parade ground.
8   Trainees should not be allowed to stray from the diving group.
9   Trainees should be advised before diving that if they do lose the diving group, they should surface and wait at the coverboat or by the snorkel cover.

10 The instructor should observe his trainees continuously and be prepared to assist in case of difficulty at any time, keeping a check of cylinder air contents, etc.

11 The speed for the descent, dive and snorkelling should not be more than that of the least capable diver.

12 In cold water or other extreme conditions, instructors should watch divers closely and not hesitate to cut the dive short if required.

13 The continuous alteration of depth should be avoided. It is best to go to the bottom at the beginning of a dive and proceed to shallower depths towards the end as trainees can often clear ears on first diving but may have difficulty on further occasions.

14 The instructor should give the signal and surface with trainees to regulate ascent rate.

15 The dive should be planned to be within easy reach of assistance if required and the return should not be with empty cylinders.

16 De-briefing and comments after dive should not be forgotten, in addition to after-use maintenance of equipment.

Further progressive training dives in open water

In order that a person can progress through the various grades of diving, there should be a continuous progression of his training and diving experience. It should be arranged for him to take part in dives which will further his experience and knowledge and allow him to qualify for the higher grades. It should also be borne in mind that even with the necessary qualifying dives for a particular grade, if there are any doubts about the person's capabilities the award should be withheld until the doubts are removed.

The standard required for a 3rd Class Diver is that he should be able to dive safely under normal conditions satisfactorily as a partner. He should not be expected at this stage to act as Dive Leader, but should be able to act as Baths Marshal for members using aqualungs.

The standard required for 2nd Class Diver is a high one; during his training he should have attained an understanding, sense of responsibility and diving competence equivalent to that of a first rate diver.

It may be found that some members, once they have qualified to dive in open water, are quite content to carry their training no further, but merely to dive under the supervision of a more experienced diver. This attitude should be watched for and every encouragement should be given to qualify for higher awards, but care should be taken to see that no diver is forced to go beyond his own limitations and capabilities.

RESCUE, LIFESAVING AND DEEP-WATER E.A.R.

It is the duty of every Club member carefully to avoid the occurrence of dangerous incidents, but if they do occur, also to know how to deal with them effectively. In this respect the Club co-operates closely with the Royal Life Saving Society.

It is obvious that the use of the aqualung and swimming aids, such as mask, fins and snorkel, raises new problems and solutions in lifesaving techniques. Despite this, the basic RLSS teachings are essential working foundations for both swimmer and diver alike. Lifesaving classes instituted within branch training programmes stimulate considerable interest amongst members, and are instructive and necessary for general watermanship.

Before any details of possible rescue techniques are studied, several points must be fully understood :

1 To offset the difficulties of wearing lead weight belts and air cylinders, the free diver has the advantage over the 'steam' swimmer of fins and face mask, and in some rescues snorkel, air supply, suit and lifejacket.

2 The snorkel diver has very great advantages of mobility, vision and easy breathing over any 'steam' swimmer.

3 In the case of the rescue of a diver by a diver, it is absolutely essential that both weight belts and aqualungs are capable of being jettisoned immediately. Unless this can be done there may be difficulty and danger in effecting a rescue. Weight belts and aqualung harnesses must have split-second 'quick-releases' capable of operation by the rescuer under the considerable difficulties of an open water rescue of a struggling or insensible companion.

4 The question of whether or not an aqualung-equipped rescuer should retain his breathing set depends largely on the circumstances. If his set still has ample remaining air, the distance to safety is not great, and he is able to effect the rescue on his back, ie with the demand valve submerged, he may well retain his aqualung. He will thus be assured of a continuous air supply even though he may be forced underwater by the struggles of the subject. If a long tow is inevitable, or his air supply is low, the rescuer should jettison his aqualung along with his weight belt and continue the rescue with mask, fins and snorkel, as practicable.

NOTE Despite any possible buoyancy of the cylinders, the water resistance and encumbrance of an aqualung is a gross and dangerous burden during a tow.

When a surfaced diver treads water furiously it is a sure sign that he is in distress and near panic; no time should be lost in giving him assistance.

It is very important that a drowning subject should, if possible, be prevented from inhaling water. Water inhaled into the lungs is rapidly absorbed into the bloodstream, probably causing irreversible changes detrimental to health and/or survival. From 60% to 100% of the blood volume can be absorbed in a few minutes. If this has taken place there is little chance of successful resuscitation, ALTHOUGH AN ATTEMPT MUST STILL BE MADE.

When swimming out to effect a rescue it is important to remember that time may decide the issue. None should be lost, *compatible with arriving on the scene in a fit state to perform a rescue*. Thus it is advisable that members should practice the fin crawl, which makes use of an overarm stroke in addition to that of the fins. This stroke gives good visibility during the approach and to some extent relieves the effort required by the leg muscles which alone will be used during the towing.

Always avoid making contact with the subject from the front. Approach cautiously from the rear and grasp him from behind; hold him firmly and keep his head above water. There should be no need to take defensive action or carry out a release, as a clutch by the subject is generally due to a failure in technique by the rescuer. It is strongly recommended, however, that all divers study and practice the techniques shown in 'Defensive Methods' and 'Releases' in the RLSS handbook—*Life Saving and Water Safety*.

If the subject is struggling frantically he will probably regain his confidence as soon as he realises that he is in capable hands. When he is somewhat quietened down he is ready for towing to shore. The rescuer must conserve energy at all times.

If the subject has stopped breathing, Expired Air Resuscitation must start at once . . . 'Seconds Count'. Do not attempt to drain water from the lungs. Commence EAR before anything else. The heart may still be beating even though breathing has stopped, and if this is so then there is a good chance of recovery. (The interval between respiration ceasing and the heart stopping is of the order of two minutes in fresh water drowning, and five minutes in sea water drowning.)

In all cases medical aid *must* be summoned immediately, but even a doctor must not interrupt artificial respiration. As the subject recovers he may vomit or regurgitate swallowed water. It is important that this is not inhaled. The importance of the 'coma position' cannot be over-emphasised here. An unconscious, but breathing subject must *at all times be placed in the coma position,* even during transport to hospital, or he may 'swallow his tongue' or choke on vomit.

Rescue methods for snorkel and free divers

All BSAC members from the level of the primary test upwards should be capable of rescuing and reviving a fellow Club member or, for that matter, anyone else. The methods of rescue given here are easy to learn and all branches should organise classes of instruction.

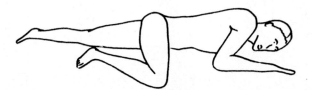

THE COMA POSITION
An unconscious, but breathing subject must at all times be placed in the coma position, even during transport to hospital.

Although it is not laid down that a 3rd Class Diver must possess a Royal Life Saving Society's Sub Aqua Bronze Medallion, it is desirable that not only a 3rd Class Diver but as many members of the Club as possible do hold this award. It is necessary to learn how to release oneself from the clutch of a drowning subject and vitally necessary to know how to administer artificial respiration.

On all occasions when a branch organises diving expeditions it is desirable that rescuers should be standing by ready to go into action. The assistance that one's companion diver can give may not be sufficient. His first responsibility is to bring the subject to the surface and keep his head above water. Then, if he cannot complete the rescue, he should signal for help, which must be immediately forthcoming.

During a rescue the subject should not use a snorkel tube as in all cases he will lie on his back in the horizontal floating position. It is advisable also that his mask should be removed so as to uncover his nose. The following four methods of rescue have been specially developed by the BSAC to be used when wearing fins, which when used correctly propel subject and rescuer with less effort than other methods.

The BSAC first method of rescue
The subject is held close against the rescuer's shoulder. His left arm is held at the elbow by the rescuer's left hand. The rescuer's right passes behind the subject and holds his right arm at the elbow. The rescuer assumes a horizontal position on his back towing the subject likewise. The subject should be held firmly and close to the rescuer.

This method may be modified for towing an aqualung subject by passing the rescuer's right arm behind the subject's head and placing the hand, with the thumb at the subject's lower lip, on the subject's chin. The rescuer's left hand holds as before. If the subject commences to struggle, the right hand can be taken from the subject's chin and a firm hold re-taken of his arm until he becomes more passive.

The BSAC second method of rescue
This method is suitable for a subject who only needs assistance due to a cramped leg muscle or general fatigue and who will co-operate with the rescuer.

The subject should be told to lie on his back and relax. The rescuer then grasps the subject's arms at the elbows so that the subject's arms

27

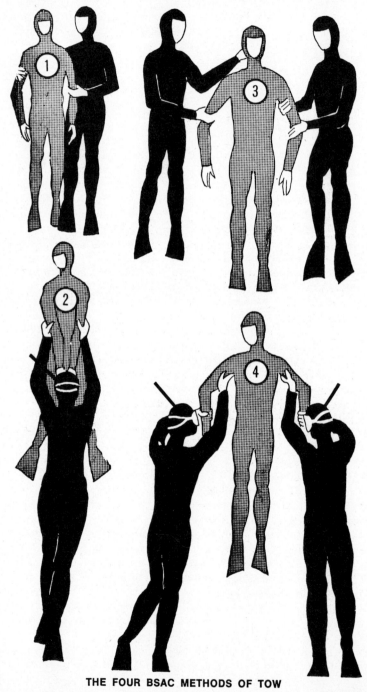

THE FOUR BSAC METHODS OF TOW

are extended in front of his chest and the rescuer's arms are extended forwards. The normal forward fin stroke is then employed by the rescuer.

The BSAC third method of rescue

This method is designed particularly for use on Club diving expeditions and is a dual method, two rescuers being used. It is suitable for a snorkel or free diver subject. The rescuers, who should be snorkel divers, swim on their backs and tow the subject on his back. The subject's mask and breathing tube or snorkel tube should be removed with his weight belt. His lung also may be removed if it is considered advisable.

The rescuers swim one on each side of the subject. The rescuer on the subject's right grasps the subject's right arm at the elbow with his right hand, palm downwards, holding it tightly against his chest. The subject's right shoulder should be close to his rescuer's left shoulder, so that the subject and rescuer are close together. With his left hand the rescuer supports the subject's head so that it will not fall back. The wearing of a lung by the subject will not prevent the rescuer from supporting the subject's head in this way.

The rescuer on the subject's left passes his right hand under the subject's upper arm, palm upwards, and grasps the subject's left arm above the elbow, holding it tightly against his chest. With his left hand he holds the subject's lower arm firmly. The subject's left shoulder should also be close to the rescuer's right shoulder so that the subject and rescuer are close together. The two rescuers then paddle their feet to the surface until they are horizontally poised and commence to tow the subject. As they are swimming on their backs they should not use snorkel tubes, but may retain their masks.

The BSAC fourth method of rescue

This method, like the third method, is suitable for diving expeditions. It is a dual method also, but is considered less suitable for an unconscious subject than method three, as there is no support for the head.

The rescuers should be snorkel divers and the subject may be a snorkel or free diver. The rescuers swim forward in the prone position, pushing the subject ahead of them on his back. The subject's mask and breathing tubes or snorkel tube should be removed. The subject's aqualung may be removed if considered advisable. His weight belt should be removed in any case. The rescuers should retain their masks and snorkel tubes.

The rescuers place themselves one on each side of the subject and facing him. The rescuer on the subject's right-hand side supports the subject by grasping the subject under the right upper arm with his right hand. With his left hand he holds the subject's right wrist. The rescuer on the subject's left-hand side supports the subject by grasping him under the left upper arm with his left hand and with his right hand he holds the subject's left wrist. The rescuers then fin forward, pushing the subject before them.

In conclusion, it should be noted that a rescuer may well be as exhausted and overstrained on arrival inshore as the person rescued, and he merits just as much attention. If he is not given this, there may well be a further incident.

The Royal Life Saving Society's Method of Extended Tow

The above methods are unsuitable or difficult when EAR must be applied because :

(a) they do not allow access to the subject's mouth or nose without changing grip

(b) the subject is bound to be passive, ie, unconscious, so that there is no need for restraints, and

(c) the subject should need no support, being buoyant due to release of his aqualung and/or weight belt, and inflation of his lifejacket.

The method recommended is therefore the RLSS Extended Tow. With one hand the rescuer must (i) cup the subject's chin, or (ii) grip his hair, or (iii) hold him by the nape of the neck, or (iv) take hold of his

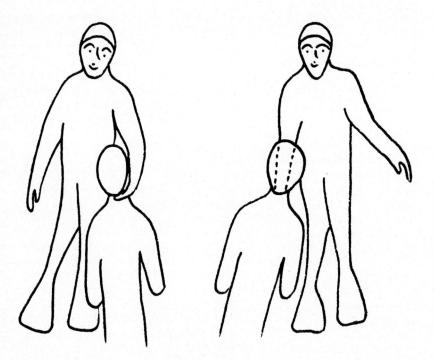

EXTENDED TOW

With one hand the rescuer must (i) cup the subject's chin, or (ii) grip his hair, or (iii) hold him by the nape of the neck, or (iv) take hold of his clothing, suit or harness in the vicinity of the nape of the neck.

clothing, suit or harness in the vicinity of the nape of the neck, providing that in so doing he does not restrict the subject's airway or lose
'extension'. The rescuer uses his spare hand to assist EAR and to
help in the tow. The rescuer fins on his back holding the subject at
arm's length. If fins are not worn the rescuer swims side stroke or life-
saving back stroke.

The rescuer removes the subject's mask and snorkel, and raises or
removes his own mask and snorkel. Partial inflation of the subject's
lifejacket is preferable to full inflation, allowing better extension of his
neck. Likewise the retention of the subject's weight belt will keep him
more vertical in the water, again making neck extension easier. In a
real rescue full buoyancy may be essential for a lift from depth, or
support of an overweighted diver. Full inflation of the lifejacket is then
essential, and retention of the subject's weight belt very inadvisable.
Methods of overcoming this difficulty are mentioned below.

Rarely should the rescuer seek extra positive buoyancy himself, beyond
possibly ditching his weight belt and/or aqualung, as an inflated life-

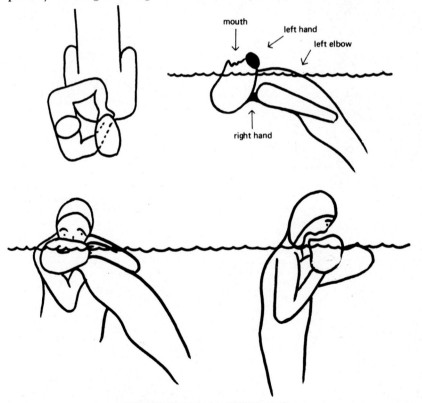

DEEP-WATER EAR METHOD 'A'

31

jacket will prevent him getting close enough to the subject to carry out EAR. It will also add to his difficulties should the subject sink again. However, if the rescuer is getting exhausted or is subject to other risks, then he *must* inflate his own jacket, but as little as he can comensurate with safety.

Deep-Water Expired Air Resuscitation

An essential preliminary to deep-water EAR is a position where support can be given if necessary, and from which EAR can be given. The rescuer must come to one side of the subject—without releasing his tow hold. There are three such methods of administering deep-water EAR, referred to as Methods A, B and C. Methods A and B use the left hand on the subject's chin, and method C the left hand on the subject's face.

Method A. The rescuer's right hand in the nape of the subject's neck keeps his head above water and provides a pivot around which the left hand tilts the head, extending the neck. The left hand also closes the

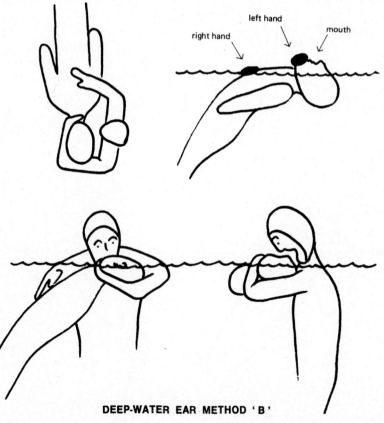

DEEP-WATER EAR METHOD ' B '

subject's mouth, and the left elbow may be used to depress the subject's chest so that sufficient extension is possible without tilting the subject's nose below the water surface. The rescuer ventilates the subject's lungs by the 'mouth to nose' method.

Method B. The rescuer's left hand cups the subject's chin, closing the mouth and extending the neck, but the left arm is crooked around the subject's head so that the rescuer is on the subject's right, and his right hand is available to depress the subject's chest to increase neck extension, or cling on to a boat or jetty, etc. Ventilation is again by the 'mouth to nose' method.

Method C. The rescuer's right hand in the nape of the subject's neck acts as a pivot. His left hand closes the subject's nose and his left wrist tilts the head to give neck extension. 'Mouth to mouth' EAR is applied.

While Method A may follow either method of extended tow, Method B

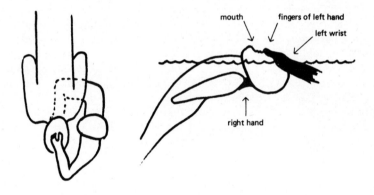

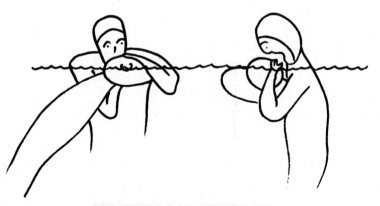

DEEP-WATER E.A.R. METHOD 'C'

can only be used after the cupped chin tow, and Method C can only be used after the nape of the neck tow.

In all three methods the whole method is easier if at the same time the subject's head is turned slightly towards the rescuer so that he need not rise so far out of the water to make his mouth seal. NB : care must be taken nòt to lose the tilt which extends the neck and opens the airway.

Remember the essentials : *Tilt* to extend the neck and open the airway, and *seal* the alternative opening to the one you wish to use. *Seal* your mouth round the chosen opening, mouth or nose, and inflate the subject's lungs. Once both seals have been made it will not matter if both subject and rescuer happen to sink back to, or even a little under the surface, but both should have airways open above water for expiration and voluntary, unaided, inspiration.

Give three or four good inflations before resuming towing. Give another two or three inflations every 15-20 seconds during the tow.

NOTE : In a real rescue circumstances may indicate variations from the above. For example : In Method C simply tilting the subject's head may not open his mouth sufficiently. In this case the rescuer's right hand would have to be removed from the nape of the subject's neck and would instead grasp the subject's jaw to open his mouth. As a bonus the rescuer's right elbow could then be used on the subject's chest, similarly to Method A to increase ' tilt '. The principle still holds, however, that whenever possible there should be no change of grip by the rescuer when changing from the tow position to the EAR position.

ARTIFICIAL RESPIRATION

Cells and Anoxia

All animal cells, including those which make up our bodies have two basic needs in order to keep alive—an energy source (such as sugar) and oxygen (with which to utilise that energy). If the organs are deprived of oxygen then in a greater or lesser time the cells of which they consist will die. However, there is great variation in their sensitivity to lack of oxygen. Thus permanent brain damage will occur after only three minutes without oxygen; the heart will only survive for about 5 minutes, the kidneys and liver about 15-30 minutes; whereas the muscles may last several hours, as they are able to utilise energy sources for a period without oxygen, unlike brain and heart cells which have no such capacity.

When a person stops breathing for some reason, then some means of artificially providing him with oxygen is urgently required if he is not to die within a few minutes. This is known as Artificial Respiration or Resuscitation, and as can be appreciated from the above the essence of all the techniques to be described below is speed in initiating treatment.

Signs of Respiratory Arrest

The signs of respiratory arrest are :
1   Absent Respirations.
2   Blue discolouration of the face and lips (Cyanosis).
3   The pulse rate is variable but is usually slow.

The causes of 'Respiratory Arrest' that you are likely to meet in diving are :
1   Asphyxia due to Drowning.
2   Acute Heart Attack.
3   Electrocution.
4   Respiratory Obstruction.
5   Carbon Monoxide poisoning.

It must be borne in mind that there are many other causes. In many cases, not only may breathing have ceased but the heart may also have stopped—'Cardiac Arrest'.

In considering how to resuscitate an unconscious victim, then, we must consider two things :
1   How to provide adequate ventilation of the lungs.
2   How to stimulate the heart and to provide an artificial blood circulation whilst the heart is stopped.

There are 4 essentials for the success of emergency resuscitation :
1   Artificial respiration must be started at the earliest possible moment.
2   The airway to the lungs must be kept clear.

3   Artificial respiration must be continued until normal breathing is restored.

4   An artificial circulation must be maintained if the heart is stopped.

Respiratory Obstruction

There may be a distinction between a person in whom breathing has ceased and one with an obstruction to his airway. In the first case the chest will not be moving; in the case of an obstruction, initially there will be violent movements of the chest wall as the victim attempts to breathe, but no air will be able to get into his lungs unless the obstruction is cleared. After a while these violent movements will cease and then it will be impossible to distinguish between the two by just looking at the subject.

Obstruction to breathing may be caused by :

1   The tongue falling back and blocking the air passage in the throat (probably the commonest cause), or by;

2   Materials such as blood, vomit, water, or even seaweed in the throat, or by;

3   Spasm of the vocal cords shutting off the airway as occurs in many cases of drowning.

For this reason the first essential in resuscitation is to clear the airway. Open the mouth and remove any solid matter from the throat with a finger. Any vomit, blood, or water in the throat is best drained by turning the patient on his side, head down. In many cases of drowning, contrary to popular belief there is little or no water in the lungs, and draining of the lungs before instituting artificial respiration is probably of little benefit and is time-wasting.

Methods of Artificial Respiration

Artificial Respiration may be applied in one of two ways. External forces may be applied to the outside of the chest (eg Sylvester Brosch), or air may be blown into the chest via the nose and mouth (eg Expired air method)—' Positive Pressure Ventilation '.

1 Expired Air Method

Movements of the chest can be induced by altering the internal pressure of the airways. By forcing air down the trachea into the lungs, they will expand; when the pressure is released the chest returns to the resting position (see below) and it is expelled. The Expired Air Method employs these principles, and is the most satisfactory form of artificial respiration, and should be that normally used. Its main advantages are :

1   Easy and effective to apply and can be done with little training.

2   Can be used in situations where other methods cannot, eg in the water, on rocks, or in a small boat.

3   Gives greater and more controlled ventilation of the lungs than other methods.

4   The operator can assess the degree of inflation of the lungs by observing the movements of the chest.

5   Less tiring and does not require strength by the operator.

6   Can be used on persons of any age, including newborn babies and infants.

It is essential before commencing that there is no respiratory obstruction and a clear airway is maintained, so this must be checked first.

a) Mouth-to-mouth Method

1   The operator should lay the subject on his back and take up a convenient position at one side level with the subject's head.

2   With one hand he should then press the head backwards and squeeze the nose. This prevents air leakage through the nose.

3   At the same time with the other hand the lower jaw should be pushed forwards and upwards. This prevents the tongue from falling back and obstructing the air passage in the throat. Occasionally this may prove difficult, in which case a clear airway may be obtained by first putting the forefingers of each hand behind the angles of the jaw and pulling steadily and firmly upwards and forwards. This provides better leverage. Once this is done one hand can be transferred to the point of the jaw whilst maintaining the position with the other, and then this hand is moved to the nose as described.

4   The operator should open his mouth wide, take a deep breath, seal his lips around the subject's mouth and exhale steadily into his lungs. If the airway is clear, air will enter the subject's lungs with little feeling of resistance and the chest wall will rise.

5   The operator then removes his mouth from the subject, turning his face towards the subject's feet. In this way one can observe the rise and fall of the chest and at the same time brings the operator's ear over the victim's mouth and nose to listen for the exhalation of air. Gurgling or noisy breathing indicates that the airway is not properly clear for one of the reasons mentioned above.

The first two minutes of inflation should be done as rapidly as possible (within the bounds of the operator's capabilities), and thereafter at a normal breathing rate of 10-15 per minute. Do not blow too forcibly, but, rather, gently and steadily, otherwise air is also forced into the stomach, which may cause a recovering subject to vomit.

b) Mouth-to-nose Method

If the patient's mouth is damaged or cannot be opened or he has no teeth, then the mouth-to-nose method can be used. This is similar to the mouth-to-mouth method except that the operator seals his lips widely over the subject's nose and closes the subject's mouth by placing the thumb on his lips. The lower jaw must be pulled forwards as before. This method may be more effective in those whose airway is difficult to maintain clear. It is also stated (on somewhat dubious evidence) that there is less risk of inflating the stomach with this method than with mouth-to-mouth.

In small children it is best to seal both mouth and nose with one's own lips, and in older children either method may be used. There are no hard and fast rules, the best guide being to use the method which seems to work best at the time.

External Cardiac Massage

In many cases of respiratory arrest the heart has also stopped—in the cases of electrocution and acute heart attack in particular this is the primary cause of the arrested breathing. This is known as 'Cardiac Arrest'. In such a situation the heart may have stopped beating entirely, or may be beating in such an irregular and inefficient manner that no blood is being pumped around the body. Whichever it may be the signs of arrest and the treatment are the same.

Signs of Cardiac Arrest

The signs of cardiac arrest are :

1 Absent pulse; 2 Absent respirations; 3 Dilating pupils; 4 Blue discolouration of the face and lips.

If the heart has stopped then cardiac massage must be instituted immediately. First hit the lower part of the breast bone (sternum) with a sharp blow with the side of the clenched fist 2 or 3 times. Occasionally this measure alone is sufficient to start the heart beating properly again, and if so then the above signs will show an improvement rapidly, provided the lungs are being properly inflated at the same time. If the heart does not appear to have started again then external cardiac massage is commenced. (Do not waste more than half a minute at the most for this initial action).

This is done as follows :

1 Place the heel of the palm (where the hand joins the wrist) on the lower end of the sternum with the other hand placed over the first one.

2 With the arms fairly straight, downwards pressure is applied with a fairly sharp movement sufficient to depress the sternum 1-2 inches and then released. This is repeated about 60 times a minute.

The heart lies behind the sternum, between it and the spine behind. When the sternum is pushed down in this manner the large chambers of the heart (ventricles) are squeezed between the two and blood is thus forced out of the heart chambers into the blood vessels. A remarkably effective artificial circulation can be provided by this method, if done properly. Care must be taken not to press too hard or sharply as ribs may be fractured, but on the other hand a few fractured ribs if a life is saved is acceptable. In fact the incidence of fractured ribs, particularly if the operator is inexperienced, is high.

It will not normally be possible, and is not advisable, to practice this manoeuvre on a conscious subject, but you can be assured that the sternum will move freely in the unconscious person.

The actions of expired air resuscitation and external cardiac massage must be co-ordinated. It is advisable to give 4-6 cardiac compressions to every breath of air; that is 10-15 respirations per minute and 60 compressions per minute. Preferably two people are needed to execute the actions, but it can just be managed with one. If a third person is present then he should time the actions and rotate with the cardiac massage operator every ten minutes.

Assessment of Resuscitation

People complain that they are not taught how to assess their efforts at resuscitation. This is because assessment is extremely difficult, and can easily be misleading to the layman (and to medical attendants). However, the following points may be helpful.

1 Return of spontaneous respiration, a good pulse, and recovery of consciousness are obvious indications of success.

2 Change of colour from blue to a more normal colour (best seen on the lips, especially the inner surface and inside the mouth). Conversely, a deepening purplish appearance shows that for some reason one's attempts are not adequate. This is most commonly due to :

a) Inadequate ventilation of the lungs due to a blocked airway (usually by the tongue)

b) Ineffective cardiac massage

c) Severe irreversible damage due to delay in instituting resuscitation.

3 Return of a pulse which can be felt at the groin. A pulse at the wrist, unfortunately, is very often not easy to detect under these circumstances (especially in a cold subject) and is therefore not a very good guide. If heart beats can be heard in the chest when the operator's ear is placed against the front of the chest wall this can be taken as an indication that at least some effective pumping is occurring. Alternatively the heart may be seen beating by movements of the chest wall, or people should be taught how to feel for a pulse in the neck or in the groin.

4 Pupils. When the victim is first seen his pupils may be very widely opened and do not contract down when the eyes are opened by raising the upper lid suddenly—'fixed dilated pupils'. This is a bad sign if it persists as it indicates severe brain damage due to lack of oxygen. Pupils which do 'react to light' when the lids are opened or a light is shone

in the eye, or which are small are signs that your efforts are probably being effective.

General

Whilst artificial respiration is taking place, the subject should be covered with a blanket or other convenient covering, but do NOT apply artificial heat to his body.

With any form of artificial respiration when the subject shows signs of breathing, the operator's rhythm should be synchronised to suit the subject. One of the biggest dangers in these emergencies is the risk of vomiting during the procedure or after recovery. This can have dire consequences if some of the vomit goes down into the air passages as can easily happen in an unconscious person. Therefore during the procedure the back of the mouth should be checked periodically as stomach contents may well get up into the throat without your being aware of it. If vomiting occurs tip the head well over to one side, turning the patient on his side and clear out fluid and solid matter with the fingers. For the same reason, upon recovery, the subject should NOT, under any circumstance, be given fluids or food for at least two hours after fully regaining consciousness except under the direction of a medical practitioner.

After the subject has regained consciousness and is breathing normally he should not be allowed to sit or stand up, but should be kept warm with coverings and laid on his side. He should be watched carefully to see that his breathing does not fail again. If it does, artificial respiration and if necessary external cardiac massage must be recommenced immediately. In all cases medical aid should be summoned at once as serious complications may still arise after normal breathing has returned, particularly in cases of drowning which are the ones you are most likely to meet. Even if recovery is rapid and appears to be complete, every case should ALWAYS be seen by a doctor at the earliest possible opportunity, preferably at a hospital where they can then be admitted for observation if necessary.

The reasons for this are several. Firstly, additional injuries received at the time of the accident may require treatment. Secondly, residual damage to the heart, kidneys or brain due to the period of anoxia may mean an extended period of hospital care for the victim. Thirdly, one of the greatest dangers after apparent complete initial recovery from salt water drowning is the development of congestion of the lungs (pulmonary oedema), which, unless rapidly and vigorously treated, may be fatal within a few hours. Fourthly, pneumonia may be a sequel particularly in those bedridden for a period following their accident. Finally, acidosis occurs rapidly during respiratory and cardiac arrest due to accumulation in the body of carbon dioxide, lactic acid, and other acids produced by metabolism (see chapter on exhaustion). If resuscitation is successful these will rapidly correct themselves, but special therapy in hospital may be necessary in those cases which survive the initial mishap but whose condition remains critical.

The decision to discontinue efforts at resuscitation should only be made by a qualified medical practitioner, unless for geographical reasons or the fact that you are alone makes this absolutely impossible. This is for two reasons; firstly, it is a difficult decision even for the medically qualified, let alone the inexperienced layman; and secondly, such a decision taken by a layman may present legal problems afterwards—doctors are legally covered (in this country) to make such decisions. If you do have to take this responsibility, and I sincerely hope this never occurs, then the signs described above may help to guide you in this extremely difficult decision.

If there is any evidence AT ALL of an improvement in the victim's condition then resuscitation efforts must continue if need be for hours.

Aids to Artificial Respiration
There are several different methods of artificial respiration and ways in which these can be applied. Certain of these employ some form of aid to simplify or assist the work of the operator. Whilst in the hands of a person experienced in their use and fully conversant with their purposes and limitations, aids can be extremely useful, it is not recommended that they be used by Club members unless they have this special training.

Moreover, it is not wise to place reliance solely upon methods that require the use of an aid, as it is possible that on the very occasion when it is required it may be lost, not available, or involve a delay in bringing it to the subject who is in need of artificial respiration.

The methods described here require no aids and can easily be taught to and used by Club members. It is obvious, however, that constant practice is the surest aid to speed and efficiency in starting and maintaining artificial respiration until a successful outcome is achieved.

Acknowledgement is made to the Royal Life Saving Society for permission to include the descriptions of expired air resuscitation in the water and the Silvester-Brosch method from their Manual 'Emergency Resuscitation'.

Techniques in Water
In each case use the mouth to nose method. Close the subject's mouth and support his jaw in the normal manner for mouth-to-nose resusci-

tation, using that hand to extend the head; *and*

Standing in Shallow Water
support the subject's trunk
either between his shoulder
blades or under his far arm-
pit with your other hand; *or*

Supported in Deep Water
support the subject with your
other arm behind his neck
with your hand gripping the
bar or side.

Note: For practice and demonstration purposes for the
above techniques, breathe
beyond the subject's far cheek.

*Swimming in Deep
Water*

Support the subject with
your free hand under
the back of his head.
Keep his face out of the
water and avoid twisting
his head. Keep the sub-
ject moving slowly with
his body in the normal
towing position.

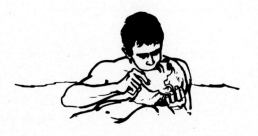

Note: For practice and demonstration purposes the rescuer's mouth
should be applied to the subject's forehead.

2 Manual Methods of Artificial Respiration

The resting position of the chest is between full inspiration and full expiration. You can test this for yourself by holding your breath in inspiration or deep expiration for a few seconds then releasing it, when your chest will return to a more comfortable position rapidly without any effort on your part. This is because the chest wall and the lungs act as opposing forces, the former tending to spring outwards and the lungs tending to collapse. At the resting position these two forces equal each other and so no effort is required to maintain the chest in that position. Thus if external pressure is applied to the chest wall the lungs tend to deflate, and when the pressure is released the chest will spring back to the resting position, pulling the lungs out with it and drawing air into them. Inspiration may be further increased by movements that expand the chest wall further. The Silvester-Brosch method employs these principles.

The Silvester-Brosch Method

This method should only be used if, for any reason, the Expired Air method cannot be used.

1 Lie the casualty on his back and quickly place suitable padding *under the shoulder blades* if immediately available. This should be thick enough to raise the shoulders so that the head just rests on the ground with the neck extended to open the airway.

2 Check for any obvious restriction or obstruction and keep the airway clear throughout.

3 Kneel on one knee just clear of the top of the casualty's head and to one side. Place your other foot beside his shoulder.

4 Grasp the casualty's wrists and cross them over the lower end of his sternum.

5 To compress the thoracic cage, rock the weight of your trunk forward with straight arms until they are vertical, exerting a smooth, evenly increasing pressure : 10 to 15 kg for an adult; 5 to 6 kg for slight women and children; 1 to 2 kg for infants.

6 Rock back releasing the pressure and move the arms with a smooth semi-circular sweep parallel to the ground until the casualty's arms are extended above his head. Stop when slight resistance is felt and do not force the casualty's arms to the ground in the extended position. Watch for the chest cage to lift as the extended position is reached.

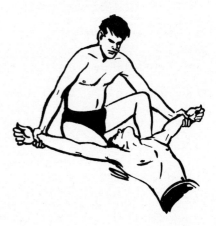

7 Return the arms along the same route and place them in the original position on the casualty's chest ready for the next compression.

8 The whole cycle should take about five seconds; one second for compression, two for extending the arms and two for their return, ie about 12 cycles per minute.

FIRST AID

The aim of first aid is :

1 To sustain life (resuscitation, control bleeding).
2 To prevent the worsening of any condition (cover wounds, immobilise fractures, place patient in proper position).
3 To promote recovery (reassure, relieve pain, handle gently, prevent chilling).

The old image of first aid as a formal drill, rigidly tied to 'fancy' methods of bandaging, etc, should be discounted and the above aims now kept in mind.

When tackling a situation where first-aid is needed, it is helpful to follow a 'check-list' of priorities so that the more serious threats to life are dealt with first. Such a list of priorities is :

1 Remove the patient from danger ⎫
2 Restore breathing ⎪ At the earliest possible moment
3 Restore heart-beat ⎬ send for assistance.
4 Stop bleeding ⎭
5 Treat other conditions, eg burns, fractures, etc.
6 Treat for shock
7 Convey the patient to hospital or recompression chamber.

No list of priorities such as the above will cover every eventuality, but it illustrates the principle. (In this case the only important deviation would be in the case of a major haemorrhage which would be dealt with first, *but quickly*.) A competent first aider will appreciate just how to apply these priorities, but for the unpractised and inexperienced the following may be written on cards to be included in the expedition first aid kit.

1

There is *massive* external bleeding.
(a) Stop the bleeding. Do not delay before :
(b) Check respiration and administer EAR if necessary.
(c) SEND FOR HELP—A LIFE IS IN DANGER.
(d) Treat burns, fractures, etc. Add further dressings if bleeding continues.
(e) If unconscious, place in the coma position and treat for shock. If conscious, treat for shock.
(f) Convey the patient to shore/recompression chamber/*hospital* immediately.

2

There is little or no external bleeding.
(a)   Check respiration and administer EAR if necessary.
(b)   Check pulse and restore heart-beat if necessary.
(c)   Stop any bleeding.
(d)   Treat burns, fractures, etc.
(e)   If unconscious, place in coma position and treat for shock.
(f)   If any of the above are serious—SEND FOR HELP—A LIFE IS IN DANGER.
(g)   Convey the patient to shore/recompression chamber/*hospital* as soon as possible.

3

There is evidence of internal bleeding . . . after a dive.
(Suspected when there is pallor, sweating, rapid feeble pulse, air hunger and often recent injury.)
(a)   Move the patient as little as possible, and make him rest.
(b)   Check respiration and administer EAR if necessary.
(c)   Stop any external bleeding.
(d)   SEND FOR HELP—A LIFE IS IN DANGER. Contact HMS *Vernon.**
(e)   Treat burns, fractures, etc.
(f)   Place the patient in the coma position, whether unconscious or not.
(g)   *Treat for shock.*
(h)   Convey the patient to shore/recompression chamber/*hospital* immediately.

*Portsmouth (0705)
> 22351 Ext. 72375 during working hours. Supt. of Diving.
> Ext. 72588 outside working hours. Officer of the Watch.

4

The patient is convulsing . . . after a dive.
(a)   Treat as appropriate under '1', '2' or '3'.
(b)   SEND FOR HELP—A LIFE IS IN DANGER. Contact HMS *Vernon.*
(c)   Restrain the patient from harming himself further.
(d)   When the patient is quiet, place him in the left coma position, whether unconscious or not.
(e)   Convey the patient to shore/recompression chamber/*hospital* by the fastest possible means.

5

The patient is acting in a drunken manner and/or has severe pains in the chest . . . after a dive.

(a) Treat as appropriate under '1', '2', '3', or '4'.
(b) SEND FOR HELP—A LIFE IS IN DANGER. Contact HMS *Vernon*.
(c) Constant supervision is essential as resuscitation may become necessary, or his condition worsen in other ways.
(d) Place the patient in the left coma position, whether unconscious or not. But if his breathing is difficult he would be better sitting up.
(e) Convey the patient to shore/recompression chamber by the fastest possible means.

6

The patient complains of other severe pains, especially in the shoulder, knee or other joint . . . after a dive.

(a) Treat as appropriate under '1', '2', '3' or '4'.
(b) CONTACT HMS *Vernon*.
(c) Place the patient in any position which is comfortable for him, unless the coma position is essential because he is unconscious, or any other condition makes it inadvisable.
(d) Keep the patient under constant close observation, his symptoms may worsen.
(e) Convey the patient to shore/recompression chamber by the fastest possible means.

The most highly recommended method of learning first-aid is to study and take the First Aid Certificate of the Red Cross, St John Ambulance Association, or the St Andrew's Ambulance Association. Courses consist of ten or twelve lectures in theoretical and practical first aid, but you do not have to join any of the above organisations in order to attend. Enquiries may be made at any of their local headquarters.

(The certificate awarded also covers the requirements for first aiders under the Factories Act, 1961, and is valid for three years.)

For those who do not wish to attend such a course in first aid, some amplification of methods of treatment is outlined below. Of necessity it cannot be complete in one chapter, and every diver, indeed every responsible adult, should read the authorised First Aid Manual of the above organisations. (It costs only about 30p.) A copy of the Manual, or the First Aid Section from Reed's Nautical Almanac, should be in every first aid kit.

1 Remove From Danger

In the diving context this is largely a matter of deep rescue and/or life-saving. As EAR can be administered in the water, treatment, or at least some part of it, may be given before the patient is removed from danger. As a general principle, however, removal from danger must be a high priority, only delayed by the necessity for the most urgent treatment to prevent imminent death.

It is worth noting that this is the time when the rescuer or first aider is himself at risk. (In 1969, the last year for which statistics are available, thirteen persons were drowned in Great Britain while attempting to rescue swimmers.)

Bear in mind at all times that where resuscitation is necessary 'seconds count'. Delay in starting resuscitation while removing the patient from danger, may result in his being beyond recovery by the time you do start.

2 Restore Breathing

The expired air method of resuscitation is the method recommended by the BSAC. It is dealt with in another chapter. Remember—if you are in doubt whether the patient is breathing or not—start EAR, it will do a normal adult no harm even if he is breathing.

If bleeding is heavy AND respiration has ceased, both conditions really need immediate attention. The recommended procedure is to rapidly place a dressing or thick pad of cloth over the wound, even if only crudely held in place, and within seconds start EAR.

3 Restore Heart-beat

If the patient is breathing, his heart will also be beating. If the patient is bleeding strongly it is probable that his heart is still beating—check this.

The method of restoring the heart-beat is described in the preceding chapter.

4 Stop Bleeding

Remember that a little blood makes a large mess and this will frighten the patient, who may, in fact, have lost relatively little blood. Severe bleeding can be stopped by pressure on the wound, or if there is a foreign body in the wound, then by pressure as near to the edges as possible. Blood escapes less quickly if the patient is sitting or lying down and also if the injured limb is raised. A dressing may be applied instead of or as soon after this as possible. The best dressing is known as a Standard Dressing. It consists of a sterile pad of gauze-covered cotton wool firmly attached to a bandage, wrapped in such a way that it remains sterile even when applied to a wound by filthy hands. Dressings may be bought medicated, although their use is best avoided as the medication may adversely affect subsequent medical treatment. The most useful sizes of Standard Dressings are large, medium and small (Numbers 9, 8 and 7).

In the absence of proper dressings, substitute materials which could be used in an emergency include most woven materials, especially cotton or linen, and paper tissues or handkerchiefs. Obviously the cleaner the material the better, but do not allow dirt to prevent the use of the only available material while the patient bleeds to death. If any dressing fails to stop bleeding do not remove or replace it, but add further dressings on top and bind them securely in place.

There is little doubt that the most effective method of stopping bleeding is the tourniquet. It is, however, so efficient that death of some or all tissues beyond it is probable. Any tourniquet must therefore be loosened every twenty minutes to allow some blood past into the blood-starved tissues, even though some may escape. It is now believed that tourniquets no longer have any use in first aid, with the possible exception, if you can get to the victim quickly enough, of an amputation such as from a shark attack. Any medical attendant MUST be told of the tourniquet immediately he arrives. Write the word ' tourniquet ' on patient's forehead with ball pen or lipstick.

Self-adhesive dressings will not stick to wet skin and may be of little use to divers. They are, however, popular for minor cuts, blisters, etc, sustained before or after diving. Some should therefore be carried, preferably in a separate container from the rest of the first aid kit (so that clean dressings, etc, are not disturbed when hunting for a ' plaster '). Individually wrapped sterile adhesive dressings are recommended.

5 Treat Other Conditions
Decompression Sickness
Symptoms will usually appear within three hours of surfacing, occasionally up to 24 hours later.

Pneumothorax
Air Embolism } Symptoms occur within seconds of
Emphysema } surfacing.

IMMEDIATE RECOMPRESSION in a chamber is necessary for the first two conditions. Emphysema usually needs no treatment.

During transport do not exceed 300 m altitude.

Transport the patient in the left coma position with the head kept low.

' Foul Air ' Poisoning
Whether carbon monoxide, other gas or oil vapour, or any combination of these the patient will probably complain of a foul taste to the air. He may suffer nausea, vomiting or headache.

Remove from exposure. Oxygen may be necessary, especially for carbon monoxide poisoning (cherry-red lips).

(Retain the air-cylinder and its contents for later air analysis.)

Fractures

If in doubt as to whether an injury is a sprain, dislocation or fracture, treat it as a fracture.

The patient will be in pain, there will be some swelling, and there is danger of further damage caused by movement of the broken ends. The best form of management is to immobilise the limb to reduce this movement. The immobilisation must itself be comfortable as well as efficacious. Where a long and/or rough journey is probable a greater degree of security is needed than for a short or gentle journey. Immobilisation may be achieved by the use of padded splints, or by strapping the broken limb to the body or a healthy limb. Triangular bandages are particularly useful in bandaging fractures and making slings. Exactly where to place the splints, bandages and padding depends on the exact location of the fracture, but broadly speaking bandages are applied (a) to secure the ends of the splints, (b) each side of the break, and (c) each side of any joint nearby. The feet are tied together for injuries of the leg and hip. Padding is applied for comfort between two limbs and between the injured limb and the splint. If no splints are available, use cushions, rolled-up clothes, etc, to support the limb in a comfortable position where it will move as little as possible.

Burns and Scalds

By their nature, burns and scalds are sterile. Make every effort to keep them so by covering them with sterile dressings. Do not apply lotions, ointments, etc, which will only have to be removed later and may hinder subsequent treatment. Do not prick blisters. Pain will be lessened if the affected part can be cooled, eg with cold water. Be prepared to treat shock, it can be severe.

Sunburn

Make the patient rest. Keep him in the shade. Give the patient fluids to drink. Seek medical attention. Serious cases should be treated as burns and scalds.

Hypothermia

Symptoms of a serious fall in the 'inner core' temperature of the body include:

    complaints of cold
    mental and physical lethargy
    mental confusion (so that the symptoms escape notice in oneself)
    muscular weakness or fatigue
    slurred speech
    shivering
    stiffness and/or pain and/or cramp in the muscles
    abnormal vision ⎱ VERY serious symptoms.
    collapse and unconsciousness ⎰

As in the treatment of shock, which is dealt with later, it is VITAL that any increase in the blood supply to the surface of the body should be avoided—it may prove fatal. Therefore, avoid the use of external heat (although a hot bath is excellent), alcohol, spiced foods and massage. (An increase in surface blood supply is always at the expense of that of the heart and brain, thus endangering life.)

Prevent further chilling. This means changing wet clothing for dry. If no dry clothes are available, do not remove his wet ones, but wrap him in plastic sheeting or a rescue blanket or similar windproof material. Keep the patient out of the wind and rain. If he is conscious and able to swallow, give him tepid or warm food or drink.

Carry the patient to safety and medical aid.

Cramp

Fear of cramp and its associated pain is perhaps more dangerous than the cramp itself. The treatment consists of stretching the affected muscle. Keeping fit and warm are perhaps the best ways of avoiding cramp.

Headache

A headache is always a symptom of something else. Alleviating the headache with drugs does not remove the cause and does not make a man fit to dive again. Most pain-killing drugs contain aspirin and/or paracetamol (or phenacetin), which, besides killing the pain, lower the body temperature. This could be serious in cold water. Therefore a diver with a headache, or a diver treating a headache, should not be allowed in the water again that day.

Stings and Bites

There is no universal antidote, one merely treats whatever symptoms appear. This means that if there is pain, ease the pain; if there is swelling, reduce it, etc. Depending on the nature and severity of the wound, be prepared to carry out EAR and cardiac massage if necessary. Get medical attention as soon as possible.

Syncope (Fainting)

In divers, syncope is due to the simultaneous occurrence of two or more of the following :

    hyperventilation

    after-effects of alcohol

    emotional disturbance, anxiety, etc

    fatigue

    hunger

    breathing pure oxygen

    incubating a febrile (feverish) illness

    poor vaso-motor tone (susceptible persons commonly faint at the thought of receiving an injection, etc)

    increased intra-pulmonary pressure (holding the breath during physical exertion).

In every case, the result is an inadequate supply of blood to the brain. Treatment consists of laying the patient flat and, if possible, raising his legs above the level of his head. Loosen any tight clothing, especially diving suits.

Sea-Sickness

The probability of a person becoming sea-sick is increased by :

> sitting in a stationary boat which is heaving in a swell
> cold
> apprehension
> unpleasant smells such as engine exhaust fumes
> the sight of another person being sick
> the after-effects of alcohol.

Treatment consists of returning the affected person to shore as soon as possible. Meanwhile, lay him down and keep him warm. If he vomits, give him a drink of cold water, this will help to remove the unpleasant taste, even though it may be brought up almost immediately.

Once sea-sickness has started, drugs by mouth are totally ineffective as they will be vomited out again. Sea-sickness pills should be taken at least half an hour before embarking on board boat. Nobody should be allowed to take such pills unless he has taken them before on a non-diving expedition and proved they have no side-effects *on him*. Each sea-sickness pill has a different effect, and success or failure with one particular brand does not necessarily mean that another brand will have the same effect.

The side-effects which may be encountered include : serious drowsiness and narcosis which would be additive to nitrogen narcosis or alcohol. If there is any doubt about the suitability of any pill, consult your doctor; do not dive on it.

6   Treat for Shock

Shock is a state of collapse *which can be fatal*. It follows severe bleeding, severe or extensive burns, severe abdominal emergencies, excessive sea-sickness and certain emotional situations.

> The patient breaks out into a cold sweat
> he is very pale
> his breathing is shallow and rapid
> he may be gasping and suffer ' air-hunger '
> the pulse rate increases (except in emotional shock)
> the pulse becomes weaker
> the patient is worried and often confused
> the patient may become unconscious and die.

The treatment is to reassure the patient, lay him down with legs higher than head and prevent chilling. (Note that preventing chilling does *not* mean making him warm—see the note on ' Hypothermia '.) Remove the patient to hospital at once.

7   Convey the Patient to Hospital

An ambulance is probably the best vehicle for this. If he is carried by any other vehicle there MUST be another attendant as well as the driver. If the patient has to wait for treatment, the attendant should stay with him for both comfort and to provide the authorities with background (possibly vital) information. He will also be able to take or telephone the latest information to the patient's family. The attendant should leave only when dismissed by the hospital or recompression authorities. In view of a possible long wait, the attendant's gear will also have to be cleared up and his family informed. Even when an ambulance attends, an attendant should accompany the patient if possible. Remember that an unconscious patient must be transported in the coma position.

First Aid Kit

All first aid kits should include simple instructions so that anyone can use them in an emergency. Suitable instructions are :

1   Department of Employment and Productivity form 1008.

2   Instruction cards like those outlined at the beginning of this chapter.

3   The section ' First Aid at Sea ' from Reed's Nautical Almanac. (It can be removed from an out-of-date volume.)

4   The First Aid Manual.

Three first aid kits are recommended, each suitable for a different situation :

(a) *The Small Kit*

This contains the irreducible minimum. It is suitable for carrying in a diver's kit-bag, and on an inflatable which is never more than half an hour from shore or other medical assistance. It could be part of the ' boat box '.

1 waterproof plastic bag

Form 1008 or other Instructions

3 large standard dressings (No 9)

2 triangular bandages

4 medium safety pins

1 large polythene bag, rescue blanket or survival bag.

When in doubt about the size of dressing or bandage to be included in a first aid kit, choose the larger; a large dressing will cover a small wound, but a small dressing is useless for a large wound. For the sake of simplicity, therefore, the small kit need only contain large dressings. A large polythene bag 2 m x 1 m, or a piece of polythene tubing taped up as a bag 2 m x 1 m, of any gauge polythene will retain as much body heat as a rescue blanket while giving the same protection against wind and rain.

Rescue blankets are aluminised melanex and reflect radar (a useful property for a small boat) and the sun's heat (useful in the tropics). They may also be used to attract the attention of rescuers.

Sams survival bag is a rescue blanket taped up as a sleeping bag.

(b) *The Large Kit*

This would be kept at base, ie on shore or a larger diving boat. It can cope with a greater number and a wider variety of accidents.

A first aid box complying with the requirements of the Factories Act 1961 for 10-50 persons would make a good foundation for this kit.

1 polythene box, tin or other suitable container
Form 1008, other instructions, or the extract from
Reed's Nautical Almanac
6 small standard dressings (No 7)
6 medium standard dressings (No 8)
6 large standard dressings (No 9)
24 assorted sterile adhesive dressings
4 triangular bandages
12 medium safety pins
1 roll Zinc Oxide Plaster 25 mm x 5 m
2 small packs of sterile cotton wool
1 50 mm or 75 mm crepe bandage
2 25 mm roller bandages
2 50 mm roller bandages
1 pair of scissors
1 large polythene bag, rescue blanket or survival bag.

The cotton wool is for miscellaneous wounds. It is better to have several small packs, rather than one big one, so the the whole stock is not rendered unsterile for one small wound.

(c) *The Medical Kit*

This is intended for use on more ambitious expeditions, holidays and voyages. It goes beyond first aid as it contains drugs, etc. The more remote the expedition, the wider the range of drugs which may be carried.

1 large box or case with compartments
Form 1008, any other suitable instructions AND
The First Aid Manual
1 lb sterile cotton wool
4 eye pads (standard dressing No 16)
1 pair splinter forceps or tweezers
1 eye bath
100 Paracetamol tablets
100 Enterovioform tablets
100 ml cetrimide antiseptic (Cetavlon)
1 oz. antiseptic ointment (Dettol ointment)
1 bottle of Milk of Magnesia
Sea-sickness pills (Marzine, Dramamine or Avomine)
(Kwells are also useful—non sedating)
1 oz bicarbonate of soda
½ lb glucose sweets
PLUS THE CONTENTS OF TWO 'LARGE KITS'.

Paracetamol is for headache and pains generally.

Enterovioform is for diarrhoea. Kaolin and morphine mixture is cheaper and available without prescription.

Cetrimide is for skin disinfection and cleansing. It is also useful for sterilising instruments.

Antiseptic ointment is for sores, stings etc.

Milk of Magnesia is for indigestion. It is also a laxative.

Bicarbonate of soda dissolved in water (1 teaspoon per pint) is useful for severe burns. It may also be used for indigestion and bathing the eyes.

Glucose is for hypoglycaemia (in diabetics).

CHAPTER TWO

PSYCHOLOGY OF DIVING

Adaptation : Dr Alan D Baddeley

The Mental Attitude : Alan V Broadhurst

ADAPTATION

When a diver leaves the surface, he enters a world which is probably more foreign to him than any other environment he will ever experience. He faces new problems on which his survival may depend, while his perception of the world around him may be impaired and distorted and his capacity for action reduced. Unless he is fully aware of these limitations, a diver will be neither comfortable, efficient nor safe.

THE SENSES

Man depends on his senses for information about the world around him. When these are required to function in water instead of air, the different physical properties involved may produce an impaired and in some cases distorted picture of his surroundings.

Vision

In this case problems are presented both by the effects of refraction, and of absorption and scattering.

First, refraction. Since the refractive index of water is four-thirds that of air, objects beneath the surface appear to be larger and nearer than they would in air (see *Underwater vision*). While it is almost certainly *possible* to learn to judge sizes and distances accurately under water, there is some doubt as to how effectively the average diver *does* learn this adaptation; however, for most practical purposes the effect does not seem to prove a very great handicap.

A more serious problem is raised by the effects of refraction in that they reduce the field of vision. The visual field is limited by the fact that light rays striking the face plate at an angle of more than about 50° from the perpendicular are reflected and do not pass through the glass, producing a tunnel vision effect which is made worse by the mask itself. Since the nose must be enclosed in the mask to allow pressurisation, the mask must either be relatively deep in which case the rubber surround has a fairly marked blinkering effect, or else the nose must be enclosed in a separate section which then tends to reduce the area which can be seen by both eyes simultaneously, an important limitation if accurate visual judgements have to be made. The blinker effect is reduced in the case of a full face mask in which the glass extends well below the nose allowing more downward vision, though this has the drawback of making a diver's vision and air supply interdependent. The visual field may also be extended by using a wrap-round face plate; this has the advantage of increasing side vision, but unfortunately it produces some distortion.

Theoretically, contact lenses provide the best solution to the problem, but there are still a number of technical difficulties to be solved before they become suitable for practical diving, and in view of their probable cost, it seems unlikely that they will replace the face mask in the near future. None of the available masks is therefore ideal and choice remains largely a matter of personal preference, the standard oval mask probably being as good a compromise as any.

In the case of absorption and scattering, water acts as a filter which reduces light intensity. Since it absorbs reds most rapidly, the available light becomes increasingly blue with depth although when the amount of available light falls below that necessary for normal day vision, the eye is no longer able to discriminate colours and all objects appear grey (see *Underwater vision*).

This process affects vision in two ways, by distorting the colour of objects at relatively shallow depths and by generally reducing visual efficiency as the amount of available light decreases. The first of these effects, although it may reduce the diver's aesthetic appreciation of his surroundings, is not a serious practical handicap. Indeed, the diver will almost certainly adapt to the increasing blueness and still be able to recognise other colours, just as one adapts to tinted sunglasses, though such appreciation is unlikely to be complete. The reduction in available light at depth is a much more serious problem, particularly in conditions of low visibility where illumination is likely to decrease very rapidly. Given time, the eye will adapt to reduced illumination and increase its efficiency quite markedly. Unfortunately, this process is likely to take at least 15 minutes before it is complete, so that a deep dive is likely to be almost over before the eyes become adapted.

This process of adaptation will occur at quite high levels of illumination, however, provided the eye is exposed only to red light. During the war fighter pilots took advantage of this fact by spending the last half hour before a night flight in purely red illumination and hence dark-adapting their eyes in advance. There is evidence that a similar advantage may occur in low-visibility diving, using a mask with a red face-plate which is put on half an hour before the dive and removed at the bottom (*see C C Hemmings and J N Lythgoe, 'Better visibility for divers'*, Triton, 1964, *vol 9, No 4, 28-32*).

The scattering of particles suspended in the water also of course reduces visibility, even under high levels of illumination, just as fog reduces visibility in air. Diving under these conditions presents special problems and even under conditions of extremely good visibility (for example, 30 metres), a diver's acuity for objects 10 metres away is reliably reduced, despite the magnifying effects of refraction, a fact which should be borne in mind when conducting searches under such apparently ideal conditions.

Touch

As visibility decreases, touch becomes increasingly important, till eventually it provides the only available information about the diver's surroundings. Even under ideal conditions, however, because of the restriction in visual field, the diver must rely on touch for locating certain crucial parts of his equipment such as the quick-release fastening on his weight belt. Since his safety may depend on this, it is essential that a diver should be familiar enough with his equipment to locate each item and manipulate it quickly and effectively.

Hearing

At present this is one of the least used of the diver's senses, since for the most part underwater communications still depend on visual signs and rope signals. The ears do, however, function perfectly well underwater, and current developments in the field of underwater communications seem likely to increase the importance of hearing to the diver.

Smell and Taste

Since the diver can smell and taste only what is in his breathing set, these senses are of little use underwater. There are two exceptions to this : the tendency of air at depth to have a somewhat metallic taste is a possible though not invariable indication of the onset of nitrogen narcosis; and certain impurities such as oil fumes in the breathing mixture may be detected by smell. If impurities are suspected, the dive must be terminated immediately.

Orientation

Our sense of bodily position depends on the combined effects of gravity and visual information. In conditions of low visibility a correctly weighted diver will be deprived of most of his normal sources of information and may become completely disoriented. In such a situation it is vital that the diver should not panic and swim off in whatever direction he guesses is upwards. There are still several available clues as to the direction of the surface including his rising bubbles, the direction of maximum brightness and the pressure of his weight belt. Failing this the weight belt can be taken off and used as a plumb line, and as a last resort, releasing the weight belt or inflating your lifejacket will at least guarantee that you move up and not down.

ENVIRONMENTAL STRESSES

The underwater environment is in many ways a hostile one and presents the diver with a number of special problems.

Weightlessness

This, the ability to move freely in three dimensions, is one of the great joys of diving, but anyone attempting to work underwater will confirm that it is not an unmixed blessing. The basic problem is lack of stability, for in the absence of a strong effect of gravity any slight movement is likely to cause the diver to drift away or roll over. Such a disadvantage may be reduced by overweighting the diver, though this can be inconvenient, since a heavy diver is likely to stir up any sediment on the bottom. Excessive weight may also make controlled descent difficult and may be dangerous unless it can be released reliably and rapidly in case of emergency. From this point of view, it is better for the diver to swim down normally weighted and take on supplementary weight at the bottom which then need not be firmly attached and can thus easily be released before ascent.

Cold

In British waters, cold presents one of the diver's greatest problems. Quite apart from the question of comfort, cold may be dangerous because of both its general effects in reducing the diver's physical and mental efficiency, and its specific numbing effects which may make impossible such vital though apparently simple tasks as operating the quick-release buckle of a weight belt. In view of this, the importance of protective clothing is obvious and is discussed in detail elsewhere (see *Protective Clothing*). The problem of keeping the hands warm is, however, a difficult one, since the wearing of gloves is likely to reduce finger dexterity almost as much as numbness from cold, and the practice of removing a glove every time the hands need to be used is hardly a satisfactory solution. Ways of somewhat reducing the numbing effects of cold are described under *Protective clothing,* and if exposure to cold is frequent, acclimatisation will occur and circulation improve. In any case it is important to bear in mind when selecting equipment, that it may have to be manipulated with numb fingers. An emergency quick-release device that relies on precise manipulation is worse than useless.

Anxiety

In view of the potential hazards, it is only natural to feel somewhat apprehensive before a dive, particularly if conditions are not ideal. A moderate amount of anxiety will probably have the desirable effect of ensuring that the diver is particularly careful in checking his equipment and preparing for the dive, and once in the water he will probably feel much less anxious. Beyond a certain point, however, anxiety can become dangerous since it tends to cause a reversion to old-established habits which are unlikely to serve a useful function underwater. Since the more recent, least practised habits are most likely to be forgotten under stress, it is vital that the basic diving skills should not only be learned during training, but should be practised till they become virtually automatic. If unchecked, anxiety may escalate into panic, the worst possible response to any underwater emergency. It goes without saying that anyone who tends to panic under stress should not dive.

Nitrogen Narcosis

When breathed at sufficient pressure, air has an intoxicating effect (see *Nitrogen Narcosis*). The subjective symptoms are in general pleasant, a feeling of relaxation and well-being coupled with a sense of detachment from reality, hence Cousteau's phrase 'the rapture of the depths'. Unfortunately, this feeling of well-being is both illusory and dangerous, since as a diver goes deeper and deeper he will become more and more confident but less and less capable.

The effects of nitrogen narcosis have been shown to be appreciable at a depth of 30 metres and are probably present to a lesser extent at shallower depths. There seems to be a fairly general reduction in efficiency extending from an impairment in reasoning ability to slowing down in speed of reaction and a decrease in manual skill. At depths of 30 metres and less, nitrogen narcosis is a problem mainly because it reduces the working efficiency of a diver. At rather greater depths it begins to become a real danger since by impairing the diver's judgement it increases the risk of accident while decreasing his ability to cope with an emergency. Finally, at depths exceeding 60 metres nitrogen narcosis becomes extremely dangerous, producing bizarre behaviour, stupor and ultimately loss of consciousness.

Such narcotic effects can be considerable reduced by breathing a mixture of oxygen and helium instead of air, but since helium is very expensive and presents rather special decompression problems it is not suitable for normal club diving. It seems likely then that nitrogen narcosis will continue to be a problem for the amateur diver.

THE MENTAL ATTITUDE

This section is concerned with the mental attitude of a diver rather than the actual techniques he employs. His psychological approach to diving and his reactions in different circumstances have a large influence on his appreciation and enjoyment both in and out of the water, as well as on his actions and self-control in unfamiliar surroundings or in an emergency.

The mental make-up and character of a person and also his original reason for taking up diving as a recreational sport at all colours his whole outlook, although training and experience can radically alter his approach to it.

Many receive their first urge to dive from interest in a popular activity, attraction to spearfishing, or fascination for a new experience. Those who become successful divers are usually those who can already swim efficiently and have a love of water. This makes a good start and such people generally take to snorkel or free diving without worry. Some people, however, will never become competent aqualung divers, but subconsciously recognising their own limitations will be content to limit their activities to the swimming pool, snorkel diving, or an occasional sea dive only. These people should never have pressure brought to bear on them to advance further than they wish. At their own stage in diving they enjoy themselves and make a useful contribution to branch and Club activities.

Breathing underwater

The human being depends for his life and the correct functioning of his physical and mental processes on his receiving a regular supply of breathable air, ie air containing the correct mixture of gases for respiration. In everyday life respiration is an automatic action performed without conscious effort, which normally only becomes noticeable during or after exercise when the stimulus of carbon dioxide produces panting or heavy breathing in the process of getting rid of the excess from the lungs.

Although breathing under normal conditions is almost unnoticed, any threat of interruption to the air supply is resisted by the individual and may manifest itself in two ways—either as a rapid increase in the breathing rate as a result of nervous excitement, or as a straightforward attempt to remove any real or imagined restriction of the air supply and a panicky fight to restore normal breathing conditions.

In diving an understanding of this basic mental attitude explains why so many beginners imagine faults in their apparatus, or that their breathing tubes are leaking; why they overbreathe and have consequent buoyancy difficulties, or are anxious to terminate a dive because of some apparently unrelated difficulty, eg a leaking suit. Most of these early troubles arise from this basic fear of an interruption to the vital supply of air. For the same reason an inexperienced diver in a condition of difficulty and stress will almost invariably try to regain the surface and once there will remove his breathing tubes and tear off his mask in the effort to regain normal breathing conditions. A rarer reason for such actions is a tendency to claustrophobia, which is discussed later.

The novice diver undergoing training and his instructor should both realise that all diving equipment, from basic equipment up to full free diving equipment, is to some degree strange, unfamiliar and unnatural. Few people can immediately accept the practice of mouth breathing only; fewer still can at once co-ordinate this with vision under water and the correct finning technique. These facts should be fully understood and accepted by instructors, and be made plain to those under instruction.

Although the actual techniques of diving, once learned, are not easily forgotten, anxiety states may well occur amongst experienced divers who have perhaps not dived for some time, or who have been involved in some diving mishap or difficult diving experience.

That this fact is recognised, particularly by the experienced divers themselves, is most important, since although fears and failures are expected in novice divers they are not in more experienced ones, and the failure of such a diver, possibly in a moment of stress when in charge of a party, could lead to disastrous results. The maintenance of 'diving trim' is thus vital and should be periodically proved by re-submission to the standard diving tests, either directly or as practice drills both in the training pool and the sea. Experienced divers should not be afraid to re-learn simple techniques that have not been used for some time, or to face the fact that their standard of diving efficiency may not be as high as others expect from them. In diving it is foolhardy and dangerous not to admit limitations in ability that may exist.

Experience is not merely the number of dives that one has accomplished or has attested in one's logbook. It should be continuous and progressive. Experience in diving leads to self-discipline, which in turn helps the diver to exercise self-control to suppress panic that might arise from an imagined or real interruption to his air supply.

The aim in diving is to attain a breathing action that is automatic and unnoticed as that when breathing under normal atmospheric conditions. Only when this has been accomplished can the diver really enjoy his diving and be able to perform other underwater tasks such as leading diving groups or training individuals, taking photographs, carrying out studies or doing other ancillary work. To arrive at such a state means that the diver must have complete confidence in his equipment, in himself, and in his ability to deal with any unusual or emergency

3

condition that may arise while underwater. This can only be achieved by using his equipment, understanding it thoroughly, and submitting it to every personal test he may think fit to prove its reliability under all circumstances and conditions. There is no short cut; experience and continuous use is the only way.

Relaxation underwater

It is fundamentally important to be mentally relaxed when diving. Most novice divers if left to their own devices when first using an aqualung will immediately fin at top speed, arms and legs flapping madly and breathing at an excessive rate. To look through the mask and into the eyes of such a person will reveal that they are blank and unseeing; he will neither see nor recognise signals and can only be stopped by physical force. In these circumstances he is merely receiving vague impressions of what he is doing. The main difficulty on the first few dives is that of inability to relax. This may be partly due to faulty breathing technique and the resultant buoyancy difficulties, and partly due to nervous tension. The two conditions are, of course, interlinked.

In the training pool these difficulties may be fairly simply overcome. Firstly the instructor must be firm and positive, take complete charge of his pupil and gain his absolute confidence. Secondly he should make sure his pupil understands the principle of the working of the aqualung, and the fact that air supply is continuous and readily available to him when he inhales. This should be demonstrated on the bath side before entering the water. Thirdly the instructor should make sure his pupil is well weighted—overweighted rather than otherwise. Fourthly he should impress on his pupil that at first he should do nothing underwater, but sink gently to the bottom, moving neither his arms nor legs, and sit there, relaxed, comfortable, and let the demand valve 'breathe' for him. Then he should enter the water with his pupil, holding one of his hands firmly and make sure his instructions are obeyed.

After a few moments of steady, relaxed breathing underwater the pupil will recognise and return an 'OK' signal. This is the time to start a very slow and gentle swim across the width of the bath, still holding the pupil's hand. Then return to the steps and leave the water. In the vast majority of cases the pupil will come out interested, relaxed and confident.

Further instructions that will help to promote underwater relaxation are : 1 always fit equipment carefully and make sure that it is comfortable—firm but not restrictive; 2 always move gently, carefully and slowly underwater; 3 concentrate on exhalation, leaving inhalation to take care of itself; 4 always weight correctly.

For the first open water dives of a novice diver, the same procedure should be adopted. The excitement of the transition from the clear familiar waters of the training pool to the unknown of open water is often sufficient to produce the same early symptoms of overbreathing and tension. Instructors should be prepared for this. When the pupil is relaxed and breathing rhythmically and confidently, and only then, should he be taken on an easy dive. He should never be taken too far, or for so long that his air supply becomes exhausted and a possibly difficult surface swim in equipment becomes necessary. During this initial dive every opportunity should be taken to draw the pupil's attention to interesting underwater features. This will help to take his mind off his breathing, and build up confidence in his equipment.

Fear of surfacing

As a diver becomes progressively more experienced he begins to recognise, perhaps as the result of past difficulties, the fact that he is generally far safer underwater than on the surface. It is not uncommon for this knowledge to produce a tendency to anxiety and even moment-ary panic when a diver first breaks surface after a dive and cannot immediately pin-point his position, orientate himself with his nearest position of safety, or sees shore or boat further away from him than expected. The moment of surfacing is not a good time to suffer such anxiety, because it is the moment of danger, when co-ordination of movement is necessary and clear thinking essential. The correct surfacing procedure helps in this respect and so does the wearing of an inflatable life jacket, but by far the best way of relieving any diver's anxiety about surfacing is to provide efficient and reliable surface cover, preferably by boat, or by snorkel cover equipped with some form of floats such as inner tubes or buoyancy bags. In conditions where it is apparent that efficient monitoring of divers by observation of their bubbles cannot be relied on, as for instance in choppy seas or in con-siderable depths of water, the use of a light signal line from a boat is the only real safeguard. Although in such conditions the wearing of an inflatable lifejacket will again provide some considerable measure of security.

It is necessary to stress that in this instance what is being discussed is the state of mind of the diver, which depends entirely on his faith in the surface safety arrangements. This faith should always be justified.

Fear of dark water

If, in addition to the various other difficulties with which he is beset, the diver is unable to see clearly or at all, he has to exercise considerable self-control to resist panic. A definite distinction exists between diving free into progressively darker water or reducing visibility towards an unknown bottom, unable to see the surface or the bottom alike, and the alternative of descending a short rope or following a guide line or predetermined marks. The former is a most dangerous practice and presents great psychological difficulties. It should be avoided whenever possible. On the other hand it is true to say that a diver following distinct guide lines or feeling familiar objects like rocks, very rapidly builds up a touch picture and can often work quickly, with reasonable efficiency and quite at ease mentally even in black waters of zero visibility.

Claustrophobia

Some people have an inherent fear of being confined in limited spaces and it is doubtful if a chronic sufferer would ever be induced to wear diving equipment or wish to take up diving. Varying degrees of claustrophobic tendencies may, however, manifest themselves in divers under certain circumstances. Conditions likely to lead to this are when a diver reaches bottom and then begins to think of the depth and weight of water above and around him and his confinement within it; or if at a greater depth he considers the difficulties of reaching the surface successfully should his air supply run out or fail. Similar effects can be induced by wearing diving suits—particularly if they are tight fitting, of heavy material or restrictive to swimming. Also if they are leaky or become subject to squeeze effects on a deeper dive.

In these cases the diver's reaction may be to regain the surface as quickly as possible or to withdraw his attention from his surroundings and to ignore the external environment and his companions. Such a diver is a danger to himself and others.

Apart from carefully watching novice divers to counteract such tendencies, they can be overcome to a large degree by diving with a trusted companion or with a signal line to the surface party.

Fear of weed

Fear of weed is well known to both skin and free divers alike. This is probably a relic of 'steam' swimming days when entanglement in weed conjured up a picture of a desperate struggle to release oneself from an unseen but very tangible danger. The sense of sight and the ability to see clearly underwater plays a great part in release from this fear. Weed underwater is generally very beautiful and a calm detached study of its pattern and growth in relation to its surroundings does much to help. Some people suffer a feeling of physical repugnance at the touch of weed, but here again this can often be alleviated, if not entirely eliminated, by visual familiarity with it.

Similar repugnance may be experienced with other forms of underwater life such as weed or animal covered rocks, fish, crab or sea anemones which is caused by their unfamiliar appearance or feel.

Conversely some divers at first think that they can treat things underwater with impunity. Whereas they would never dream of grasping a nettle or picking up a hedgehog without care, they will nevertheless underwater take hold of creatures or plunge their hands into unseen holes. It is not surprising if they emerge from the water with minor cuts, stings and bites. How to adjust oneself to the underwater world has to be learnt from experience and from other divers.

General

The dividing line between comfortable confidence and panic when diving is a very thin one. The diver is in an alien element depending for his life on the correct functioning of a piece of mechanical equipment. He is, however, subconsciously acutely aware of the dangers resulting from any interruption to his source of air supply or his inability to regain the surface. Any strange or new occurrence, an inexplicable sound, an unidentified object or touch, is liable to make him react far more strongly than he would when above the surface. Such a reaction need not necessarily be dangerous if he can control it, and impose the required self-discipline to avoid any tendency to panic. Knowledge, training, experience and through them confidence in both his equipment and himself can reduce the dangers to a minimum.

The gradual build-up of this confidence and experience through the process of the training schedules provides the greatest safeguard against psychological difficulties in diving.

CHAPTER THREE

PHYSICS

The Sea : Dr J Woods

Effects of Pressure : M K Todd

Buoyancy : Dr J Woods

Vision Underwater : Dr John N Lythgoe

THE SEA

What makes the sea behave in the way it does? Why do the tides rise and fall? What are the mechanisms of the currents? The factors covered by these questions, as well as many others, and the complex interactions between all of them go to make up the physical nature of the sea in which we dive. Their study is quite as fascinating as any other aspect of the under water environment: the sea-bed; its animals and plants; the archaeological clues to man's history, and so on. At the same time, the diver with a firm grasp of the mechanisms of the sea—insofar as they are understood—is better able to appreciate the reasons for some of the physical phenomena he encounters on and beneath the surface.

The tides

First we must consider the forces which produce the rise and fall of level. The British diver is familiar with twice-daily (semi-diurnal) tides whose range varies over a twice-monthly cycle between maximum 'Spring' tides and minimum 'Neap' tides. The semi-diurnal period of the tide results from the redistribution of the world's surface water caused by the gravitational attraction of the Moon and, to a lesser extent, the Sun. As Figure 1 shows, the surface of the oceans is raised above the mean level at a point directly below the attracting body and at the corresponding position on the opposite side of the globe. As the Earth rotates about its axis the tidal 'bulge' sweeps round so that every point encounters a high tide twice a day. This process was analysed by Newton some three hundred years ago: he was able to explain the monthly cycle of Springs and Neaps by combining the effects of the Lunar tide which has a period of 12:48 hours and the Solar tide of 12 hours. While in principle these should combine to give Spring tides when the Sun and Moon are aligned at New and Full Moon, in practice there is a lag of, typically, a few days (depending upon the geographical location). The theoretical ratio between the Lunar and Solar tides is about 2:1, giving a ratio of about $2\frac{3}{4}$:1 between the ranges at Springs and Neaps. The reason for the considerable difference between this theoretical value and that found at a given locality will be examined below.

So far we have considered the pattern that tides would exhibit on a featureless, evenly inundated globe. In practice the water is divided into seas and oceans of varying sizes, shapes and depths with the result that the range of tides varies considerably from one place to another. The necessary studies of the response of particular water basins form the major part of contemporary tidal research. Recently the availability of high-speed electronic computers with large storage capacity has permitted theoretical computations on the tides in actual seas, in contrast to the earlier, rather unrealistic mathematical shapes such as squares and circles.

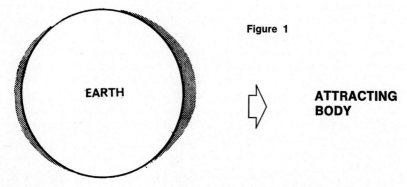

Figure 1

Tidal bulges on an evenly inundated earth in the gravitational field of a single body.

The problem may best be demonstrated by means of an everyday observation in the home. If a nearly full teacup is tilted, then rapidly replaced on a level surface, the liquid will rock from side to side with a decreasing amplitude, but a constant frequency. If the teacup is now gently rocked from side to side at this 'natural frequency' the amplitude of the sloshing motion will steadily increase until the tea spills over the side. If, however, the experiment is repeated at a different frequency, either faster or slower, the surface of the tea does not slosh so strongly from side to side and may break up into a confusion of waves.

Further experiments will satisfy the reader that there is, in fact, a series of sharply defined frequencies, all multiples of the natural frequency, which also induce a regular tidal motion in the teacup—these are called harmonics. If the experiment is repeated with a larger container, a washing-up bowl for instance, the natural frequency will be lower, while even lower frequencies will be found for the water in a bath or swimming pool. Clearly the natural frequency of the water basin depends upon its dimensions and shape. This phenomenon is called 'resonance'. If the driving force has a frequency different from the natural frequency (or some harmonic) the tide produced will have a reduced range, the precise value depending upon the difference in frequencies and the strength of the driving force.

The tides in a sea or ocean will depend, therefore, upon how closely the semi-diurnal driving force matches the natural period of the water mass. If the resonant frequency is closer to the 12 :48 lunar period than the 12 hour solar period, then the lunar tide will be relatively stronger, and vice versa. This has a corresponding effect upon the ratio of the ranges of Neaps and Springs.

Even quite small features on the edge of the oceans can produce a strong local resonance which gives tides out of all proportion to the oceanic tide. The most famous example is the Bay of Fundy, which resonates almost exactly to the semi-diurnal rhythm to give a tidal range of 17 metres at Springs. Other effects can enhance the tides locally; for example, shoaling of the bottom or narrowing of a channel or bay into which the tide floods—both these phenomena contribute towards the very large tides at St Malo (11 metres at Springs). More sophisticated theory is required to explain the double tides at Southampton—little did King Canute appreciate that his striking demonstration exploited a unique non-linear phenomenon.

These then are the major principles behind variations in the tides at different places. Several important factors have been left out of the simple description given above; for example, the rotation of the Earth alters the tides from a 'to and fro' motion in each basin to a rotary wave which swings around the basin's edge (this may also be examined at home with the aid of a teacup or washing-up bowl). Nor has mention been made of the tidal currents which transport the great mass of water for every tide, or of the frictional resistance of the seabed. These factors must be the subject of further reading in the texts recommended later.

CURRENTS

Although, from the diver's point of view, all currents require precautions, it is the variation of current speed and direction which need particular attention. The regular cycle of tidal currents are the strongest encountered in British waters, but because they are predictable they do not present such a problem as the wind-driven currents which fluctuate with the weather. So, leaving the diver to become familiar with the published values for tidal currents (eg, in *Reed's Nautical Almanac*), this section will examine the features of wind currents.

Wind-driven currents

Ekman's classic theory, published in 1905, concerned the effect of wind drag on a sea in which temperature changes rapidly with depth. Although, as we shall see later, this limitation may be quite severe, the Ekman theory has been remarkably successful. It makes two main predictions. Firstly, that the current speed shall decrease exponentially with depth—in an example quoted in *The Oceans* (p 496—see over) the current speed decreases by a factor of three over a depth of 20 metres. The second prediction concerns the direction of the current, which, because of the rotation of the Earth, does not match that of the wind, but rotates in an 'Ekman Spiral' as shown in Figure 2. The surface water moves at an angle of 45° (measured clockwise in the Northern Hemisphere and anticlockwise in the Southern) to the direction of the wind; the water below flows in directions, the angle with the wind of which increases steadily with depth—in the example quoted above the current of 15 metres depth makes an angle of 90° with the wind direction. The theory predicts that the current should directly oppose the wind at a depth where its speed has fallen to about 4% of the surface value.

Figure 2

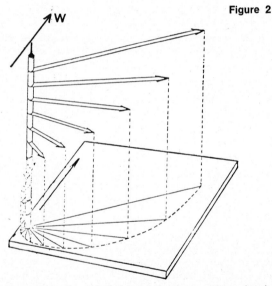

Schematic representation of a wind current in deep water, showing the decrease in velocity and change of direction at regular intervals of depth (the Ekman Spiral). W indicates direction of wind.

The precise shape of the Ekman Spiral in any given situation will depend largely upon the vertical eddy viscosity at the various levels. This 'eddy viscosity' determines the flow of a liquid when it is turbulent; in many ways it may be compared with the 'dynamic viscosity' which determines the rate of smooth or laminar flow (when there is no turbulence). The 'viscosity' of a turbulent fluid may be many hundred times larger than for laminar flow. The precise value will depend on density variations across the current and also upon the strength of the current itself. One of the major problems of contemporary oceanography is to unravel this complicated situation. Suffice to say here that when the current is strong and very turbulent, the eddy viscosity will be large and the wind-driven current will penetrate deeper. Generally, however, the wind current will be effectively terminated, after completing only a fraction of the Ekman Spiral, at the thermocline, where the eddy viscosity decreases sharply giving a slippery layer. There is almost always a large change in the current at a thermocline—an important consideration for divers.

One of the most important questions that a theory of wind currents must answer is 'how rapidly will a change in the wind be followed by a corresponding change in the wind-driven current?' Approximate answers (the first by Ekman, himself) indicate that the response time is comparable with the duration of a longish dive. Of course the diver is most vulnerable near the surface, where the current, and consequently the change, is most pronounced. However, even when the wind remains steady the surface party must be prepared for divers to surface after a considerable drift in midwater—in a direction that cannot be predicted on the basis of the surface current.

WAVES

An understanding of waves on the sea surface requires the use of refined mathematical techniques and covers such a broad range of studies that the subject can only be introduced here. Fortunately, the decision whether to dive or not is usually reduced to an assessment of whether it is too rough for the diving boat to put to sea. Physical oceanography has, with one exception discussed below, little to add to the practical experience of those familiar with handling small boats.

It is evident to the most casual observer that waves are created by the wind and that stronger winds give longer and higher waves. A storm in the Atlantic Ocean, for instance, breaks up the sea into a confused, fluctuating shape, which may be analysed statistically into sinusoidal waves with a whole spectrum of different wavelengths. As these waves travel out from the storm centre the longer waves travel fastest across the ocean surface and arrive at Western Atlantic coasts to herald the coming of rough seas and stormy weather. A deep water wave travels by virtue of a circular motion of the water near the surface. Figure 3 shows how the radius of the circle executed by any particular particle of water (and hence its speed) decreases with depth. Theoretically the diameter of the orbits at a depth equal to one-half the wavelength is only 4% of the corresponding diameter at the surface. This explains why a diver at, say, 30 metres can be quite unaware of the development of a rough sea following a change in the weather. (An experienced diver will notice a decrease in the light as the sky becomes overcast and will visit the surface to check that it is safe to continue diving.)

From the description given above, we see that the energy of a wave is spread through a layer of water whose depth is comparable with the wavelength. When waves approach shallow water this energy is concentrated into the available depth making the height increase and the speed decrease, both of which increase the steepness of the wave. The increase in wave height is known as 'ground-swell', while the deceleration 'refracts' the waves so that they tend to run up a beach square-on regardless of their original direction. In the end the wave becomes so steep that it breaks, either by plunging over in a graceful arc or in a less spectacular spill down the leading edge.

Finally, we must consider the combination of several waves of different sizes and often from different sources. In its simplest form this is described by the traditional saying that 'every seventh wave is larger

Figure 3

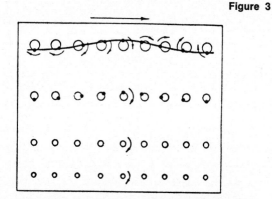

The orbital motions of water under a surface wave.
[After: Kinsman, Wind Waves Prentice Hall.]

Figure 4

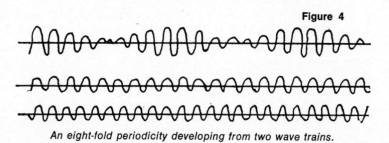

An eight-fold periodicity developing from two wave trains.

than the rest'. This observation may be interpreted in terms of the combination of two regular trains of waves arriving on a beach. Figure 4 shows how a seven-fold periodicity may be generated by a slight difference in the two wavelengths, but, of course, any number may result—the traditional 'seven' had, no doubt, a mystical origin. In a rough sea composed of a wide range of wavelengths, there will be no simple periodicity, but it can be shown that there is a statistical 'probability' that the waves will combine to produce a 'freak' wave of unusual height. Though rare, these freak waves do considerable damage to ships—even large tankers have been tossed tens of yards by them—and they have been held responsible for sweeping holidaymakers out to sea. Clearly the possibility of a freak wave, which can overturn a small diving boat, must be considered when assessing whether the sea is too rough for diving.

DENSITY

The diver will encounter variations in the density caused by changes of temperature and salinity (the concentration of dissolved salt). These will be considered in turn.

TEMPERATURE

Geographical and seasonal differences in sea temperature determine to a large extent where diving is most enjoyable and the failings of British waters compared with, say, the Mediterranean are well known. However, superimposed upon these broad climatological features there are rapid fluctuations cause largely by changes in the weather over the sea. The most regular mechanism is the diurnal rhythm of heating and cooling, but changes in wind-speed, humidity, air temperature and cloud cover also cause changes in the sea temperature throughout a surface layer whose depth approximately matches that available to the diver.

The most striking feature of the temperature structure in this surface layer, the thermocline, has already been mentioned for its importance in limiting the depth of wind-driven currents. There is no really satisfactory theory to explain the development of thermoclines so, apart from stating briefly that their existence and form depend on the modification of the turbulence in the sea by density gradients, this section will present a description, rather than an explanation, of their principal features.

By definition, a thermocline is any region of the ocean where the temperature changes more rapidly with depth than the water either immediately above or below. A rather weak thermocline exists at a depth of some thousands of metres throughout the oceans of the world, but far stronger temperature gradients develop near the surface during the summer. In the Mediterranean, for instance, temperature changes of four or five degrees over a few metres are common at depths of a 30 metres or less. Figure 5 shows a series of temperature profiles measured off Malta during August 1965. The left-hand curves (for 16th August) show that the temperature was almost constant from the surface down to a depth of 30 metres, where it decreased rapidly at the 'summer thermocline', which is a fairly constant feature of the temperature structure. The remaining curves illustrate the development of a series of shallower, but quite intense, thermoclines, whose depths show some persistence from one day to the next despite quite large changes during any single day.

These 'transient' thermoclines are probably initiated by changes in the weather—a fresh breeze springing up or perhaps clouds covering the the sun for a brief period. Their persistence demonstrates that it is easy to form a thermocline, but difficult to dissipate it; in fact, it is generally believed (though there is no direct evidence) that transients last until convection wipes them out in a great upheaval of the sea, lasting perhaps only an hour or so. Considerable efforts are being made to understand the erosion of transients. If current ideas are correct, the seasonal thermocline marks the maximum depth to which convection penetrates at any given time of the year. In which case, the temperature profile for 16th August shows the result of intense convection during the previous night and the following sets of temperature profiles indicate that similar convection did not occur during the next four days.

A diver can detect the presence of a thermocline by feeling the sharp temperature discontinuity or by seeing the change in refractive index. Usually it is possible to see the two layers of water mixing together in eddies a few centimetres across. When the water masses above and below the thermocline move in different directions, as is often the case, they may carry different concentrations of plankton and other suspended material; often in coastal regions the water above the top transient is heavily contaminated with sewage, while the lower water, which has come from a different direction, is quite clear.

Internal Waves

Just as surface waves are the result of a rise and fall in the interface between seawater of density about 1 g/ml and air about 0.001 g/ml, there can also be waves on a thermocline, which is the interface between cold water and warm water with a density difference of 1 part in 1,000 or 10,000. These 'internal waves' are regular features of the ocean, being present to some extent all the time. Because the density difference across the thermocline is so small they are very large and very slow-moving compared with surface waves, but like surface waves they can travel greater distances without diminishing their amplitude. The orbital

Figure 5

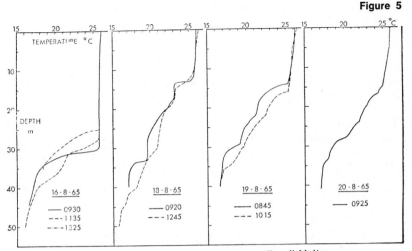

Temperature profiles measured one mile off Malta.
[from Woods and Fosbery, Proc. Symp. Underwater Ass. Malta '65]

motion of the water following an internal wave is correspondingly slow and, although the amplitude of the waves on a deep thermocline may reach a hundred feet or more, the radius of the orbit decreases to a negligible size below the surface, so that there is no detectable disturbance on the surface apart from a 'slick' of glassy water over the subsiding thermocline.

The origin of internal waves is uncertain, but they are probably generated by the tides, during storms and by the current shear across the thermocline (just as a wind blowing over the surface gives surface waves). They may be recognised by measuring the temperature profile of the sea at the same point every five minutes or so; some of the changes in the profiles in Figure 5 may be explained by internal waves. Divers have reported seeing internal waves on a particularly visible thermocline and the rise and fall of the thermocline is often detected by regular fluctuations of the temperature near the seabed—particularly if a diver stays in roughly the same place for an hour or so. It is said that Red Sea pearl fishers use the internal waves reaching them ahead of an approaching storm as a warning to pack up work and retire to the shelter of the harbour before the storm arrives.

Internal waves exhibit all the non-linear features of surface waves; they 'break' on a beach after developing internal ground swell and, just as whitecaps are formed on the sea surface in a strong wind, the internal waves develop agonisingly slow-motion internal breakers when the current shear across the thermocline becomes sufficiently strong.

SALINITY

With the exceptions considered below, salinity plays a minor role in causing rapid density fluctuations in the surface region of the sea. Because the solubility of salt varies very little with temperature, fluctuations in the sea's temperature structure are not materially modified by secondary changes in salinity. The exceptions all arise from changes at the very surface of the sea.

Evaporation

The sea is continually giving water vapour into the atmosphere, but the rate of evaporation is considerably faster when the air is dry and when a wind blows over the sea. The evaporation reaches a peak when white crests develop during stormy weather. Evaporation increases the salinity and hence the density of the surface. In a highly turbulent, well-mixed sea, the extra salt is rapidly diffused into the water below, but when the mixing rate is slow the dense, salty layer may accumulate on the surface until there is sufficient to trigger off convection, when plumes of salty water sink down until they meet colder water of equal density. Because evaporation is accompanied by cooling, the surface density reaches this critical value even faster.

Freezing

When seawater freezes much of the salt in it is rejected by the ice, which is in consequence surrounded by increasingly salty, dense water. Again this may lead to convection, although in this case the latent heat liberated during the freezing process acts against the density rise by warming the sea.

Melting

When sea ice melts it forms a pool of fresh water, which floats on the sea. Eventually this fresh water mixes with the seawater, but until this happens the two are separated by a 'halocline', which is the salinity equivalent of a 'thermocline'.

Precipitation

When rain, snow or hail falls on to the sea a similar layer of fresh water forms on the surface giving a temporary halocline.

Other sources of fresh water

Haloclines are frequently found in estuaries or near sewer outlets, where fresh water runs on to the surface of the sea. A not infrequent phenomenon is the occurrence of freshwater springs under the surface of the sea. The buoyant fresh water welling up to the surface in a continuous plume can sometimes be spotted from the coast. Occasionally ships detect these freshwater plumes with their echo-sounders—and mistakenly report the presence of shallows.

The reader requiring a more rigorous or more detailed treatment should refer to one or other of the standard works on physical oceanography. Every keen diver should be familiar with the classic text of oceanography *The Oceans* by Sverdrup, Johnson & Fleming. The non-specialist may prefer the easily-read narrative of King's *Oceanography for Geographers,* while at the other end of the spectrum, Defant's *Physical Oceanography* provides a comprehensive textbook for those with a formal schooling in physics and mathematics. Finally, I would refer the diver who is keen to read about the very latest research in oceanography to an exciting three-volume work edited by Hill and called *The Sea*. Here we are reminded that our knowledge of the sea is in a state of rapid flux and that each of the topics outlined above forms the subject of current research in laboratories throughout the world.

THE EFFECTS OF PRESSURE

The function of the aqualung is dependent on the fundamental laws of pressure, and an understanding of these laws and their implications is necessary for a proper appreciation of the problems facing the diver as a result of the changes in pressure due to descending into the water or surfacing from depth.

Pressure

At sea-level our bodies are subjected to atmospheric pressure, due to the weight of the atmosphere above us. This pressure remains fairly constant and is taken as being equal to 1 bar (1 b), but the pressure decreases as the altitude increases, diminishing to about $\frac{1}{2}$ b at approximately 5000 m.

The increase or decrease in pressure due to changes in depth during diving is far more significant, the pressure changing by 1 b for a change in depth of 10 m. Water is virtually incompressible and the pressure is due to the body supporting the combined weight of the water and the atmosphere above it. Pressure can be measured with a gauge. If this gauge is calibrated with respect to a perfect vacuum then it will read absolute pressure (1 b on the surface, 2 b at 10 m, 3 b at 20 m etc). Most depth gauges are calibrated with respect to atmospheric pressure and they read relative or 'gauge' pressure (0 at surface, 1 b at 10 m and so on). This distinction is important and must be taken into account when calculating changes in pressure due to changes in depth.

Absolute Pressure = Relative Pressure + Atmospheric Pressure.

Effect of pressure on gases

The air that we breathe is composed of approximately 78.05% nitrogen, 21.00% oxygen, 0.03 to 0.3% carbon dioxide and traces of other gases. It is affected by the physical laws which govern the behaviour of gases.

Boyle's Law

This states that the volume of a gas is inversely proportional to the absolute pressure. So, if the pressure is doubled the volume will be halved, if the pressure increases 10-fold then the volume is divided by 10.

As can be seen, the rate of change in volume with depth is greatest at the approach to the surface—the volume doubling from 10 m depth to the surface. This rapid change in volume must be borne in mind when surfacing from below if an embolism is to be avoided and also explains why frequent ear-clearing is necessary on the first part of a descent from the surface. The change in volume with depth has a marked effect

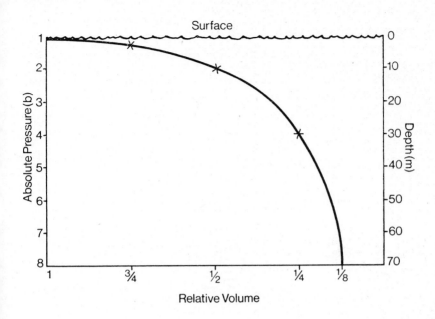

Relative Volume

on buoyancy—particularly if the diver is wearing a wet-suit, and a suitable adjustment of the weight-belt before diving deep may be called for.

Law of partial pressures

When a mixture of gases is under pressure, each constituent gas exerts a 'partial pressure' in proportion to its percentage of the mixture. This is the same as saying that the partial pressure of a gas in a mixture is the product of the absolute pressure of the mixture and the volume percentage of that gas. Thus the partial pressure of nitrogen at atmospheric pressure is 1 b x 78/100 = 0.78 b.

At a depth of 20 m the partial pressure of nitrogen in the air being breathed is 3 b x 78/100 = 2.34 b.

As the overall pressure increases so the partial pressure of the constituent gases increases.

When a gas is brought into contact with a liquid (eg, when the air in the lungs comes into contact with the blood) then some of the gas will dissolve in the liquid. The amount that will dissolve and the rate at

85

which this takes place is dependent upon several factors—the pressure of the gas in the liquid, the contact area between gas and liquid, the temperature, the maximum solubility of the gas in the liquid. As the gas nears saturation amount, so the rate of solution decreases. If gas has dissolved in a liquid, and if the prevailing conditions are varied, then the amount of dissolved gas will also vary.

BUOYANCY

Archimedes' Law states that any object immersed in a fluid suffers an upthrust equal to the weight of fluid it displaces, ie, whose volume it occupies. In the atmosphere, this force is exploited to support a hydrogen-filled balloon; while in the sea the immensely heavy pressure sphere of a bathyscaphe is supported by the buoyancy of a petrol-filled sheet metal float above it.

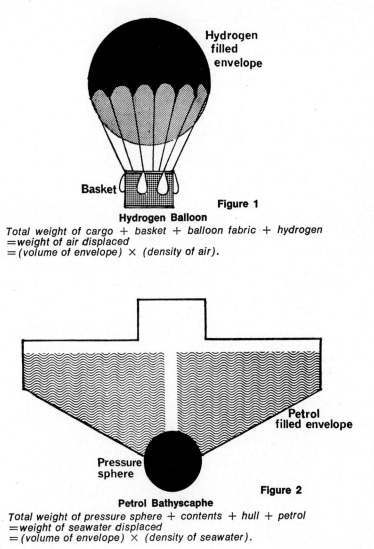

Hydrogen filled envelope

Basket

Figure 1

Hydrogen Balloon

Total weight of cargo + basket + balloon fabric + hydrogen
=weight of air displaced
= (volume of envelope) × (density of air).

Petrol filled envelope

Pressure sphere

Figure 2

Petrol Bathyscaphe

Total weight of pressure sphere + contents + hull + petrol
=weight of seawater displaced
= (volume of envelope) × (density of seawater).

Ships which float on the sea surface are designed to submerge to the *plimsoll line,* ie the weight of water displaced by the volume under the *plimsoll line* just equals the total weight of the ship and its cargo—its *displacement.* In fact, there are several lines to allow for small, but significant differences in density between, for instance, WNA (Winter North Atlantic) and TF (Tropical Fresh).

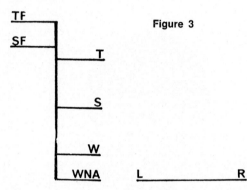

Figure 3

Standard merchant shipping load lines indicating differences in the density of the sea.

A free diver seeks to adjust his buoyancy to suit the varying requirements of his diving. In the vast majority of situations he will try to attain neutral buoyancy, ie a precise equality between his total weight and the upthrust due to the displaced water. In achieving this balance, he must consider a variety of different factors, some of which he can control, some he cannot. One of the major successes of free diving is the ability of the unaided human body to counter the inevitable changes of buoyancy that occur during a dive. These are dominated by two effects, which act quite differently from each other :

Change of weight. A 1700 l compressed air bottle contains about 2 kg of air when full and less than 1% of this figure when empty. Thus, a diver starting with 1700 l of air will end his dive some 2 kg lighter. This excess buoyancy can be a considerable embarrassment at the end of a dive, especially when decompressing or returning along the bottom to avoid heavy waves on the surface.

Change of volume. A rubber diving suit, whether it is a foam wet suit or a dry suit covering woollens, reduces heat loss from the body by interposing an insulating layer of air between skin and water. The volume of this trapped air varies in inverse proportion to the hydrostatic pressure acting on it (see *hydrostatic pressure* and *Boyle's law*) so that, at a depth of 30 metres the air will occupy only one quarter of its volume at the surface. Taking a 5 mm thick neoprene suit designed to cover an average body surface area of about 1.3 m³, we obtain a volume of about 3 litres, of which perhaps 1 litre is in the form of air bubbles at a pressure of one bar. This volume displaces approximately 3 kg of water at the surface, but at a depth of 20 m the air is compressed to one 1 litre in which case it will displace 2 kg less than at the surface (this buoyancy will be regained during the ascent).

The free diver has a variety of methods of countering these inevitable changes in buoyancy. By swimming downwards if too light, or upward if too heavy, he can overcome an imbalance of several kilogrammes, but this is extremely tiring and is strongly to be discouraged. A less tiring method of balancing changes of buoyancy is provided by controlling one's breathing. The human lungs contain on average about 4.5 litres when fully extended and a residential volume of about 1.5 litres after complete exhalation. Thus, the diver can vary his volume by as much as three litres simply by breathing in and out; this is equivalent to a change of three kg of displaced water. The range of normal breathing covers only the middle 20% of this range, so that a neutrally balanced diver breathing normally will experience a regular change of buoyancy from about half a kilogramme too light, when he breathes in, to half a kilogramme too heavy when he breathes out. But by controlled breathing he can maintain an average change in his buoyancy of up to one and a half kilogrammes.

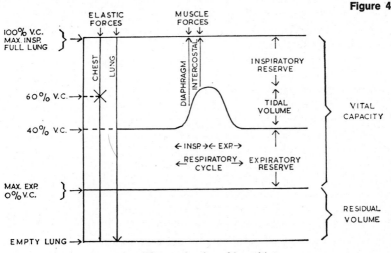

Figure 4

The mechanics of breathing

Illustration taken from Underwater Medicine *by Sgn Rear Admiral Stanley Miles*

Really deep breaths retained for all but brief periods of exhalation followed by immediate inhalation will make the diver about 1 kg more buoyant than when he breathes naturally. The converse, short shallow breaths designed to reduce one's buoyancy, is less easy and may lead to panting.

A new but not recommended technique for controlling buoyancy, which is gaining rapidly in popularity, consists of a lifejacket that may be filled from its own small cylinder of air, or vented into the sea, to provide a change in the diver's total displacement. Of course, this system suffers from the pressure-volume changes which have already been discussed when dealing with diving suits : when descending, the bag is compressed so losing buoyancy and vice versa. The diver must compensate for this hydrostatic instability by carefully adjusting the contents of the bag whenever descending or, more important, ascending. As we shall see later, this control is most critical when near the surface. (See section *Lifejackets*.)

So far, we have only considered methods for adjusting buoyancy continually during a dive. Now we must consider how much constant ballast should be carried in the form of lead weights on a quick-release belt. This is really a matter of philosophy based on physics : in general, it is more convenient to be slightly overweight during the early stages of a dive (both to assist the initial descent and to help keep on the bottom once there) than to be too light a the end of a dive, which will probably be in shallow water. So one carries sufficient ballast to ensure neutral buoyancy at a depth of, say, 5 m with empty cylinders. To achieve this, the diver with a 2000 litre cylinder should aim to be about 1.5 kg heavy when on the surface at the start of his dive.

The use of buoyancy for lifting

One of the most convenient ways to lift a heavy object from the sea bed is to fill one or more plastic buckets with the exhaled air from one's aqualung. This system has the particular merit of affording a constant-buoyancy system at low cost. An air-filled 12.5 litre bucket displaces 12.5 kg of water, so if its mass is 2 kg, the net buoyancy will be 10.5 kg. As the object rises, the air in the bucket will expand and the excess will flow freely from underneath, leaving the displacement, and hence the buoyancy, constant. In general, it is best to use slightly too little buoyancy when raising a heavy object by this method, the remainder being supplied by pulling on a rope from the surface. Otherwise, if the buoyancy exceeds the object's weight, it will rise up with increasing speed until the buckets break surface, overturn and fill with water, with disastrous results.

If, on the other hand, it is decided to used closed bags or balloons, they must be provided with an exhaust valve to allow the expanding air to escape as the object rises. These bags should always be blown up taut on the bottom; if an oversize, partially filled bag is used, its buoyancy will increase as it approaches the surface giving a spectacular, but quite uncontrolled, ascent.

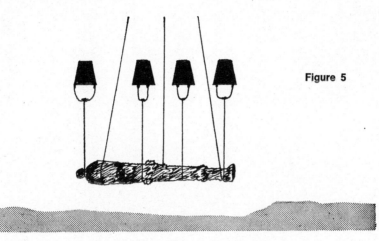

Figure 5

Balancing the weight of a heavy object with air-filled buckets and lifting with ropes.

Hydrostatic pressure

This is defined as the weight of fluid lying on top of a horizontal surface of given area. Thus, the earth's atmosphere gives a pressure of 100 kilonewtons per square metre at sea level. In Britain, we usually call this pressure *one bar*. If we descend below the surface of the sea, there will be an increase of pressure due to the weight of water over us. This gives a further pressure of one bar for every 10 m. Thus, at a depth of 10 m the total hydrostatic pressure is two bars and at 30 m the pressure is four bars.

Fluid pressure has the particular property of acting in all directions; thus, 30 m down the body is subjected evenly to four bars all over and in all directions. The reader will recognise that this is so when he considers the pressure of the water inside an underwater cave : although it may be largely covered with rock, not water, the pressure inside will exactly equal that of the open sea at the same depth, the pressure being transmitted horizontally (see Figure 6).

As the human body consists largely of liquid, it takes up the ambient hydrostatic pressure without any decrease in volume, but the spaces that contain air (for example the lungs) will be compressed unless they are artificially filled with air of pressure equal to that of the surrounding water. This is the purpose of the aqualung demand valve.

A practical use of buoyancy for lifting a heavy object.

Although the total pressure on an object in the sea equals that due to the weight of both the water above it and the atmosphere above that, the *net* pressure on the glass of a diver's watch, for instance, will be equal only to that part which is due to the water, because the inside contains air at atmospheric pressure. Because many pressure gauges are designed to register zero at sea level for the same reason, this is often referred to as *gauge pressure*. Sometimes a container designed to go underwater will be *pumped up* to pressures of more than one atmospheric in order further to reduce the net pressure on its walls. The ultimate in internal pressurisation of this kind is provided for some camera cases, which are connected to a miniature aqualung, complete with demand valve, which maintains the pressure on the walls. With modern materials and seals, however, this is seldom, if ever, necessary.

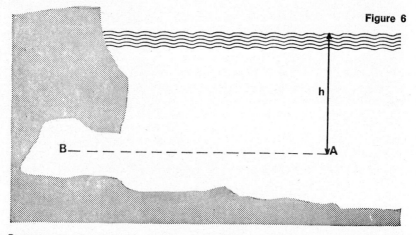

Figure 6

Pressure at point B inside the cave equals that at point A at the same depth in open sea.

Gas laws

Boyle's Law. When a gas is compressed, its volume varies in inverse proportions to its pressure. Thus, an inverted bucket which is full of air at the surface where the pressure is one bar will be only half full at a depth of 10 m, where the total pressure is two bars, and only a quarter full at 30 m (four bars). This is illustrated by the diagram, where we see that the fractional change in the gas volume for a given change of depth decreases with depth. Thus, a change of 10 m near the surface halves the volume, while the same 10 m drop at 60 m only reduces the volume by a factor of one seventh.

This is particularly important for divers. For example, when swimming at 5 m, the diver must clear his ears every time he swims over a sea bed feature of more than a metre in height, but at 30 m, the same vertical movement will not give sufficient percentage change in pressure (and hence in volume) for this to be necessary. For similar reasons, almost all the decompression after a deep dive occurs very near the surface.

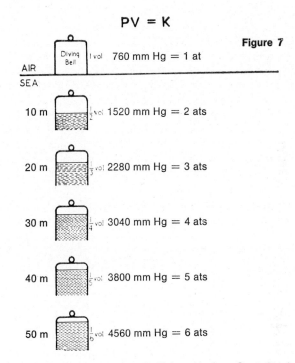

PV = K

Figure 7

AIR

Depth	Volume	Pressure
SEA	1 vol	760 mm Hg = 1 at
10 m	$\frac{1}{2}$ vol	1520 mm Hg = 2 ats
20 m	$\frac{1}{3}$ vol	2280 mm Hg = 3 ats
30 m	$\frac{1}{4}$ vol	3040 mm Hg = 4 ats
40 m	$\frac{1}{5}$ vol	3800 mm Hg = 5 ats
50 m	$\frac{1}{6}$ vol	4560 mm Hg = 6 ats

Illustration taken from Underwater Medicine *by Sgn Capt Stanley* Miles

Because a diver must breathe air at the same pressure as the surrounding water, he extracts more air per breath from his bottles when deep. Thus a supply of air that lasts for 60 minutes at a depth of 10 m will only last 30 minutes at 30 m, assuming the same rate of breathing. Furthermore, the density of the air he breathes at 30 m will be twice that at 10 m and four times that at the surface. At even greater depths, the muscles of the lungs experience difficulty in working against the increased drag resulting from this dense air. It is particularly important to design demand valves so that they do not add to this drag at high pressures; generally speaking a demand valve that has been designed for economy of air at medium depths is unsuitable for deep diving, and vice versa.

Dalton's Law of Partial Pressures. Air is a mixture of nitrogen ($78\frac{1}{2}$%), oxygen (21%) and carbon dioxide (about 0.1%) with small percentages of inert gases, such as argon and contamination from organic and industrial sources in proportions which vary widely with locality. Dalton's Law states that for practical purposes each of these constituents acts independently of the others.

Specifically, the total pressure of the gas equals the sum of the partial pressures that each member has and would have if the others were absent. Thus, while at sea level the partial pressure of oxygen is approximately one-fifth bar and nitrogen is approximately four-fifths bar, the air breathed by a diver 40 m below the surface contains nitrogen at four bars and oxygen at one bar, the total pressure being five bars. The importance of this Law lies in the fact that the physiological effect of a gas depends upon its pressure or, when in a mixture such as air, upon the partial pressure, which, according to Dalton, is quite independent of the presence or absence of any of the other gases. In fact, for deep diving the nitrogen may be replaced by helium at the same partial pressure without any change in the physiological effects of the other gases.

It is particularly important to remember that contamination from, for instance, the exhaust of a compressor, though present in harmless quantities at the surface, may become a serious hazard at depth where its partial pressure is higher.

VISION UNDERWATER

When a swimmer without apparatus goes underwater, his vision becomes inadequate in three distinct ways. Firstly, his eyes are unable to focus and only blurred impressions remain; secondly, it gets rapidly darker as he descends until there is not enough light to see by, and thirdly, visual contrasts are so reduced that even if an object could be brought into focus and even if there were enough light to see by it, it can scarcely be distinguished from the water background. The problem of focusing has been virtually solved by the invention of the face mask which must be one of the most significant in diving. The reduction of light intensity with depth can also be coped with to some extent, but the loss of visual contrasts underwater is a stubborn problem and very little can yet be done about it.

When the eye is working normally in air, light is focused by the curved cornea and by the lens on to the light-sensitive retina (Figure 1).

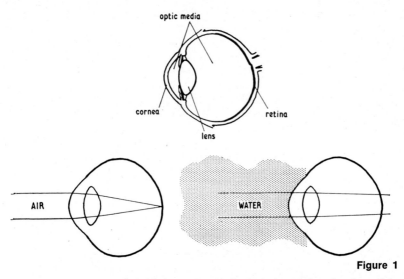

Figure 1

Diagrammatic cross-section of the eye and its focusing action in air and in water.

This focusing depends on the fact that a light ray passing from one medium to another is bent or refracted to an extent determined by the difference in the refractive index of the two media. Air has a very low refractive index while the optical media in the eye have rather high ones. Thus a ray of light entering the eye is refracted at the cornea of the eye and this is where the main focusing power of the eye is found. The partially focused light then passes through the lens which has itself

4

a rather higher refractive index than the media in which it is embedded. Unlike the cornea, the curvature of the lens can be altered, and it is in this way that we can focus at will on near or distant objects. As the main imaging power of the eye lies at the air-cornea boundary, the power to focus depends on the difference in refractive index between air and the optical media. The naked eye cannot focus underwater as water and the optical media have rather similar refractive indices and the focusing power of the cornea is much reduced. The lens lacks the power to complete what the cornea has failed to do and the eye cannot focus on any object at all.

The solution is to imprison an air-space in front of the cornea and thus allow it to function properly. This is the principle of the face mask and most types of underwater contact lenses. The slight disadvantage of this system is that light passing obliquely through the face plate will be refracted in its passage from the water, through the glass, into the imprisoned air within. This has the result of making an object in the water appear to be at $\frac{3}{4}$ its true distance (Figure 2). As the object is optically nearer, a larger image of it will be projected on the retina, but this does not necessarily mean that it will seem to be bigger. On land a near object is not judged to be bigger than an identical object further away, because distance is unconsciously taken into account when estimates of true size are made. Underwater, the increase in image size should be offset by a decrease in the apparent distance of the object. An object underwater should therefore appear to be nearer but

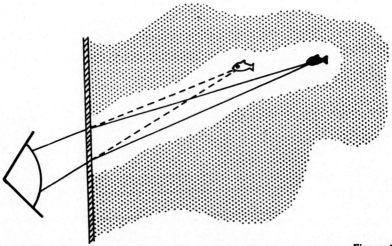

Figure 2

The way in which objects appear nearer underwater when a face mask is worn.

not bigger than on land. Nevertheless, an inexperienced diver frequently judges things underwater to be bigger than they really are and this may be because he does not unconsciously compare the size of the retinal image with the optical distance of the object, but rather because he compares image size to true distance which he has judged by some independent means.

Contact lenses are being developed for underwater use although they are not yet on the open market. They either depend on the air space principle of the face mask, when a small cap containing air is cemented to the outside of the contact glass, or they have a small lens of very highly refractive material embedded in the contact glass. In its simple form the air-space type has the advantage that it allows equally good vision on land as underwater, but is rather bulky. The lens type cannot be worn in air but has less bulk. Neither type has yet been perfected sufficiently to allow extended periods of wear and they do not give the protection against cold and polluted water provided by the face mask. Nevertheless, contact lenses do provide a wider field of view than the standard mask and the elimination of the inner glass surface of the face plate with its scratches, condensation and water drops should make a useful contribution to the clarity of vision underwater.

Scattered light and contrast reduction

A distant object underwater is usually detected because it is either a little darker or a little brighter than the background it is seen against. This brightness contrast is very important in the study of underwater vision and it is defined by the equation :

$$\text{Contrast} = \frac{\text{Object brightness—background brightness}}{\text{background brightness}}$$

Contrasts are low underwater because much of the image-forming light from an object is either scattered out of the light path or absorbed by the water before it reaches the eye, whilst daylight is scattered out of its downward path into the eye thus interposing a veil of brightness between the object and the eye. It is this scattered daylight which is responsible for the brightness of the water background. Taking the results of absorption and scatter together, bright objects become darker and dark objects become brighter as they recede until neither can be distinguished from the water background. The rate at which this happens depends upon the rate that a beam of light is diffused and attenuated by the water and upon the direction of sight. Obviously if the rate of contrast decrease remains the same, the distance that an object can recede before it becomes invisible depends on the original contrast with the water background.

Figure 3 shows how the distance at which a grey object becomes invisible depends upon the object brightness (here measured by the percentage of white light reflected from the object). The low point of the curve represents the object brightness which exactly matches the water background. Although this point is very variable in position, the object presenting the greatest contrast with the water background must be either black or white and in virtually every case it is white.

A close black object has a brightness of zero and therefore the contrast is —1 irrespective of the background brightness. As man can generally detect contrasts greater than about .02 in good light and with large targets, the distance at which a large black object can just be seen depends only upon the rate at which contrast decreases in water. *Thus the distance at which a black body greater in area than 1 sq ft can just be seen when viewed horizontally is an excellent standard method for measuring the visibility.*

In practice, a good way to make the measurement is for two divers wearing black suits to stretch a measuring tape between them. The 'black body' distance being that at which it just becomes impossible to decide the position of the co-diver's limbs in the water.

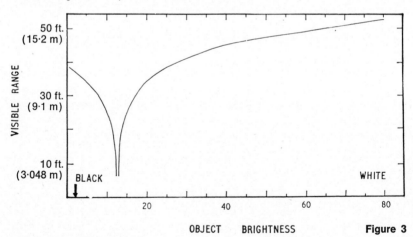

OBJECT   BRIGHTNESS   **Figure 3**

The range at which objects of different brightness can be detected when viewed horizontally underwater. Objects which exactly match the water background in brightness are nearly invisible; those which are white can be seen at the greatest distance.
(This diagram was calculated from actual sightings using painted grey targets 37 sq cm in area at 16 M in Broad Bay, Stornoway.)

The reduction of light with depth and the sensitivity of the eye
The rate at which daylight is absorbed by different bodies of water varies greatly and depends on the amount of dissolved and suspended matter in the water. In Britain it is common enough to find it too dark to see

at 50 feet (15 metres), whilst in the Mediterranean this limit is still far off at the deepest aqualung depth. The eye is able to cope with great differences in light intensity by switching between its two visual systems, one adapted for use during the day and the other at night. In day vision relatively bright light is needed but colours can be seen and there is a good perception of contrast and detail. Night vision is much more sensitive to low light intensities but colour vision is lost and there is some reduction in the ability to distinguish contrasts and detail. It takes between 20 and 30 minutes for an eye adapted to bright light to achieve maximum sensitivity in very dim light. In diving terms this means that a dive into darker water is usually completed before the eye has had time to reach its greatest sensitivity.

In biological diving where a torch can upset the animals being observed, a technique has been successfully used to overcome the slow rate of dark adaptation. The technique takes advantage of the fact that the night vision system is quite insensitive to red light and thus if a well fitted red visor is worn for the 25 minutes before a dive and only removed at depth, the night vision system reacts as though it were dark and adapts accordingly. It has been estimated that this technique provides a 30 per cent greater working depth when no torch is used.

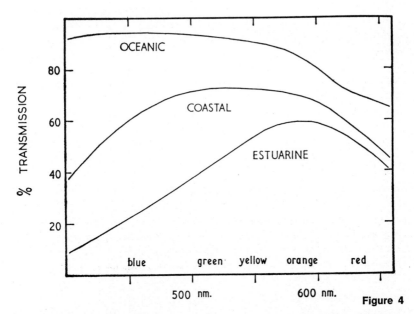

Figure 4

The percentage of light of different colours absorbed for each metre of depth by different types of sea water. Data from N G Jerlov (1951) Rep Swed deep Sea Exped Phys and Chem.

Colour underwater

The eye is sensitive to a band of radiation extending in wavelength from about 350 nanometers (1 nm = 10⁻⁹ metres) to about 750 nm. When all wavelengths are present in about equal amounts the sensation of white is produced, but when a narrow band of wavelengths predominates, the sensation of colour is produced. The relationship between colour and wavelength is shown along the horizontal axis in Figure 4.

Pure water absorbs most red and orange light, less yellow, still less green and relatively little blue light. Therefore the deeper daylight penetrates into pure ocean water the poorer it becomes in red light relative to blue. Inshore waters, on the other hand, are usually stained by the yellow products of vegetable decay. These substances are very persistent and have the property of absorbing much blue light, less green and very little yellow or red. If these yellow substances are present in quantity they act as such strong light filters as to over-ride the blue filtering properties of pure water and the reddish-brown colour of freshwater lochs and burns results. If the yellow stain is rather more diluted, the red and yellow light is absorbed by the water and the blue by the yellow substances and this leaves green as the colour least absorbed. This is the explanation for the green colour of the water around our coasts.

This colour-filter action of a water mass is chiefly responsible for the fact that colours appear different below the surface. An object is coloured because it absorbs some wavelengths more than others. The wavelengths that it does not absorb but reflects are responsible for its colour. For instance, at about 30 metres in the Mediterranean the water has absorbed most of the red light so that an object which is red on the surface because it absorbs all save red light will not be exposed to the only wavelengths it reflects and will thus appear black. In reddish-brown peat-stained water the blue is absorbed more than the red (although both are absorbed more rapidly than in pure water) and it is the blue object which appears black.

Painting objects to be conspicuous underwater

To begin with a distinction must be drawn between objects which can be seen at a distance underwater and those which are conspicuous when seen at close range lying amongst weed or stone on the bottom. In the former case it is the brightness contrast which is much the most important, and in the latter case it is more usually a combination of colour and brightness contrast which renders an object conspicuous.

Safety considerations usually require divers to go down in pairs and it is important for one diver to see the other at the farthest possible distance. It has already been explained why an object presenting the highest brightness contrast with the water background will be visible at the greatest distance. In practice it is white objects which present the greatest contrast with the water background in all directions except directly upwards when black will be best. *This leads to the suggestion that large areas of equipment should be painted white whilst the suit should be black. On the other hand, parts which break the surface whilst swimming should be painted the colour which shows up best against the sea. Fluorescent orange might be the best choice here.*

In all except peaty water fluorescent oranges and reds show up with great brilliance at close range. This is because fluorescent pigments have the ability to absorb the short wavelength light at the blue end of the spectrum and re-emit longer wavelength light at the red end.

A series of tests were carried out to ascertain the most visible colours underwater around Britain. This then applies to green waters and not necessarily to Mediterranean waters or brown peaty water such as Loch Ness or Bala.

The colours for test were :

Fluorescent : Yellow-Green (a pure yellow is not possible in fluorescent colours).

Orange.

Red.

Normal :   Yellow.

Orange.

Red.

Black.

BS 630 Grey.

White.

The results indicated that yellow is always poor; and the present cylinder grey is also always poor. Fluorescent orange is good for horizontal paths of sight in shallow dirty water (vis about 1.5 metres), but poor in deep water and probably clear water too. It is difficult to ascertain the circumstances where maximum visibility is vital. The most likely is looking downwards or sideways trying to find a lost diver.

Current indications for coloration for all circumstances would be as follows.

Hood—Fluorescent orange.

Suit—Black.

Cylinders, harness straps etc—White.

Table of the Most Visible Colours in Various Situations

BRITISH COASTAL WATERS

	Daytime, shallow		Deep, or at night	
	Good Vis	Poor Vis	Good Vis	Poor Vis
Looking horizontally	White	Black or Fluorescent orange	White	White
Looking down	White	White	White	White
Looking up	Black	Black	Black	Black

CHAPTER FOUR

MEDICAL

Fitness and Medical Certificates :
Dr John Betts

Ears and Sinuses : Sgn Lt-Cdr J Murray Young

Respiration and Anoxia :
Sgn Lt-Cdr J Murray Young

Exhaustion : Dr John Betts

Burst Lung and Ascent Hazards : R L F Darby

Decompression Sickness : H Val Hempleman

Carbon Monoxide Poisoning : Leo Zanelli

Nitrogen Absorption : George F Brookes

Nitrogen Narcosis : P B Bennett, PhD.BSc.
MIBiol

Carbon Dioxide Poisoning :
Sgn Lt-Cdr D H Elliott

Oxygen Poisoning : J Bevan, MSc.

Air Analysis : P Freeland

FITNESS AND MEDICAL CERTIFICATES

Fitness for Diving

The vague term 'fitness' is often bandied about without it being realised that it may take different forms. Thus the lean fitness of a 30 metre sprinter is not that of the Channel swimmer with its accent on moderate obesity and long-term muscular effect nor yet, to take an extreme, that of the Japanese wrestler where immense bulk and muscularity are at a premium. Fortunately, diving is compatible with a large range of body builds, with the exception of gross obesity, and the individual, moreover, may limit his diving to areas which are not too physically demanding for him.

Fitness may be subdivided under three headings. Firstly, the rather negative aspect of ensuring that various diseases or deformities incompatible with diving are absent, this being to a large extent the purpose of the medical examination, and secondly to ensure that the individual can maintain sufficient power output (physical efficiency) to cope with the possible demands upon him. Diving, with all the shifting and wearing of heavy equipment involved, is equivalent in its demands to labouring as an occupation, and in tidal waters swimming with equipment involves a work level equal to running on dry land. The third component of fitness is the acquisition of the mental and physical reflexes appropriate to the sport concerned. In the case of diving the appropriate re-actions to different situations are acquired at practice drills during the course of the training programme and then reinforced by actual diving under supervision.

While an intelligent individual could undoubtedly learn most of the essential drills during a few hours training, their use will not be automatic when first learnt and they will be soon lost again unless reinforced by further practice or actual use. Similarly the more experienced diver may find his diving technique rusty after the winter lay-off, while his physical efficiency may also have deteriorated if he has an office job and no alternative winter exercise or sport. This has proved a reliable recipe for trouble in the past and some form of physical exercise and practice of the basic underwater drills are a good investment before resuming active diving.

General Medical Examination

The medical examination should ideally be carried out by a doctor conversant with the requirements of diving and in possession of the diver's past medical history, or, since this is not always possible, his own general practitioner, who should be asked to give an account of any abnormalities found so that if there is any doubt about their effect on the man's fitness, a decision can be given by a suitably experienced doctor. A routine general medical examination is required with additional attention being paid to the ears, and sinuses. The individual's past medical history must be checked, particularly for any major illnesses or accidents, particularly any involving attendance at or admission to hospital, ear, nose and throat conditions such as otitis media (infection of the middle ear), sinusitis, mental illness, epilepsy, asthma, diabetes, and any drugs regularly taken.

It is impossible to discuss all the effects of every possible ailment on diving in a short chapter but in most cases the answer will be self evident. A few problems, however, are of particular importance.

The Nervous System

Epilepsy: Any event producing unconsciousness underwater has a high mortality. Thus epilepsy must completely disbar a man from diving. Where, however, an individual has been off treatment and free from all attacks for over five years, this rule may possibly be relaxed, bearing in mind, however, that epileptics tend to conceal their disability. He should, of course, never use an oxygen or mixture set, with which even normal individuals are at risk of having convulsions.

Mental illness: Part mental illness should not disbar a man from diving, although it may raise some doubt as to his motivation for diving, such as a desire to prove one's self! Current treatment of the milder degrees of depression and anxiety need not prevent training although open water diving should be prohibited until treatment has been successfully completed, since the illness may affect judgment and many modern drugs used in treatment can adversely affect the body's reaction to stress and cold.

Respiratory System

An X-ray as well as examination of the chest is essential. Healed lung disease is no disability except insofar as it produces reduced effort tolerance or areas of abnormal lung tissues liable to produce air trapping. A common example of a condition producing air trapping is the lung cyst, which may be present from birth or be the result of disease. Although compressed at the beginning of a dive it will refill with compressed air as the dive continues but on the ascent may prove to have too small an opening to empty rapidly with the result that the excess air is forced into the bloodstream producing an air embolism. Any condition which produces severe narrowing of bronchus or bronchioles may produce the same effect. All such conditions absolutely preclude diving as does active chest disease of any type.

Asthma : Although theoretically a hazard, attacks of asthma do not seem to occur in the relatively clean air of the coast or when breathing the highly purified air supplied by an aqualung. It should be checked that the subject's effort tolerance has not significantly been diminished by his asthma.

Cerebrovascular System

Minor degrees of valvular disease of the heart may be ignored provided that the individual's physical efficiency is adequate.

Hypertension (high blood pressure) : Minor degrees are not of importance. Probably the dividing line lies about the level of 140 mm mercury systilic (peak) pressure and 100 mm diastolic (lowest) pressure. Above this no one should be accepted without careful enquiry into its effect on their exercise tolerance and into any associated illness such as coronary arterial disease. Certainly hypertension sufficient to warrant continuous control by drugs should not be accepted.

Coronary arterial disease : There is considerable evidence from accident statistics that the exertion and stress of underwater swimming is particularly prone to provoke coronary thrombosis where there is coronary disease and that these attacks are generally fatal. Therefore, where there is hypertension, or a history of chest pain on exertion (angina) or heavy smoking, especially in the middle-aged candidate, an electrocardiogram, if possible taken during exertion, should be done. No individual with evidence of coronary disease, including previous coronary thrombosis or angina, should be permitted to dive.

Diabetes

Diabetes when controlled by diet or tablets is normally acceptable although the cardiovascular system should merit careful scrutiny in view of the accelerated degeneration associated with the disease. A problem arises when the individual is having insulin injections which may produce unconsciousness through hypoglycaemic attacks (abnormally low blood sugar). Provided that such attacks do not occur or, if they do, the sufferer has some warning symptoms, diving may be permitted. An emergency supply of sugar or glucose should always be carried while diving. Attacks sometimes occur because of omission to eat regular meals through seasickness.

Teeth

These should be adequate to grip a mouthpiece. Partial dentures firmly anchored to sound teeth are acceptable. Full dentures should be removed while diving, since there is a definite risk of them coming adrift and impeding breathing.

Ear, Nose and Throat

Attention should be paid to the ears and sinuses since these are a common source of trouble, in particular past ear infections and sinusitis should be enquired about. As well as checking that the tympanic membranes are intact, they should be observed while the subject ' clears his ears ' to confirm that there is no obstruction of the Eustachican tubes.

Otitis media (inflammation of the middle ear) : Old otitis media which has cleared up and the drum healed over is quite acceptable. Where there is chronic infection or discharge, diving would almost certainly provoke a flare-up and be dangerous. The difficult case is one where the infection has cleared but left the individual with a persistent perforation of the drum. While undoubtedly many people have successfully dived with such a perforation, there is some danger of starting a fresh attack of otitis media or even mastoid infection and also of provoking uncontrollable vertigo as cold water enters the ear. Since most of these cases would be suitable subjects for plastic repair of the ear drum, it is far preferable that this be done before they attempt to dive.

Otitis externa : This is an infection or dermatitis of the outer ear passage and is not a disqualification, but affected individuals must take additional care over normal hygiene, rinsing the ear with fresh water and carefully drying it after diving.

Sinusitis : It is difficult to predict the response of an individual subject with sinusitis to diving. Some have small inadequate openings into their sinuses or poor drainage and get sinus squeeze or fresh attacks of sinusitis, while on the contrary others actually benefit from diving, the to and fro movement of compressed air presumably helping to wash out mucus from the sinuses. Thus cautious experiment may be permitted in the milder case.

Exercise Tolerance

Ideally, the examination should include a test of physical fitness or exercise tolerance. Various tests based on the rate of recovery of the pulse after a standard exercise have been devised, such as the Harvard step test. These may give misleading results if apprehension has accelerated the heartbeat prior to the test, and in addition are somewhat time consuming. At present the BSAC swimming tests, particularly those involving swimming 50 yds with a 10 lb weightbelt and treading water for one minute with hands above head form an effective substitute for a formal test of effort tolerance.

Special Tests

As stated, the chest X-ray is an essential part of any medical examination. The electrocardiogram should not be done routinely but in selected cases, as mentioned.

Lung function tests such as the vital capacity (see page 119) the peak expiratory flow rate and the one-second forced expiratory volume (FEV_1) are used by professional units to assess pulmonary efficiency but are not generally available.

Temporary Unfitness

Any infection of the ears, sinuses, respiratory tract and lungs produces temporary unfitness for diving.

In the ears and sinuses the movement of compressed air will help to spread the infection far and wide, converting a mild infection into a serious one, while there is considerable evidence that bacteria and viruses actually multiply far more quickly when the oxygen partial pressure is raised by diving.

The same effect occurs in the lungs where bronchitis and pneumonia have been known to become fulminating in their rapid deterioration under pressure.

It should not be overlooked that sedative drugs, particularly alcohol, sleeping tablets and some types of seasickness cures may persist in the body for 12 to 24 hours and greatly increase nitrogen narcosis or even produce its effects at unexpectedly shallow depths.

Review

The individual should ideally be examined prior to diving and then, barring any severe illness intervening, the frequency with which he is reviewed should be related to his age.

EARS AND SINUSES

The Ear

The ear is the organ of hearing and is also concerned with balance and position sense. It can be described as having outer, middle and inner portions and is shown diagrammatically in Figure 1.

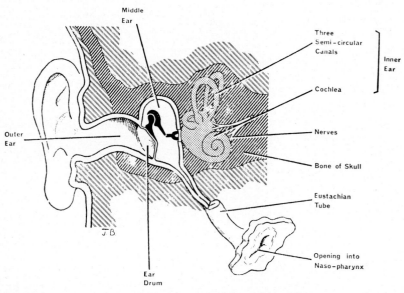

Figure 1   *Diagram of the ear and Eustachian tube*

The outer ear consists of the externally visible ear and the 'external auditory canal' which is closed off at its inner end by the ear-drum. This portion is open to the air and its purpose is to collect sound waves and direct them to the cone-shaped ear-drum which will therefore be made to vibrate.

The middle ear is an air-filled space mostly surrounded by bone. Part of its outer wall is formed by the ear-drum, and the air-space is connected by the Eustachian tube to the air passages which lie behind the nose (the naso-pharynx). Running across the centre of the middle ear is a chain of three small bones (the ossicles) which transmit the vibrations of the ear-drum to the inner ear.

The inner ear is filled entirely with fluid and is embedded in the bone of the skull. The cochlea (Figure 1) receives vibrations from the ossicles and converts them into nerve impulses which are sent to the brain and there perceived as sounds.

The semi-circular canals are usually considered as part of the inner ear although they take no part in hearing. They are of major importance for a sense of balance and enable one to determine one's position in space, but their function can be upset by factors which affect the middle ear (see later—Vertigo and Disorientation).

The Sinuses

The sinuses are air-filled spaces within the bones of the skull and are mostly connected to the inside of the nose (the nasal cavity). The largest (Figure 2) are the frontal sinuses, in the bone over the eyes, and the maxillany sinuses in the cheek bones. Others, which are not shown in the figure, occupy positions in the mid-line of the skull behind the root of the nose.

The mastoid bone, which is the hard protruberance behind the ear-lobe, also contains a number of small air-spaces which connect with each other and with the middle ear air-space.

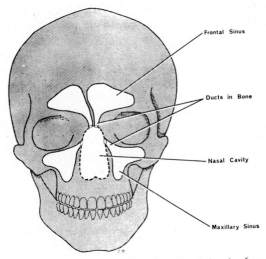

Figure 2   *Diagram showing the position that the main air sinuses occupy in the bone of the skull*

The Effects of Pressure

The outer ear is normally in easy communication with the atmosphere via the external auditory canal and therefore pressure in it will remain equal to that of the surroundings. If the canal should be blocked with wax this must be removed (under medical supervision *only*) and no ear-plugs or anything that may obstruct the outer ear should ever be worn while diving.

The middle ear is an air-filled space and will therefore be affected by pressure changes. On first descent into the water the increasing pressure will be transmitted throughout the outer ear to the ear-drum which will tend to be pushed inwards towards the middle ear. To counter-balance this, air at the increased pressure must be admitted to the middle ear via the Eustachian tube. As shown in Figure 1, the opening of the Eustachian tube into the naso-pharynx is normally closed so that air cannot pass up to the middle ear unless some positive action is taken to open the tube. This is a knack which is easy for some people but which requires much practice in others and is commonly brought about by swallowing or by the Valsalva manoeuvre (holding the nose, shutting the mouth, and gradually increasing the air pressure within the naso-pharynx by forced expiration.) When the Eustachian tube has been opened, air will rush into the middle ear and the ears will be felt to 'pop', this process being called 'clearing the ears'.

When pressure is increasing, the ears must be repeatedly cleared at a rate which will depend upon the rate of descent into the water and the actual depth. If clearing is not carried out, the difference in pressure across the ear drum will stretch it and cause pain and eventually will burst the drum. (Cases have been recorded where the pressure of 3 metres of sea-water has been sufficient to burst an ear-drum.) Experience will soon tell a diver how often to clear his ears but it is important to clear them before descending to a depth where pain occurs; pain is a danger signal and a sign that some damage has already been caused. If pain does occur the diver must ascend until the pain has gone and then must clear his ears; descent can then be continued, clearing more frequently than on the first attempt. If he is still unable to clear his ears, or if pain returns on the continued descent, the dive must be abandoned. During an ascent, the decrease in water pressure will cause the air in the middle ear to expand and, if the pressure is not relieved, the ear-drum could again be burst. The anatomy of the Eustachian tube is such that its connection at the middle ear is permanently open and so air has no difficulty in passing down the tube and equalising pressure. This act is helped by swallowing but will occur passively. The Valsalva manoeuvre should not be performed during the ascent as this will hinder ear clearing.

The inner ear contains no air-space and so is not directly affected by pressure changes.

The sinus ducts are tubes which run in bone and are always open in health and thus no positive action is required to clear the sinuses. The diver usually has no sensation of the passage of air into or out of the sinuses.

The Effects of Disease

The Eustachian tubes and sinus ducts are all lined with living membranes. When any cells are subjected to disease or irritation they will become inflamed and swollen and hence the membranes of a person suffering from a cold or hay-fever will become swollen. The degree of swelling is often sufficient to completely block the sinus ducts and make it impossible to open the Eustachian tubes and gives rise to the 'blocked-up' feeling and headaches which are common in the early stages of a cold.

No person should ever attempt to dive when they cannot clear their ears easily, as even a shallow dive with blocked ears or sinuses can cause such pain as to certainly be a great distraction and possibly cause loss of consciousness.

The anatomy of the Eustachian tube (described above) is responsible for the fact that 99.9% of all cases of blocked ears give trouble on the descent, with increasing pressure. Most cases of sinus pain (67%) also occur on descent but one third of cases who have got down to depth without trouble have pain on the ascent. A quick 'trial dip' is therefore no sure guarantee of fitness to dive after a cold, especially if the diver has had previous sinus trouble, but in most cases the sinuses will clear if the ears can be cleared.

A blocked sinus duct will cause pain and often local tenderness of the bone over a sinus. If a duct blocks during the ascent the diver should, if his air supply and decompression time allow, descend again until the pain goes and then re-ascend more slowly. If the diver must continue to the surface, the air in his sinus will continue to try to expand and will cause increasing pain and an increasing force which will usually succeed in blowing the obstruction out of the duct. This will immediately allow the pressures to equalize and will ease the pain and usually the diver will find blood-stained fluid coming from his nose. Any such occurrence should be followed by a lay-off from diving until sinus symptoms have disappeared.

Tablets and nose drops or sprays should not be used, except under medical advice, as an aid to clearing ears or sinuses during open-sea dives. This is because, firstly, the effect of the drug may wear off during the time at depth and the diver may have trouble on the ascent.

Secondly, some such drugs have side-effects and may cause drowsiness; the appearance of side-effects varies markedly between individuals and from day to day in the same individual and can never be predicted.

The outer ear may become infected and become sore with a fluid discharge from the external auditory canal and diving must not occur until medical advice has been taken. This infected condition is commonly brought about by not drying the ears properly after a dive, with the result that the lining of the canal becomes saturated and 'soggy' and loses its natural protective qualities. It is not advisable to push anything into the canal deeper than a finger will normally reach, but all excess moisture must be shaken out as soon as possible after leaving the water.

MEDICAL

Vertigo and Disorientation

Vertigo and disorientation are the names for the conditions in which the world appears to be spinning around you and all sense of position or direction is lost. These symptoms are brought about by a disturbance of the function of the semi-circular canals of the inner ear.

If the ears have become partially blocked, the sudden large pressure change on clearing can cause vertigo which is usually momentary but can be very disturbing. Sudden temperature changes in the ear can give the same effect and this can happen at any time during a dive when cold water gets to the ear-drum; the water will rapidly be warmed by body heat and the vertigo will usually disappear in 30-60 seconds.

There are other causes of this condition and the advice of an experienced diver or of a doctor should be sought when it occurs.

RESPIRATION AND ANOXIA

Metabolism and Respiration

The body is composed of millions of separate cells, each of which carries out a particular function. Some types of cells are widely distributed throughout the body while others are highly specialised and grouped together into organs such as the brain, liver, kidney or lungs. In order to live and grow each cell needs a steady supply of food and oxygen which it uses to supply energy. This process is called metabolism and in a very simplied form follows the equation

$$\text{Food} + \text{oxygen} \rightarrow \text{energy} + \text{water} + \text{carbon dioxide.}$$

Not all of the food taken in is used in this process and that unwanted is partly released from the body as faeces and partly excreted by the kidneys, together with the water produced in metabolism, as urine. Water is also lost by evaporation of sweat from the skin and as water vapour in the breath.

Respiration is the process whereby oxygen (O_2) is transported from the atmosphere to the cells for use in metabolism and carbon dioxide (CO_2) is removed from the cells to the atmosphere. Respiration therefore includes the act of breathing, the uptake of O_2 by the blood at the lungs, the transplant of O_2 to the cells by the circulation and pumping action of the heart, the uptake of O_2 by the cells from the blood, and the reverse process for CO_2.

The Heart and Circulation

The heart consists of four chambers and can be thought of as two separate pumps (Figure 1). The two chambers on the right side of the heart from a pump supplying blood at low pressure to the lungs via the pulmonary arteries. In the lungs the blood passes through the microscopic vessels called capillaries and is then collected in the pulmonary veins and returned to the left side of the heart. The two chambers of the left heart form a high pressure pump which supplies blood via the arteries to the capillaries of the rest of the body, from whence it is collected in the veins and returned to the right heart. Between the two chambers of each side of the heart and on the output side of each lower chamber there are flaps which act as non-return valves.

The heart is mainly composed of muscle and acts by contraction of this muscle in a rhythmical fashion. Contraction of the heart will squeeze out some of the blood contained within it and the valves will ensure that the expelled blood is pumped into the arteries. On relaxation of the heart muscle, blood will flow into the heart from the veins. The amount of blood pumped out at each contraction will depend upon the volume of the lower chambers and the strength of the muscular contraction.

117

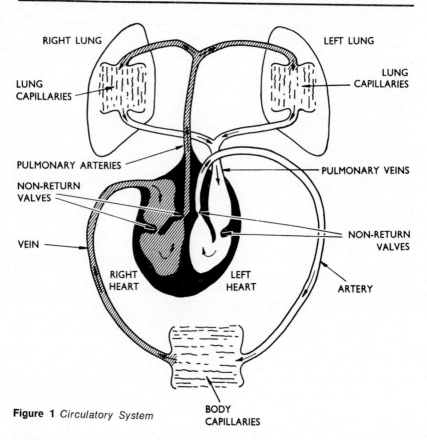

Figure 1 *Circulatory System*

Lungs

The lungs are the organ for interchange of gases between the atmosphere and the blood and consist basically of two air-sacs, situated in the chest, connected by the windpipe (trachea) to the atmosphere via the mouth and nose. Each lung is enclosed in a membrane (pleura) which protects it and allows it to move freely over a similar membrane which covers the inside of the ribcage, the space between the two membranes (the pleural cavity) being completely obliterated in health except for a small amount of lubricating fluid. The lungs have elastic properties, like a balloon, and will always tend to contract away from the chest wall but, because of the absence of any gas in the pleural cavity, the lungs cling to the chest wall in the same way that a rubber disc will stick to a flat surface.

Contraction of the muscles between the ribs and the muscles of the diaphragm will raise the ribs and lower the diaphragm and cause an expansion of the volume of the chest. The lungs will follow the chest movement and therefore there will be a lowered gas pressure within them which will draw air in from the outside atmosphere. Relaxation of this muscular effort will, under normal conditions, allow the diaphragm to rise and the ribcage to fall passively under the action of gravity, and, aided by the elastic recoil of the lungs, will decrease the volume of the chest, raise the pressure within it and force gas out to the atmosphere again.

The pattern of the airways inside the chest can be compared with the branching structure of a tree. As the trachea enters the chest it divides into two, and each airway (bronchus) supplies one lung. Each bronchus then divides to supply the lobes of the lung and at each division the size of the airway becomes smaller. Further divisions and sub-divisions occur until millions of small twigs are formed (bronchioles) and, on each twig, bud-like protrusions form the blind end of the airways (the alveoli). The total surface area of these alveoli, which are the places where gases are exchanged between the blood and the air in the lungs, has been estimated in adult man to be about the area of a tennis court. The alveoli are separated from the blood in the lung capillaries only by the thin membranes which form their respective walls.

In an average man the greatest volume of gas that the lungs will hold when fully expanded (the total lung capacity) is about 6 litres but not all of this volume is used in respiration. When at rest and breathing quietly the volume of air moved into and out of the lungs on each breath (the tidal volume) is about 0.5 litre and at the end of a normal breath out (expiration) the lungs still contain about 2.5 litres. During exercise the tidal volume increases, both by having a bigger expiration and a bigger breath in (inspiration), until it may reach as much as 3 litres with maximum exercise. If you first give a maximum expiration and then measure the volume of a maximum inspiration it will be about 4.5 litres; the value obtained is called the vital capacity and denotes the maximum volume of air that can be moved into or out of the lungs in one breath. The difference between the total lung capacity and the vital capacity, about 1.5 litres, is called the residual volume and represents the gas which cannot be expelled from the lungs, even by a maximum expiration.

The residual volume is of great importance when considering the effects of change of pressure on the lungs. For example, a breath-holding diver who breathes in to total lung capacity (say 6 litres) on the surface at 1 bar absolute pressure (1 b) and then descends to 30 metres (4 b) will have decreased his lung volume to a quarter, 1.5 litres, because the pressure has increased fourfold (Boyle's Law). His lungs now only hold their residual volume and if he descends further the increased pressure will compress his chest more than nature intended and he will suffer from 'the squeeze'. Again, if a diver attempts a

free ascent from below 30 metres (ie over 4 b) without breathing out
on the way up, even if he has breathed out to his residual volume before
leaving bottom, by the time he has reached the surface his residual
volume of 1.5 litres will have expanded to more than 6 litres, ie to
more than his total lung capacity, and he will suffer from pulmonary
barotrauma.

Blood and Gaseous Exchange

The adult body contains about 5 litres of blood which is composed of
a fluid (plasma) within which are carried specialised cells. The plasma
also contains a substance in solution which forms the main constituent
(fibrin) of a blood clot when a blood vessel is damaged. Plasma without
fibrin is a slightly yellowish thin fluid (serum) and is most commonly
seen oozing from a graze.

The main type of cell contained in the plasma is the 'red' cell which
contains within it a substance called haemoglobin which has the property
of combining chemically with oxygen; there are normally about 5
million red cells per cubic millimetre of blood. The other cells which
do not contain haemoglobin are the 'white' cells which have special
functions concerned mostly with the combating of infection within the
body; there are about 7,500 of these cells in every cubic millimetre of
blood. As the blood passes through the lungs, oxygen will combine with
the haemoglobin in the red cells and the amount of oxygen which com-
bines will depend upon the pressure of oxygen present in the lungs. The
air we normally breathe contains 79% nitrogen (N_2) and 21% O_2 with
a trace of CO_2 and at sea level the total pressure of gas is 1 ata, which
is equivalent to 760 millimetres of mercury (mm.Hg.). Oxygen will
contribute 21% of this total pressure and so there will be 21% of 760
$= 160$ mm.Hg. pressure of O_2 in air and this is called the partial pressure of oxygen (Po_2). (Nitrogen will have a partial pressure (Pn_2) of
79% of $760 = 600$ mm.Hg.). When haemoglobin is chemically combined
with the maximum possible amount of O_2 it is said to be 100%
saturated at a Po_2 of 160 mm.Hg. Arterial blood is normally about 98%
saturated.

The oxygenated blood coming from the lungs will be carried by the
circulation via the heart to the body capillaries. The tissues of the body
will have been using oxygen in metabolism and so the Po_2 in the tissue
cells will be lower than in the newly-arrived blood. Any gas will always
move (diffuse) from an area of high pressure towards an area of low
pressure and so oxygen will diffuse out of the blood capillaries into the
tissues. As the haemoglobin gives up its oxygen it changes colour and
obtains a noticeable blue tint. Also because of metabolism there will be
a greater partial pressure of carbon dioxide (Pco_2) in the tissue cells than
in the blood so CO_2 will diffuse into the blood where it mostly forms
a chemical compound, sodium bicarbonate.

This blueish blood will then be collected in the veins and returned via the heart to the lungs. The blood now will have a lower Po_2 and a higher Pco_2 than the air in the alveoli so O_2 will diffuse into the blood from the lungs and combine again with the haemoglobin, causing it to change back to the bright red colour of arterial blood. At the same time the CO_2 will be released from its chemical combination and will diffuse out into the lungs to be expelled from the body during the next expiration which will usually consist of about 17% O_2, 4% CO_2 and 79% N_2. Nitrogen is said to be an inert gas because it takes no part in normal metabolism and therefore, provided the total pressure remains unchanged, ie the P_{N_2} is constant, the amount expired is the same as the amount inspired because the body is already fully saturated with nitrogen at this P_{N_2} (but see *Decompression* and *Nitrogen Narcosis*).

As metabolism concerns a chemical reaction between food products and oxygen, the cells need a supply of food to be brought to them and this is also carried by the blood. The full metabolic reaction takes place by stages and some steps can only be carried out in specialised cells such as those of the liver. It simplifies matters therefore to say that the blood carries ' metabolites ' from the cells of the body at the same time as it transports O_2 and CO_2.

Anoxia and Hypoxia

Anoxia means total lack of oxygen and hypoxia means a reduced amount of oxygen and both conditions will cause death or decreased efficiency of the cells of the body. It will be obvious from the descriptions given above that continuing life depends on the combined actions of the heart, blood and lungs. If the heart stops the cells of the body will eventually use up all the O_2 in their immediate vicinity and then die of anoxia; if the heart is inefficient, either through disease or in-born defects, it will not be strong enough to pump sufficient blood around the body and the cells will suffer from hypoxia. If the blood volume is decreased because of bleeding (haemorrhage) or if the normal quantity of haemoglobin is reduced (as in anaemia) the amount of oxygen that can be carried to the cells will be reduced and again the body will suffer.

Some substances can poison the blood and interfere with the carriage of oxygen. The most important is carbon monoxide (CO) which is found in domestic gas supplies and in the exhaust of internal combustion engines (eg petrol or diesel driven compressors). Carbon monoxide also reacts chemically with the haemogoblin of the blood, but much more powerfully than does oxygen, so that the blood will always pick up CO in preference to O_2 and this CO is retained for possibly hours. Therefore if CO is present the amount of haemoglobin available for the carriage of O_2 will be reduced and the cells of the body will again be subjected to hypoxia. At the same time, CO combining with haemoglobin causes it to become a very bright cherry red and the affected person becomes very noticeably red in the face.

If the interchange of gases at the lungs is interfered with, either because breathing has stopped or because the lungs are blocked (eg by a foreign body such as a denture-plate), the body will go on using oxygen by metabolism and gradually reduce the blood Po_2 producing a blueish tinge of the skin (cyanosis), especially of the lips and nail-beds, which is characteristic of such cases of asphyxia. If the obstruction is not rapidly removed the body will suffer from O_2 lack and eventually die.

Lastly, the air breathed into the lungs must contain sufficient Po_2 for the body's needs or else again cyanosis will occur and eventually death of all the cells of the body through anoxia. The air breathed must also contain a smaller Pco_2 than is found in the veins of the body so that a pressure difference is still present to cause CO_2 to diffuse into the air in the lungs. If not, CO_2 will accumulate within the body and cause ill-effects and eventual death.

The cells of the body vary in their sensitivity to hypoxia and in the time needed to cause damage from which they cannot recover. The cells of the brain are the most sensitive and, if the heart stops and the body is becoming hypoxic through the continuation of normal metabolism, the brain is likely to be irreparably damaged in four minutes. Other tissues are much more resistant and a muscle will eventually recover its full strength and function even if its blood supply has been stopped for 20-30 minutes. However, efficient muscles are useless if the brain is so damaged that it is no longer capable of properly controlling them and therefore four minutes must be considered the limit of time available for restoring normal carriage of oxygen to the body.

Effects of Exercise

The rate at which metabolism is carried out in any group of cells depends on the amount of energy being used. Thus an exercising muscle will use much more energy than one at rest and hence the rate of O_2 consumption and CO_2 production will be increased during exercise. If the circulation and respiration remained unchanged in exercise there would again be an increasing degree of O_2 lack in the cells because oxygen usage would be greater than the supply.

The circulation and respiration rates are therefore very finely controlled in the body to ensure that the supply of oxygen and food, and the rate of removal of CO_2 and other metabolites, at the cells is always sufficient whatever their rate of metabolism. These control processes are automatic and subconscious but the normal control of respiration can be consciously over-ruled for a short time, eg in speaking, eating and breath-holding.

(i) Control of circulation

The circulation rate is largely determined by the heart. Like any pump, the output from the heart (cardiac output) will be given by multiplying the volume ejected from the heart on each contraction (stroke volume) and the number of contractions per minute (pulse rate). When exercise occurs nervous impulses are sent to the heart to increase the pulse rate and this can rise from the average level at rest of 60-70 beats/min to 180-200 beats/min (see Table 1). At the same time the heart will slightly dilate and increase its stroke volume so that an overall four-fold or five-fold increase in cardiac output can result.

The circulation rate can locally be increased very much more than this however by alterations in the distribution of the blood within the

	Rest	Moderate Work	Maximum Exercise
Pulse rate (beats/min.)	60-70	100	180-200
Cardiac output (1./min.)	4-5	6-8	20-25
Tidal volume (litres)	0.5	1.5	3.0
Respiratory rate (per min.)	12-14	20	35
Total expired ventilation (1./min.)	6-7	30	100-110
Oxygen consumption (1./min.)	0.25	1.2	4.0-4.5
Carbon dioxide production (1./min.)	0.20	1.0	3.5-4.0

Table 1.   Effects of exercise. All figures are average values. There is considerable variation between individuals. Moderate work may be taken as walking on the flat at 4 mph or swimming at 0.75 knot which is a medium pace for average swimmers.

body. Not all cells increase their metabolism at the same time and, by contraction or dilation of small arteries, blood can be diverted from those cells at rest to those which are active. Thus after a heavy meal the stomach and intestines are very busy digesting food and blood is diverted from other places, such as the muscles, into the abdomen to increase the oxygen supply. When taking physical exercise blood is diverted away from non-active areas such as the intestines and skin and concentrated on the active muscles, and the circulation rate to, say, the muscles of the legs can be multiplied twenty-fold when comparing the resting and exercising states. (If exercise is taken after a heavy meal, the circulation finds itself with conflicting needs from two different systems of the body and compromises between the two. As with any compromise, the solution must be a less than optimum effort in both directions so the result in this case is a reduction of physical exercise capability—and indigestion!)

(ii) Control of respiration
The amount of respiration is found by multiplying the tidal volume and the rate of breathing (the respiratory rate), and is usually described as the total expired ventilation measured in litres per minute (1./min.). At rest the respiratory rate is normally 12-14 breaths per minute and the tidal volume about 0.5 litres so that the total expired ventilation is 6-7 1./min. (Table 1). During exercise the respiratory rate and the tidal volume both increase so that total expired ventilation may reach 100-110 1./min.

Exchange of gases between the air and the blood in the lungs only occurs in the alveoli but at each inspiration gas has first to fill the airways (the branches and twigs of the bronchial tree) before it can reach the alveoli. Therefore at the end of inspiration the airways will be filled with gas that takes no part in the gaseous exchange and is expelled, unaltered, on the next expiration. The volume of the airways (the "dead space') is a nearly constant quantity for an individual but varies, roughly with chest size, between individuals and is of the order of 0.15 litre. The volume of gas per minute available for interchange of gases (the 'effective' or 'alveolar ventilation') will therefore be less than the total expired ventilation by an amount which is determined by the dead space times the respiratory rate. Any piece of equipment (eg a snorkel tube) which increases the dead space must decrease the effective ventilation and decrease the ability of the body to interchange O_2 and CO_2 at the lungs, causing the P_{O_2} in the blood to tend to fall and the P_{CO_2} to rise.

The body contains specialised receptor cells which sense any change in blood gas pressures and will cause an increase or a decrease in the total expired ventilation to return the blood gas partial pressures to normal values. The most powerful stimulus to breathing is the P_{CO_2} and this is kept remarkably constant in the body throughout the whole range of activities. Under experimental laboratory conditions it is possible to show that the total expired ventilation will more than double if the P_{CO_2} in the lungs rises by 1 mm.Hg. from its normal value of 40 mm.Hg. Also, if by deliberate over-breathing (hyperventilation) you wash out more CO_2 from the lungs than is being produced by the body and thus cause a fall in P_{CO_2}, the stimulus to breathe is greatly diminished and breathing may even stop for a while until the P_{CO_2} is restored to its normal value by continuing metabolism. A low Po_2 can also stimulate respiration but the effects are barely noticeable until the Po_2 in the inspired air has decreased to below about 100 mm.Hg. when the ventilation will increase to enable the blood in the lung capillaries to absorb more oxygen.

The level of ventilation is also affected by nerve impulses from the joints and muscles so that, at the start of exercise, the ventilation is increased almost immediately to cope with the increased amount of CO_2 the body will produce because of the exercise. When this increased Pco_2 appears in the blood some quarter of a minute later, there is a further increase in ventilation because of stimulation of the specialised receptor cells. At the end of an exercise period, there is again a very rapid decrease in the level of ventilation followed by a slower return to normal as the Pco_2 regains its original value. Nerve impulses from the lung tissues, diaphragm and ribcage also affect ventilation and maintain the regularity of respiration and control the relationship between tidal volume and respiratory rate.

(iii) Oxygen consumption and carbon dioxide production

Oxygen consumption when completely at rest is about 0.25 1./min. (Table 1). During exercise, as metabolism increases to provide more energy, O_2 consumption must also rise and the average person will achieve a maximum of about 4.5 1./min. when working as hard as possible. The maximum O_2 consumption varies with the degrees of fitness and the size of the individual and consumptions of about 6.0 1./min. have been measured in Olympic athletes. During a dive the consumption will be varying with the degree of activity and the overall oxygen usage will normally be about 1.0 1./min.

Carbon dioxide production is closely linked with oxygen consumption because of the metabolic equation and is measured as the amount of CO_2 breathed out in litres per minute. This amount will be affected by the volume of the total expired ventilation. The ratio between CO_2 production and O_2 consumption will therefore vary under different conditions but as a general rule CO_2 production can be taken as being 0.8 times the O_2 consumption.

It is important to remember that O_2 consumption and CO_2 production are values that are unaffected by the depth of a dive. If a diver is performing a constant rate of work and has a total expired ventilation of 20 1./min. at the surface (1 ata), he will still have a ventilation of 20 1./min. at 10 metres (2 ata) but this gas volume will be equivalent to 40 1./min. when measured on the surface. Thus, for a constant rate of work, the ' surface equivalent ' ventilation will increase with depth. However, a constant rate of work will have a constant rate of energy usage and, because the production of energy is basically a chemical reaction, this will require a constant number of molecules of oxygen per minute under all conditions. If the work being done requires each minute a number of O_2 molecules which occupy a volume of 1 litre at 1 ata, they will only occupy 0.5 litre if measured at 2 ata but the 'surface equivalent' O_2 consumption will still be 1 1./min. and thus is independent of depth.

The body does contain a small store of oxygen, in the blood haemoglobin, in the gas in the lungs, and in a special compound found in muscles. This O_2 store is sufficient to support the body for short bursts of exercise and, for example, top-class sprinters rarely breathe during a hundred yds race. The O_2 store can also be used in situations where the O_2 consumption is greater than the amount of oxygen being taken up by the body, such as in fast swimming in an emergency. However, such exercise will have produced an increase in P_{CO_2} in the body and decreased the total P_{O_2} much below normal ie have produced an 'oxygen debt'. The specialised receptors will react to these changed conditions and after the exercise is over will increase the respiration until the P_{CO_2} has returned to its normal value and the O_2 store has been replenished and the repayment of the oxygen debt has been completed.

Effects of increased pressure

The body is mostly composed of watery fluids and water can be said to be incompressible; certainly it is not affected by the pressure at present foreseen in diving. The air-containing cavities within the body (lungs, ears, sinuses) will however be compressed with increasing pressure according to Boyle's Law and to avoid ill-effects they must be filled with gas at the same pressure as that of the surrounding water (see *Ears and Sinuses*).

The effects of pressure on the circulation will vary with the position of the body in the water and are difficult to assess but certainly are less in degree and importance than the effects of exercise. Anyone who is medically and physically fit to take hard exercise will not suffer any circulatory embarrassment in the water.

The effects on respiration arise from several factors. As mentioned above, the supply of gas to the diver must be at a pressure close to the water pressure over his chest so that there is no pressure difference across the chest wall. The pattern of respiration tends to change when underwater because the effect of gravity is hidden amongst the conflicting pressure variations and the act of expiration can no longer be the passive action seen in the normal situation. Gas has usually to be actively and consciously expressed from the lungs and this skill sometimes is difficult for the new diver to learn as it requires confidence in oneself and one's equipment. Complaints about shortage of gas can sometimes be observed to be not because of lack of gas flow from the breathing set but because the diver has not been expiring sufficiently and his chest is so 'blown-up' that he cannot physically expand his chest any further to breathe in. As pressure increases so does the density of a gas and it becomes heavier and more sticky and therefore more difficult to move. To obtain the same amount of ventilation under pressure as at the surface will therefore require more work to be done and this can become a serious embarrassment to the diver. For example, experiments show that at 30 metres (4 ata) the maximum volume of air that the average man can move into and out of his lungs in one minute (the maximum breathing capacity) is half that which he could attain at the surface. Although at 30 metres the O_2 partial pressure is four times normal and therefore there is no shortage of O_2, the volume of ventilation required to remove CO_2 from the body is not changed. As the maximum breathing capacity is halved at 30 metres so will be the maximum amount of CO_2 that can be removed per minute. If the body Pco_2 is to remain at its original value this means that the maximum possible exercise at 30 metres will also be half that attainable on the surface. Most types of breathing apparatus cause a mechanical increase in breathing resistance and an increased dead space and this will further restrict respiration as well as increasing the need for respiration. With increasing depth the maximum breathing capacity and the exercise capacity will be further decreased and this is a factor in determining the maximum depth obtainable breathing air.

The solution to this problem is to use a breathing mixture such as oxy-helium (O_2/He) which has a much smaller density. The work of breathing and the apparatus resistance are much decreased and breathing O_2/He at 90 metres is very similar to breathing air at 30 metres.

EXHAUSTION

Definition
Exhaustion is a symptom more easily recognised than defined, but may be described as a condition in which the diver or individual has reached a point where he is unable to respond adequately either physically or mentally to further demands on him. In its physical form, it is usually characterised by deep, laboured breathing. It is dangerous because any inability to respond to the demands of diving is liable to result in drowning.

Causes
Physical Exertion. Swimming at a moderate pace, even with the assistance of fins, is equivalent to running or heavy work on land. As explained in the chapter on 'The Body', muscular exertion results in an increased blood flow to the muscles actually at work to carry oxygen to them and remove waste products. Efficient as this mechanism is, it is unable to provide sufficient oxygen for heavy exertion, and once a muscle has used up the small store of oxygen contained in its own haemoglobin-like pigment, myohaemoglobin (responsible for the reddish-brown colour of muscles), it has two methods of continuing to function for a short time without an oxygen supply. Firstly, there are special phosphate compounds which store rapidly available energy in small amounts and can be used for muscular contraction. These can be quickly reformed when once again sufficient oxygen is available. Secondly, there is a much larger reserve, provided by the break-down of glucose into lactic acids, an energy-giving process which does not require oxygen at the time, but which eventually requires oxygen to consume the lactic acid produced, a comparatively slow process compared to the first. In the meantime, the lactic acid appears in the blood stream, producing an acidosis which stimulates the respiratory centre in the brain and causes a great increase in pulmonary ventilation—the deep laboured breathing referred to as being characteristic of physical exhaustion.

It follows from this that the most efficient technique both from the point of view of avoiding exhaustion and minimizing air consumption, is to swim at a moderate rate, thus avoiding running into severe oxygen debt and incurring the distress and unnecessarily high air consumption produced by the accumulation of lactic acid in the blood. If heavy exertion should be unavoidable, then short bursts of activity with frequent rest periods are the best technique.

Depth. As depth is increased, the density of the air breathed increases, as does the work involved in breathing. At 30 metres the diver's maximum ventilation rate is halved, and at 45 metres it is down to about one third, and his work capacity correspondingly reduced because of inability to eliminate sufficient carbon dioxide. In addition, further restrictions on breathing are imposed by the inadequacies of demand valves.

At depth, then, it becomes increasingly essential to swim slowly and easily, and avoid heavy exertion in any form, which not only will be wasteful of air but in addition lead to exhaustion under water. There is also considerable evidence that if early symptoms of this are ignored, then the accumulated carbon dioxide not only aggravates nitrogen narcosis, but also increases the probability of decompression sickness.

Hypothermia (lowered body temperature). (For detailed discussion of hypothermia, see the chapter on protective clothing.)

Loss of body heat, from inadequate or poorly fitting diving suits, results not only in physical discomfort but in slow mental reactions and loss of ability to think clearly, loss of muscle power in chilled limbs and if allowed to continue, eventually ends in coma and death. In lesser degree, it is an important but often unrecognised cause of exhaustion and a silent, contributing factor in many accidents. To press on and disregard the physical discomfort of feeling chilled is thus not only foolhardy but dangerous.

Decompression. Fatigue and mental tiredness is a well recognised symptom of decompression sickness, and may be the only symptom resulting from a dive which was near or just exceeded the no-stop limit, or in which the recommended rate of ascent was exceeded, or in which decompression was inadequate.

Mental fatigue. A diving week-end may entail a combination of physical and mental work that will tax the strength of even the fittest. An early morning start, followed by a long drive to the coast, the assembly of boats and other equipment on site, and the organisation of diving in addition to the normal exertion of the dive itself, all combine to produce fatigue. Particularly at risk are dives later in the day and the return journey home.

Treatment of exertion exhaustion. This is the type of exhaustion most likely to produce a crisis while diving and is recognised by a great increase in the rate and depth of breathing, sometimes to the point at which the demand valve is unable to cope, 'beating the lung'. This situation can occur as the result of poor dive planning, leaving the diver downstream of his boat or other point of return and necessitating a heavy swim upstream against the current, at a time when his air supply is running low. It is essential in this predicament to reduce one's effort, and consequently the demand for air. This can only be achieved by physical rest and relaxation, while at the same time taking such steps as are possible to minimize the danger involved. The technique is to :—

1   Stop finning and any other activities and rest with the demand valve below the level of the chest, ie, in normal swimming position with

mouth-held single hose valves and lying on the back with twin hose valves. This ensures that air is supplied at positive pressure and lessens the work of breathing.

2   If possible grab hold of some stationary object in order to avoid being swept yet further away from one's diving base. If this is not possible, ie, at the surface, in mid-water, or on a sandy bottom, then relax and drift with the current, making sure, however, when in deep water that one does not sink too far.

3   Concentrate on controlling the breathing rhythm, which should, ideally, be deep and slow.

4   Once breathing is under control, it is usually wiser to abandon the dive and ascend to the surface, dropping the weight belt or inflating lifejacket to assist the ascent if necessary.

5   At the surface, unless out of air, continue to breathe from the lung, since if the change-over to snorkel is mismanaged in the stress of the moment, the heavy breathing will ensure that any water inhaled will be carried deep into the lungs and initiate drowning. The mask also should be kept in position.

6   Give distress signal.

Novices may find the degree of self control demanded by this technique beyond them, and if in shallow water they may surface before carrying out the rest of the drill. They should retain the demand valve mouthpiece if possible, unless out of air, to avoid inhalation of water.

Avoidance of Exhaustion. A good diving technique demands that diver exertion be minimized, both to avoid exhaustion and to conserve air supplies. In particular the effects of tide and current should be taken into account.

Physical fitness is important, as fit divers need less air for a given amount of exertion. Conversely illness, particularly coughs and colds, may considerably reduce physical efficiency and increase the liability to exhaustion.

When diving from a moored boat a floating safety line should be trailed astern, so that divers in difficulty will be able to avoid being swept farther away while they relax to regain their breathing rhythm.

After care. Shock may follow exhaustion and need treatment with rest, warmth, hot drinks, and if chilled a hot bath later.

BURST LUNG AND ASCENT HAZARDS

The mechanics of burst lung are simple. If the pressure of air within the lungs is allowed to rise compared with surrounding pressure the relative increase in internal pressure distends the lungs causing them to stretch fully to their limit of elasticity. Once this point is reached a further increase in relative pressure within the lungs builds up sufficient force to burst the lung and allow air to spill out. Pulmonary Barotrauma (Pulmonary—of the lungs, Barotrauma—pressure damage) is the medical name given to this condition. When the point of maximum stretch has been reached—this point is beyond that which can be achieved by a normal maximum inhalation—the additional pressure the lung can tolerate unaided is equivalent to the pressure of about 1.5 metres of water. It follows, therefore, that burst lung is always a risk when compressed air breathing apparatus is used underwater at almost any depth.

Situations where burst lung is a risk occur frequently in sports diving. The diver must be aware of these situations and familiar with the procedures necessary to reduce the risk to a minimum.

There is no 'medical mystique' about the basic cause of burst lung. Burst lung is always caused by a relative excess of air pressure within the lungs. A relative excess of air pressure in the lungs can be brought about if the pressure in the lungs remains constant when the surrounding pressure falls. This is the situation that would arise if air at 'bottom pressure' was retained in a diver's lungs during his ascent.

A diver coming up from depth in the normal manner and breathing naturally from his breathing apparatus is not usually troubled by air at 'bottom pressure' being retained in his lungs when his surrounding pressure is decreasing. This is because there is plenty of time and opportunity for the expanding 'bottom pressure' air to escape with the exhaled air during the natural breathing cycle. If however, the diver was suffering from a lung disorder which trapped 'bottom pressure' air in a small diseased section of his lung, then even a normal ascent would present an unacceptable risk in spite of the fact that the major part of his lungs could vent unhindered. This is one of the reasons why a diver should keep in good physical condition and undergo regular medical checks with chest X-ray.

A burst lung can happen to anyone ascending more than a few metres, irrespective of the maximum depth and duration of the dive. Using a normal rate of ascent and ascent procedure the risk, given healthy lungs, is very small indeed. Any increase in the rate of ascent or enforced variation to the natural breathing rhythm during ascent increases the risk of burst lung.

Emergency ascent procedures are dealt with in another chapter but all expose the diver to a more rapid than normal decrease in surrounding pressure or to an alteration of his breathing rhythm, or both. If a diver, before discarding his breathing apparatus to make a solo emergency ascent, fills his lungs with air from the breathing apparatus, he must consciously and continuously exhale during the ascent. He must exhale to allow the 'bottom pressure' air expanding in his lungs to escape. If the diver makes the ascent at a constant speed he will need to allow for the fact that the air in his lungs will expand at a greater rate as he nears the surface, and will therefore need to be exhaled at a greater rate to avoid a pressure build up.

Theoretically, if an emergency ascent was made from a depth of 30 metres and the diver forcibly exhaled to the fullest extent possible before commencing the ascent and then held his breath, the residual 'bottom pressure' air left in his lungs would only be sufficient to just fill his lungs completely when the surrounding pressure was reduced to surface pressure. Under these circumstances any over-distention of the lungs would be impossible. As a technique this would only be valid for depths up to 30 metres, and even then would leave the diver with a strong desire to breathe and a general feeling of discomfort during the ascent. It also imposes upon the diver the additional burden of assessing his depth accurately in relation to the 30 metre limit, an assessment he may not be able to give the necessary attention to in an emergency situation. If he should misjudge the depth and attempt to use this technique from a depth greater than 30 metres, then the chances of his being aware when his lungs are 'full to bursting' during the latter stages of the ascent are small. This is because the 'full to bursting' signal, known as the Hering-Breuer reflex, is very weak in man.

A diver faced with an emergency ascent must remember that as the pressure surrounding him falls during the ascent the air in his lungs will expand and must be allowed to escape. This can be accomplished by pursing the lips in the 'whistling position' and consciously and continuously blowing out during the ascent, increasing the exhalation as the surface is neared. If the 'bottom pressure' air in the lungs is vented off in this manner as it expands, then no discomfort will be felt during the ascent. Since the expanding air being 'whistled' away carries with it any excess carbon dioxide produced in the lungs, there will be no desire to breathe in.

A complete understanding of the technique and, through this understanding, personal confidence in the ability to carry it out, are the most important factors in achieving a relaxed, comfortable, safe emergency ascent without breathing apparatus, should the situation ever arise.

An assisted ascent, where two divers ascend sharing one breathing apparatus need not expose the divers to a much greater risk of burst lung than a normal ascent if the assisted ascent is made at the normal rate, and if the divers are competent and relaxed enough to be able to establish a shared breathing rhythm close to their natural rhythm.

Even so, in the special circumstances of an assisted ascent there is a tendency for each diver to take a deeper than normal breath before handing the mouthpiece to his partner. The deeper than normal breath is then followed by a longer than normal delay in the breathing cycle. Because the ascent is continuing during this delay the surrounding pressure will fall. Air in the lungs will expand and should be consciously vented off by the divers between mouthpiece exchanges to reduce the risk of a dangerous pressure build up.

The snorkeller who attempts to prolong his dive by taking a breath underwater from the breathing apparatus of a companion diver puts himself at the same risk as a diver making a solo emergency ascent. This risk, is not acceptable under normal conditions and the practice should be avoided.

A diver in the swimming pool is not exempt from the dangers of burst lung if he breathes from underwater breathing apparatus at a depth of more than a few metres. If a trainee, having swum down to a breathing set on the pool bottom, attempted to fit the equipment but failed after taking one good breath from it and then decided to surface for a repeat attempt, he could be starting the ascent with his lungs already expanded beyond the normal maximum. This would be the case if at the time he took the breath the demand valve diaphragm was at a greater depth than his lungs. If the pool was a deep one and the trainee did not exhale on the ascent, the risk of burst lung would increase from the possible to the probable.

The rule to reduce the risk of burst lung when a diver ascends with 'bottom pressure' air in his lungs is always the same whether the ascent is made in the swimming pool or in open water. The 'bottom pressure' air in the lungs must be allowed to expand and escape during the ascent. This venting, which occurs naturally with the breathing cycle during a normal ascent, will have to be made by the conscious effort of the diver 'whistling' air out continuously during the ascent. The symptoms that a burst lung has occurred differ according to what has happened to the air which has burst through the lung tissues.

Air Embolism is the condition which arises if air from the ruptured lung finds its way into the blood circulatory system. Bubbles of air (emboli) form in the blood stream and where they become lodged, prevent further supplies of blood, and therefore essential oxygen, being carried to any dependent tissues beyond that point.

If the blood supply to the heart muscle is blocked the result is a heart attack.

If the blood supply to the brain is impaired dramatic symptoms may develop quickly. The diver may lose consciousness upon reaching the surface, or shortly afterwards, and suffer irreversible brain tissue damage and subsequent death unless recompressed (usually 6 bars absolute) in a Compression Chamber within seconds—within minutes will be too slow.

Almost any part of the blood circulation can be affected by an air embolism. In consequence any of the body systems or functions which rely upon an unrestricted blood supply can undergo partial or complete failure. The range of symptoms presented is wide including giddiness (vertigo), patches of numbness, partial paralysis and defects in speech or vision. So wide is the range of possible symptoms that any abnormal behaviour by a diver upon, or shortly after, surfacing, particularly if he has just completed an emergency ascent, must be taken as the symptom of an embolism. Even in the case of the less dramatic symptoms it may prove necessary to commence treatment by means of recompression in a compression chamber within a matter of seconds if permanent disablement or death is to be avoided.

Spontaneous Pneumothorax is the condition which arises if air bursts through the lung lining and collects between the lungs and the chest wall (pleural cavity). If this occurs when the diver is at depth the entrapped air expanding during the ascent may collapse the lung. The symptoms present in the surfaced diver may be : shortness of breath; a cough, perhaps with small amount of blood or a nose bleed; or he may complain of a pain in the chest. In severe cases extensive collapse of the lungs, perhaps aggravated by the physical displacement and consequent embarrassment of the heart, can cause death. Qualified surgery using a hollow needle (cannula) can be employed to release the entrapped air as it expands during the therapeutic decompression which follows. Further hospital treatment will be necessary to deal with the collapsed lung.

Interstitial Emphysema is the condition which arises if air from the ruptured lung gets into the mass of tissues within the chest cavity. Air may spread under the skin at the base of the neck giving a crackling effect (crepitation) if the skin is touched. Symptoms are similar to those of pneumothorax and like them may only become apparent during the therapeutic decompression of a suspected case of air embolism or serious decompression sickness (bends). Treatment may require recompression in a compression chamber. The difficulty of removing the air by surgical means coupled with the slow natural absorption and dispersal rate from these tissues may make the therapeutic decompression a slow procedure.

Treatment for a diver showing any symptoms of burst lung is recompression in a compression chamber. Although subsequently it may become apparent that the condition did not need recompression, the fact that symptoms of burst lung were present meant that lung tissues had been ruptured and air may have been present in the blood stream making seconds vital.

When the diver has been recompressed in a compression chamber to a depth at which all symptoms are relieved, or to a maximum of 6 atmospheres absolute, expert medical advice can be sought to identify the exact problem. If the original diagnosis of burst lung is proved to be wrong, no harm has been done and the diver can be brought back to surface pressure on a regular repeat dive decompression schedule. If the diagnosis was correct, or if the symptoms proved to be those of serious decompression sickness, prompt recompression could well have saved a life.

If no recompression facilities are available and a diver has surfaced showing symptoms of burst lung, the situation is grave. Recompression by sending the diver down again in the water is not recommened. The effects of cold and the limits imposed by the equipment usually used by the sports diver make the procedure impractical, apart from any other medical considerations. The only answer is recompression in a compression chamber and all effort should be directed towards this end.

During the delay in getting specialist medical advice or the diver to a compression chamber he should be positioned comfortably resting on his left side with the head slightly lower than the feet—in the hope that any free air bubbles in the blood will tend to rise away from the heart and brain. Oxygen may be beneficial where there is respiratory distress or irregularities in the blood circulatory system.

Practising solo emergency ascents as part of the normal diving training for a sports diver is a matter for controversy. In earlier years the BSAC training programme included solo emergency ascent practise but does not do so today (1971). Current medical opinion opposes such practise unless recompression facilities and qualified medical assistance are immediately available at the surface.

The dilemma to be resolved is whether more divers would be lost practising the correct solo emergency ascent procedure than by using the established but unpractised procedure when the actual emergencies arise.

DECOMPRESSION SICKNESS

Before giving an outline of the difficulties of safely decompressing a diver following his time underwater, it will be advisable to re-examine briefly the basic physics and physiology of his situation.

Atmospheric pressure

This pressure varies slightly from day to day, but the normal pressure at sea level is 1 bar, or 10 metres of sea water. In other words, before anyone commences a descent into the sea, he already has a total pressure equivalent to 10 metres of sea water pressing equally in all directions on his body. It is very important to remember that we are already living at pressure before we descend into the sea and further increase the pressure upon ourselves. Gauges as used by divers only record the extra pressure due to descent into the sea and this pressure sensibly enough is termed the *gauge pressure,* but the actual total pressure on the diver is called the *absolute pressure.*

Increase of pressure

If a balloon full of air at atmospheric pressure is taken to a pressure of 10 metres (two bars absolute) below the surface of the sea, then according to Boyle's Law* the volume will be halved. Similarly, to reduce the volume once more by a half, it will be necessary to double the pressure again and descend to 4 bars absolute pressure which is equivalent to 30 metres under the sea. Thus, to diminish the original volume to one half of its original value it is necessary to descend 10 metres, but to halve the volume at 10 metres it is necessary to descend a further 20 metres. In other words the expansion or contraction of gas pockets is much greater for a given change of depth when near the surface than when deep down. This observation is very important to the theory of decompression, and to the practical aspects of ear clearing, breath holding, etc.

Water pressure

Water is impossible to compress to any extent except by enormous pressures which do not interest the diver.

The human body consists of incompressible solids and liquids which enclose a few gas cavities in communication with the external atmosphere. Consequently pressure alone will cause the human body no distress whatsoever provided sufficient suitable gas is supplied to the gas cavities (lungs, ears, etc) to prevent them changing their volumes beyond their normal limits.

* Boyle's Law—Pressure × Volume = Constant.

Composition of gases breathed

Air is, of course, by far the commonest gas breathed by the diver, and it consists of 21 per cent oxygen and 79 per cent nitrogen. At atmospheric pressure, the pressure of oxygen is 0.21 bars in addition to 0.79 bars of nitrogen. At 10 bars absolute pressure of air, the pressure of oxygen is 2.1 bars and of nitrogen 7.9 bars, ie 21 per cent of 10 bars and 79 per cent of 10 bars respectively. In some semi-closed or closed breathing sets, mixtures of oxygen and nitrogen other than air are used. Values common here and in the United States are $32\frac{1}{2}$ per cent oxygen and $67\frac{1}{2}$ per cent nitrogen; 40 per cent oxygen and 60 per cent nitrogen, or 60 per cent oxygen and 40 per cent nitrogen. If a diver is breathing 40 per cent oxygen and 60 per cent nitrogen from his breathing bag and his oxygen consumption is temporarily ignored, then at 5.0 bars absolute pressure—40 metres under the sea—the pressure of oxygen in his bag is 5×0.4 (40 per cent) bars, ie 2.0 bars. The remaining 3.0 bars pressure is nitrogen. Thus the oxygen pressure in his breathing bag at 40 metres is very nearly the same as the diver on air at 10 bars absolute or 90 metres under the sea. For reasons which will be discussed later, it is very advantageous from the point of view of the risk of decompression sickness to have as much oxygen pressure in the breathing medium as possible, but as with many other things it is possible to have too much of a good thing. It has been generally agreed that pressures of oxygen in excess of 2.0 bars are not to be breathed by the diver for more than a few minutes. From the examples given above it may be seen that a 40 per cent oxygen, 60 per cent nitrogen mixture is dangerous from the point of view of its oxygen pressure at depths greater than 40 metres and air has an unacceptable oxygen pressure at 90 metres depth.

Respiration and Circulation

The chest wall with its ribs and muscles, the diaphragm, and other muscles take part in forming a pump-like mechanism for drawing air in and out of the lungs. The lungs themselves fill the chest cavity and there is normally no space between the outer lung surface and the surrounding chest wall and diaphragm. The only normal separation is a thin film of fluid which permits the lungs to move freely over the chest wall as chest expansion and contraction occurs. The lungs may be regarded as two elastic bags containing air passages communicating with millions of tiny distensible air sacs. Air that enters the lungs via the wind-pipe (trachea) due to chest expansion, flows down all the main air passages and enters into these tiny air sacs. Each of these air sacs (alveoli) is lined with an extremely thin transparent membrane and this in turn is surrounded by a network of very small blood vessels called capillaries. These blood vessels make up what is termed the capillary bed of the lungs and it is this capillary bed which is responsible for supplying fresh arterial blood to the tissues of the body.

It is very necessary to appreciate the remarkable efficiency of the lungs in promoting rapid exchange of gas between the surrounding air and the capillary bed. If the whole of the area of the lining of the alveoli and capillary bed were to be spread out flat on the ground it would cover an area about 10 metres by 10 metres, or 50 times the surface area of the skin. This enormous area with air on one side and blood on the other separated by a very thin membrane is capable of promoting very rapid exchange of gases between the blood and the air. In fact, only fractions of a second are necessary to alter the gas composition of the blood leaving the lungs when the gas composition of the alveoli is changed. From the diver's standpoint this is a crucial factor as it means that the moment descent into the sea commences and he starts breathing compressed air, then the body is being supplied by blood from his lungs with a full quota of air dissolved in it. There is very little delay in transmitting the effects of a gas change to the arterial blood supply. Similarly, on decompressing the diver, there is almost no delay in losing excess gas dissolved in the blood passing through the lungs.

When the blood leaves the lungs it flows through the heart and is pumped out via the main arteries to all parts of the body. The pulsation of these thick elastic walled pipes can be felt where they near the body surface. The arteries diminish in diameter as they approach a particular area of the body to which they are bringing fresh blood. Eventually they become very thin walled tubes with non-elastic walls and their diameter has been reduced to the order of 1/100 of a millimetre. These very thin-walled vessels are blood capillaries, and across their walls the exchange of gases takes place. The fresh arterial blood changes its composition and acquires the tissue waste products. After passage through the capillary bed nearly all the arterial driving pressure is lost and the blood is collected into the veins and returned to the heart where it is pumped through the lungs, and the cycle commences again.

From this outline picture of the circulation it is necessary to emphasise several points of importance to the diver and to his safe decompression. Firstly, all tissues are supplied directly by arterial blood, which has come straight from the lungs, via the heart. Secondly, the number of capillaries in a tissue varies very considerably with the type and activity of the tissue. Taking muscle as an example it has been established that a resting muscle has 200 capillaries open per square millimetre but that an active muscle has as many as 2500 capillaries open per square millimetre. The tissues depend upon the density of the capillary network for their nutriment, and active tissues such as the brain, the kidneys, and the heart, have very dense supplies, whereas tissues such as cartilage, tendon and fat, are only poorly supplied. Thirdly, as with the lungs, it must be noted that the passage of blood through a capillary takes the order of one second, but that the time for the complete exchange of the dissolved gases between the blood and tissues takes only fractions of a second. Thus one of the principal factors determining the amount of dissolved gas delivered to a tissue is the rate of blood-flow through the tissue, and this is dependent upon the number of open capillaries.

Now, it is equally clear that if a tissue with a poor blood supply is adjacent to a tissue with an extremely good blood supply, then some exchange of dissolved gas will occur between the two. The situation is analogous to the flow of heat. If one imagines large numbers of pipes inserted into a metal block, then if hot water is passed down these pipes the metal block will start to heat up. The parts of the block with the largest number of pipes per unit volume will obviously warm up the quickest but the heat will also spread by conduction from these hot regions to adjacent colder regions which are not as well supplied with hot water pipes. Thus the circulation of blood—or of hot water in the example given—is not the sole factor determining the distribution of dissolved gas or heat. This demonstrates the point that the location of the tissue as well as it blood supply is important.

The prevention of decompression sickness
From the above physics and physiology the basic points have been reviewed to permit a description of the major factors influencing the onset and prevention of decompression sickness.

In the very early days of diving it soon became realised that when one descended into the sea wearing a flexible suit there were a number of untoward happenings that could occur on releasing the air pressure and returning to atmospheric pressure. Names such as diver's palsy, chokes, staggers and bends were used to describe various of the more easily recognisable forms of these ill effects following a dive. Two factors were mainly involved, namely depth and time. A long period at a depth in excess of 10 metres or a short stay at a deep depth both seemed equally likely to provoke trouble. Similar findings were emerging from studies of caisson workers and tunnellers who were exposed to raised pressures of air comparable to those of the diver. Many of the earlier descriptions were confused pictures of various phenomena. For instance, divers who were supplied from the surface by hand-turned air pumps may have had the same volume of air regardless of their depth; consequently, many of them were inadequately ventilated inside their helmets. Naturally they arrived back after such a dive feeling dizzy and sick. Again, depth control was not as good as it should have been. A diver who altered his depth by dropping off his stage would have a sudden increase in pressure which would reduce the volume of air in his suit and helmet (Boyle's Law), and this would give his body what was descriptively termed a *squeeze*. Some *squeezes* were sufficiently severe to kill the diver, whereas others merely bruised him, particularly over the shoulders where his head got rammed into the helmet by the sudden reduction in air volume inside the helmet.

In the early part of this century, thanks largely to the pioneer work of a Frenchman, P Bert, and an Englishman, J S Haldane, many of these various mechanical and physiological factors had been assigned to their proper sources and the following situation became apparent. It is necessary for a diver to be supplied with sufficient pure air; he must be kept reasonably warm; depth control must be good, and any mouthpieces fitted with valves must present a low resistance to breathing.

When these basic physical requirements had been fulfilled, a large number of post-dive ill effects disappeared. There now remained ill effects solely attributable to the depth and time course of the dive. Over the years these have settled into the following classifications.

a   *Air embolism.* This is the condition in which air bubbles reach the circulation via some direct mechanical rupture in the lungs. Holding one's breath at, say, 30 metres (four bars absolute) and then rising towards the surface with the breath still held back will cause expansion of the gas contained in the lungs. Ascent to 10 metres (two bars absolute) would double the air volume. If there are not sufficient empty lung alveoli to take up this extra gas then pressure will be brought to bear on the delicate lung lining which will easily tear and rupture. This gas now finds its way into blood vessels and it often tracks between the lungs inside the chest cavity.

b   *Cardio-vascular and central nervous system involvement.* Shortly after a dive, or sometimes during decompression, the diver may find acute difficulty in breathing, accompanied by a tight feeling across the chest. This is called *the chokes* and the name is very descriptive. It is an extremely serious form of decompression sickness that is never seen nowadays except as a result of a diving accident or a gross mismanagement of a decompression. Treatment immediately is imperative or death rapidly ensues. The chokes are caused by bubbles appearing in the blood in large numbers. They block the circulation to the lungs, preventing effective breathing, and they accumulate in the heart as a froth with the result that the heart cannot pump correctly.

Also very serious but fortunately fairly rare are cases where divers surface and then shortly afterwards begin to complain of weakness in their limbs, particularly the legs, and then find they cannot move the affected limbs. There is generally no pain with this form of decompression sickness, but the diver is obviously a very sick man judging by his pallor and the shocked appearance that accompanies his limb paralysis. Here again, as with the chokes, immediate recompression is the effective answer. To delay treatment is to risk permanent damage to the central nervous system which will leave permanent after-effects. There are sometimes other forms of central nervous system involvement such as ' tunnel ' vision, the loss of certain nerve reflexes, partial temporary blindness, and indefinable ' woolly ' or ' fluffy ' feelings in limbs. In all these cases there is no pain present normally, but the man does not feel right in himself and he usually looks pale and shocked. Recompression as soon as possible is essential to avoid the risk of permanent after-effects.

It must be emphasised that the chokes and central nervous system decompression sickness are only seen after gross departures from normal diving practice, but a word of caution is necessary : diving accidents do occur in the best regulated circumstances, as when someone gets fouled up at depth or attacked by a sea creature. In these emergency situations, it is as well to know the risks involved in the various alternative procedures that may present themselves.

The bends
This is by far the most common form of decompression sickness encountered these days. The bends are pains in or around a joint or sometimes deeply in a muscle. They are most commonly felt around knee or shoulder joints and can vary in intensity from excruciating pain to transient mild aches which have been given the name of *niggles*. Bends very rarely attack a diver immediately he has finished his dive. There is a delay period of anything between a few minutes to several hours after the dive before any pains begin. A delay of 20 to 60 minutes accounts for the great majority of the bends. Many of the aches and pains of low intensity, ie the niggles, are tolerated and ignored by most divers. In fact, it is quite possible for the amateur to confuse niggles with the muscle aches and pains which may follow hard physical effort by a man not in training. There is, however, no possibility of ignoring a severe attack of the bends. The only satisfactory form of relief is obtained by recompression.

Itches, rashes and pressure bruising
In addition to true bends, described above, there are certain after-effects often given the name of *skinbends*. These are itches, which vary in severity and can be intensely irritating for up to one hour afterwards: rashes, which can appear on almost any part of the body and cover varying areas of skin; and pressure bruising and skin mottling, which to the untrained eye have the appearance of an ordinary bruised area of skin. All these effects may be rapidly reversed upon recompression but are generally ignored and not recompressed except when accompanied by other signs and symptoms of a more serious character.

Bone Necrosis
This, it is generally assumed, is caused by a blockage of the nutrient vessels of the bone by bubbles formed during decompression, and can result in a weakening in the mechanical strength of the bone involved. This is not liable to cause any real trouble to the diver unless the affected

141

bone is at the joint surface when collapse of this surface can occur with all the resulting pain and disablement following such a calamity. Very fortunately, the condition is almost unknown in the ordinary diver and only seems prevalent amongst caisson and tunnel workers who work in compressed air for many hours a day, five days a week, for several months. It is just mentioned here for the sake of completeness and also to sound a word of caution to anyone thinking of the undersea house concept of diving.

Squeezes and nips

If using a suit with an air gap between the body and the suit then descent to depths reduces the volume of this trapped gas and may cause the suit to wrinkle and trap folds of flesh. These nips by the suit can be quite painful and sore afterwards and must not be confused with true decompression sickness effects.

The position is now defined both as regards a classification of the forms of decompression sickness and the main physical variables involved. It is now necessary to evolve some ideas on the actual causes of decompression sickness and on methods of prevention. All the serious forms of decompression sickness (chokes, staggers, etc) are avoided by the methods used to prevent the appearance of the less serious forms (bends, itches, etc). Thus, avoiding the bends is the major task, and if this can be done successfully the serious forms of decompression sickness will be so rare that they may be ignored for all practical purposes.

The causes of the bends

If a diver descends to 30 metres under the sea he commences breathing air at this very increased pressure. Almost immediately blood with a full quota of dissolved gas in it is pumped from the lungs to the tissues of the body. These various tissues all have different numbers of open capillaries and, therefore, they all saturate with dissolved gas at different rates. Those with a good blood supply saturate rapidly, and those with a poor blood supply saturate slowly. If, after a few minutes at 30 metres, it was possible to examine the gas content of the tissues of the diver's body it would be found that such parts as the kidney, heart, and lungs had a very large amount of gas in them, whereas cartilage, tendon, and other such tissues had a comparatively small amount of gas. Now, allow the diver to stay at 30 metres for a further hour and imagine re-examining the state of his tissues. All those organs with a good blood supply, the kidney, heart, etc, would have the same dissolved gas content as on the previous analysis performed after only a few minutes, but those that are poorly supplied with blood would have gained an appreciable amount. Eventually, after many hours of exposure, all tissues would reach a gas content beyond which they would no longer change.

It is now necessary to examine how this acquisition of gas affects the decompression problem. Many years ago it was shown that if animals die as a result of severe attack of decompression sickness then large numbers of bubbles are found in the blood vessels and tissues. Analysis of the gas in these bubbles reveals that it consists almost entirely of nitrogen. It is the inert gas content of the breathing medium that causes nearly all the decompression sickness problems of the diver. If one could dive on oxygen alone, the difficulties of decompression would be very much less. The trouble is, of course, as explained earlier, that once the oxygen pressure in the breathing medium exceeds 2.0 bars there is a risk of oxygen poisoning effects occurring, especially in a diver doing hard underwater work. Nevertheless, there are considerable decompression advantages for a diver breathing oxygen-rich mixtures whilst at depth. Once it had been realised that the nitrogen content of the air was the main cause of the bubbles seen during severe attacks of decompression sickness, it became of importance to discover the speed with which nitrogen entered and left the body. This problem was approached in two ways. Firstly, nitrogen gas elimination from the body was measured in the following manner. A man at atmospheric pressure was fitted with an oxygen breathing apparatus. As he breathed pure oxygen from his apparatus his exhaled breath contained nitrogen gas which was being washed out of his body. The nitrogen had been acquired through previous living at one atmosphere pressure in ordinary air conditioning 79% N_2, 21% O_2. Measurements, at convenient intervals, were made of the nitrogen content of the exhaled breath. In this way the speed of removal of nitrogen from the body was obtained (Figure 1). Secondly, nitrogen uptake was estimated by actually decompressing men and plotting a curve showing their sensitivity to attacks of bends. This was carried out as follows. For example, a dive duration of 25 minutes was chosen. Divers were then rapidly compressed in air to, say, 24 metres and kept there, working hard, for the agreed period of 25 minutes after which they were rapidly decompressed at 18 metres per minute back to the surface (atmospheric pressure). When this proved to be a perfectly safe procedure for a group of healthy young men, the pressure was raised the next time they tried this 25-minute dive. So they all now performed a dive of 25 minutes at 27 metres with no stops on the way back to atmospheric pressure. Again this proved to be safe. The next dive was 25 minutes at 30 metres which gave marginal trouble in a small percentage of men, ie mild transient attacks of the niggles. This was an indication that after 25 minutes at 30 metres most normal men had acquired just sufficient nitrogen to be tolerated on immediate return to atmospheric pressure. Having established this point, another time was chosen, say 60 minutes. Here it was found that most normal men would tolerate 18 metres before coming near to trouble. Thus, it is now possible to say that 60 minutes at 18 metres also gives just sufficient nitrogen to permit rapid safe return to

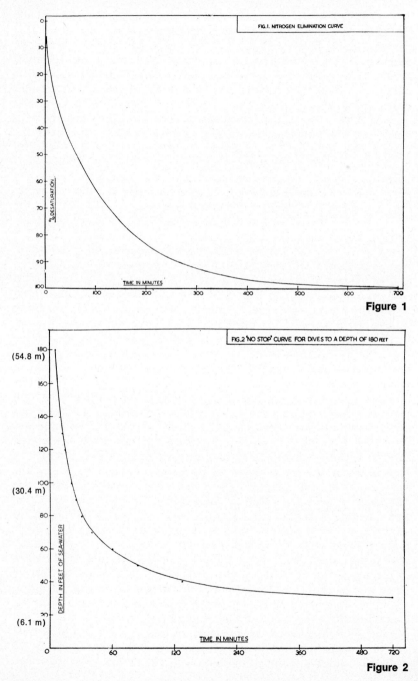

Figure 1

Figure 2

atmospheric pressure. A curve can be constructed showing the various pressures one can go to safely and how long one can stay there without causing any decompression problem. This is called the *no-stop* curve for man (see Figure 2). The shape and time-course of this curve and the nitrogen elimination curve can be shown to be identical within the experimental limits. Thus, there is obtained data showing the connection between the rate of uptake of gas by the body and the decompression performance. All the main facts are now available for calculating a decompression procedure using the limits of performance that have been obtained.

It is at this point that a digression must be made to assess the position regarding the various decompression tables available throughout the world. Suppose a diver wishes to go to 30 metres and stay at this depth for the maximum length of time which just allows him to return to the surface without decompression, he will see the following different international calculations. The Royal Navy's table will allow a 20-minute dive, the United States Navy will allow 25 minutes, and some Italian tables will allow 30 minutes. The diver may then decide to use that routine which allows him to stay 30 minutes and apparently surface in safety. Why not? The answer is fivefold. Firstly, it very much depends where the constructor of a decompression schedule sets his safety limits; secondly, what sort of men he has used to obtain his basic data; thirdly, the sort of work they performed whilst at depth; fourthly, the water conditions (temperature, etc), and, finally, the way the decompression procedure was performed.

It can be seen that the Royal Navy's tables are the most conservative, and for hard underwater work in northern waters they are undoubtedly the best proposition. Even so, a word of warning is necessary. If the diver is in a position to do dives beyond the black line of the table he must expect some risk of mild decompression sickness.

Repetitive dives are a difficult problem. The number of possible combinations available concerning depth and time of the first dive, the time interval on the surface, and the depth and time of the second dive, is enormous. Therefore, unless the diver has a decompression computer the rules adopted have to be crude and they must err on the safe side. For about 12 hours after his first dive, a man will be losing from his tissues the dissolved gas he acquired during his exposure to pressure. Consequently, if he wants to dive again within 12 hours of completing his first dive, there is residual gas in his body tissues which will be added to the gas he acquires on his second dive. This means that the second dive must have a decompression which takes this into account.

There are quite complex procedures which may be adopted for this, and as a result of the mental work involved it is possible to save decompression time in some instances. If a diver wishes to dive for 20 minutes at 30 metres and one hour later to repeat this dive, then, using the present RN method, the bottom times of the two dives would be added together, and the decompression given to the second dive would be for 40 minutes at 30 metres. Some other procedures are far more complicated than this, but the differences between the more complex error-prone routines and the simple principle of adding the bottom times are really very marginal over most of the usual combinations of pressure and time available to the amateur. Only when carrying out very dissimilar dives with surface intervals over one hour is there a distinct advantage in the more complex procedures.

CARBON MONOXIDE POISONING

Carbon monoxide is a dangerous gas present in the exhaust fumes of an internal combustion engine. It is even lethal breathed at atmospheric pressure. Should the compressor charging the cylinder be badly sited so as to allow exhaust fumes to enter the inlet, carbon monoxide will enter the cylinders. Air thus contaminated will reduce the oxygen-carrying power of the blood, causing, initially, mental confusion and ultimately loss of consciousness.

Symptoms include weakness, exhaustion with breathlessness, dizziness, and fainting. Despite the fact that the victim's blood will be low in oxygen, their lips will not appear blue—as with usual oxygen lack—but cherry red.

Where available, treatment includes pure oxygen, preferably in a compression chamber. And where unconsciousness has occurred artificial respiration in some form might be needed.

Carbon monoxide contamination is one of the most likely ways in which a cylinder of compressed air can be rendered dangerous. The number of clubs owning compressors is increasing all the time, and in some cases the people operating the equipment are totally unqualified to do so. There is also the fact that compressors, by virtue of the noise they make, are often located in a confined space that minimises the noise travel—and not a site that has been selected with a view to safety. In such cases it is often easy for carbon monoxide fumes to contaminate the air. It is even important to keep check on wind direction—a compressor exhaust rendered quite safe when the wind is westerly could well be dangerously sited when the wind is easterly.

Regular air analysis should be normal procedure for any compressor owner or operator.

See also *Air Analysis* and *BSAC Paper No* 1.

NITROGEN ABSORPTION

During normal breathing at rest, blood flowing through the capillaries of the lungs is subjected to the air in the alveoli. The main constituent gases of the alveolar air are dissolved in the plasma of the blood in proportion to their partial pressures, which depend on the concentration of the gases in the alveolar air and the absolute pressure of the air. In considering nitrogen absorption we are not concerned with chemical changes in the blood, but only with a simple solution of nitrogen in the plasma.

If a diver makes a descent and the pressure of the air he breathes is increased to two atmospheres, the partial pressure of nitrogen breathed will be twice as great as it was at the surface with an air pressure of only one atmosphere, and twice as much nitrogen can be dissolved in the blood.

Some of the nitrogen dissolved in the blood passes into the fatty tissues, particularly those of the brain and spinal cord which contain a high proportion of special forms of fat. When the partial pressure of nitrogen in the alveolar air is increased as the diver descends, this nitrogen dissolved in fat and other tissues will also be increased. For this increase of nitrogen concentration in all the tissues of the body to take place some time must elapse, dependent on the blood flow to the various tissues. (A diver carrying out heavy exercise will absorb more nitrogen than one at rest and the muscles being used will be those most affected.) Thus the amount of nitrogen in the tissues depends on the depth, duration of the dive and the exertion of the diver.

If a diver breathes air in which the partial pressure of the nitrogen is doubled for sufficient time, the total nitrogen dissolved in the tissues will also be doubled.

As the pressure is gradually decreased, the body tissues will no longer be able to hold the extra nitrogen which will be liberated into the blood and then breathed out through the lungs. If, however, the partial pressure of nitrogen has been maintained for some time at a high level, and it is then suddenly reduced, the nitrogen will come out of solution quicker than it can be carried away by the blood to the lungs and the nitrogen will form bubbles in the tissues and in the blood.

A clearer understanding of the process involved may be gained from an analogy. In the manufacture of soda water, the bottle is pressurised to several atmospheres with carbon dioxide gas which is absorbed by the drink. Yet the bottle appears to contain ordinary water. If the cork is removed slowly the gas will be heard issuing out under pressure, with very little disturbance of the liquid. Should the cork be removed quickly the drink immediately bubbles and froths in its effort to give up the dissolved gas. Applying this analogy to diving: the diver is the bottle; his blood, the soda water; and the compressed air breathed in, the gas. As long as the diver stays under pressure his blood will resemble the soda water with the cork secure. Should he ascend too quickly, allowing a rapid drop of pressure in the lungs, his blood will bubble and froth in a similar manner to the suddenly uncorked soda water.

The bubbles so formed may interfere with the normal workings of the body. For instance, bubbles in the fatty tissue and synovial membranes around the joints leads to the stretching of the nerve endings in these tissues. Pain around them gives rise to the condition known as the bends, or more generally, decompression sickness. This is no new condition and has been an industrial hazard for some time. It gets is name ' the bends ' from the fact that one of the symptoms of persons suffering from this complaint is the severe pain in the limbs causing the victim to double up in anguish and be unable to straighten the affected joints. Bubbles liberated in the spinal cord are even more serious and may cause paralysis. They may also be liberated in the brain, giving rise to cerebral bends. In the most severe cases, large bubbles are collected in the chambers of the heart and the person dies.

The main symptoms of the condition may occur immediately on ascending or in other cases any time up to six hours after the dive. The commonest symptom is local pain, usually in the legs, and sometimes in the arms. Dizziness, paralysis, shortness of breath, itching, swelling and rash on the skin, and in extreme cases, unconsciousness, are associated conditions.

The rates at which nitrogen is absorbed and given off through respiration vary with individuals and with the same individual on different occasions. It is also affected by such factors as age, fatigue, obesity and alcohol intake. About 12 hours is usually required to get rid of all excess nitrogen absorbed in the human body.

Bubbles will not form provided the pressure of nitrogen is not allowed to exceed twice the ambient pressure. In order to prevent this two-to-one ratio of pressure being exceeded, the diver must undergo decompression, that is, to make a slow and controlled ascent to the surface in order to allow sufficient time for the excess nitrogen to be removed from the system.

Recompression

Should a diver contract the bends, the treatment is to force the bubbles in the blood back into solution by means of recompression, followed by a long decompression according to special tables drawn up for this purpose. This must be carried out under expert medical attention. Any inept attempts to give emergency treatment in the water may cause serious and permanent injury. Treatment should be carried out as soon as possible after the symptoms have been observed, as damage may follow should the condition be left to develop. If prompt attention is given a complete cure can be expected, but should delay or constant recurrence of the sickness with improper treatment prevent the bubbles being completely re-absorbed in solution, even though they may be so reduced in size that the symptoms disappear on recompression, a cure cannot be affected.

Every officer in charge of an expedition should know the location of the nearest recompression chamber and the best method of reaching it without delay.

NITROGEN NARCOSIS

The two basic components of compressed air are oxygen (21%) and nitrogen (79%). At sufficiently increased pressures, the nitrogen component is responsible for the production of a form of narcosis similar to that produced by alcoholic intoxication, the early stages of oxygen lack or to being anaesthetised by the dentist with nitrous oxide.

The signs and symptoms are characterised by feelings of elation and well-being associated with a sense of detachment from reality with a dangerous over-confidence, an uncontrolled desire to laugh and a tingling numbness of the lips, gums and legs. Sight, sound and smell perception may be affected. More commonly there will be an inability to make correct and rapid decisions or concentrate. Errors may be made in writing information or reading, accompanied by memory defects and dizziness. Intellectual functions are affected most and manual dexterity to a lesser extent.

Novices or sensitive subjects will be affected by the narcosis at 30 metres. As the condition is proportional to the nitrogen partial pressure, the severity of the narcosis increases rapidly with depth until at 75 metres the condition is severe and may be accompanied by even more bizarre signs and symptoms such as stupor, voice reverberation, hallucinations, sense of impending blackout, maniac or depressive states, a sense of levitation and disorganisation of the sense of time with a characteristic 'dead pan' change in facial appearance and eventually loss of consciousness.

Narcosis is a significant danger to the diver since it increases the risk of accident but also decreases the ability to cope with emergencies. Many fatal accidents have occurred to divers who chose either to ignore its dangers or foolishly attempted depth records.

The onset of narcosis is rapid, usually reaching a maximum in a few minutes and there is, as with alcohol, a wide variability of sensitivity between different individuals. Frequent exposure to compressed air induces some adaptation and the diver is less affected.

Recovery also is rapid, the extent of the narcosis decreasing as the diver ascends. There are no after effects, except possibly an inability to remember what occurred while narcotic.

Generally the narcosis is more severe when underwater than in simulated pressure chamber diving and is potentiated by alcohol, fatigue, ill health, apprehension and hard work.

The narcosis may be prevented by substituting helium for nitrogen in the breathing mixture but this gas has disadvantages of its own such as expense, body temperature regulation and special decompression requirements which make it unsuitable for club use.

Narcosis must therefore be recognised as a significant danger and *could* be minimised by the following rules :

1 Restrict diving to less than 30 metres unless, at the instigation of the Branch Diving Officer, special preparation and precautions have been taken. Even then it is not to be recommended, except for the fit, very experienced and well trained individual and certainly not alone.

2 If affected, return immediately to a shallower depth.

3 Take as many decisions as possible prior to the dive, eg maximum time permissible on the bottom, decompression required, minimum air required for the ascent and action to be taken in an emergency.

Further Reading:

(a) The Narcotic Effects of Air. P B Bennett. Science Journal, *4*, 53-58, 1968.

(b) The Aetiology of Compressed Air Intoxication and Inert Gas Narcosis. P B Bennett. Pergamon Press, Oxford, 1966.

(c) Inert Gas Narcosis. Ch. 7 in, The Physiology and Medicine of Diving and Compressed Air Work. Edited by P B Bennett and D H Elliott. Balliere, Tyndall and Cassell, London.

CARBON DIOXIDE POISONING

Carbon dioxide is a waste product of the body and if it cannot be eliminated through the lungs it will accumulate in the body and its concentration in the blood will increase. A rise in carbon dioxide partial pressure will first stimulate the respiratory centre and cause an increase in the depth and rate of respiration. Further accumulation may cause a headache and, if it continues, the sensation of breathlessness becomes greater and greater until confusion occurs and, in an extreme case, consciousness is lost.

A period of heavy work or vigorous swimming can soon cause breathlessness and at this stage the mechanical inadequacy of the demand valve is such that the diver may 'beat the lung', the time lag in the mechanism preventing continuous heavy panting. If this occurs the diver must rest and make every effort to increase his depth of breathing and to regain a slower rhythm. The technique, which may call for a major application of will power, is as follows :

> Stop finning and all other movement. Relax completely in such a position that the demand valve is below the level of the centre of the chest, thus increasing the supply of air at positive pressure. Hold on to some fixed object, if mid-water, drift. Start attempting to control exhalation and let inhalation take care of itself until normal rhythm is restored.

The more severe manifestations are not likely to occur with an open-circuit set but are a further hazard of a rebreathing apparatus. Respiratory distress may occur in a similar manner after heavy physical effort and the essential procedure is just the same : relax and breathe deeply. The accumulation of carbon dioxide is aggravated if attention is not paid to respiratory dead space. A certain amount of gas from the lungs never leaves the body at the end of expiration but is drawn back into the lungs, with its content of carbon dioxide, at the beginning of the next breath. When the volume of the airway is increased by the volume of the mouthpiece or an oro-nasal mask, a greater tidal volume, a deeper breath in, is needed to obtain the usual amount of fresh air. Thus, particularly with the oxygen apparatus, a period of quick shallow panting can be very inefficient at eliminating carbon dioxide. With the rebreathing apparatus carbon dioxide can also build up when the soda-lime is not functioning properly or becomes exhausted. The only action is to flush the counter lung with fresh oxygen and surface immediately. After carbon dioxide poisoning there may be a persistent headache, the subject may appear flushed and he may vomit, but there are no serious consequences.

OXYGEN POISONING

Oxygen is essential to our lives. We must have an adequate supply of oxygen in order to carry on living and there is absolutely no substitute for it. How, then, can oxygen, on which we depend so completely, ever be regarded as a poison? Perhaps the simplest answer is that you can have too much of a good thing.

This chapter is concerned with explaining how, when and where oxygen can be a poison to us. *What is more important, it will show that so long as we use only compressed air in our aqualungs we will be completely free of any possibility of oxygen poisoning in all normal club diving.*

Now, even though we will never really meet the problem of oxygen poisoning (or 'oxygen toxicity', as it is often called), there are two good reasons why it is very important to be able to understand the problem. First, it will allow us to see for ourselves why the Club prohibits the use of 'oxygen' or 'oxygen-enriched' breathing equipment in conventional Club diving. Second, once we know how a very rich oxygen supply affects our bodies, we will be able to understand several other most important aspects of a diver breathing underwater.

What is oxygen poisoning?

There are 2 basic types :

a Acute oxygen poisoning
b Chronic oxygen poisoning

'Acute' here means a short-term effect whilst 'Chronic' means a long-term effect.

Acute oxygen poisoning

This is the more important type to the diver because he would seldom, if ever, be exposed to a high enough oxygen partial pressure for a sufficiently long period to suffer from chronic oxygen poisoning.

The following is a list of possible symptoms of acute oxygen poisoning which may be experienced by a diver :

a Lip twitching and twitching of other facial muscles.
b Dizziness (vertigo).
c Feeling sick (nausea).
d Unusual tiredness.
e Disturbances of breathing, eg, overbreathing (hyperpnoea), temporary stoppage (apnoea) or difficulty in breathing (dyspnoea).
f Unusual mental states, eg euphoria.
g Disturbances of sight, eg 'tunnel vision'.
h Unconsciousness and general convulsions similar to a major (*grand mal*) epileptic fit.

154

By far the most dangerous symptoms to a diver are the unconsciousness and convulsions since such conditions could easily lead to his losing the mouthpiece and drowning. The other symptoms may or may not occur prior to the onset of convulsions, and experience shows that in the case of divers there is most often *no warning whatsoever* before convulsive seizure and unconsciousness interrupts their dive.

Oxygen Convulsions

A diver succumbing to oxygen convulsions would become unconscious and enter the 'tonic phase'. During this phase which lasts some half to two minutes the diver would arch backwards as all his voluntary muscles contracted simultaneously and completely, his body thus becoming quite rigid. Following immediately after the tonic phase would come the 'clonic phase' which is the familiar convulsive stage. This is when the diver would jerk violently and spasmodically perhaps for two to three minutes. As the clonic phase subsided the diver would pass into a relaxed, though exhausted and unconscious, stage called the 'post convulsive depression'.

Thus, three distinct phases are embarked upon by the unsuspecting diver :

a Tonic phase (rigid).

b Clonic phase (convulsive).

c Post convulsive depression phase (relaxed).

Once the series is begun there is no means of stopping the natural progression through to the post convulsive depression phase.

The next events could depend on what had happened to the diver during his preceding performance. First, if he had lost his mouthpiece he would most certainly have drowned without a chance of recovering consciousness.

Second if he had retained his mouthpiece and continued oxygen-breathing at the same, or an even deeper depth, he would have undertaken an 'encore' or perhaps several 'encores' before death by oxygen poisoning brought down the final curtain. The diver's 'encores' would consist of clonic phases of increasing frequency interspersed by post convulsive depression phases.

Third, if the diver was fortunate enough to be accompanied by a buddy-diver who brought him to the surface before he drowned, he would have a good chance of surviving. The correct action to be taken by a rescuer would be to return the stricken diver to air breathing as soon as possible and thenceforth to support the unconscious diver on the surface until he was either picked up or the rescuer himself landed the subject. Once the stricken diver returned to air breathing he may or may not have another convulsion. In some cases, however, it has been observed that the return to air breathing or even reduction of the partial pressure of oxygen (for example, by ascending) has apparently induced worsening of symptoms and even precipitated convulsions. The diver would slowly recover consciousness over five to 30 minutes after returning to air breathing but he should not be regarded as having 'revived' since he would be in an exhausted state, mentally confused and likely to become unconscious or fall asleep without warning.

No permanent neurological injury would normally be expected to have occurred as a direct cause of one or two convulsions. However, the violent muscular contractions which occur during the tonic and clonic phases are so complete (a condition which would never occur in normal life) that the forces exerted could occasionally tear the muscle tissue itself, tear its tendons from their bone insertions or even break the very bones to which they are attached. After such strenuous, though unconscious effort, it is no wonder that the body is so physically exhausted after a convulsion. In fact, there is often a strong desire to fall asleep if the diver had regained consciousness shortly after returning to air breathing. In other cases, the diver may pass from the unconscious 'depression' phase straight into the sleeping phase. There is no harm in this and it is even beneficial so long as he can be kept warm and safe from further accidents. When he regains consciousness he should be talked to calmly, reassuringly and in simple terms; warm clothing should be provided as soon as possible. He would have no recollection of his previous experiences (amnesia) from the time when he became unconscious or perhaps even a little while before that.

One important item remains to be noted: the diver would be automatically holding his breath (apnoeic) during the tonic phase and consequently it would be hazardous to try and bring him to the surface during this brief period due to the danger of burst lung (pulmonary barotrauma). Even though it would be more difficult to surface a convulsing body rather than a rigid one it would be safer to await the onset of the clonic or convulsing phase before ascending. However, the tonic phase is rarely noticed underwater and the attention of the buddy-diver is most likely to be first drawn by the convulsions so that there is unlikely to have to be a need to wait before surfacing. It should not require emphasis here that great care would have to be exercised whilst in the proximity of a convulsing diver since his movements would be most violent and unpredictable.

When might a diver suffer acute oxygen poisoning?

Acute oxygen poisoning occurs when a particularly high concentration of oxygen appears in the blood and brain. This is brought about by breathing a gas mixture with a particularly high partial pressure of oxygen. From many years' experience, the Royal Navy has established a maximum permissible partial pressure for oxygen in breathing gas for divers (1.75 bars absolute). Thus the depth to which a breathing gas may be used will depend on its concentration of oxygen. A high oxygen concentration will have a shallow limit as follows :

100% oxygen limited to 8 metres.
60% oxygen limited to 21 metres.
40% oxygen limited to 37 metres.

It is interesting to note that for a mixture of 21% oxygen in nitrogen (that is air) the partial pressure of oxygen at 80 metres is the same as in 100% oxygen at 8 metres so that the possibility of oxygen poisoning can be added to nitrogen narcosis as a barrier to diving deeper than 82 metres with air. Certain types of modern deep-diving breathing equipment automatically changes the oxygen concentration in the breathing gas mixture as the diver varies his depth, thus maintaining a constant and safe partial pressure of oxygen.

Oxygen poisoning does not occur immediately the diver goes to depth. There is a delay or ' latent period ' whilst the oxygen reaching the brain gradually builds up. Logically, the higher the partial pressure of oxygen (due to deeper depth or richer gas mixture) then the shorter the latent period. It is unfortunate, however, that *it is impossible to predict* the latent period or even an individual diver's susceptibility to acute oxygen poisoning. This is because of the enormous variation which one finds in most physiological functions. Both susceptibility and latency vary widely from individual to individual and even in a single individual from day to day. Certain broad generalisations can, however, be made in some cases. For example, it is known that fatigue, stress, hard work, high carbon dioxide concentrations, cold water, ' hang-over ' and bad physical fitness increase susceptibility and reduce the latency to acute oxygen poisoning.

The mechanism of oxygen poisoning

To understand the mechanism of oxygen poisoning we must first know what role oxygen plays in the functioning of the body.

This is basically quite simple. Consider living tissue (such as we are made of) as an energy producing system analagous to, say, the petrol engine in a car. We can say that the food we eat and drink is just like the petrol fuel of the engine and that the air we breathe is like the air drawn into the engine via the carburettor. Beneath the car's bonnet the petrol and air are mixed and ignited. The resultant explosive reaction liberates energy previously chemically bound up in the petrol. This energy is used to drive various mechanisms in the car such as turning the drive wheels and driving a water pump.

Meanwhile, back in the body, the crude food has been ' refined ' by the processes of digestion and transported by the blood to all the living tissues of the body along with the oxygen obtained from the air in the lungs. The cells which make up the living tissues accept the food and oxygen and cause them to react together to liberate the energy chemically bound up in the food. Obviously, we could not tolerate millions of little explosions inside our tissues as in an engine so we do it by very clever chemical techniques which collectively, with all the other intricate chemical reactions of the body involved in keeping us alive, are termed the processes of 'metabolism'. The resulting energy liberated from the food is used to drive various processes of the body such as contracting muscles or boosting nerve impulses along their special pathways.

To return now to oxygen poisoning, we know that if a car's carburettor is badly tuned, to give a mixture with too much air then the engine will not run properly and will probably splutter and stall. Similarly, if there is too much oxygen reaching the living cells of our bodies then the 'chemical engines' or more precisely 'metabolic reactions' will also splutter and stall. Different tissues of the body with different functions will have varying degrees of susceptibility to oxygen poisoning. One of the most susceptible tissues is that of the brain and this is why the apparent symptoms of acute oxygen poisoning are of the neurological type. As various nerve cells in the brain begin to 'splutter' they send out all the wrong messages which give rise to the various symptoms of acute oxygen poisoning. In the case of oxygen convulsions the abnormal brain activity is similar to the abnormal activity associated with the convulsions in an epileptic.

Chronic oxygen poisoning

This form of poisoning can be suffered at partial pressures of oxygen lower than that required to produce 'acute' oxygen poisoning but the time taken to onset of symptoms is generally much longer. This particular type manifests itself initially as soreness of the upper respiratory tract. As the lungs themselves become further irritated by the high oxygen, there develops a condition similar to pneumonia, with congestion, coughing and considerable discomfort.

In conventional club diving (that is, using compressed air) there is no risk whatsoever of suffering from chronic oxygen poisoning. Even if a diver used pure oxygen there would be no real risk if normal diving practice was employed. Chronic oxygen poisoning would only be expected to be seen in certain clinical conditions when, say, hospital patients breathe oxygen or oxygen-rich mixtures for very long periods, perhaps days. More pertinent to the diver, would be the case of a saturation dive involving perhaps living in an underwater habitat. In this case the diver would be exposed to a high pressure gas environment for days or even weeks. Thus if the oxygen partial pressure of the gas was too high then he would be a likely candidate for chronic oxygen poisoning.

If 100% oxygen is breathed at atmospheric pressure (that is at a partial pressure of 1 bar absolute) the irritation would be experienced probably within 24 hours. 60% oxygen at atmospheric pressure (partial pressure of 0.6 bars absolute) appears to be safe to be breathed indefinitely without ill effect to most people.

The mechanism of chronic oxygen poisoning is basically similar to that of acute oxygen poisoning. However, in the chronic form where the tissues of the body are having to function in an abnormally high concentration of oxygen over a long period it appears that the most sensitive tissue is the delicate lining of the air pathways within the lungs and throat. Other tissues such as brain, kidney, liver, etc, would eventually suffer if the exposure was not terminated.

Oxygen and the blood

The blood is entirely responsible for the transport of oxygen to various regions of the body. Having evolved to function as such over millions of years it has come to be very good at it. In fact the chemical in the red corpuscles (haemoglobin) responsible for picking the oxygen up at the lungs becomes 97% saturated with oxygen in a fraction of a second whilst breathing air at atmospheric pressure. It would be reasonable to question how the blood manages to carry the excess oxygen around the body when the usual carrier (haemoglobin) is already almost fully saturated. The answer quite simply is that although the haemoglobin carries very little more than the normal quantities of oxygen as it circulates in the blood stream, the amount of oxygen in simple solution in the blood plasma (which is normally very little) rises enormously. Thus the body has no means of avoiding excess quantities of oxygen entering the blood stream and hence the rest of the body.

Advantages of pure oxygen or oxygen-rich breathing equipment

a   Construction of the breathing equipment is simple and the set is easy to produce.

b   The set is relatively light and compact.

c   Longer duration. The limitation is usually imposed by the ' life ' of the carbon dioxide absorbent rather than the compressed gas supply.

d   Closed circuit breathing equipment produces no bubbles. For example, necessary when dealing with acoustic mines.

Disadvantages

a   Severely limited in depth (8 metres for pure oxygen).

b   Danger of acute oxygen poisoning with probable lethal consequences.

c   Danger of 'dilution hypoxia' (unconsciousness followed probably by asphyxia or drowning). This insidious danger occurs when for some reasons the breathing gas provides too low a partial pressure of oxygen to sustain consciousness due to its accidental dilution, usually by nitrogen. Nitrogen can easily ' contaminate ' the breathing gas either by insufficient flushing of air out of the set before use or by gradual diffusion out of solution from the body into the lungs during the course of a dive. Since the body cannot adequately detect an insufficient supply of oxygen, the unsuspecting diver might become unconscious without warning due to lack of oxygen (hypoxia).

d   Danger of oxygen fires and explosions. Oil explodes spontaneously in the presence of high pressure oxygen.

e   Danger of receiving a ' cocktail '. If water enters the expiratory tube and reaches the soda lime carbon dioxide absorbent there is an instantaneous reaction producing a highly caustic foam which immediately froths up the breathing tube and can severely burn the mouth, lungs, stomach, etc, perhaps with lethal consequences.

In conclusion it would be pertinent to include another item of information derived from the diving experience of the Royal Navy. The Royal Navy has a definite requirement to use pure oxygen and oxygen-rich breathing equipment and thus has had a vast amount of experience in most forms of breathing equipment. The men who use this type of equipment are professionals in every sense of the word supported by the very best standards of training. Nevertheless, about 70% of the diving accidents within the Royal Navy, excluding decompression sickness, occur to divers using pure oxygen or oxygen-rich breathing equipment. Thus it can be seen that use of this equipment can only be justified when the end justifies the means and then only when extra-special organisation and facilities are available to cater for the possibility of the occurrence of a diving accident.

Summary

The main points to remember are as follows :

a   Oxygen poisoning *does not occur* in normal club diving, that is when using compressed air for breathing.

b   Oxygen poisoning is a problem associated with the use of pure oxygen or oxygen-rich breathing equipment.

c   There are two basic types of oxygen poisoning :

    (1)   Acute oxygen poisoning, and

    (2)   Chronic oxygen poisoning.

d   Acute oxygen poisoning is the more dangerous form to the diver since it can, without warning, induce unconsciousness, convulsions and therefore very probably, drowning.

e   Acute oxygen poisoning is brought about by breathing oxygen partial pressures in excess of approximately 1.75 bars absolute for a short time (minutes).

f   Chronic oxygen poisoning only occurs in people exposed to high oxygen partial pressures, say in excess of 0.6 bars absolute, for very long periods which are well beyond the range of normal dive durations.

g Chronic oxygen poisoning produces symptoms similar to those of pneumonia.

h Having considered both the advantages and disadvantages of oxygen and oxygen-rich breathing equipment the British Sub Aqua Club has banned the use of this type of equipment for all normal club diving.

6

AIR ANALYSIS

Air Analysis using Portable Detectors

Before the advent of the BS 4001 specification for divers' air, which was one of the standards used in compiling the new BSAC standard, analysis carried out by outside laboratories was sometimes unreliable and to varying standards. Even after the British Standard became available, the problem still remained that due to the difficulties of obtaining an analysis, these were often carried out at too infrequent intervals. It is therefore recommended that whether or not outside facilities are used for a periodic check analysis, the regular air testing should be carried out on the spot by the air station itself.

The most likely source of contamination to be met with is oil vapour, and the easiest check for this at present available is as follows: A sheet of 'Baryta' or 'Varityper Composition' paper (both of which possess extreme surface whiteness) is placed on a suitable flat surface. The cylinder under investigation is placed valve downwards over the paper and the valve opened to a degree of blast which is judged by experience to be just short of that which will tear the paper to shreds. The blast is maintained for 30 seconds before shutting off. The paper is then examined under a source fairly high in ultra-violet content (the ends of a fluorescent lamp appear very satisfactory). The paper should be viewed *across* as well as at right angles to the surface, and if no oil stains are visible the air source is, until more scientific measuring techniques become available, accepted as oil free.

Other possible contaminants require the use of a sensitive gas detector, such as the MSA-Auer Toxic Gas Detector or the Dräger Multi-Gas Detector. These simple units, which vary in price from about £13 to £23 or more, work on the principle of a calibrated charge of the air under test being passed at specified flow rate through a test tube containing a chemical colour-sensitive to the gas under investigation. The two detectors mentioned are of the most modern type which are calibrated by length of stain on the chemical carried in the test tube.

The earlier devices which were calibrated on degree of colour change, which required somewhat skilled colour matching for accuracy, though by no means obsolete are now becoming obsolescent. It should be noted that with all such devices the air is not taken direct from the cylinder or compressor, but is used to fill a flexible sampling bag from which the samples are then drawn by the hand pump of the gas detector.

Three further general points are perhaps worth noting. Firstly, the tubes are usually specific to a gas and contain filters to remove gases other than that under investigation. Secondly, the tubes are heat sensitive and therefore must *not* be used to test the output from a compressor, only a cool bottle (via a sampling bag). Thirdly, various vapours (notably sulphuric acid with CO tubes) are released into the hand pump during the course of a test, and this must therefore be thoroughly pumped out before another test is completed.

Final Note:

When the contamination level is, on test, getting rather high, *even though it may still be within the limits specified,* the compressor operator should investigate the source of contamination at once, as it indicates a deterioration in some manner of the equipment concerned, which will doubtless get worse rather than better if ignored at this stage.

Bibliography:
BSAC Paper No 1
Underwater Swimming—An Advanced Handbook (Kaye Ward, Chapter 4).

CHAPTER FIVE

EQUIPMENT

Basic Equipment : M K Todd

Protective Clothing : Dr John Betts

The Weight Belt : Leo Zanelli

Principles of the Aqualung : R B Campbell

Air Cylinders and Recharging : Dr P Baker
and R B Campbell

Diving Accessories : G T Skuse

Lifejackets : Leo Zanelli

Maintenance of Equipment : F Lock

BASIC EQUIPMENT

The basic equipment of the diver consists of fins, mask and snorkel. There are many different makes and patterns available, and an appreciation of their function will help the trainee to make a more reasoned choice.

Fins

The fins are used to improve the propulsive power of the legs so that the arms need not be used for swimming. The beginner would be well advised to avoid the very long or very flexible types which can cause excessive leg fatigue and/or cramp. Fins are available with angled blades and with cut-out flaps, with strap fixings and with shoe fitting. Which to select is mainly a matter of personal preference but the advice of experienced members of the branch might well be sought. Choose a pair of fins that are comfortable; if too tight they may cause cramp and if too loose they may be lost during finning. Remember that the fins you buy will be worn over a pair of neoprene bootees on open-water dives and this should be allowed for when deciding on the size to select. Many people wear neoprene bootees or socks in the swimming pool to avoid their fins being too loose. An alternative is to keep the fins in place with the aid of a pair of fin-retaining straps. Many of the modern makes of fins are manufactured from two separate kinds of rubber—a stiff one for the blade and a softer one for the foot fitting, and these have the advantage of comfort without sacrificing efficiency. Fins can also be obtained in material which will float—perhaps a good thing should the fin come loose (which it should not!).

Masks

The function of the mask is to enable the diver to see clearly beneath the surface of the water, since the eyes can only focus correctly when looking through air and the mask facilitates this. Goggles should NOT be used since pressure resulting from depth cannot be equalised through the nose with such devices. Full-face masks are not favoured; they can be difficult to clear of water and to keep the glass clear. Masks with attached snorkels are also to be avoided.

The 'window' of the mask should be of toughened glass, NEVER ordinary glass, to avoid damage to the face in the event of an accident. Plastic is used in some masks but this suffers from the disadvantage that it scratches easily and sometimes is difficult to keep clear. The glass of the mask is normally prevented from misting-up by the old-fashioned but effective technique of rubbing the glass with saliva prior to the commencement of the dive, but don't forget to rinse it out with clean water before fitting!

Ear clearing is allowed for in the mask by recesses on either side of the nose which enable the nose to be pinched from outside the mask. It is essential, therefore, to ensure that the mask is fitted with these nose-pinching recesses. Many masks are now fitted with drain valves which enable water to be expelled from the mask without having to remove it. During training the diver is shown how to clear the mask without the drain valve, so its presence is a personal preference rather than a necessity.

It is important that the mask should be a comfortable, water-tight fit on the face. This can be checked by placing the mask on the face without using the retaining strap, and sucking through the nose to hold the mask on the face without leakage of air—if the mask stays in position easily it is a good fit.

There are many different designs of mask on the market at widely differing prices. Get a mask that is comfortable, water-tight and gives you a wide field of vision. Faces vary considerably in contour, so try several types of mask before making your choice.

Snorkels

The snorkel tube enables the diver on the surface to breathe without having to lift his head out of the water, as the 'steam' swimmer must. There are many types and shapes available, but probably the simplest single-bend or 'J' type is the most satisfactory. The tube should be just long enough to clear the water—if too long it is unwieldy and uncomfortable and may be difficult to clear. The diameter should be large enough not to interfere with easy breathing, but not so large that clearing becomes difficult. Avoid tubes that have unnecessary complications such as double-bends and/or fitted valves, the latter can be a hazard in that the valves have been known to stick or leak.

To prevent the tube being lost and also to avoid it pulling excessively on the mouthpiece, it should be fitted *under* the strap of the mask or it can be fixed to the strap of the mask by a rubber band. Some divers prefer to fit the snorkel under the mask-strap and avoid losing it by having a lanyard tied to the tube and fitted around the neck.

PROTECTIVE CLOTHING

Cold water has always been a problem for divers, and one that many of us regularly meet. Although a resting unclothed man can stand low temperatures in still air, he is quite incapable of adapting himself similarly to cold water. This is due to the vastly greater heat loss during immersion; in fact, man is unable to maintain a normal body temperature at rest in water much cooler than a lukewarm domestic bath (96° F). Cooling of the body, more precisely termed hypothermia, at first calls into play protective measures by the body to conserve heat: the small blood vessels to the skin, especially of the hands, feet and limbs, are closed. These parts are allowed to cool while the temperature of other more vital organs is preserved. This protective mechanism is not, however, so effective in the head and neck, where such vital organs as the brain and spinal cord are near the surface. Later, shivering occurs as a means of producing extra heat, and when this defence fails the deep body temperature begins to fall with a consequent slowing of reflexes and movement, and an impairment of thought and judgment. Eventually coma and death from drowning, or arrest of the heart, results.

The graph illustrates how a man will survive from 40 minutes to two hours in water at 40° F, and from two hours to indefinitely at 60° F. The variation in survival time at each temperature (the marginal zone of

Figure 1

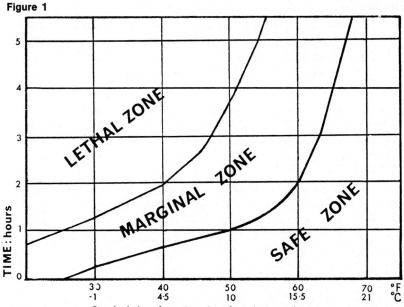

Survival time in water at various temperatures.

the graph) is due to differences in build from person to person and to the amount of extra body heat generated by exertion such as swimming. Those well endowed with a natural covering of fat will survive far longer than the small and skinny, and vigorous exercise also has a protective effect by promoting body heat production. Thus each summer we have the spectacle of channel swimmers flailing their way across the Straits of Dover unscathed, in conditions where the thin and less fit would soon succumb.

Unfortunately the present day aqualung with its limited air capacity places a premium on slow unhurried movement in order to conserve air, while obesity as a method of keeping warm has little to commend it, as it usually betrays a lack of physical fitness.

It follows from this that for comfort and safety a diver will need some form of protective clothing for all but the warmest of tropical waters. In addition to its prime purpose of providing thermal insulation, the clothing also gives welcome physical protection against abrasions from rocks, coral, jagged metal and similar hazards.

There are two basic types of diving dress, the dry suit and the wet suit. Neither of these is completely satisfactory and they each have different fields of usefulness.

Dry Suit

The dry suit is loose fitting and is made of rubber sheet or rubberised fabric with thin rubber seals at the neck and wrists to exclude water. In itself rubber is a poor insulator but the suit is worn with sufficient woollen underclothing underneath to provide the required protection.

Dry suits commonly available are of two main types as follows :

The one-piece, neck entry, suit is a robust outfit entered via the neck of the suit and sealed after entry either by a separate and easily replaceable thin rubber neck seal or a hood which is clamped to the suit by a 'dog collar' at the neck. Its disadvantages are the need for assistance to get into it, and the bulk of its collar.

The two-piece suit consists of jacket, trousers and cummerbund. They are joined together at the waist by thin sheet rubber seals which are rolled together after entry and held in place by the cummerbund. While these suits are easier to put on, the large thin seals are easily damaged and, because they are glued to the suit, difficult to replace. The bulk of the rolled up seal is inconvenient at the waist where weight belt and aqualung are frequently fastened.

Other types of dry suit exist, differing mainly in the method of entry and manner of sealing the suit.

Difficulties in the use of dry suits mainly arise from compression or the escape of air trapped in the suit. As the diver descends and pressure rises the volume of this air decreases in accordance with Boyle's law. As the air volume shrinks, the suit is pressed more and more tightly to the diver. It compresses his clothing and becomes rigid, and the so-called 'squeeze' effect results. Ultimately, when the clothing cannot be compressed any more, the air pressure in the suit can no longer be affected by outside pressure and a relative vacuum is produced. This causes bursting of small blood vessels in the skin which also becomes pinched in folds of the clothing. When a hood is worn instead of a neck seal, bleeding into the external ear passage may result—known as 're-versed ears'. The compression of air in the suit also results in consider-able loss of buoyancy.

These difficulties can be circumvented in two ways. The simplest is merely to commence the dive with a surplus of air in the suit which will be compressed at the expected depth of the dive to a comfortable volume. Provided a shot line or anchor rope is available to assist in overcoming the excessive buoyancy during the initial stages of the descent, this is a satisfactory solution.

A more elegant way is to provide some method of inflating the suit at depth as required. This can be from a small compressed air cylinder operated by a hand wheel, or by taking a supply from the aqualung. This system has the additional advantage of providing a considerable degree of control over buoyancy. On ascent surplus air has to be bled off, usually via the cuff seals. Some may prefer to have valves at neck and ankles to do this automatically, but in practice these valves often leak water into the suit.

A logical development from this idea has been the French constant volume suit in which the half face mask is an integral part of the hood. To inflate his suit the diver has merely to blow air past the edges of his mask. Surplus air is vented through valves at ankles and head.

Flooding of a dry suit after a tear can be a serious problem not merely because of the sudden chilling but also from the rapid loss of buoyancy which may result, especially if automatic vent valves are fitted.

Dry suits are particularly valuable for long periods of diving especially when in dirty, cold or polluted waters.

The wet suit

In this, no attempt is made to make it watertight, and in contrast to the dry suit it is essential that it be a good fit to minimise the amount of cold water entering the suit.

The most primitive and still useful form of wet suit was the wearing of warm woollen clothing—sweater, combinations, socks and gloves—preferably with some close-woven garment on top to diminish water flow through the material. This will give a quite useful increase in comfort and endurance over the unprotected diver.

A development of this, the porous sponge rubber suit, was more elegant but otherwise worked in the same manner, but this has now been entirely superseded by the use of expanded foam Neoprene. This material consists of a dense foam of nitrogen bubbles in Neoprene rubber. There is a skin of smooth Neoprene on one or both sides and, often to give additional strength and ease in dressing, nylon material is bonded to the surface. Neoprene is supple, light, a good heat insulator and easily tailored. Usually a complete suit comprises jacket and trousers with separate hood, gloves and boots of the same material. For cold water use an undervest of Neoprene is often added. Flow of water through the suit is reduced to a minimum by skintight fitting and by giving a generous overlap between different parts of the suit. The jacket is fitted with a jock strap to prevent its being pulled away from the trousers in use, and usually it has a zip down the front to facilitate dressing.

The advantages of Neoprene suits include comfort, ease of dressing with comparative elegance, easy manufacture and repair, good physical protection of diver, and buoyancy.

Figure 2

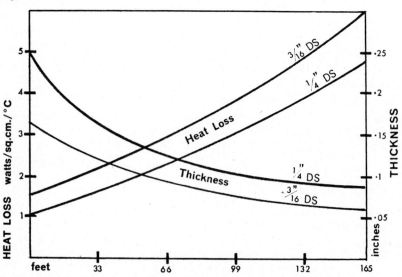

Variation in Heat Loss and Thickness of Neoprene with depth.

In spite of its almost universal use for club diving, Neoprene suffers from some drawbacks, all associated with the compression of the nitrogen in the foam under pressure. This causes thinning of the material at depth with resulting loss of buoyancy and effectiveness as a protection against cold. The material halves its thickness at a depth of 20 metres and is down to a third at 53 metres. Heat loss varies rather more than this, being double at 20 metres and four times bigger at 53 metres. Thus a suit which gives adequate protection at the surface may be quite inadequate during a dive. Fortunately the effect of this is not so serious as might be imagined because the aqualung has a somewhat parallel loss of endurance with increasing depth and the diver runs out of air before he is dangerously chilled. Nonetheless, with the advent of larger capacity breathing sets and the extension of the diving season further into the winter this is becoming a bigger problem.

Buoyancy varies considerably with depth, being halved at 10 metres and down to one-tenth at 53 metres. Thus a diver needing a 9 kilogramme weight belt at the surface for neutral buoyancy will be some 8 kilogrammes overweight at 53 metres. In practice, of course, a diver uses the weight he will require to achieve neutral buoyancy at the planned depth of his dive. This leaves him with useful excess buoyancy at the surface. What is less desirable, however, is that if he descends deeper than expected he becomes negatively buoyant and sinks. In deep water, especially in poor visibility, he may be overcome by narcosis before realising what is happening. This has caused several disasters in the past. When decompression stops are needed, it may be advisable to tolerate some excess weight at the bottom. This will enable the diver who has surfaced some way from the boat to swim back to the shot line at his correct decompression depth without being forced to surface by excessive buoyancy.

Care of suits

The rubber seals of dry suits and the inside of unlined Neoprene suits should be dusted with talc before dressing. Nylon lined suits do not need this preparation but are easier to put on if dry.

After use all types of suit should be rinsed free of salt and dirt, and dried, and all unlined rubber and Neoprene lightly dusted with talc before storage. They should never be left in the sun, stored in a hot place or be allowed to become contaminated with oil or grease, all of which deteriorate rubber and the adhesives used in bonding suits.

Hands

While many divers prefer to use bare hands as much as possible, it is advisable, because of softening of the skin on immersion, to wear some form of protection such as cotton or leather gloves. Cold water is a good anaesthetic and it is all too easy to spoil a holiday by cutting oneself unawares on some snag. Remember that cuts and abrasions exposed to salt water heal slowly and often scar badly.

Adequate thermal protection of the hands in cold water is a difficult problem due to the large surface area exposed by the fingers. Mitts are relatively warm but difficult to do useful work with. They can, however, be taken off as necessary for short periods. Five-finger foam Neoprene gloves are available but not really adequate in cold water.

Head and neck

As explained before, the head and neck are a serious source of heat loss. It is essential that the hood, if of Neoprene, is at least as thick as the suit itself. With a hooded dry suit a balaclava helmet may be worn underneath to increase protection. With a hoodless dry suit the use of a foam Neoprene hood is probably the best solution. In spite of these measures, full protection of the head is not possible because of the need to use a mask and mouthpiece.

General hints

It is equally essential to avoid chilling before and after diving. Adequate weatherproof clothing should be worn on board boat or while waiting around on cold and windy beaches. Wet diving gear should be discarded immediately after use unless required as a temporary protection from foul weather. Hot water poured through the suit will go some way towards restoring body heat while a supply of hot drinks will do much to restore morale.

Any diver who looks or feels cold, especially if he is shivering uncontrollably, may well have suffered a fall in body temperature. It is difficult to confirm the diagnosis unless a rectal temperature is taken and shows a reading below 97.4°F (normal rectal temperature 99.4°F), but as a working rule any diver who feels cold and is shivering uncontrollably should be treated as suffering from hypothermia and rewarmed as above. A severe case should be put in a warm bath as soon as possible. It should be remembered that it can take two or three hours for body temperature to be restored and in the meantime reactions are slowed and judgment impaired. This may be doubly dangerous when decisions affecting other people's safety are required or if a car has to be driven home.

BIBLIOGRAPHY

L G C E Pugh,
  O G Edholm *et al.*
W R Keatinge

W R Keatinge

A Physiological Study of Channel Swimming. Clinical Science 1960. Volume 19. Page 257.
Death After Shipwreck (Lakonia Disaster). British Medical Journal, 1965. Volume 2. **P 1537-1540.**
Survival in Cold Water. Blackwell Scientific Publications. 1969.

THE WEIGHT BELT

The buoyancy of protective clothing is such that some form of weighting is needed if the diver is to obtain neutral buoyancy underwater. This is usually achieved by wearing a weight belt. Lead weights are added to the belt until the correct buoyancy is arrived at. It is impossible, by this means, to be correctly weighted at all depths as the suit's buoyancy varies with depth. In any case, experienced divers have individual preferences; some prefer to be slightly buoyant, some neutral, and some prefer to be slightly heavy. For the novice, however, heavy weighting is dangerous.

It is important that a weight belt should be comfortable. Make sure that the belt is reasonably wide—a narrow belt cuts in and can be very uncomfortable. Likewise the weights should be fitted flush with the inside and protrude outside so that there is nothing pressing into the diver.

The main function of weights is to assist the diver to descend. So it follows that if he should wish to surface in a hurry, or be exhausted on the surface, he must be able to dispense with them quickly. A weight belt should possess an efficient quick-release. An ordinary belt strung with lumps of lead is potentially lethal. The belt must be able to be released in a single movement, and the release mechanism should be easy to locate with bulky gloves on. A small spring or tape is of little or no value in this case if it cannot be found and grasped easily with gloved, frozen hands. A weight belt should fit snugly—if it doesn't it is likely to ' revolve ' round your waist; and when you want to get rid of your weights in a hurry the release mechanism might be located somewhere around your back and inaccessible.

If you have need to get rid of your weight belt, don't just pull the release and let the belt drop—it will probably snag in your knife or some other item of equipment. When you have released the belt, keep hold of it, then *throw it away*. In other words, hold it at arm's length before dropping it, so that it does not snag on anything.

The weights should be able to be fitted, or removed, easily; otherwise there might be a tendency to leave them on when they should be removed, leaving the diver dangerously heavy.

PRINCIPLES OF THE AQUALUNG

History

The first diving regulator was designed in the 1860s by two French engineers, Benoit Rouquayrol and Auguste Denarouze. It is of great credit to these two pioneers that their regulator contained virtually all the basic design details that we still use today. What was lacking in 1860 was the availability of lightweight cylinders of adequate capacity to give the diver a useful underwater endurance. Rouquayrol and Denarouze had to make do with cylinders of only 30 bars pressure rating, a pressure at which we now consider our cylinders to be virtually empty! To boost the endurance of the 'Aerophore' as it was named, it had to be used in conjunction with an air line to keep the cylinder topped up. As such the equipment had little advantage over the standard copper-helmet diving suit, and development of the system did not proceed.

By the 1930s fins and goggles had appeared but the swimmer's underwater endurance was still limited to his own breath-holding capacity. It was at this stage that Jacques Cousteau became interested in the sport of underwater swimming and began experimenting with underwater breathing apparatus. In company with Frederic Dumas he tried several systems from a simple hand-pumped air line to a rudimentary oxygen re-breathing set. The air line was very restrictive and the oxygen set unreliable and dangerous.

However, by the 1940s manufacturers of gas cylinders had at last produced cylinders which were light enough to be carried on a man's back and still contain a useful supply of air. Another Frenchman, Commander Le Prieur, designed a free diving set, supplied from cylinders, but this fed the air to the diver in continous flow and had to be manually regulated. Cousteau tried this set but realised that there was still room for much improvement.

What was needed was a 'Demand Valve'. A valve that fed air to the diver only when demanded, ie, when the diver required to breathe in. It was to shut off while the diver breathed out, be automatic in operation, and cope with changes in pressure due to depth. How was this achieved?

In 1943 Cousteau's searches led him to be introduced to Emile Gagnan. Gagnan was already working on gas regulators, some of which were used to allow the war-time Paris taxis to run on coal gas. Gagnan studied Cousteau's problems and produced a demand valve which worked well on the surface but gushed continuously when submerged. Experiments continued and the secret of success discovered. It was essential that the exhaust valve be placed immediately adjacent to the demand diaphragm, this feature was lacking in the Rouquayrol-Denarouze valve.

With this feature incorporated Cousteau and Gagnan had produced the true demand valve. The partnership of Cousteau-Gagnan was to continue to produce other demand valves. The sport of sub-aqua diving was born and a new name coined—the 'AQUA-LUNG'.

Strictly the term 'AQUA-LUNG' should only be applied to those products of the Cousteau-Gagnan team, but the name has tended to be applied to all types of free diving apparatus. If we continue to do so now I hope that this will not be regarded as plagiarism but rather as a tribute to the pioneering of Jacques Cousteau and Emile Gagnan and recognition that their experiments helped to create a new sport.

Basic Principles

What were those secrets that the early experimenters had to uncover and which, today, we take for granted? Attempts to breathe surface air through elongated tubes had soon shown that man himself could not draw air down to any significant depth. It was necessary for the air to be pumped down to him until the pressure of the air he breathed equalled the pressure of the surrounding water. This is the principle of the standard diving suit.

As the diver descends deeper so the water pressure increases and the air delivery pressure must also be increased to stay in equilibrium. Conversely, as the diver ascends the water pressure decreases and again it is necessary for the regulator to adjust the air to match the lower pressure. A further effect of the increased air pressure at depth is that the density of the air delivered is also increased. At 30 metres depth the absolute pressure is 4 bars, ie, four times the pressure of the atmosphere on the surface. The density of the delivered air will also be four times greater than surface air. The regulator must allow this 'thicker' air to flow through the various passageways without restriction.

If we accept that 60 metres is the absolute limit for sport diving then the air needs to be delivered at 7 times the surface pressure and density. To give a margin of safety the regulator must be capable of functioning at even greater pressures. Not all regulators are recommended for use at such extreme depths.

For economy the air needs to be delivered to the diver only when he demands it—hence the term 'Demand Valve'. The regulator must be automatic in operation, triggered off by the initial suction of the in-taking breath. Nothing is quite so tiring as having to breathe against a restriction so the action of the regulator needs to be initiated by only a very slight inhalation, equivalent of sucking half an inch of water up a straw. The onset of the air flow must be gentle and match the diver's natural breathing rhythm, starting slowly, reaching a maximum about half way through the breath and then decreasing to zero again. Air should not be forced down the diver's throat, and yet for ease of breathing the air flow should be self-sustaining all the time the diver is inhaling.

When the diver stops breathing in the air delivery must also stop and remain so whilst the diver pauses and then exhales. There should be little resistance to the exhalation, for this can also prove to be very tiring. The air delivery must re-commence as soon as the diver commences his next inhalation.

Cousteau and Gagnan discovered that the demand valve was sensitive to the relative positions of the exhaust valve and demand diaphragm and that these two components must be positioned immediately adjacent to each other for correct operation of the regulator.

The remaining factor is the position of the demand valve relative to the diver's lungs. Ideally both should be subjected to identical water pressure but this is not possible to achieve at all times. Luckily the diver can cope with the varying effects providing they are kept within reasonable limits. The correct positioning of the demand valve will be discussed later in this chapter.

Types of Demand Valves

Although the air cylinder is a very essential component of the 'Aqualung' it has a passive role and so in this chapter we will concentrate on the functions of the demand valves.

Demand valves may be divided, visually, into two types; the Twin Hose, back mounted valve, and the Single Hose, mouthpiece held valve. The valves may be further categorised into 'Single Stage' or 'Double Stage' valves. These terms describe the number of stages in which the air pressure is reduced from the high pressure, stored in the cylinder, to the low pressure breathed by the diver. With the 'Single Stage' valve the air pressure is reduced in one step, ie, there is only one controlling orifice. A 'Double Stage' valve reduces the pressure in two steps. First the air pressure is reduced from cylinder pressure to an intermediate pressure, usually around 7 bars, this pressure is then reduced at the main demand diaphragm to the breathing pressure required by the diver.

Twin Hose demand valves may be either single or double stage. Single Hose demand valves are normally double stage, although one design has been produced which is single stage. This was originally intended for use with a full-face mask where the stiffness of the high pressure delivery hose was of no significance.

Some demand valves have been described as 'Three Stage'. Now, whilst it would be quite possible to produce such a valve most of those so described are mis-named. The so-called third stage is often only the interstage relief valve.

Other descriptive terms are 'upstream' and 'downstream' valves. These expressions refer to the main controlling valve orifice, operated by the demand diaphragm. An 'upstream' valve is one in which the controlling orifice faces towards the oncoming air stream and the sealing face of the valve head prevents the air entering the orifice until the valve is actuated. The valve head is in fact on the upstream side of the orifice. The air pressure tends to force shut this type of valve and when used as the second stage of a double stage valve then an interstage relief valve must be provided to protect the valve in case of leakage of high pressure air past the first stage.

A 'downstream' valve is one in which the controlling orifice faces away from the oncoming air stream and the sealing face of the valve head prevents the air from leaving the orifice, ie, the valve head is downstream of the orifice. The air pressure tends to open this type of valve and it is kept shut by means of a spring. When used in a double stage valve inadvertent overpressurisation will cause the valve to lift and so it acts as its own relief valve.

The first stage of a double stage valve may be either 'diaphragm' or 'piston' action. With the former the first stage pressure is controlled by a thick laminated rubber fabric diaphragm which bears down on the metering valve. With the latter the diaphragm and its associated components are replaced by a single metal piston. The head of the piston senses the interstage pressure and the stem of the piston forms the metering face. The function of all these various components will be explained as we consider each type of demand valve in detail. With single hose demand valves upstream (tilt) valves appear to be associated with diaphragm action first stages and the downstream second stages with piston action first stages. There is no fundamental reason why this should be so and either type of first or second stage will function with the other—with due regard to the provision of relief valves with upstream second stages.

Twin Hose, Single Stage Demand Valves

Figure 1 shows diagramatically the construction of a twin hose, single stage demand valve. The main casing consists of two chambers separated by a thin rubber diaphragm. One chamber is open to the water; this chamber also contains the exhaust valve. The other chamber contains a system of levers which transmit the movement of the diaphragm to the metering valve. The metering valve is contained in the high pressure body which clamps directly on to the cylinder pillar valve. A corrugated hose leads from the air chamber to the mouthpiece and a second hose carries the exhaust air back to the non-return valve in the water chamber.

When the cylinder is turned on the air first flows through a fine filter—this is usually a porous sintered bronze disc—and into the high pressure body. For the moment the high pressure air cannot pass the metering valve which is held shut by a spring. A small pin rests on the top of the metering valve and the lever system rests on top of the pin. To open the metering valve the levers must be depressed. When the diver commences to inhale the first effect is to create a very slight suction in the air chamber; this pulls down the diaphragm thus compressing the levers and opening the metering valve. Air now flows into the chamber and along the hose to the diver's mouthpiece.

In modern regulators the incoming air is deliberately blown into the delivery hose as a fast moving jet. This is to produce a venturi effect. In our requirements for an ideal demand valve we mentioned that for ease of breathing the air flow should be self-sustaining. Without the venturi effect the diver needs to keep sucking for the entire breath. With the venturi the speed of the air jet entering the hose tends to suck the rest of the air from the chamber, this keeps the diaphragm depressed and the main valve open sustaining the air flow. The design of the venturi is very critical for one can have too much of a good thing and blast too much air at the diver.

When the diver's inhalation stops the pressure in the air chamber rises slightly, lifting the diaphragm; this relaxes the levers and the main valve closes, shutting off the air delivery.

As well as being sensitive to changes of pressure caused by the diver's breathing the main diaphragm is also sensitive to changes of pressure caused by variations in depth. When the regulator is submerged the water chamber floods. The pressure of the water depresses the diaphragm causing the levers to open the main valve. The incoming air will raise the pressure in the air chamber and when the air pressure equals the water pressure the diaphragm will have moved back to its neutral position and the main valve will close. This action will take place automatically without any attention from the diver and without any interference of the breathing action which will be superimposed.

Non-return valves are fitted on either side of the mouthpiece of modern demand valves. These non-return valves prevent water entering the delivery hose should the mouthpiece become flooded. They also prevent any water in the exhaust hose from flowing back into the mouthpiece. Similarly they prevent stale air being drawn back. When clearing NRV fitted mouthpieces it is only necessary to blow the small amount of water from the mouthpiece itself and into the exhaust hose before commencing to breathe from the regulator. Older demand valves did not have this facility and the hoses could flood completely. With these valves it is necessary to clear both hoses of water before recommencing breathing. Even non-return valves can fail so don't neglect your flooded hose drills!

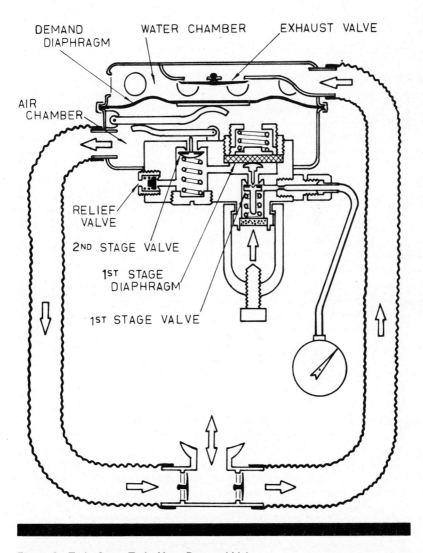

DEMAND DIAPHRAGM

WATER CHAMBER

EXHAUST VALVE

AIR CHAMBER

RELIEF VALVE

2ND STAGE VALVE

1ST STAGE DIAPHRAGM

1ST STAGE VALVE

Figure 2   Twin Stage Twin Hose Demand Valve

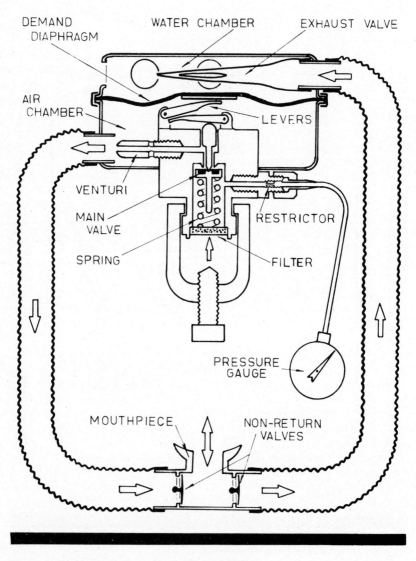

Figure 1 Single Stage Twin Hose Demand Valve

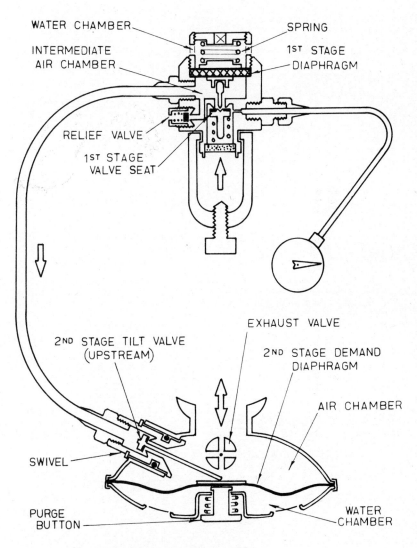

Figure 3 Twin Stage Single Hose Demand Valve
(Diaphragm and Upstream Action)

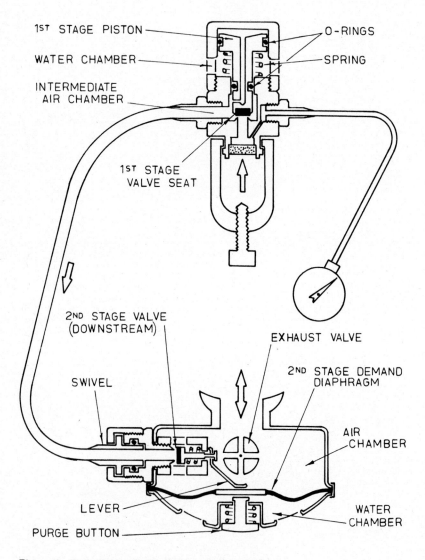

Figure 4 Twin Stage Single Hose Demand Valve
(Piston and Downstream Action)

The exhaust hose leads from the mouthpiece back to the demand valve casing and vents the expired air through the final exhaust valve into the water chamber. The air escapes through the same holes which admit the water to the chamber.

An accessory to the demand valve is the contents gauge; this shows the air pressure remaining in the cylinder. A tapping is taken from the high pressure body of the regulator and fed, via a flexible hose, to the gauge. The connection at the regulator contains a deliberate restriction so that in the event of the gauge hose bursting the loss of air will not be rapid. In some demand valves this restrictor takes the form of a small screw inside the connection : the air has to flow along the threads of the screw in order to reach the gauge. These screws should not be discarded. In other demand valves the connecting passage is drilled only as a very tiny hole.

Two Stage Valves

The single stage demand valve contains all the essential features for an underwater breathing apparatus but it is sensitive to the changes of air pressure in the cylinder. The double stage valve was developed to overcome this effect. The demand (second) stage functions as described for the single stage valve. However, instead of drawing air directly from the cylinder at a steadily decreasing pressure the demand stage is supplied with air at a constant, reduced, pressure. This intermediate pressure is usually controlled at around 6-8 bars. The reducing valve which controls this pressure is the first stage of the regulator.

To say that the intermediate pressure is held constant is an oversimplification. The pressure is actually held at a constant pressure above the surrounding water pressure. In this respect the first, reducing, stage is similar to the second, demand, stage as it also consists of two chambers separated now by a thick rubber fabric diaphragm. One side of the diaphragm bears on the first stage metering valve, the other side of the diaphragm is open to water pressure and also has a heavy spring bearing against it. This spring tends to keep the metering valve open.

When the air is turned on it flows past the open metering valve and into the intermediate chamber. Air continues to flow until the pressure in the chamber has risen sufficiently to overcome the combined force of the spring and water pressure. At this point the diaphragm will have moved to a neutral position and the metering valve will close.

When the diver inhales the demand stage opens as before and the air pressure in the intermediate chamber will start to fall. This will cause the first stage valve to open and air will flow from the cylinder to the diver. The first stage closes when the demanded flow ceases and the intermediate pressure rises to its predetermined level.

Some form of relief valve must be fitted to the intermediate chamber to vent off any excess pressure should the first stage valve fail to seal correctly. If an 'upstream' demand stage is used then a separate relief valve is necessary but a 'downstream' demand stage will act as its own relief valve.

The double stage, twin hose demand valve is very similar to the single stage version with the first stage, reducing, valve contained in the same casing as the demand stage.

The relief valve may be arranged to vent overboard or possibly to vent into the main air chamber where the vented air may be breathed by the diver. Ordinarily the relief valve leakage, if it exists at all, will be very slight.

Perhaps this is a good point to mention that if the relief valve is found to be leaking then the fault lies with the first stage valve, and screwing down the relief valve will not cure the trouble although it may hide it for a while. Whilst it is unlikely that the casing around the first stage valve will burst even if the intermediate pressure rises to cylinder pressure, the demand stage valve will not be able to open against the excessive pressure.

From Figure 2 it will be seen that the first stage diaphragm does not necessarily have to have direct contact with the water. As the demand stage air chamber automatically equalises to the water pressure then this air pressure may also be used to actuate the first stage diaphragm.

Single Hose, Two Stage Valves

With these types of demand valves the two stages are separate. The first stage, reducing, valve clamps directly to the cylinder pillar valve. A smooth bore hose carries the air to the demand stage which is built into the mouthpiece. The hose acts as the intermediate pressure chamber. The exhaust valve is also contained in the mouthpiece adjacent to the demand diaphragm. There is no need for an exhaust hose.

Relief valves, when needed, are fitted at the first stage and vent overboard. Again a warning about leaking relief valves, in this case screwing down the relief valve will not hide the excess pressure for long . . . the hose will burst! These hoses are of medium pressure rating, and while they will withstand pressures several times greater than the predetermined first stage pressure they will not withstand cylinder pressure.

Figure 3 shows a common type of single hose demand valve with a diaphragm action first stage and an upstream, tilt valve, demand stage. The tilt valve is so named because movement of the demand diaphragm does not lift the valve head off its seat but instead tilts it to one side.

Figure 4 shows another type which is becoming popular. This has a piston action first stage with a downstream demand stage. There is only one moving part in the first stage. The spring, plus water pressure, pushes on the underside of the piston head and lifts the stem, which forms the actual metering valve, off the valve seat. Air then flows through the orifice and into the hose. The piston stem is hollow and the air pressure is also transmitted to the top of the piston. When this air pressure has reached the predetermined level it will overcome the combined spring and water pressure and the piston will move down to close the valve. The piston head and stem are sealed with O-rings and also incorporate plastic wiper rings to keep the sliding surfaces free of silt.

The downstream demand stage consists of a spring-loaded plunger sealing against the main orifice. Usually a single lever bears against the demand diaphragm and movement of this lever, initiated by the diaphragm, lifts the plunger to admit air to the mouthpiece.

Venturi action is achieved in mouthpiece regulators by deflecting the air flow from the inlet orifice to the mouthpiece proper by means of baffles.

Positioning of Demand Valves
1   Twin Hose Regulators

Ideally the demand valve should be sensing the identical water pressure as the diver's lungs. With twin hose demand valves the height of the cylinder in the harness should be adjusted so that the demand valve is level with the diver's shoulder blades, just below the nape of the neck. In this position the demand valve is level with the diver's lungs in the vertical position. When the diver is swimming normally, face down in a horizontal plane, the demand valve is only at a slightly less pressure than the diver's lungs. The very slight drag that this produces on the air delivery is of no significance; it might be noticed at the initial intake of breath but will be eliminated by the venturi action as soon as the air starts to flow.

If the diver lies on his back the demand valve is subjected to a greater pressure than his lungs. In this position the regulator will deliver air very readily but not so forcibly that the diver cannot control it. This effect may be used to advantage if the diver has become short of breath.

2   Single Hose Regulators

The reaction of single hose regulators is different. They are not sensitive to the positioning of the cylinder.

With the demand stage just in front of the diver's mouth they are at their best position when the diver is swimming horizontally, face down. The natural tendency is for the diver to tilt his head slightly upward and the demand valve and the diver's lungs are then substantially on the same level. If there is any bias it will be for the demand valve to be at a slightly greater pressure and delivering air readily. This is the most noticeable difference between single and twin hose regulators.

When standing vertically the mouthpiece demand valve is subjected to slightly less water pressure than the diver's lungs, but, as with the twin hose regulator, the difference is not so great as to make any significant alteration in the performance of the regulator.

The trick of swimming on one's back produces no advantage with the single hose regulator. On the contrary, it makes it more difficult to breathe.

AIR CYLINDERS AND RECHARGING

Cylinders

In order to provide the air for a free diver to breathe under water in sufficient volume and at the required pressures, cylinders (colloquially referred to as bottles) are carried on his back. These bottles may be of any convenient size, but for ease of management and transport, the smaller and lighter they are—consistent with safety and adequacy of air supply —the better. Those normally used with underwater breathing apparatus are often slightly buoyant and, without the other equipment associated with them, will float.

The size or capacity of a bottle is usually expressed in cubic feet or litres. This does not refer to its actual internal volume, but to the volume of air at atmospheric pressure ('free air') which must be compressed into the cylinder to bring it to its rated safe working pressure. Thus it is impossible to determine the physical size of an aqualung bottle, or other type of gas cylinder, from its capacity alone; it is also necessary to know the pressure to which it is normally charged.

Of the various factors contributing to the deterioration of the steel compressed air cylinders used for aqualungs for free diving, rust is the biggest danger. The problem of preventing rusting of the outside of the cylinder is relatively simple. A good sea-water resisting paint over a zinc spray priming undercoat will protect the bottle for long periods.

Any rust that does accumulate may be removed by gentle wire brushing and treatment with a rust-removing compound prior to further priming and painting. The exterior paint on cylinders may be protected during transport and diving by placing them in a suitable canvas jacket.

The prevention of rusting inside the cylinder is rather more difficult and no really satisfactory solution has yet been devised. Rusting may, however, be avoided to a great degree by using dry air for filling the bottles, filling slowly and keeping stored bottles in a filled condition.

When aqualung cylinders are charged by use of a compressor, a silica gel or alumina filter will absorb much of the moisture, but it is still necessary to fill slowly in order to prevent unnecessary heat and subsequent internal condensation when the metal cools.

All aqualung bottles should be tested regularly by a competent authority. At present British Home Office regulations require that cylinders for underwater breathing apparatus shall be manufactured according to approved specification and shall be tested at least once every two years. These regulations include strict instructions on the testing and use of such cylinders. In the case of new cylinders provided with aqualungs the purchaser should satisfy himself regarding the relevant manufacturer's and test certificates.

The methods adopted for the testing of cylinders is of interest. The on/off valve is unscrewed and the bottle inspected internally with a powerful light for rust. If rust is found the cylinder is sand-blasted. The pressure test itself is carried out by filling the cylinder with water, immersing it in a water tank and increasing the pressure of the water in the cylinder to 50 per cent above its working pressure, for steel cylinders, and almost 100 per cent for aluminium alloy. The use of water instead of air in the cylinder and the surrounding water blanket greatly minimises the danger in the event of a cylinder failure and burst.

The test pressure is maintained for 30 seconds, and the expansion of the cylinder is accurately measured. After the pressure is released another reading is taken and the cylinder should have returned to its pre-set dimensions, although a 10 per cent set of the expansion figure is allowed. After an hydraulic test such as this, the cylinder must be thoroughly dried by heat. Cylinder valves are replaced with a lead capsule inserted to ensure a good air seal.

Whenever a cylinder is presented for charging, it is the responsibility of the fillers to assure themselves that the cylinder has been tested within the stipulated period. Cylinders should not be charged unless they are painted grey, with black and white quarters at one end.

Purchasers of second-hand aqualungs or bottles should make sure that all the necessary tests have been carried out before buying—certainly before using them, and that the bottles are painted in the standard colours as described above.

Cylinders should never be filled beyond their rated safe working pressure. They should invariably be stored in well-ventilated rooms and should be protected from heat and from extreme cold. Cylinders should never be left empty with the valve open as, by accident, sea or other water may enter. Furthermore, due to temperature changes, air will pass through the open valve carrying moisture which will condense on the inside of the cylinder walls causing rust. When not in use cylinders should be stored with at least a small pressure of air in them. This will avoid the possibility of open valves with consequent condensation and will also enable any dust to be blown out of the valve before the cylinder is recharged.

The mishandling of cylinders subjects them to severe stresses and they should always be treated carefully, particularly during transit. For example, they should not be allowed to roll about on the floor of a vehicle. In fact, statutory regulations govern their transport; the Gas Cylinders (Conveyance) Regulations, 1931, state that 'cylinders shall be so conveyed as not to project beyond the sides or ends of the vehicle.

Adequate means shall be taken to prevent the cylinders falling off the vehicle.'

Valves should be kept clean, as dirty water, grit and other foreign bodies can cause leakage at the joints. Oil or grease should never be applied to cylinder valves or anywhere which may come into contact with high-pressure air. There is risk of an explosion under conditions of heat and pressure.

Whilst cylinders are quite safe in normal use, an explosion can be extremely violent and very probably lethal.

Pillar Valves

A Pillar valve is more than a mere tap that turns your air supply on or off and it deserves better treatment than it usually gets. For a start it should be washed with fresh water after each dive; many are never washed, with the result that dried salt accumulates in the spindle gland. Salt is very abrasive and will cause the spindle to become stiff in operation. Pillar valves should be lubricated periodically, at least once a season. Silicone grease only should be used for this purpose to avoid the dangers caused by mineral greases reacting with the oxygen content of high pressure air.

If a pillar valve cannot be turned readily by hand then something is wrong with it. It may be salt deposit in the spindle gland; the onset of this can be avoided by washing the valve regularly. There is an advantage in leaving the regulator in place and hosing down the regulator, pillar valve and cylinder all in one go. The pillar valve can then be left open exposing more of the spindle stem than otherwise. Stiffness may also be caused by lack of lubrication on the spindle threads, in which case the valve should be stripped and re-lubricated. If this point is ignored the screw thread will ultimately seize up and strip; this may mean the replacement of the whole valve.

Unbalanced Valves

The commonest pattern of pillar valve is the 'unbalanced' type, as shown in Figure 1. With this type the spindle and valve head are in one piece and the spindle screws directly into the valve body. This means that the nylon valve pad rotates against the valve seat as it seals and so is liable to wear, particularly if screwed down very hard.

The term 'unbalanced' means that the thrust of the high pressure air is attempting to blow the valve head off the valve body. This force has to be resisted by the actuating thread and it means that there is always an extra frictional load on the thread and in consequence it will wear relatively quickly; lack of lubrication will aggravate the condition. Once the screw thread in the valve body is worn there is no alternative but to replace the whole valve.

Figure 1 Unbalanced Valve

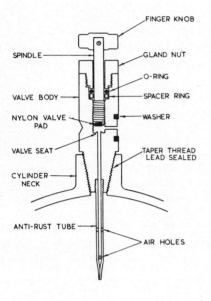

FINGER KNOB

SPINDLE

GLAND NUT

O-RING

VALVE BODY

SPACER RING

NYLON VALVE PAD

WASHER

VALVE SEAT

TAPER THREAD LEAD SEALED

CYLINDER NECK

ANTI-RUST TUBE

AIR HOLES

Figure 2 Glandless Valve

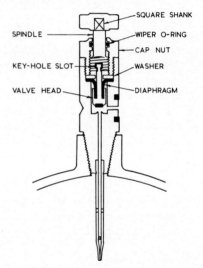

SQUARE SHANK

SPINDLE

WIPER O-RING

CAP NUT

KEY-HOLE SLOT

WASHER

VALVE HEAD

DIAPHRAGM

Figure 3 Balanced Valve

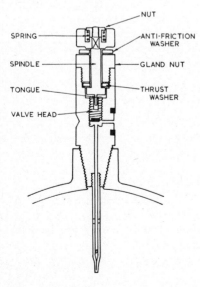

NUT

SPRING

ANTI-FRICTION WASHER

SPINDLE

GLAND NUT

TONGUE

THRUST WASHER

VALVE HEAD

The spindle assembly can be removed from these valves by backing off the gland nut, unscrewing the spindle at the same time. The condition of the screw threads can be seen. Unfortunately it is not so easy to re-assemble. Attempts to replace the spindle assembly in one piece are very likely to cause the spindle O-ring to be trapped and cut. The spindle assembly should be taken apart, which necessitates removing the finger knob. The assembly will now pull apart; the components should all be washed and cleaned, then lightly lubricated.

Re-assemble by first screwing the spindle into the valve body, then slip on the metal spacer ring followed by the O-ring, push these two down into the recess around the spindle using a blunt rod to avoid cutting the O-ring. Now screw home the gland nut and finally re-pin the finger knob in position.

Glandless Valves

Although still an unbalanced valve this type, shown in Figure 2, is more complex and has some advantages over the simpler variety. In the first place the valve head does not rotate with the spindle. This reduces the wear on the valve pad as it is not dragged around the valve seat. The high pressure air is prevented from escaping up the spindle by a bell-shaped diaphragm which is attached to the valve head. The actuating screw thread is contained in the cap nut and, being of larger diameter than in the previous design, is not so prone to wear. Even if the thread did seize it only means a replacement of the cap nut and spindle, not the whole valve. The top O-ring does not seal hp air but serves as a wiper ring to prevent ingress of salt and sand to the screw thread; it should be inspected closely and replaced when worn. To strip this kind of valve first close the valve lightly then remove the cap nut, withdrawing the whole spindle and valve head assembly. A sharp tug may be necessary if the rubber diaphragm proves to be stuck. Screw in the spindle so that the valve head may be disengaged from the 'key-hole' slot. Continue screwing the spindle into the cap nut until the plastic finger knob is pushed off, the spindle may now be separated from the cap nut and all the components cleaned and re-lubricated. Have a look at that wiper ring.

Re-assemble the components into the cap nut, taking care not to forget the large metal washer between the cap nut and rubber diaphragm. Bring the diaphragm back into contact with the cap nut but do not squeeze it. Now insert the assembly back into the valve body and lightly tighten the cap nut, 'open' the valve to lift the valve head clear of the valve seat and then complete tightening of the cap nut.

The valve depicted is the Sealion, manufactured by Submarine Products Ltd. The manufacturers point out that the plastic finger knob is intended to shatter if struck a heavy blow; it is easy to replace a broken knob but more difficult to replace a bent spindle. (So carry a spare knob!)

Balanced Valves

Figure 3 shows the third variety, the 'balanced' valve. The valve head although separate from the spindle still rotates with it, being driven by a tongue and groove connection. This rotates the valve head but also allows it to move axially along the screw thread without the spindle following it. When the valve is 'open' the hp air flows past the thread of the valve head so that it is completely surrounded, with the result that there is no extra thrust exerted on the thread. Instead this thrust is taken on a PTFE (PolyTetraFluoroEthylene, since you asked!) washer behind the shoulder on the spindle. Since there is no axial thrust on the valve head it is considered to be in a 'balanced' condition.

While the valve head moves axially, independently of the spindle, it cannot move so far as to come out of engagement. The fact that the operating spindle does not move in or out when the valve is used indicates that is is a balanced type.

Unscrewing the gland nut will allow the whole spindle assembly to be withdrawn, the valve head will remain in the valve body. Dismantle the spindle assembly by removing the little nut inside the finger knob, watch out for the spring! Having separated these components use the spindle to withdraw the valve head from the body. Wash and clean all components, particularly the spindle and gland nut as these have no wiper ring and will have a heavy salt deposit.

After re-lubricating replace all components, in order, in the valve body. Insert the valve head followed by the spindle, thrust washer, gland nut, anti-friction washer, finger knob, spring and nut. The spring nut should be two turns short of coil-binding the spring.

Anti Rust Tubes

A small tube extends from the base of all pillar valves into the cylinder. This is the anti rust tube, its purpose is to prevent particles of rust, even water, being drawn into the valve. Without the tube it will be readily seen that as soon as the cylinder is inverted all loose rust or water would be funnelled into the pillar valve and hence to the regulator and you. The anti rust tube allows this foreign matter to lie harmlessly in the shoulder of the cylinder while the air is drawn from a point above it.

Cylinder Threads

The inlet to most cylinders is still a tapered thread and it is not advisable for unskilled 'mechanics' to attempt to remove the pillar valve. Although excessive tightening is not necessary when fitting pillar valves it often takes considerable effort to get them out again after a couple of seasons' use. The chromium finish of the valve is slippery and will cause a spanner to skid and it is all too easy to crush the metal around the washer groove and ruin the sealing face. In many cases the shape of the pillar valve does not allow normal spanners to be used.

The taper thread is made pressure tight by wrapping it in a lead foil cup, or with PTFE tape, prior to screwing it into the cylinder. As the pillar valve is tightened down the lead foil, or PTFE tape, flows around the threads completely sealing the two mating halves. The torque required to fit the pillar valve is no more that that needed to tighten an ordinary nut of comparable size. If excessive torque is used there is a danger that the neck of the cylinder will be strained or the thread damaged. Extra long spanners may be needed to extract an old pillar valve but they should not be needed to insert new ones.

Siebe Gorman cylinders have a different taper thread to others and care should be taken not to fit the cylinder with an incorrect valve.

Aluminium cylinders and some of the new steel cylinders have a parallel threaded neck. The corresponding pillar valve has a shoulder which screws down onto the neck of the cylinder. Sealing is achieved by an O-ring placed between this shoulder and the cylinder neck. There is less strain on the necks of such cylinders, hence its use on aluminium cylinders.

The compression of the O-ring acts as a friction grip between the two components and when the cylinder is charged the frictional force on the O-ring and thread is such that it could not be unscrewed unwittingly.

The great advantage of a parallel threaded cylinder is that it allows a larger diameter hole through which the internal condition of the cylinder may be inspected.

Recharging

High pressure air cylinders used for diving can be recharged in two ways, namely, from a compressor or a decanting cylinder. The ideal system would incorporate both these methods thus ensuring a ready supply of air at any time.

Although it is important that a knowledge of the fundamentals of recharging techniques should be imparted to the average Club diver, it must be stressed that the actual operation and maintenance of compressors and decanting systems is highly specialised and should, therefore, be left to competent personnel.

Simple Compressor Theory

'The operation of compressing air produces heat.' This statement describes the fundamental problem of maintaining high efficiencies in air compressors, ie, the more this compression heating can be reduced, the higher will be the efficiency.

EQUIPMENT

Figure A

Adiabatic & Isothermal Compression

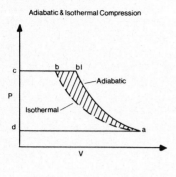

Figure B

Multi-Stage Compression

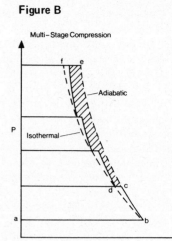

Figure C

Basic Compressor Layout

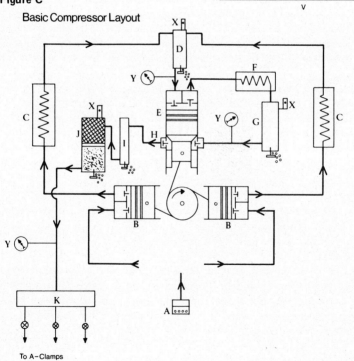

Air can be compressed in many ways, the two most relevant systems being isothermal and adiabatic compression :

(i) *Isothermal compression*—An isothermal air compression is one in which all the heat of compression is dissipated and the final temperature is equal to the initial value. This type of compression is only possible if the cycle of time is extremely slow. (See the dotted line 'ab' of Figure A.)

(ii) *Adiabatic compression*—An adiabatic air compression is one in which the majority of the heat of compression is contained within the air itself. This is the type of compression encountered in practical air compressors. (See the full line 'abl' of Figure A.)

Figure 1 shows the P-V diagram for a compressor cycle; 'da' represents the suction stroke, 'ab' or 'abl' represents the compression stroke and 'bc' or 'blc' represents the constant pressure discharge. As the work required to produce such a cycle is proportional to the area within the curve 'abcd', it will be seen that an isothermal compression requires less work and is therefore more efficient. When the air is eventually cooled after an adiabatic compression, the volume will be reduced and hence, the nearer a compressor can approximate isothermal conditions, the more air it will deliver.

In order to achieve conditions approximating to isothermal compression, modern compressor units pump air in a number of stages. The P-V diagram for a four-stage compressor is shown in Figure B. The dotted line 'bf' is the isothermal; the object is to keep the compression as near to isothermal as possible. In the first stage the air is compressed adiabatically to 'c'; it is then cooled at constant pressure by an intercooler until the temperature is reduced to the initial value if possible; this is represented by the constant pressure line 'cd'. For complete intercooling, the point 'd' is on the isothermal line 'bf'. The air is then drawn into the next cylinder for the second stage of its compressions and the process is repeated. Thus it will be seen that each stage increases the pressure of the air whilst the initial temperature is maintained at the end. Throughout the whole process the isothermal line has been approximated to in steps. If the compression reached by all these stages had taken place in a single stage, the compression line would have followed the adiabatic line 'be'; hence the work saved is that shown by the shaded area.

Basic Compressor Design

(i) *The compressor*

An air compressor suitable for charging diving cylinders basically consists of a crankshaft which drives a number of pistons dependent upon the number of compression stages. The reciprocating motion of each piston pumps air through inlet and outlet valves at the end of each cylinder. These valves are simple, air-flow operated, poppet types.

(ii)   *Compressor layout and charging circuit*

Figure C shows a simple layout for a three-stage air-cooled compressor. The air enters at the filter 'A' and is drawn into the first stage cylinder 'B'. At first stage pressure, the air is pumped through intercoolers 'C' and the water separator 'D' and thence to the second stage cylinder 'E'. At second stage pressure, the air is then pumped through a further intercooler 'F' and water separator 'G' to the final duplexed cylinder 'H'. Air at the final outlet pressure then passes through the final water separator 'I' and then through the composite chemical filter 'J'. The last passage of the air is through the manifold 'K' to the high pressure hoses and 'A' clamps to the diving cylinders.

The intercoolers 'C' and 'F' are usually made from coiled copper pipes situated in an external air stream which is derived from a fan mounted on the end of the unit's crankshaft. The water separators 'D', 'G' and 'I', are usually simple cylindrical chambers in which the air flow changes direction thereby letting any water vapour condense onto the walls and drain down to the outlet cock where it is periodically discharged to atmosphere. The chemical filter 'J' usually contains Silica Gel or Activated Alumina and Activated Charcoal separated by a thick felt pad.

In order to prevent damage to the compressor by over pressurisation, relief ('X') valves are situated at the entry to the second and third stages. Another relief valve is situated in the final pressure line which is set to the final pressure desired in the diving cylinders.

Although the above description is for a three-stage air-cooled unit, the same type of circuit is used in all compressors with minor differences, eg, with a water-cooled unit intercoolers will usually be in part of the main block casting and thus cooled by the same water that flows around the cylinders.

Filter Systems

In order to maintain a consistent supply of pure air from a compressor, it is essential that an efficient and trouble-free filtering system should be employed.

The most efficient air filtering media are manufactured from absorbant materials, that is, materials whose granular form has an extremely high surface area to attract particles of contamination. The most common materials used are Silica Gel or Activated Alumina for removing moisture and Activated Charcoal for removing oil mist and colours (when constructing or recharging a filter, it is essential that the Activated Charcoal should be situated downstream from the desiccating material in order to ensure efficient absorption of oil mist etc . . .). A rather more efficient filtering medium than those described above is Molecular Sieve (Activated Zeolites) with a granule size of 13X; this material will remove both water vapour and oil mist but has the disadvantage of high cost.

The composition of a typical filter for an average size compressor could be described as follows :

1   12.5 mm thick felt pad at inlet.
2   Silica Gel (self indicating type)—at least 100 mm depth.
    OR Activated Alumina—at least 100 mm depth.
3   Activated Charcoal—at least 100 mm depth.
4   13X Molecular Seive—about 50 mm depth.
5   12.5 mm thick felt pad at outlet.

One of the most important points concerning filtering systems is that of regular maintenance. The simplest way to assess the time interval between replacing the filter elements is to use self indicating Silica Gel which changes colour as it becomes saturated with water. With a new compressor, the filter life can be established by repeated inspection (approx every ten hours running time) of the Silica Gel—the whole element including felt pads should be replaced immediately a definite colour change is observed.

Lubrication

In order to ensure that a compressor is satisfactorily lubricated it is essential that any manufacturers' recommendations should be followed. In general, most compressors that are used for filling diving cylinders are lubricated with mineral based, medium viscosity index oils which are not prone to emulsification. Liquid paraffin, vegetable oils, motor oils and medical oils should normally be avoided.

(For further information on compressor lubrication see *BSAC Paper No* 1.)

Compressor Operation and Maintenance

The golden rule for compressor operation and maintenance is to always read the manufacturers' manual before attempting to start and run a compressor. There are, however, a few general points relating to operating procedures which are outlined in the following :—   .

1   Always ensure that no obnoxious fumes can flow into the air inlet. This is particularly important with a portable unit driven by either a petrol or deisel engine where incorrect positioning with regard to the prevailing wind direction can cause carbon monoxide to be drawn into the air inlet from the engine exhaust; any concentration of CO above 10 ppm (parts per million) will render the air outside the standards laid down by the BSAC.

2 If the compressor is new, an air testing kit should be available so that the purity of air delivered can be established. The BSAC standard for air purity is as follows :—

BSAC TABLE OF AIR PURITY STANDARDS—1971

Nitrogen	As atmospheric air
Oxygen	21% $\pm$ 0.5%
Carbon Dioxide	0.03% (300 ppm)
Carbon Monoxide	10 ppm
Oil	1 mg per M^3
Water	As dry as possible and not give rise to condensation at temperatures above 40°F.
Solid Particles Dust etc	Lack of residue on a Whatman 40 filter after passing 5,000 cc of air†
Odour and Taste	Freedom from both
Nitrogen Dioxide and Nitrous Oxide	NIL (under 1 ppm)

† Whatman 40 filter, rated as fast and of mean pore size 3.4 to 5 microns.

3 With all compressors, it is essential that the drain taps on the inter-stage separators should be cracked open at regular intervals; these taps should be left open as long as the water and oil emulsification (white in colour) flows out. Failure to do this will result in the early saturation of the final chemical filter and therefore the possibility of moisture in the cylinders.

4 If anything unusual occurs during the filling operation such as overheating, air leaks etc . . . the compressor should be immediately shut down and the cause determined by an experienced person.

With regard to compressor maintenance, it is essential that only competent personnel should undertake servicing procedures even if only the simplest of faults is involved. In addition to the manufacturers' recommendations, a regular check should be kept upon the oil level and filter system combined with frequent checks of air purity using a suitable testing kit. *Remember*—a little time spent regularly can save the inconvenience of a complete shut down later.

Choosing a Compressor

When deciding upon a compressor, a consideration of the following points will be found useful :—

1 The compressor must supply air free from oil, water, dust and contamination by other gases, or exhaust fumes.

2 It should supply air up to the maximum working pressure of the cylinders used or likely to be used.

3 It should have an output rate such that filling does not occupy an unreasonable time.

4 It should be so designed and constructed that it will run for reasonable periods between overhaul, and be inherently safe.

5 The system of drive should be simple and safe.

6 It should have a high efficiency, and spares should be readily obtainable.

7 If portability is required, the output will be limited to about 280 litre/min at the most.

If cost is a limitation, then the solution might be to purchase a second-hand compressor which can be subsequently reconditioned and modified to supply breathing air by fitting a suitable filter system. If this is the case, then it is essential that expert advice is obtained.

Decanting

Aqualung cylinders—referred to in this section by their colloquial name of bottles—may be filled by a system known as decanting. This is the procedure of transferring air into bottles from one or more larger cylinders.

At present the cylinders most commonly used in Britain are of 1100 l and 2000 l capacity. These figures are the volumes of free air (ie at normal atmospheric pressure, 1 b) which the bottle will hold when at its rated working pressure. Normally a 1100 l bottle is rated at 120 b and a 2000 l bottle at 150 b.

The two common sizes of cylinders supplied by British Oxygen Gases Ltd to branches for decanting purposes have capacities of 3100 l and 4600 l of free air at the nominal minimum pressure of 120 b.

It would appear at first sight that as a 4600 l cylinder contains four times as much air as a single 1100 l bottle that it should be possible to fill four bottles from the one large cylinder. This is not so; if 1100 l of air is removed from a 4600 l cylinder the remaining 3500 l will occupy the same space as occupied by the 4600 l and there must therefore be a considerable lowering of the pressure of 120 b.

The bottle will only hold 1100 l at 120 b and, as the pressure in the cylinder.has already fallen below this figure a second 1100 l filled from this cylinder will obviously not reach the required working pressure of 120 b.

To help overcome this problem the technique of decanting is employed. Briefly it involves coupling a number of cylinders together by a high pressure piping arrangement called a manifold, and progressively filling the bottles from the cylinders in ascending order of cylinder pressure.

A manifold can be of any convenient size, connecting any number of cylinders to any number of bottles. It may be a simple connection of pipes or each outlet may be equipped with a valve. Pressure gauges may also be incorporated at various points to check pressures in the cylinders or bottles. A bleed-off valve in the manifold is an advantage so that prior to removing a bottle, the manifold is at atmospheric pressure; if an attempt is made to remove a bottle when there is hp air in the 'manifold the bottle washer may be blown out.

The more cylinders there are connected to the manifold the more air can be used from them and the less number of connection changes necessary, thus simplifying and speeding up the decanting process. More than one bottle may be filled at the same time by using multiple outlets, thereby reducing the overall time required.

Manifolds should be constructed from piping and fittings designed for high pressure working. A burst union or valve can produce fatal results. At least one loop of not less than six inches diameter should be formed in each metal pipe. This permits flexing of the pipe without excessive bending. Continuous bending work hardens copper, causing it to become brittle and requiring frequent annealing to prevent fracture. Manifolds should only be made by persons competent with high pressure fittings and both piping and fittings should be tested every two years as recommended in BS4001 Part 1, Care and Maintenance of Underwater Breathing Apparatus '.

When air is compressed, heat is generated, and when pressure is reduced heat is lost. This fact can be used to indicate the direction in which air is flowing between the cylinder and bottle. By placing the hand on the neck or shoulder of the bottle being charged it will be felt to be getting warm, whilst the cylinder from which it is being filled will become cool. If the rate at which the air is being exchanged is too rapid the bottle will heat up extremely quickly, quicker, in fact, than it can be cooled by the atmosphere, and it may become dangerously overheated. Decanting should always be done slowly so that the bottle never becomes more than slightly warm.

Decanting technique

For the purpose of description it will be assumed that a bank of six cylinders is available, together with a manifold for coupling three cylinders and a single outlet connector with an 'A' clamp for attaching to a bottle. It is also assumed that there are a number of bottles, not completely empty, to be filled.

The remaining pressures in the bottles should be checked, they should be numbered with the highest pressure bottle as one and the others in decreasing order of pressure.

The three cylinders should then be connected to the manifold, having first ensured that all unions on the cylinders and manifold are free from dirt, grit, oil, grease and crossed threads. This is of the greatest importance, as dirt and grit will cause leaks and oil or grease in contact with high pressure air may cause a serious explosion.

Bottle one should be connected to the 'A' clamp and its valve left closed. With the proper spanner open one of the cylinder valves slowly (cracking is the technical expression) and check for leaks. The pressure in this cylinder and the other two should be checked individually and chalked on the cylinders.

With all cylinder valves closed, slowly open bottle one until the air remaining in the bottle and in the manifold have equalised. The cylinder with the lowest pressure should be slowly cracked until the pressure gauge in the manifold shows no further rise in pressure, or when the air flow ceases, the cylinder valve is then closed and the residual pressure in the cylinder is rechalked. The pressure gauge will show also the pressure in the bottle and if necessary the second cylinder can be cracked.

If the cylinders are at various pressures, having been used before, then equalise the bottle with the lowest pressure cylinder first; of course if a bottle has a higher pressure than the lowest pressure cylinder, it is pointless to use it since air will flow from the bottle to the cylinder.

Bottle one valve is now closed and either the manifold bleed valve is cracked or the 'A' clamp slowly unscrewed until all air has leaked out of the manifold and the 'A' clamp can be safely undone.

Bottle two is now connected and the process repeated. As the filling progresses in this way it will be found necessary to crack number three cylinder to reach the required maximum pressure in the bottles. Eventually it will be found impossible to approach maximum bottle pressure by using number three cylinder, and at this stage the manifold must be transferred to cylinders number two, three and four, and so on.

If a gauge is not fitted in the manifold, great care must be taken when filling to avoid overcharging a bottle and immediately a bottle is filled it should be checked with a pressure gauge, either on a demand valve or on a separate special 'A' clamp.

From the foregoing it will be realised the importance of numbering the cylinders in use, so that the lowest number indicates the lowest pressure. In the same way the numbering of the bottles so that the lowest number indicates the first bottle to be filled, ie the bottle containing the highest pressure air, will be appreciated. This method prevents wastage of time and air.

The simple rule when decanting ·from several cylinders is always to ensure that a bottle is filled from a cylinder whose pressure is least different from that in the bottle, or, conversely, when decanting from a cylinder into a series of bottles, the order of filling of the series should be the order of the bottle pressures from the highest to the lowest.

To illustrate this point consider four 1100 l bottles with pressures of 60, 50, 10 and 0 bars respectively, to be filled from one cylinder of 3100 l. The figures are as follows :

							Final pressure in both bars
From 120 to 60 bars	...	...	...	...	...		104
„ 104 „ 50 „	...	...	...	...	...		89
„ 89 „ 10 „	...	...	...	...	...		68
„ 68 „ 0 „	...	...	...	...	...		50

Compare these final pressures with :

							Final pressure in both bars
From 120 to 0 bars	...	...	...	...	...		88
„ 88 „ 10 „	...	...	...	...	...		67
„ 67 „ 50 „	...	...	...	...	...		62
„ 60 bottle	...	...	...	...	...		60

In the first method 50 b remains in the cylinder, so more air has been removed from it than in the second method, if a series of cylinders are used then gains are made at each decant and as well as using more air from the cylinder higher bottle pressures are obviously obtained.

Points to remember when decanting

High pressure air is lethal and should be handled with care. All fittings should be clean and free from oil and grease before any connections are made. Manifold nipples and threads must be undamaged and all connections secure.

Bottles must not be filled at an excessive rate. If the rate is too fast, the air temperature is raised and when the bottle subsequently cools the air pressure drops, sometimes by as much as 15 per cent. Excessive filling rates can also damage flexible rubber manifolds, leading to blocked pipes and valves.

The air temperature rise in a bottle with pressure increase during charging is about one degree C per 0.25 b. If decanting is done slowly the heat produced is conducted away through the bottle wall by the outside air. With adequate cooling of the bottle, a charging rate of 25 b per minute can be used. A simple check on the filling rate is never allow the bottle to become uncomfortably hot to the touch.

Leaks should never be cured by the use of a hammer nor undue force on the manifold couplings or unions. Fittings should be undone and checked for damage or dirt, then retightened. Attempts to make fittings work more easily by grease or oil should never be tried as these in contact with high pressure air can cause explosions. Damaged threads should be cleaned up with the appropriate taps or dies.

Before disconnecting any part of the decant system check that all bottles and cylinders are turned off. The manifold must be disconnected slowly as there may be a considerable quantity of high pressure air still inside.

Conclusion

It must be emphasised that the procedures and descriptions outlined in this section are only intended as an introduction to the principles involved. Further information can be obtained from publications such as *BSAC Paper No* 1 and only when such further information has been thoroughly digested and understood should any attempt be made to run, service or, in fact, have anything to do with the recharging of high pressure air cylinders.

Note : The BSAC Air Purity Table 1971 on page 200 is the latest. It differs from the Table in *BSAC Paper No* 1 in the assessment of water vapour.

DIVING ACCESSORIES

Accessories include any item carried by the diver besides basic kit, aqualung and suit. It has been the practice in the past to regard life-jackets as accessories, but as they are now regarded as fundamental items of equipment they are dealt with elsewhere. Accessories must be of the best possible quality and reliability, but this does not mean they must be expensive or have to be purchased ready-made. More than any other diving equipment they lend themselves to 'do it yourself' manufacture. Individual ingenuity has full rein, as will appear in this chapter. Just how many accessories are of interest will depend on the individual diver, his interests and his finances, but those included in the first group, the major accessories, are necessities rather than accessories. The major accessories will therefore include : knife, compass, depth-gauge, watch and contents gauge. They must be treated with respect, they are each in turn liable to be responsible for your life—or its loss. The minor accessories include, but are not limited to : fluorescent hoods, divers' marker buoys and reels, miniflares, buddy-lines, torch, slate and pencil, fish-ring, specimen containers, lifting bags, 'bug-bag', crab-hook, aqua-plane and ankle-straps.

MAJOR ACCESSORIES
Knife

It is often difficult to assess the priority of each accessory, but the knife is certainly at the top. Every diver in open water must carry a knife, its main purpose being for cutting entangling nets, line or rope, lesser uses, although possibly more frequent, including stabbing fish, levering off shellfish, hammering or screwdriving etc. At the same time a knife is a dangerous thing and it must be treated with respect. A good diver's knife is of solid construction and quite heavy weight. The blade is usually made of stainless steel, despite the fact that stainless steel does not hold a good edge for long. If a good knife steel were used it would be unable to stand up to the highly corrosive conditions met in diving. Hidden corrosion of the tang inside the handle is very likely.

It is a curious fact, but I have found even a stainless steel blade to benefit from oiling, especially for the first few dives, and at regular intervals thereafter. In any case knives need honing regularly, and this provides an opportunity for cleaning and oiling as well. By the way it pays to keep your knife clean, after all if you must cut yourself one day it is better to do so with a clean blade, rather than one smeared with stale fish guts! The blade should have one ordinary cutting edge, often· needed for fine lines, and one saw edge of more use on larger lines and ropes. A sharp point is usual at the end, although some divers prefer a screwdriver blade. The blade must be thick enough not to bend at all with the heaviest use to which·it may be put.

The handle may be made of metal or hard rubber, with a cross hilt to protect the hand. Floating knives have a use in boats, but they are not recommended for divers, imagine yourself trapped on the bottom by line, and you let the knife go . . . This of course brings us to the subject of lanyards. Lanyards are recommended for the better security of the knife, if there is a suitable ring for attachment of the line. Diving knives should be made with divers in mind, but this does not prevent the production of lightweight knives well suited for stabbing fish, but of little use in a real emergency. If you should ever adapt a knife for diving, remember the corrosive effect of salt on the blade and the tang, and the softening effect of water on the handle; remember further that you may be unable to curve your gloved hand round a tiny handle.

At all times when not actually in use the knife must be sheathed. The habit of carrying your knife at the ready throughout the dive is strongly to be deprecated, both for your own safety, and for that of your buddy, remember your skin becomes softened during immersion. The sheath must be of suitable material and design so that it is not cut when removing or replacing the knife. Removal should be easy and quick, but at the same time the knife should be secure against accidental loss. Some form of rubber or neoprene ring attached to the sheath will secure the knife when slipped over the handle. A suitable ring can be manufactured from scraps of 5 mm expanded neoprene. The sheath itself must not be attached to any equipment liable to be jettisoned in

A suitable heavyweight knife and sheath. Note the rubber ring to secure the knife in its sheath.

an emergency. This usually means strapping it to one leg just above the ankle, or putting it on a special belt. This belt is worn under the weightbelt and *all* other harnesses, and does *not* have a quick release buckle.

The Magnetic Compass

Underwater the sense of direction is easily lost, especially when it is time to return to shore or boat. Whilst it may be possible to surface and return visually, there are a number of occasions when this may be dangerous, such as when decompression is required, or when the surface is being churned up by myriads of water-skiers. In sight of the bottom the experienced diver will navigate by noting the ripples in the sand, or the way the weed is moved by the tide, or merely by noting familiar ' landmarks ' etc, but eventually only the possession of a suitable compass will bring him to safety.

Let us be quite clear just what a compass is, and what it can do. The Earth acts as a giant magnet, attracting to its poles other freely swinging magnets. Unfortunately the North Magnetic Pole is not at the True navigational pole, and this means that a compass needle does not point to True North. The amount by which the compass varies is called Magnetic Variation. It is known for each place on the Earth's surface, and therefore correction can be applied if necessary. If therefore it is necessary to swim or steer a particular True bearing, correction can be applied (about 10°). Unfortunately the presence of any stray iron and steel in the boat or on the diver, or undiscovered underground, causes deviation by an unknown amount. By a process of ' swinging the compass ' it is possible to find out just how much magnetic deviation there is at each point of the compass, but a correction card has to be carried round all the time. Both variation and deviation are vital factors in boat navigation, but it is customary for divers to ignore both, and simply use the compass on one bearing to keep to a straight line. With the diver fully equipped and away from the boat and its motor, he takes the bearing himself, and it is then a perfectly accurate method of keeping to a straight line. (NB because of deviation the opposite bearing may not be exactly 180° different!) Conclusion : a magnetic compass permits a diver to swim a straight line. Only with specialist knowledge can it be used to obtain an actual bearing, or for real navigation.

In use a wrist compass must not collapse under pressure, and it must not swing too freely. If the compass is oil-filled it is both pressure-proof, and excessive swinging of the needle is damped down. Because of the difficulty of keeping level under water the needle should still swing freely when the compass has quite a tilt on it. The possession of a moveable ' lubber-line ' removes the need for the diver to memorise his bearing. It also makes it easier to follow any bearing.

Depth Gauges

On the face of it a depth gauge is only used to satisfy our curiosity, provide something to boast about, or ensure we have achieved the depth specified for a particular test. There is a much more serious aspect of depth. Absolute depth must be known together with time to enable us to avoid decompression by ascending before the 'no-stop time' is up, or to ensure correct decompression at the end of extended dives. Our lives and health depend on this.

Two principal kinds of depth gauge may be met, the so-called capillary gauge or bathymeter, and the Bourdon tube gauge. The former is cheap, easily made and the most accurate at shallow depths. It depends on Boyle's Law which, simply put, says that to double the pressure of a gas halves its volume. If a gas, usually air, is in a rigid tube open to pressure and water at one end, and closed at the other, the water will enter the tube as depth and pressure increase. Thus a 16 cm long tube will show a water surface movement of 8 cm at 10 metres, but only another 4 cm at 30 metres. Temperature also affects the volume of gases, so the bathymeter will be inaccurate, showing extra depth, if a warm gauge is immersed in cold water.

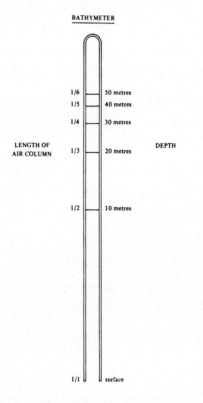

BATHYMETER

LENGTH OF AIR COLUMN		DEPTH
1/6		50 metres
1/5		40 metres
1/4		30 metres
1/3		20 metres
1/2		10 metres
1/1		surface

If making a bathymeter, out of glass-tubing for example, the diameter of the bore matters little over 2 mm, but 3 mm is usual. The position of the markings along the length is critical. Whatever the length, the column of air will contract to :

one half its original length at 10 metres (2 bars absolute)
one third its original length at 20 metres (3 b)
one quarter its original length at 30 metres (4 b)
one fifth its original length at 40 metres (5 b)
one sixth its original length at 50 metres (6 b) etc, etc.

It does not matter whether the tube is straight, 'U-shaped' or circular. Mechanical gauges use a Bourdon tube. This is a curved metal tube which attempts to straighten itself when pressure is applied to its cavity. Linkage is attached to its closed end moving a needle over the dial to indicate pressure and therefore, in this context, depth. The dial is only calibrated in depths. In some of these gauges the Bourdon tube is open to the water via a simple mesh filter. In time this filter or possibly the tube itself may clog with salt or silt. Washing or even prolonged soaking in freshwater after use is absolutely vital. In some the filter can be removed and cleaned, while in others when the filter/tube clogs the whole thing must be returned for servicing. At least one make of gauge is sealed and oil-filled. The sea pressure acts on the case, which acts on the oil, which acts on the Bourdon tube. Salt and silt pose no problems.

In any depth gauge large clear luminous markings help in the dark, and a recording needle may appeal to many. NB if a magnet is carried to

A depth gauge of the sealed kind where water does not enter the 'works' at all.

re-set this needle, beware of its effect on your compass. Finally note . . . few depth gauges are accurate to within 5% and in any case 9 metres of seawater is equivalent to a depth of 10 metres freshwater because of their different densities.

Watches

Besides being necessary for decompression, a watch is necessary for dive planning so that you are not caught out cold and out of air far from home.

There are two main requirements for diving watches—they must be waterproof, and there must be some way of recording elapsed time, usually a moveable bezel. Sad to say accuracy is a poor third as even the cheapest watch will not lose as much as a minute an hour which is the minimum necessary accuracy. If a watch has been properly designed and correctly assembled it will not leak. Why then do so many leak? They usually do so because of damage to the crown (winder) or crystal (glass). Leaks are rarely gross, being noticeable as condensation on the inside of the crystal after a dive. The necessary precautions are obvious —do not apply undue pressure or force to either the crown or crystal at any time. The design of some watches allows for the crown to be securely home when not actually in use. Automatic winding mechanisms are an advantage, they reduce the usage of the crown and possible wear on the seal. A diving watch should be covered by a guarantee which specifies the test pressure or its depth equivalent, and this should be at least 90 metres.

The bezel on some cheap watches rotates without check and can therefore be accidentally re-set underwater . . . choose a watch which has a positive method of preventing accidental rotation other than simple stiffness. All figures must be simple and clear. At least twelve o'clock, and the bezel zero must be large and unequivocal. A good luminous paint is now used on most diving watches, so a black dial gives the greatest contrast underwater. Fancy watches with a multiplicity of markings on the dial and/or the bezel should be avoided, they could cause confusion in the dark, or under conditions of nitrogen narcosis. A diving watch can be the most expensive single piece of diving equipment; it need not be. Very many of the cheaper watches may prove adequate. The results of the Club's ' Watch Which ' published in 1968 gave the conclusion that ' even if you buy an internationally famous watch costing over £50 you still stand a fair chance of finding it full of water when you start your decompression schedule after a deep dive when your life depends upon an accurate knowledge of the time.'

A leather watch strap will not last many dives. A plastic one like those designed for tropical use is much better. Stainless steel sprung bands are very good, although on some the catch is a weak point, and on others the springs in the links are the weak point. On the whole stainless steel spring straps are to be preferred, they are more comfortable to wear.

Contents Gauges

Unless you calibrate your own gauge for your own cylinder, this is a misnomer. The gauge only indicates the pressure of the contents, and only by deduction the actual contents. For example any cylinder at half its working pressure is only half full, at one quarter pressure it is one quarter full, etc.

Contents gauges work on the Bourdon tube principle already explained. The gauge is usually attached to the demand valve by a flexible high pressure hose. (This is British practice, continental divers relying more on reserves.) Should the gauge or tube fracture a rapid and possibly dangerous loss of air would result. It is therefore ESSENTIAL that a narrow bore restrictor valve be fitted at the demand-valve end. This is usually built into the demand valve itself, but if it can be removed make sure it is always replaced. This restrictor will have no effect on the pressure recorded, but would considerably reduce the volume of air escaping after damage, enabling the diver to surface before all his air vanishes.

When ' cracking ' the cylinder the sudden surge of pressure could fracture the Bourdon tube or its connections, allowing high pressure to enter the gauge body. This might cause the gauge glass to explode with consequent danger to the diver and his companions. You do not therefore look directly at the gauge, or point it at anyone else, until after you have cracked the cylinder and the pressure in the gauge has risen to its maximum. To avoid such an accident the better gauges have a pressure relief valve or plug set into the back of the case—don't look at this

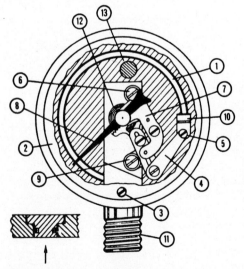

1. Bourdon Tube
2. Dial
3. Dial Fixing Screw
4. Link
5. Link Screw
6. Locking Pillar
7. Movement
8. Pointer
9. Reset Pillar
10. Shoe
11. Stem
12. Hair Spring
13. Relief Valve
   (also shown
   cross-section)

Sectional Drawing of a Pressure Gauge Movement

either while cracking the cylinder. Some gauges are filled with glycerol to damp needle movement. Never remove or replace this with anything else, especially oil. Pressure gauges are not items of equipment the ordinary diver should service or repair himself at any time, nor should pressure gauges meant for use out of water be adapted for use underwater, even if they are the right size and fitting, and cover the correct range.

MINOR ACCESSORIES

Fluorescent Hoods

The increasing use of inflatables and other boats with the safety party at sea-level has brought home to many the difficulty of seeing black-helmeted divers on the surface. This difficulty might not arise if divers were to dive with surface marker buoys, but the fact remains that they do. One answer to this is to make the helmet more visible by painting the actual hood with flexible fluorescent paint. Another answer is to use overhoods made of a fluorescent material. These hoods may be purchased ready-made, or made at home. One pattern is illustrated. It is elasticated loosely round the neck to fit, instead of using 'pop-fasteners' or 'velcro' as the commercial hoods do.

Diver's Marker Buoys, Surface Floats (Blob-Buoys)

These floats are used to indicate to the surface party the position of each pair of divers beneath the surface, especially in conditions where bubbles cannot be seen breaking the surface, or when several parties are underwater. It is worth noting that the use of surface floats is not cissy, the Royal Navy practice it . . . 'It is most desirable, particularly with deep swimmers, that the equipment (surface floats) should be used whenever operational requirements permit'. (BR155, Admiralty Diving Manual.)

The following broad specification has been drawn up :

1 A surface marker must be clearly visible on the surface, therefore must present a sufficiently large surface area in high visibility colouring or pattern. Alternatively the buoy can support a mast and flag which will aid long distance visibility.

2 A suitable length of line must attach the buoy to a reel carried by the diver. A light floating line will reduce the risk of snagging. (The Royal Navy recommend a small 'apple float' on the line, two metres from the swimmer.) Recommended length of line is one and one third times the maximum depth likely to be encountered.

3 There must be a reel for the line, carried by the diver, who can pay out just sufficient line to keep the marker buoy on the surface but with the line fairly taught.

Some divers claim that carrying around the reel during the dive is inconvenient, but this is easily outweighed by the advantage of having the boat-cover in constant attendance. (Obviously coping with a surface line when diving on wrecks would present a problem, but this is not

*Fluorescent hood (photograph).
This is a home-made hood made
from the pattern below.*

*Fluorescent hood (diagram). Two pieces like this are cut out and sewn
together round the edges. An inch wide strip is sewn round the inside, as
shown by the dotted lines, so that elastic can be threaded through.*

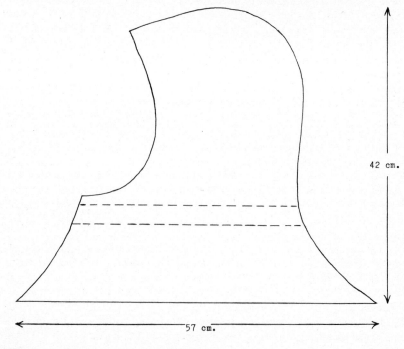

214

really the type of diving for which marker buoys are intended to be used.) It is important that companion divers stay close to the diver carrying the reel at all times, and particularly when surfacing. When surfacing the line must be reeled in during the ascent so the buoy is always directly over the divers.

Where a boat is following closely, flying the Diving Flag, a marker buoy of the orange plastic mooring buoy type is adequate. If diving among other mooring buoys or farther away from the boat or safety party on the shore a more elaborate float is required, as illustrated, incorporating a diving flag. These floats are not intended to support a diver in an emergency. They do not replace lifejackets.

When collecting shellfish or other specimens a collecting bag may usefully be hung under the marker buoy, if the buoy has sufficient buoyancy to spare.

Lifebuoy lights for use in rescuing men overboard, or small boats adrift, have been on the open market for a few years. These have an appeal for use by divers as a surface marker buoy for night diving. It is important to note that as manufactured they are designed to draw attention . . . they invite investigation which is generally what a diver does not want. If one of these, eg, the Seaflash or Sunbeam is used, either change the clear plastic cone or the bulb for an amber one. Remember white, green and red lights have other significance at sea. It is further essential that the inshore fishermen and local Coastguard should be informed just what this unusual light is, and a surface cover boat must keep close attendance. See the surface cover itself carries the appropriate lights, both navigational and those indicating underwater work.

Miniflares

Primarily intended for use on small boats, they have proved suitable for carrying on the person, even at depth, although they may only be discharged at the surface. One kind consists of a pen-type projector and eight screw-on red cartridges, all fitted into a moulded plastic holder. When fired a single star shell is ejected to a high altitude similar in a way to a miniature Verey pistol. It is important to note that the projector and flares require the possession of a Firearm Certificate, obtainable free for this purpose from your local police station. This is not transferable, neither are the projector nor flares. They are very much personal accessories and are highly recommended.

Buddy Lines

A buddy line is 3 to 4 metres (5 metres in the RN) of line joining a pair of divers. It provides a means of communication between buddies. It is recommended that the line be attached to each diver by means of snap-hooks on the line, and metal rings securely stitched to armbands worn on the upper arm. (See 'Ropes and Roping'.)

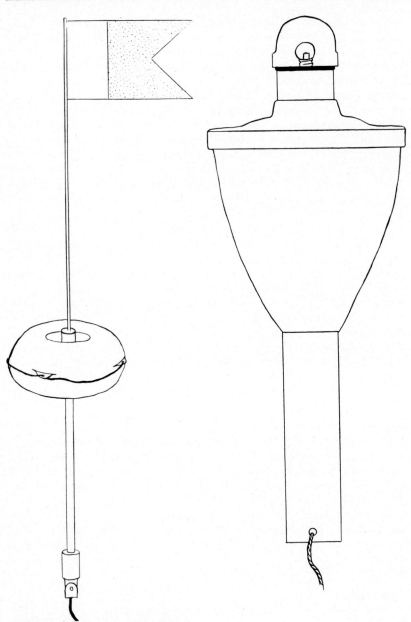

Diver's marker buoy. The float is orange plastic. Note the lifeline round the float, and the weight at the bottom of the mast. (After a design by Don Hilliard.)

Sunbeam lifebuoy light. The whole buoy is about 35 cm long.

Torches

Essential for night diving, a torch is a comfort on dull days, when deep, or in dark water. A proper diving torch is essential for regular night diving, or underwater work. The rubber covered kind of torch may successfully be waterproofed by the use of hose-clips around the glass etc. Some torches affect buoyancy; take appropriate action when diving with such a torch.

Slate and Pencil

This is a means of recording or passing information underwater. An odd piece of Perspex roughened with sandpaper will take ordinary pencil underwater. Even better is an opaque white plastic such as Formica. This does not need roughening with sandpaper. Useful sizes, depending on the amount of writing expected, are 15 cm by 20 cm, or 20 cm by 30 cm.

Fish Ring

A fish ring is a convenient way of carrying speared or knifed fish, other than on the spear or knife itself. The ring is usually a loop of stainless steel wire which can be threaded through the mouth and out of the gills of fish, and then hooked to itself to make a closed ring. An alternative version is a 15 cm brass rod welded to braided nylon line. This is also threaded through the mouth and gills then through a loop in the tail of the nylon line, thus 'lassooing' the first fish caught. Subsequent fish are merely threaded onto the line.

Specimen Containers

Generally speaking long clear polythene bags make the best containers for small specimens taken underwater. The bags are more easily opened if a little water is introduced into each bag before leaving the surface. When the specimen has been captured and placed in the bag, the neck may be knotted, or doubled over and closed with an elastic band. For larger specimens a nylon mesh shopping bag is ideal.

Lifting Bags

Used to lift heavy objects from the bottom, they are not common items of equipment. They must be strong enough, and attached sufficiently securely to their lines, for their lifting capacity. Remember one litre of water weighs one kilogram—displace this litre with air and get one kilogram buoyancy. This also gives a clue as to the method of testing their strength. Any lifting bag should be capable of being filled completely with water and suspended by its lines in air without breaking in any way. This is exactly the strain it will get when filled with air underwater. Any open-necked bag which is strong enough will do. If it does not have adequate lines attached it can be held in a net bag.

Taken down empty it is attached to the object to be raised, and is then filled with air, usually from the diver's mouthpiece. If the bag is not completely full when lift commences, the air will expand on the way up, lift will increase and the rate of ascent will accelerate. This could be dangerous, so it is safer to have several small bags each full, rather than one enormous bag only partly full. All the bags mentioned above remain open at one end all the time, so they are self-venting. Sealed bags with pressure relief valves, rather like constant volume life-jackets, are often used commercially.

Bug-Bag

The 'bug-bag', as the Americans call it, is a bag for crabs, lobsters, crawfish etc. For the usual few specimens a nylon mesh shopping bag or an onion bag will do. A drawstring will help secure the mouth. An angler's folding keep-net is also good, if more expensive, no draw-string being necessary. A useful addition is a snap-hook on the knife belt, if worn, so that the bug-bag may be hitched on, leaving both hands free for diving.

Crab Hook

This is a short metal rod, hooked at one end, used for getting crabs and lobsters out of their holes. It is not a good accessory as too many crabs and lobsters are left to die in their holes after unsuccessful opera-tions. Remember shellfish may not be taken by spearing or stabbing.

Aqua-Plane

This is a shaped flat piece of wood usually with two handles. When towed slowly behind a boat it enables a diver to control his depth and cover a great deal of ground without swimming. It is an invaluable aid to searching a fairly flat bottom. A considerable length of line is neces-sary for the diver to keep near the bottom.

Ankle-Straps, Fin Retainers or Fixe Palmes

These are 'Y-shaped' rubber straps which are slipped over the fin and ankle to prevent loss of the fins. Ankle straps may be purchased, or made from scraps of expanded neoprene. It is also possible to cut them out of old motorcycle inner tubes.

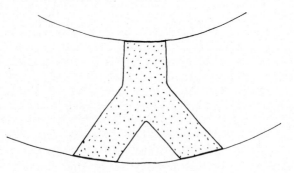

Ankle straps can be cut out of a motorcycle inner tube as shown here.

LIFEJACKETS

There are two main types of lifejacket used by European divers, the SLJ (Surface Lifejacket) and the ABLJ (Adjustable Buoyancy Lifejacket). There is also in common use in the South Pacific area a variety called a buoyancy compensator; but as it can only be inflated orally it has no practical application. We are concerned here only with lifejackets that are inflated by mechanical means primarily.

The SLJ, as its name implies, is mainly concerned with surface buoyancy. It is inflated by means of a (non-breathable) gas cartridge of the type used for filling soda syphons. The cartridge only contains enough gas to fill the jacket fully on the surface of the water, so, at a depth of, say, 10 metres its volume, and buoyancy, will be roughly halved and at 30 metres its volume and buoyancy will be about one quarter of that at the surface. In practice this means that a SLJ with a buoyancy of 5 kilos on the surface will be reduced to a lifting capacity of 1.5 kilos at about 30 metres.

You may think that a buoyancy of 1.5 kilos at this depth is better than nothing—and so it is—but there is another factor to take into account. At this depth a wet suit will also only have one quarter of its surface buoyancy, and with the average diver this means that he will be negatively buoyant with a fully inflated SLJ at 30 metres unless he drops his weight belt. And even if he does that, the rest of his equipment might well anchor him to the bottom regardless.

It follows, then, that the SLJ, while ideal for surface watersports, is far from ideal for the diver. Mind you, it is better than nothing. The SLJ was, for many years, the only lifejacket available for divers and as such has proved a valuable item of equipment. It still is where cash is the prime consideration and in this case the expression ' your money or your life ' often has real meaning.

The ABLJ has evolved because of the divers' need for a lifejacket that can adjust to full buoyancy at any depth down to about 50 metres. This of course entailed particular problems in design and function. To obtain full buoyancy at all depths an ABLJ had to have a cylinder with a larger capacity than the SLJ. This was originally achieved by fitting the ABLJ with a cylinder that could be re-filled from a standard aqualung cylinder; this had the added advantage of providing breathing air for the diver in exceptional emergencies. Nowadays virtually all ABLJ's utilize the principle of a separate cylinder of compressed air for inflation. There is also an ABLJ on the market that inflates the jacket direct from the divers aqualung cylinder by means of a hose connection extended from the pressure gauge hose.

Another problem the ABLJ had to cope with was the fact that air compressed at depth expands as it rises to the surface. So all ABLJ's are fitted with a pressure relief valve that lets the excess air bleed off to prevent the jacket bursting.

Those, briefly, are the reasons for classifying lifejackets into two separate types. The ABLJ, having been designed for divers, would seem to be the obvious choice for all divers but, unfortunately, there are other problems And these are caused by that most variable and unreliable piece of diving equipment—the diver!

Because the ABLJ will jet a diver to the surface in something like 15 seconds from some 20 metres there are the obvious dangers of embolism and/or decompression sickness; and in the context of novices using one the main danger is embolism in one of its forms. To use an ABLJ a diver should be well trained and experienced. In most clubs the procedure is followed of letting new members only use a SLJ until the diving officer considers they are fit enough to use an ABLJ. Some clubs even have courses for using the ABLJ. Limiting beginners to a SLJ has the obvious merit that novices are not allowed to go deep anyway, and so have less need of an ABLJ, which in any case is of more use to the experienced diver who is inclined to go deeper.

So now we know that the ABLJ has the merit of surfacing a diver from depths as deep as 50 metres, and that some of the problems lie in this rapid ascent. Are there any other aspects for the diver to know? Well, there are several, but the main one is—once you're on the way up, can you stop? Or at least slow down?

As I said, all ABLJ's are fitted with a relief valve for releasing excess air. Some valves are integral with the breathing hoses which are provided for utilizing the jackets' supply of air in an emergency, or for oral inflation, while some valves are a separate unit. There is usually provided a method of bleeding off additional air so that an ascending diver (having closed the inflation cylinder) can slow down or, by venting off completely, stop. This is very important because you never know what you might be surfacing under, particularly in low visibility. This additional bleed off is achieved by different means in various jackets and the amount of bleed off varies widely. With some jackets it is not possible to do more than slow down the ascent, while others enable you to come to a complete halt within several feet. The ability to stop your ascent within a few feet is an important safety factor.

Then there is the question of the capacity of the cylinder. These also vary. The more a cylinder contains the greater will be the depth from which it can quickly haul you up. All the ABLJ's currently available in

An ABLJ hits the surface.   Photo: Leo Zanelli

Britain will bring a diver up from a depth around 50 metres, so this is no problem—but we still have the problem of the diver! Lifejackets, as their name implies, are for emergencies, and should only be used as such. But some divers fall into the habit of continually adjusting their buoyancy by short bursts from the cylinder so that buoyancy is neutral at depth. Admittedly, in skilful hands this makes a more comfortable dive, but at the expense of the safety margin. There is no way of checking the contents of the ABLJ cylinder and you might well be nearing the end of a dive, run into trouble, and have insufficient air available for full inflation. As most cylinders are designed for maximum buoyancy at a maximum of 50 metres, if you use up half your air you reduce its effectiveness to 30 metres. Halve it again and your safe depth is only 15 metres. And it only takes a few turns of the tap to reach this stage. Remember, lifejackets are for emergencies; don't waste valuable lifting power for the sake of convenience. This does not necessarily apply to ABLJ's that are inflated direct from the aqualung cylinder.

There is no valid excuse for not wearing a suitable lifejacket for diving. Some people complain about the expense, but there are too many divers around with gleaming twin sets and tatty lifejackets—or none at all. Far better to stick to one cylinder and a good lifejacket if finance is the criterion. And in the case of the extremists who complain at the expense anyway, I can only say: If you can't afford the game, take up tennis or something. We are dealing here with human life and every diver has the right to expect that his buddy, who would have to come to his aid in an emergency, should be suitably equipped. So make the purchase of a suitable lifejacket a first priority. If you can't afford the money for an ABLJ, buy a SLJ and convert it. Diving shops supply excellent conversion kits. This also applies to beginners. Don't be afraid to purchase a SLJ because you think you won't need it when you are more experienced. Buy a SLJ and convert it when the time is ripe to use an ABLJ.

All ABLJ's currently on the market will bring a diver up from a depth of over 50 metres, but they don't inflate fully at that depth. In fact the depth of maximum inflation varies with the contents of the inflation cylinder. For those of you who can't be bothered with mathematical computations there is a very rough-and-ready way of assessing the maximum depth at which your jacket will inflate fully, and that is to see how many times the cylinder will inflate the jacket. The average will be 4—5 times. Each time the jacket is inflated, calculate it as 10 metres of depth. So you can see that the average depth is about 50 metres. As I said, the system is not frightfully accurate, but it does serve as a rough guide.

As mentioned, there are really two types of ABLJ. The most common uses a separate cylinder for inflation and the other uses a direct feed from the aqualung cylinder—usually via the contents gauge hose. For convenience we shall call them a Cylinder ABLJ and a Direct ABLJ (and if you think things are getting a little confusing, you are lucky that we won't be bringing in buoyancy compensators). They both have advantages and disadvantages.

The Cylinder ABLJ has the advantage of being a separate unit that functions independently of the scuba unit and is perfectly adequate for most diving providing you realise the potential disadvantages, which are more human than mechanical. First, get into the habit of filling the cylinder before every dive. No matter if you know it's already full —do it again. None of us are perfect, and I well remember a dive several years ago when I didn't bother to check my ABLJ cylinder; there was no need, you see, I KNEW it was full. At the end of the dive I opened the cylinder to help me lift a fair sized anchor I had found—and it was empty! And talking about lifting anchors, the cylinder ABLJ is an emergency lifting device, NOT a general purpose buoyancy adjuster, although it will perform this function. Once you start using the cylinder for purposes other than emergencies you are running into potential danger, particularly if you are deep, because you just don't know how much air there is left. Then there is the charging clamp. Some jackets have a charging clamp that is an integral part of the cylinder, but some have a separate clamp which can get lost. And if it does get lost or mislaid the diver invariably takes a chance and dives regardless. As for the cylinder itself, it is charged, and emptied, much too fast to avoid condensation. Would you fill your aqualung cylinder in a few seconds? Or discharge it similarly? Of course you wouldn't, but it happens all the time to ABLJ cylinders. Admittedly, the cylinders being smaller the walls are proportionately thicker, but it will pay to attend to this point and get the cylinder interior checked regularly. Of course, if it has parallel threads, 'O' ring sealed, you can do this yourself.

Briefly, the disadvantages of the cylinder ABLJ are :

1 You have no check of the contents if it is used underwater as a buoyancy adjustor; or you might forget to charge it.
2 You can mis-lay the charging clamp (this does not apply to all models).
3 The cylinder needs frequent checks (apart from the condensation problem, if a cylinder is emptied and the jacket has some water in it, this can seep into the cylinder. Some cylinders have one-way valves, but these are not always effective under pressure).
4 There is a definite limit to the depth from which the jacket will bring you up. But this a technical detail which should never need apply to the amateur diver.

Direct feed ABLJ's—and here we are talking about the type which uses the pressure gauge tube—have the advantage of virtually unlimited air. You have a check on the amount available by means of your pressure gauge. With a direct ABLJ you can adjust your buoyancy or use it as a lifting device and still know that you have sufficient air for an emergency. That is, providing your gauge is accurate!

The disadvantages are complex. Most gauge tubes are fitted with a restrictor device. These are fitted so that, in the event of a hose rupturing, the air will not flood out at the break and deprive the diver of air. If the ABLJ is to function at its optimum efficiency, this restrictor must be removed because it also restricts the flow of air into the jacket. Sometimes the restrictor has a large throat, and the jacket inflates quite quickly when the cylinder is fully inflated, but very slowly when the cylinder pressure is low. It is often said, and by people who should know better, that the direct ABLJ cannot function if you run out of air in the normal way. This is not strictly true. Just because the diver can't suck any air through the mouthpiece at, say, 30 metres, it doesn't mean that there is no air in the cylinder because, usually, if he ascends a few feet he can get another breath or two as the pressure decreases. And this air will usually provide lift, depending on the demand valve being used. If the demand valve is very efficient it will use virtually the last scrap of air, leaving you with little or no lifting 'power', but if the demand value is one of those cheap models which can't function at 30 metres when you are starting on the red, then there is plenty of air left to lift you to the surface, and more.

So, from a safety angle the paradox is that the better the demand valve, the less safe is the direct ABLJ. I have tried several types of demand valves with a direct ABLJ at depths and I can vouch that, in general, the twin hose two-stage demand valve is so efficient that you can breath your air down to the point where there is little or no lift available for the jacket. On the other hand, the average single hose, or twin hose single-stage, usually leave enough air—even if you are gasping for breath —to give you some lift.

So, the disadvantages of the direct ABLJ are :

1 You have to remove the restrictor valve for optimum efficiency.
2 If you suck your mouthpiece dry at depth, you do not know how much—if any—lifting power there is.
3 Your gauge tube must frequently be checked, because if it ruptures you are left without the means of providing the jacket with air.

At this point some divers will have made the mental note that the safest system must be a direct ABLJ with a cylinder attached. The 'hairy' divers might sneer at this combination of 'belt & braces' but, at least, it stops your trousers from falling down!

It must be mentioned that some demand valves are so constructed that a direct ABLJ cannot be used properly. This is usually the case when the valve has some sort of restrictor built integrally into the mechanism.

The National Diving Committee recommend the ABLJ type of lifejacket for use by all fully trained divers—those entrusted to the organisation of open water training. In these hands it is certainly the safest type available and it is particularly recommended that they should employ this type of jacket.

The following rules for use are recommended :

1 Always charge the lifejacket cylinder before a dive to ensure maximum reliability. (Ensuring that you charge to the correct pressure.)

2 Always wear the lifejacket so the breathing set and/or weight belt can be jettisoned while leaving the lifejacket secure.

3 If commencing dive on snorkel inflate lifejacket by mouth and deflate by venting before diving. If the cylinder is used *before* the dive, the air supply available is obviously reduced.

4 If, on arrival at depth, weighting is neutralised by allowing air into the jacket, remember that this air should be vented before or during ascent, in order to avoid too rapid an ascent.

5 Unless in emergency, always open cylinder tap very slowly. Always shut off after use, *never* leave tap open.

6 *Never* use the lifejacket for a fast ascent, except in an emergency, and then exhale forcibly during the ascent.

7 After a fast ascent from a dive requiring decompression, or which is close to decompression limits, return immediately to a depth equivalent to half the absolute pressure from which the ascent was made, then ascend at the rate laid down in the decompression tables. Remember to add the time between the beginning of the emergency ascent and the return to half absolute pressure to the calculated duration of the dive.

The following training is recommended for owners of such lifejackets. The drills should be carried out in a swimming pool or in a maximum of 3 metres of sheltered water. During all drills the diver should be closely covered by a companion who also wears a breathing set, and is ready to give assistance.

The following instructions are reprinted from the National Diving Committee's report on lifejackets.

1 Enter water wearing normal weight and breathing set. Practice standard surfacing drill plus inflation of lifejacket after surfacing. Practice surface swimming on front and back wearing jacket inflated. Practice mouth inflation and deflation by venting.

2 Practice surface tow with rescuer wearing lifejacket inflated.

3   Enter water wearing 2.5 kilos excess weight, adjust buoyancy by slowly leaking air from jacket cylinder to jacket. Vent air completely on bottom, swim to surface, inflate jacket on surface.

4   To practice breathing from lifejacket, sit on pool bottom wearing breathing set, weight belt with 5 kilos excess weight draped across lap, assistance at hand. Take breath from set—release set mouthpiece— place jacket mouthpiece in position—release small amount of air into the bag from cylinder—breathe out through nose—breathe in air in bag—breathe out through nose—continue cycle. Ideally the air should be breathed in as soon as it reaches the top of the bag in order to cause minimum change in buoyancy. Repeat exercise, decreasing weight until normal weighting is reached.

5   Practice rapid emergency ascents are not recommended but users should be instructed to exhale forcibly throughout such ascent.

MAINTENANCE OF EQUIPMENT

The sea is a healthy medium, but not for equipment. Neoprene, rubber and metal will deteriorate very quickly if neglected. Even swimming pool water can assist deterioration owing to the presence of chlorine.

Sun will also cause rapid deterioration, so equipment should always be placed in the shade, never in direct sunlight.

Frequent checks and thorough washing of equipment in fresh water will help to prolong its useful life and, more important, minimise the risk of failure. Well-kept equipment is also less expensive! Careful maintenance and routine checks will ensure a longer life.

Long storage may perish rubber and neoprene, but this can be minimised by washing thoroughly in fresh water, drying carefully, and dusting with french chalk. For very long periods of storage wrap in newspaper or brown paper—but never in polythene bags.

Each item must be given individual attention for the best results, and the following notes should help to keep your equipment in peak condition and give you confidence in your gear by minimising troubles arising from poor maintenance.

Mask. The head strap should be inspected from time to time to see if it is in good condition where the adjustments are made on either side. If the mask should need to be replaced, keep the strap, if it is in good condition, for use as a spare. The face-plate should be cleared and polished from time to time. Sealing edges of masks after a time will show signs of perishing around the edges, but the lip of single-seal masks can be prolonged by carefully cutting the edge with a sharp pair of scissors.

Fins. Frequently check to see if there are signs of splitting. When splits do occur, throw the fin away and use the good one as a spare. It is dangerous to attempt vulcanising because it is usually unsuccessful—and a diver with only one fin could be in serious trouble.

Snorkel Tubes. A simple item, but it still needs careful attention. Metal tubes that are badly dented or cracked should be replaced before going on a dive. Check to see that mouthpiece is firmly attached, as various makes will work loose and can be easily lost during a dive.

Some makes have a ring at the bend of the tube for a lanyard. The ring will invariably get rubbed through by the cord, or broken because of sudden jerking, and could cause the loss of the snorkel. The ring should thus be watched for signs of wear.

Wet Suits. Very careful attention should be given to this essential item of equipment.

Tapes covering seams have a habit of lifting off the suit. These should be glued back in position as soon as possible. Suits should be inspected after every dive for wear and tear and attended to as soon as possible, because tears have a habit of growing. In the case of large tears it is sometimes best to cut out the torn part and replace with a new strip of neoprene.

Nylon- and towelling-lined suits should be dried inside out after washing. Suits should be thoroughly rinsed in fresh water after a dive and dried gently.

Glueing should be carried out only when the suit is absolutely dry.

Dry Suits. Should be checked for holes and wear before every dive and patched in time to allow the adhesive to set properly.

Weight Belt. Often neglected, this item requires careful attention. To lose a weight belt on a dive means the abrupt termination of the dive; while a badly twisted buckle, or frayed webbing, could be a danger if it snags. Where rivets are fitted they should be inspected regularly as the webbing can rot or fray around this point. Repairs are best carried out with waxed thread. Frayed webbing, of course, can get snagged in various parts of your equipment.

Aqualung. The same attention should be given to the webbing of the harness as in the case of a weight belt.

Cylinders should be given regular checks for rust, and where this appears it must be removed by rubbing very softly with fine sandpaper. NEVER use a file or like instrument for removing rust as this might weaken the cylinder by removing too much metal. When the rust has been removed, cover by touching up with paint.

The cylinder neck should be checked where the pillar valve is fitted, as rust can develop at this point.

The tap should be checked for leaks when turning off and on. If it does leak, the cylinder should have a new tap or valve fitted. If the tap becomes difficult to turn off and on, never grease or oil the tap as certain lubricants can cause a spontaneous explosion when in contact with high pressure gases; or contaminate the air. Never screw the tap down too hard as this could damage the internal seal. The same applies when unscrewing it.

Always take care when handling a cylinder. An exploding cylinder has the same effect as a bomb. Also take care that the pillar valve does not get knocked when the cylinder is stored or handled.

Before fitting the demand valve on to the cylinder, see that the washer or 'O' ring on the pillar valve is in good condition. Replace if worn or marked.

The demand valve must be given the care required of all mechanical devices. It should be serviced yearly.

When washing a demand valve, ALWAYS keep a thumb or finger placed over the high pressure inlet. The plastic covers often supplied will allow water to seep through.

Tubes and hoses must be inspected regularly, before and after every dive. Check all metal clips and fittings to see if they are cutting into the rubber, and check rubber for splitting and general deterioration. If possible, remove twin tubes for washing and hang up to dry. Single hose tubes should be replaced every two years or when showing signs of wear.

Pressure gauges should be frequently checked against a fellow diver's by attaching in turn to the same cylinder. If the glass appears misty it should be replaced or returned for servicing immediately.

Knife. Even though the majority are made of stainless steel, the knife should be looked after and rinsed after every dive.

Smear the blade with grease while storing, but wipe it clean before returning it to the sheath before a dive.

Plastic straps in particular should be regularly inspected if the sheath is attached by this method.

Compasses and Depth Gauges. Again, straps should be checked for wear and splitting.

Depth gauges and compasses should be regularly checked for accuracy.

Lifejackets. Surface lifejackets (SLJ's) equipped with CO_2 cartridges should be frequently checked and the cartridge taken out, washed, and examined.

Occasionally blow up the jacket and immerse in a bath of water to check for leaks. Never throw the jacket about, because a jarring could cause the CO_2 cylinder to be released.

Adjustable buoyancy lifejackets (ABLJ's) should receive similar attention. Frequently check hose clips and other fittings. The tube that connects the air supply to the jacket itself should be checked for a secure fit—otherwise the tube could blow out when the jacket is inflated. The cylinder, if this is the source of air, should be checked regularly for rust, especially on the inside, because the rapid filling and emptying causes more condensation than usual.

CHAPTER SIX

TECHNIQUES

Snorkel Diving : Kendall McDonald

Aqualung Use and Buoyancy Control : R B Campbell

Surfacing Drill : 1 Ascent Procedure, Leo Zanelli;
2 Emergency Ascents, R Vallintine

Signals : Roger M Bruce

Ropes and Roping Methods : Lt Cdr Alan Bax RN

Underwater Navigation : Brian Booth

Decompression in Practice : P Garner

Low Visibility : National Diving Committee

Deep Diving : Charles Ellis

Air Endurance : George F Brookes

Diving Under Ice : Leo Zanelli

Night Diving : D Robertson, 1st Class Diver

Cave Diving : Dr K Pearce

Spearfishing : Philip T Smith

SNORKEL DIVING

You can swim. If you can't you have no business reading this chapter for we are not going to teach you to do that. What it is intended to do here is to provide you with the basic knowledge without which you cannot go any further in your diving training.

The standard of swimming that you must have reached will enable you to pass easily the BSAC Swimming Test, which is as follows.

1 200 yards freestyle.

2 100 yards backstroke.

3 50 yards wearing a 10 lb weightbelt (the weight may be reduced for junior members, women, or those with a low buoyancy index).

4 Float on back for five minutes with hand and leg movement allowed.

5 Tread water with the hands above the head for one minute.

6 Recover six objects from the deep end of the training pool using only one dive per object.

Having done those tests at one time and in the order specified, you will at least be able to swim well enough to carry on. And though you may consider some of the following information too simple for you, it would be as well to read it carefully—a conceited diver can easily become a dead one.

The basic equipment for snorkel diving—mask, fins and snorkel tube—is dealt with technically in the equipment section of this manual, and you should read that before buying. Assuming that you have, we are now going to learn the right way to use it both on the surface and underwater. The preliminary lessons should take place in a swimming pool.

First, put on the mask the right way up and make sure that no long hair is caught in the seal around your face; water will pour in through the tiniest channel. Test for water-tightness by inhaling through your nose— if no air gets in, neither will water. Now put the breathing tube, or snorkel, into your mouth, having first slipped the open end under the rubber strap of the mask. Stand in the water and put your face under the surface. If you go too deep, water will rush into your mouth through the top end of the snorkel. Experiment and you will find a happy medium. Don't look straight down. Try looking forward and downward. In this position the snorkel end will remain above the surface.

Now move into deeper water until you are about chest-deep and start swimming. Don't try anything too complicated; your normal stroke will do (the side-stroke makes things a bit difficult, but it can be done).

All this exertion will have made your face-mask mist over. There are three ways of stopping this. The simplest way is to spit into the mask before you put it on, rub the saliva around over the glass, and then wash

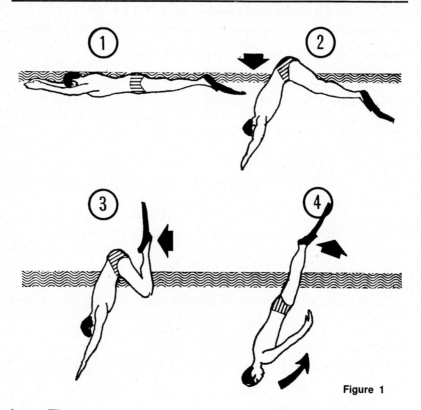

Figure 1

it out. The second method is to rub a slice of potato over the glass in the same way. The third method is to use a piece of wet seaweed.

You may also have noticed that your jaw is aching from holding the snorkel mouthpiece. Try to relax. As long as your lips are well round the mouthpiece it shouldn't leak; you don't have to clench it in your teeth. Neither should the snorkel wobble about, held as it should be by the mask-strap. Carry on swimming and soon you will find that you're not so conscious of the problems of the mask and tube. In fact, after a time you will almost forget you have them on.

You will notice that so far we haven't mentioned that fine new pair of fins you brought along with you. There is a reason for that. Fins, or flippers, are an aid to swimming underwater; they are not essential at this stage.

Well, after some practice, you will be able to use the mask and snorkel on the surface. Next we must talk about diving, and diving properly, with this equipment and fins on. There is only one completely satisfactory way to do this and that is to imitate the duck's dive, a quick flipover, when he feeds from the surface. The duck's dive, however, is limited to putting his head, neck and shoulders beneath the surface. We want to get the whole of our bodies submerged and to dive down without causing any splash or disturbance. It's not difficult. It only needs practice. But we must get it right or we'll spend the rest of our diving days frightening everything underwater before we get down to see it.

Yes, water is going to pour down the snorkel. It will be distracting at this stage, so take the tube out of your mouth for a while and swim along the surface wearing only your mask. Gently, no hurry. Now stop swimming with your hands and at the same time try to touch your knees with your head. A good pulling stroke then with your hands should have you completely underwater. If you haven't got under, it may be because you have taken too deep a breath before ducking. Filling your lungs completely may make you too buoyant. How much air should you take in? Well, when you're beginning, about the same amount as you would if someone let off a firework right behind you. Silly suggestion? It isn't really, for when you are frightened you don't take in a great lung-filling breath but a small one. And that's enough if you want to sink underwater smoothly and silently. If this doesn't work at first, try again and again. Now try lifting your legs into the air so that they are in a straight line with your body at the same time as you put your head under. You should just slide quietly down. Though this kind of dive becomes second nature to you after a time, everyone went through the splashing stage, so don't worry and just keep trying.

Though it will probably not happen in the ordinary swimming pool there are deep pools where your ears may start to hurt as you dive down. At this stage all we are going to do is to issue you with a strict warning about this : *do not go any deeper if your ears begin to hurt and return to the surface at the first sign of pain.* We will deal with the reasons for this ear pain a little further in this chapter and the way to avoid it. For the moment we are concentrating in shallow water on getting you completely used to diving from the surface.

Assuming that you can manage to make a fairly smooth entry you must start to do away with the pulling stroke with your hands that first got you underwater. You should find this fairly simple to stop. Bending from the waist and lifting your feet into the air at the same time should send you sliding downwards smoothly and without splash. Your hands can now merely point the way downward without being used to pull you under. When you have mastered this, add fins to your equipment, still leaving off your snorkel. The stroke to use with your fins is the up-and-down crawl kick, but let your knees bend a little and also point your toes. Try not to break water with the fins as you go along. Now try a duck dive and you should quickly slide underwater. That's the weight of the fins, added to that of your legs and your feet, pushing you under. Once there you will notice what control those fins give you underwater.

Keep the same stroke as you did on the surface, increasing the sweep of the kick a bit, and you will be fairly skimming over the tiles on the pool bottom. Try finning on the surface again without splashing, then repeat the exercise with your snorkel on. You'll find that breathing through this is a great relief compared with having to move your head around to take sideways gulps of air without it. Don't forget to put the tube under the face mask-strap.

Next, off you go and duck dive—and be prepared for the breathing tube to fill up with water. To avoid getting this into your throat and choking, take a breath through your snorkel just before you submerge and then close your throat. When you come up, having saved a little bit of air, blow the water out of the tube with a sharp puff and then carry on swimming along the surface. Don't be put off if you fail to get all the water out of the snorkel the first time. If you don't clear it, just spit the whole mouthpiece out and take a gulp of air through your mouth in the ordinary way. Some divers do this all through their diving lives, but this is silly and it makes repeated dives very difficult.

What do we mean by 'closing your throat'? This sounds difficult and, medically speaking, is probably impossible, but practically speaking it is something like the action you take when gargling: let the water run down the tube, let it fill your mouth, but don't let it go further. It will become second nature to you after a while, although some divers try stopping the water coming into their mouths by sticking their tongues into the mouthpiece. This isn't very satisfactory, so persevere. Finally, as you become more expert underwater, try to make your fin strokes much more sweeping: you should feel that your legs are moving in long sweeping strokes from the hips.

This initial training will take place in a swimming pool and usually you will afterwards go off for a drink with other members of your club, more often than not to a tavern that your committee has 'adopted'. It is here that you will probably be taught some of the things you must know before you go any further with your diving. Some thing will already be puzzling you. Do you remember, for instance, the point about not diving any deeper if your ears hurt? Well, this is what it is all about: The depth at which you get a pain in your ears can vary, depending on the person concerned, from about 3 metres onwards. Although the pain at any depth is slight at first, it is meant as a warning—a warning that the water pressure on the outside of your eardrum is becoming too great. If you push on and ignore the pain, which will get more intense, your eardrum will break. This sounds serious, and it can be, but the side-effects of the break are nastier. Cold water could spurt through the break and affect your sense of balance. Underwater everything would then begin to spin, and you may also feel sick. You will certainly feel giddy and you will not be much better off if you struggle up to the surface until the cold water in your ear has warmed up and reached normal temperature.

A broken or punctured eardrum must be treated by a doctor as soon as possible. He will certainly stop you diving for some time. There may be no after effects, but the trouble is that infection often sets in and treatment may be a long business. This all seems rather terrible, but don't let it put you off diving. If there were no simple way to avoid broken eardrums, all divers would either be confined to very shallow water or they would all have injured ears. This is obviously not true, so let's see how to overcome or remove the trouble.

The pain, as we said earlier, was caused by the pressure of the water on the eardrum becoming too great. Obviously the best thing to do would be to apply the equivalent pressure of air on the other side of the drum, the inside, pressing back at the water. And that is what we do.

There is a simple experiment you can carry out at this moment provided you haven't got a bad cold. Pinch your nose between thumb and forefinger, then try to blow out through your nose. You will hear your ears click, pop, or give a little squeak. This is what divers call ' clearing your ears '. If you find hearing a little difficult afterwards, try swallowing and you'll be back to normal. This is exactly the same sort of thing most people do in a fast lift; they swallow to clear their ears without even thinking about it. In some aircraft you'll find the same problem, and if you learn to clear your ears properly underwater at least you'll never have trouble in an aircraft again.

The procedure underwater is simply that directly you feel that pain you ' clear your ears '. When you get very experienced, you don't even wait for the pain, but you just keep on clearing automatically on the way down. How? Either by building up pressure inside your nose so that air creeps up the Eustachian tubes to the inside of the eardrum, or by swallowing. Even with a mask covering your nose completely, there are two simple ways to do this. The first is to hold the mask firmly on to your face with one hand and blow out hard through your nose. Pressure inside your mask will now do the trick. The second is to push the soft rubber of the rim of your mask under your nose upwards to block off your nose before you sniff out. Some masks, you will find, have inlets in the rubber around your nose so that you can actually grip your nose through the rubber before blowing down it. Swallowing can also work, and some people find that rubbing the skin behind your ear at the same time as swallowing will help.

A few words of caution. Firstly, *treat your ears gently*. Don't blow too hard down your nose for it is possible to damage your eardrum or sinuses by putting on too much pressure. If your ears won't clear, don't try to force them, and if difficulty persists go and see your doctor. It may only be that an excess of wax needs syringing out. Secondly, *don't dive if you have a cold.* If you try to force your ears to clear when you have a cold, you may be pushing mucus into places it shouldn't go. A good test of whether your ears are fit for diving on any particular day is to try them gently before you enter the water. If they won't clear in air, they certainly won't underwater. Thirdly, *don't use ear-plugs under any circumstances.* They are on the market for surface swimmers who need ear protection for some reason or another; they are not for divers. They can be forced into your ear by water pressure when you dive and cause the eardrum to explode outward.

One last thing before you move on to more advanced diving, assuming that you have thoroughly learnt how to use mask, fins and snorkel in safety : as you snorkel dive, you will find that the deeper you go the more buoyancy you lose. This can be a positive advantage, but you must be prepared for it, for although you may have had to struggle madly in the past to get down the first few metres you will now find that you sink even quicker as you pass the 6 metre mark. This is because the air in your lungs which has acted as a float in the past is now being compressed and does not have the same lift. So you are going to find it a little more difficult to swim up from deeper waters.

While dealing with snorkelling in deeper waters, you should note the following points :

Your mask will start to press hard on your face as you go deeper. This discomfort is easily cured by a snort of air through your nose into your mask equalising the pressure.

Always hold your mask on to your face when entering the water—even if you are just slipping in from the side of the swimming bath. It is surprising how easy it is to flood or lose the mask altogether when entering the water quickly.

If your mask does fill with water, there is no need to take your mask right off when you surface. Opening the lower lip of the mask will drain away the water quickly.

When surfacing after a dive—any kind of dive—look up and make sure the surface is clear. In murky water hold one hand above the head so that it is your hand and not your head that hits the bottom of that boat! Most masks are not wide-angle, so twirl round in the water as you approach the surface. In other words, make sure your surfacing point is clear in all directions. This applies just as much in a crowded swimming pool as anywhere else.

Remember the golden rule of snorkelling is to be relaxed. Speed through the water is relatively unimportant.

How long can anyone stay underwater? Well, it all depends on the person, but when you know that spearfishing champions regularly dive to depths of over 30 metres, helped down with weightbelts, you will realise that it is far longer than any beginner can hope to manage. At any rate, breath-holding contests and attempts to swim underwater longer and farther than anyone else are completely banned by the British Sub Aqua Club. There is only one end to that sort of thing : some winner, somewhere, is never going to surface in time to collect his bets!

What you must also *not* do in your understandable attempts to dive deeper and more cleanly as you progress is to boost the amount of air in your lungs before diving. This is called hyperventilation and it involves taking a number of very deep breaths before submerging in order to flush some of the carbon dioxide out of your system. The danger is that this can easily lead to unconsciousness underwater because you will not feel the same desire to breathe when the air supply in your lungs runs out. The physiological reasons for this, together with the factors involved in ear clearing, are dealt with in detail in the medical section of this manual and you must make a study of this.

Well, you are now on the road to becoming a diver. In fact, you are one already if you have digested this chapter and have become proficient with mask, fins and snorkel. A fair number of warnings have been given here, but for good reason. There is safe diving and suicide diving, and only one of them ought to be taught.

Note to instructors

We have dealt with the various pieces of basic equipment in the order chosen for obvious reasons. It is debatable, however, whether you should tell your pupils all the details about ear-clearing before they actually enter the water. If you are using a pool that is 5 metres or more deep, then obviously you must, but in our opinion such a depth of water should not be used for the real beginners for whom this chapter is intended. Basically, it must be left to you to decide whether or not your pupil is of sufficient intelligence and calm enough at the beginning of diving training to take in the problems of the Eustachian tubes. Generally, we feel, this is more likely to be understood if properly taught later on . . .

AQUALUNG USE AND BUOYANCY CONTROL

In the preceeding chapter we explained the mechanical functioning of the demand valve. Now we must consider the manner in which the aqualung is used, and here we are considering the whole assembly of demand valve, cylinder, harness, weight belt and mask.

Fitting the Demand Valve

The first consideration when assembling an aqualung is the state of charge of the cylinder. If the demand valve is fitted with a contents gauge then this check will be covered in the course of assembly, but if otherwise, then it will be necessary to check the cylinder with an independent gauge first.

Before fitting the demand valve to the cylinder ensure that the sealing washer, or O-ring, is in good condition and confirm that the pillar valve is clear by blowing off a short puff of air. Check that the filter in the demand valve is serviceable, then slip the demand valve clamp over the pillar valve and position the spigot on the sealing washer. Lightly tighten the clamp screw and re-check that the spigot is correctly seated and not bearing on the metal edges of the pillar valve—this done, completely tighten the clamp screw.

Open the pillar valve slowly to admit air to the demand valve. Do not look directly at the contents gauge during the period that the pressure is rising. When the pressure has stabilised note the state of charge of the cylinder : is it adequate for the intended dive? Check over the valve for air leaks. In the event of leakage from the sealing washer, turn off the pillar valve and discharge the air from the demand valve before reseating the valve.

With the demand valve correctly seated, and with the pillar valve fully open, check for air delivery. Blow hard into the mouthpiece to dispel any dust or water before breathing in. Take several deep breaths to confirm that the valve is functioning correctly.

Close the pillar valve and watch the contents gauge, if it starts to drop then there is an air leak on the high pressure side of the assembly, locate and correct it. Otherwise, continue to breathe from the shut-off set until all air is exhausted. At this point it should not be possible to suck any more air through the demand valve. If some air can be sucked through then there is a leak on the low pressure side. This may be a puncture in the convoluted or main diaphragm, or possibly a faulty exhaust valve. Locate and correct the fault before diving.

Wearing the Harness

The harness should be in good condition with all buckles and stitching intact. Put on the cylinder and harness and adjust the straps to the correct fit. The straps should be snug. When on dry land the weight of the set is taken by the shoulder straps but this is not so in the water when the set is bearing on the diver's back. The set must be held secure in this position. Compression of the suit with depth will cause the straps to slacken, so start with them tight to offset this effect.

The aqualung is put on after the life jacket and great care must be taken to ensure that neither interferes with the other. The inflatable portion of the life jacket must not, under any circumstances, be trapped under any harness or weight belt. With all harness straps tightened, operate the quick release buckle—with one hand only!

The height of the cylinder in the harness should be such that the demand valve is in line with the diver's shoulder blades, just below the base of the neck. Incorrect positioning of the cylinder will cause difficulties in breathing, particularly with twin hose demand valves. Too high and the air flow will be restricted, too low and the air will be blown at the diver. Too high a position will also cause the demand valve to strike the back of the diver's head.

When using twin hose demand valves, identify the two hoses. Grasp one tube, squeeze it and blow out through the mouthpiece. If you can in fact blow out then, obviously, you are grasping the intake hose; if not, then it must be the exhaust hose. Normally, the intake hose is on the right hand side and exhaust on the left. This little test may be easily made, even underwater. Single hose demand valves only have an intake hose and this, too, is usually situated on the right.

The contents gauge and hose should pass under one arm and be threaded through a shoulder strap so that it is conveniently positioned in front of the diver for reading. It should not be allowed to swing free for it may become trapped in a crevice, with dangerous results.

Wearing the Weight Belt

Fit the weight belt, having regard for the correct weights needed (see Buoyancy Control) and adjust it to a snug fit. Make sure the weights are distributed comfortably. Above all check the belt for an effective and obvious quick release buckle. Test it before diving.

Buddy Check

All these adjustments should be made well before the planned dive in time for any necessary corrections to be made. Alterations to harnesses etc are difficult to make in a small, rocking, boat.

At the same time as checking over your own equipment check your buddy's also. Both divers should be well aware of the type of harness and quick release buckles being used by the other. The operation of the quick release buckles must be obvious for they have to be released by someone else in an emergency.

TECHNIQUES

Pool Training

Buoyancy Control : Now, everything ready? Don't forget fins, mask and snorkel! Slip quietly into the water, shallow end, and trim for neutral buoyancy. Adjust the weights progressively until it is possible to lie still, face down, on the bottom of the pool, and by breathing in to start rising and by breathing out to sink back down again. When confident try the exercise in the deep end and finally try it in mid-water, ie without actually touching the bottom of the pool.

Mask Clearing: Mask clearing calls for disciplined breathing. For a start the novice should practice swimming underwater without a mask, whilst breathing from the aqualung. Ultimately he should be able to do this with eyes open and without holding his nose.

Now submerge, wearing a mask, and remove it underwater. To help break the suction of the mask blow into it, through your nose, as you lift it off your face. Replace the mask by placing it firmly on your face *before* slipping the strap over your head. Keep a hand on the topmost edge of the mask and press it gently against your forehead. Do not press too hard or the rubber seal will distort and become ineffective. Tilt your head well back and look up at the surface (if you bang your head on the demand valve it is your own fault, the cylinder's mounted too high!). Exhale steadily through your nose and the water will be blown out of the lower edges of the mask.

Another method is to lie on one side and hold the uppermost side of the mask, blowing the water out the other side. Purge valves are fitted to some masks and these make life all too easy. In an upright position, hold the top of the mask and exhale gently and the water will be flushed out the purge valve. Don't allow yourself to become complacent with this simplicity, practice with masks without purge valves.

Mouthpiece Removal: A diver should have no fear of taking out his mouthpiece underwater. The technique varies slightly between twin-hose and single-hose demand valves and a competent diver should be able to cope with either type.

a   *Twin-hose Valves:* Modern demand valves are fitted with non-return valves on either side of the mouthpiece to prevent the hoses from flooding. However, non-return valves can fail so all divers should be capable of clearing flooded hoses. You have already identified the exhaust hose (so when replacing the mouthpiece roll on to your side so the exhaust hose is lowest and then blow out vigourously while continuing to roll on to your back. This will carry the water down the exhaust tube and out the exhaust valve.

Practice mouthpiece removal in the pool. Take a breath and then remove the mouthpiece. Hold the mouthpiece at head height and air will flow freely from it. Lower the mouthpiece to chest level and the flow will stop. Replace the mouthpiece by holding it head high so that the air is flowing. Tilt it towards your face and lower it into your mouth. Blow out to expel any remaining water, rolling to the left as necessary.

When swimming on the surface with the mouthpiece removed it will be necessary to prevent it gushing air. Simply hold the mouthpiece down below chest level.

If you lose grip on the hoses underwater they will float up above your head, gushing air. To regain them, execute a backward roll and the hoses will then appear above your face where they can be grasped and replaced as before. Do not attempt a sideways roll as this will wrap the hoses around the back of the demand valve.

b *Single-hose Valves:* Only the actual mouthpiece portion of the single-hose demand valve can flood. Water cannot enter the delivery hose.

Submerge in the pool and remove the mouthpiece. Tilt it so that the mouth orifice is uppermost and it will discharge air, invert it and the air flow will stop. This will happen regardless at what height the valve is held. To clear and replace a mouthpiece demand valve hold it at head height, with the orifice tilted downward. Press the purge button and air will start to flow, expelling the water in the valve. Lower the valve into your mouth, blow out to rid the valve of any remaining water, then carry on breathing.

When diving wear the neck stap provided with this type of demand valve to prevent misplacing the valve. Should you lose contact with the valve, say, during a buddy-breathing exercise, remember that it is situated on the right hand side. Roll to the right, slightly head down, then back to the face down position. The demand valve should then swing over your right shoulder and within the grasp of your hand. Clear and replace as before.

Weight Belt Jettison: The weight belt is a safety device and it is intended to be discarded if necessary, but not indiscriminately! Once your weight belt has gone you are on your way to the surface and are no longer capable of diving to any depth.

Practice unfastening the quick release buckle so that you can remove and replace the belt underwater *without* dropping it. Remove the belt and place it on the pool bottom and ascend to the surface, breathing out all the time. (See Emergency Ascents.) Dive to retrieve the belt and fit without surfacing.

Also practice removing the belt on the surface, treading water and handing it up to someone on the pool side. If you drop a belt at sea it will be lost so don't drop it in the pool either! In pool work it is advisable to keep two hands on the belt but confirm that you can jettison the belt by a single handed operation. In an emergency you may need to hold on to something, or someone, with the other hand.

Aqualung Removal

a *On the Surface:* First remove the weight belt. Change over to breathing on the snorkel and release the neck strap. In the case of twin-hose demand valves pass the hoses back over your head.

Grip one shoulder strap firmly, with single-hose valves this should be that shoulder over which the hose lies. With the other hand, operate the quick release buckle and check that all straps fall clear. Now, swing the cylinder around to the front. Close the pillar valve if the demand valve is gushing air. Hand the straps up to someone at the pool side (in reality to someone in a boat). Only relinquish your grip on the set when they have confirmed their hold.

b *Submerged:* A set with a single-hose demand valve may be removed underwater in a similar manner to the above but it is not so convenient for twin-hose valves.

A drill suitable for both types is as follows: The diver sits on the pool bottom and unfastening his weight belt then drapes it across his lap. (For this test it will help to be weighted for negative buoyancy.) He grasps one shoulder strap while releasing the harness buckle with the other hand and ensuring that all straps, and particularly the jock strap, are free. The mouthpiece strap should be undone but do not relinquish the mouthpiece yet! Place both hands on their respective shoulder straps and pull the cylinder up over the diver's head and down in front to lay the set between his legs.

The diver should be breathing shallowly at this stage to reduce his buoyancy. He now leans forward to lay the cylinder flat on the pool bottom, with the demand valve towards him. He removes the weight belt from his lap and drapes it across the cylinder, but still keeps a hold on the belt for the moment. One final breath from the demand valve and then he relinquishes the mouthpiece and tucks it beneath the pillar valve. The last stage is to remove his mask and release his grip on the weight belt—exhaling vigorously while ascending.

Aqualung Retrieval: To retrieve the aqualung, dive from the surface to approach the set from the demand valve end. Grasp both weight belt and cylinder simultaneously and tuck them into your lap in a crouched position. Release the mouthpiece, purge or clear it as necessary, and commence breathing from the set. Slide the weight belt from the cylinder and place it across your lap, assuming a sitting position at the same time. Find and fit the face mask.

Now, being able to see clearly, check the cylinder harness. A negatively buoyant cylinder may be laid down in front of the diver. A buoyant cylinder should be held in front, in an inverted position. Spread out the straps and grasp the cylinder with both hands inside the shoulder strap position. Swing the cylinder up and over your head. As you bring it down your back release the grip on the cylinder and spread your arms upward and outward through the shoulder straps. Flex your shoulders and reach behind you to pull the cylinder down into position. Position the waist straps and hold them with one hand while the other threads the jock strap between your legs. Now fasten the quick release buckle.

Slide the weight belt from your lap to around your waist and fasten it. Re-check all straps and position of cylinder before swimming off.

General Note: All these exercises have been devised to give the diver absolute confidence in his equipment and his own ability. Loss or derangement of equipment can occur underwater but with this training behind him the diver should have no problem in taking corrective action.

Buoyancy Control

Buoyancy control is an essential technique in competent diving. Nothing is quite so frustrating as to be too buoyant and to be continually struggling to remain submerged. Conversely there are very real dangers in being too heavy, particularly when in deep water.

Neutral buoyancy, neither rising nor sinking, would appear to be the ideal state to achieve and certainly this is the basis for Buoyancy Control, but, as we shall show, it is not possible to maintain a state of neutral buoyancy at all stages of a dive. It is to be able to cope with the variations in buoyancy which are encountered that we must master the technique of Buoyancy Control.

The factors which have a varying effect on the buoyancy of a diver are :

1 The diver's breathing and lung capacity.
2 The capacity of the air cylinders.
3 The depth of the dive.
4 The type and condition of suit worn.

Let us consider these factors in turn.

Breathing and Lung Capacity

The effect of breathing on Buoyancy Control is easily demonstrated in the swimming pool and is the first exercise in learning the technique. The novice diver is required to trim his buoyancy to achieve a neutral condition. This he does by progressively altering the amount of weight on his belt until he reaches a condition when by breathing in he will start to rise off the bottom of the pool and by breathing out will sink back down again.

With an average depth of breathing the diver can vary his buoyancy either side of neutral buoyancy. With deep inhalation and exhalation he may achieve a variation of 1.5 kilograms.

This is a factor over which the diver has complete control and will ultimately become automatic in maintaining equilibrium underwater.

Cylinder Capacity

Compressed air has a significant weight. At the end of a dive virtually all this air will have been expended and our diver will be that much lighter, and that much more buoyant.

Let us return to our novice diver in the pool. When he did his first exercise in Buoyancy Control it was at the beginning of the training session with a full cylinder. Now let him repeat the exercise at the end of the session with an empty (well, almost!) cylinder. The weights he first used are now insufficient for him to achieve neutral buoyancy and he will need to add more to compensate for the expended air.

This increase in buoyancy as air is expended is a gradual process so the diver is not usually aware that a change in buoyancy is taking place. In any case, it would not be practical to be continually altering weights during the course of a dive and so a diver must learn to cope with this effect by other means, as we will explain.

Depth and Suits

The 3rd and 4th factors are so interelated that we will deal with them simultaneously. We should be aquainted with Boyle's Law, which explains how gases compress under pressure. Now, our wet suits contain a great quantity of gas in the form of individual bubbles in the neoprene and a dry suit encloses air in the underclothing.

As the diver descends the pressure of the water compresses the air in the suit and so reduces its buoyancy. So a suit, say, of 8 kilos buoyancy on the surface will be reduced to 4 kilos buoyancy at 10 metres and to 2 kilos at 30 metres. This buoyancy will be regained when the diver ascends. A point to remember is that the more material there is in a wet suit the greater the initial buoyancy and the greater the change in buoyancy with depth.

Wet suits also lose buoyancy with age as the foam cells break down. This effect is so gradual that it passes unnoticed until the diver acquires a new suit and then the increase in buoyancy is very marked.

Having considered the factors influencing Buoyancy Control in isolation let us now consider their combined effect as experienced by a diver.

Snorkel Diving

The snorkeller has two variations in buoyancy with which to contend. Both are a function of depth and are related to Boyle's Law. The first effect is the compression of the diver's lungs and the second is the compression of his suit.

Unlike the aqualung diver the snorkeller's lungs are compressed by the pressure of water about him, this causes a loss in buoyancy, such that even an ordinary swimmer, without wet suit, will become negatively buoyant at 3 to 6 metres depth. The snorkeller's wet suit will also lose buoyancy at the same time.

So the deeper the snorkeller dives the greater his loss of buoyancy. Too great a loss of buoyancy will create difficulties in regaining the surface. For safety the snorkeller should trim for neutral buoyancy at his operating depth, thus allowing himself to be positively buoyant on the surface. In this manner he may swim submerged with the least effort assured of an easy ascent to the surface and the capability of resting buoyantly on the surface between dives.

Aqualung Diving

The aqualung diver starts from the surface with a full cylinder, as he descends his suit becomes progressively less buoyant, and when he first settles on the bottom he is at his least buoyant condition with a significant weight of air in the cylinder and much reduced buoyancy from the suit. Unlike the snorkeller his lungs have not compressed but instead he has a cyclic variation in buoyancy caused by his own breathing. By controlling the depth of his breathing the diver can offset some of the initial loss in buoyancy, ie at the beginning of a dive he needs to breath deeper, inflating his lungs fuller, than towards the end of the dive. This is, in any case, a fairly natural reaction. Very deep breaths will help the diver float over obstacles and similarly deep exhalations will cause him to sink rapidly.

Further counteraction to this loss of buoyancy is achieved by the angle at which the diver swims. Swimming at a positive angle, ie head up, will generate lift and combined with the breath control this should be sufficient to maintain a stable position. If it is not then some adjustment of the weights should have been made.

As our diver continues to swim around the sea bed he is becoming progressively more buoyant as air is expended from his cylinder. Once again breath control, lessening the depth of his breathing, and angle of swimming, changing gradually from a positive, head up, angle to a negative, head down, angle should offset this effect.

Finally our diver makes his ascent, buoyancy is regained by his wet suit as the depth of water decreases and he reaches the surface, now in his most buoyant condition, with most of the air expended from his cylinder. Again, for safety, he should now be positively buoyant so he may rest quietly on the surface if necessary.

So if our diver trims for neutral buoyancy, with a full cylinder, on the surface, at the start of the dive, he will then experience a negatively buoyant condition during the initial stages of the dive. This will progressively lessen and towards the end of the dive he may become slightly positively buoyant again. Then in making his ascent he will definitely become buoyant as he reaches the surface. The amount of buoyancy will depend on the capacity of the set and the amount of air expended.

Novice divers should test this effect of loss of buoyancy with depth by practice dives down an anchor line.

Salt Water or Fresh?

This is not likely to be a varying factor, unless you are diving in river estuaries, but it is one that must be taken into account if changing from one location to another. Fresh water affords slightly less buoyancy than salt and so a sea diver must beware and reduce his weights before undertaking a dive in fresh water. The amount a diver will need to alter his weights will depend on his physical size but an average person would need to reduce his weights by around 3 kilos when changing from salt water to fresh water diving. Conversely a lake diver would need to add that amount when diving in the sea.

Deep Diving

With deep diving there comes a stage when the changes in buoyancy of the suit cannot be counteracted by the diver. The foregoing notes are applicable to depths of the order 10 metres. At 20 metres and certainly at 30 metre depths it is necessary to reduce weight before commencing the dive. Thus starting the dive in a positively buoyant condition and attaining neutral buoyancy near the bottom.

The reduction in weight needed will be dependent on the suit worn. Basically, the more material contained in the suit the greater the change in buoyancy with depth and therefore the greater the reduction in weight needed. Weight reductions of the order of 2-3 kilos should be expected for each additional 10 metres of depth.

Lifejackets

What about the use of adjustable buoyancy lifejackets in attaining neutral buoyancy, someone may ask. As lifejackets are the subject of a separate chapter we will not be delving into the matter now. However, it should be remembered that the use of adjustable buoyancy lifejackets should always be supplementary to Buoyancy Control and should never be considered as an alternative to the correct technique.

SURFACING DRILL

PART 1

Ascent Procedures

Free, and Buoyant, ascent practise should only be carried out under close supervision and with a compression chamber on the spot—a situation impossible for most divers. This creates an obvious problem because training to proficiency is usually achieved by constant practise, and proficiency is even more important in the case of emergency rescues. When an emergency occurs underwater an element of excitement, panic or fear is bound to appear in the prospective rescuer, and under these conditions a person will react correctly only if able to perform the rescue procedure automatically—virtually without thinking. This is where the value of training comes in.

Although one should not practise Free and Buoyant ascents, there is much that can be drilled or taught in the safety of a swimming pool or lecture room. Weight belt release is one.

Training should include practise in emergency weight belt release—both on oneself and on another diver—*while fully equipped for diving*. It is no use practising in the pool in swimming trunks; the drill is only of value when you are fully equipped with bulky suits, snaggable accessories and gloves.

Divers should be thoroughly aquainted with the rules of ascent procedure. This is particularly important in view of the lack of practical training for various types. Divers should be able to quote the procedure for all types of ascent on demand. Questioning could be instituted at lectures, and by DO's during verbal examination. During lectures, diagrams or, better still, actual equipment, should be shown of the various types of quick-release on weight belts, and the methods of inflation on different makes of lifejacket.

Assisted Ascent practise is encouraged at the shallower levels but—and although this is repeated elsewhere, it is well worth repeating—it should only be carried out on actual dives by divers who have practised regularly together. In the event of diving with virtual strangers, or divers who have not practised the technique with you, it might be better to carry out a free ascent. It is, unfortunately, something that your DO or instructor cannot decide for you. And you will only have a split second in which to make your decision. Far better to keep in practise, so that you will know exactly what to do should the event occur.

Normal Ascent

1 The 'Going up' signal must be exchanged with your partner.
2 Fin upwards watching exhaust bubbles and partner.
3 Maintain speed of approximate speed of small bubbles.

4   Breathe normally all the time.

5   Look up and watch out for surface obstacles.

6   In poor visibility, hold hand above head—in this case your other hand should be holding your partner.

7   Immediately on surfacing, turn a complete circle in case a boat or other possible danger should be approaching.

8   Exchange 'OK' signals with partner.

9   Signal 'OK', or otherwise, to lookout.

DEEP RESCUE : An ascent from depth carrying an unconscious diver is a difficult procedure. The decreased buoyancy of the protective clothing renders both divers heavy and if, as in this case, only one diver is finning, a lot of leg power is needed to overcome the initial inertia unless additional buoyancy is obtained. The difficulty of formulating a set of rules for rescue ascent procedure is mainly caused by the diversity of diving equipment. The divers may be wearing adjustable buoyancy life jackets, surface life jackets or no jackets at all. Thus, the rules have to take into account these variations and tend to look unwieldy. See also Deep Rescue Test.

1   Assess the situation quickly (is the victim trapped by something; be wary if he is struggling and approach from the rear).

2   Take hold of victim (from behind if he is struggling).

3   (a) If either diver is wearing an adjustable buoyancy lifejacket this should be inflated (only one, preferably the victim's).

     (b) If surface lifejackets, or no lifejackets, are worn, disregard these and slip victim's weight belt. If this is difficult or does not supply enough buoyancy, slip own weight belt (remember, if you slip your weight belt and not his he will be heavy and you will be light, if you lose your grip on him he will sink and you will be unable to get back down). If buoyancy is still not adequate and surface lifejacket(s) are worn, inflate them (victim's first).

4   The victim's mouthpiece and mask should, if possible, be kept in position.

5   If the victim is not exhaling, press his diaphragm to ensure that he does.

6   The rescuer should not try to over-exert himself. This is important.

7   Nearing the surface, look out for surface obstructions.

8   In poor visibility hold one hand above head.

PART 2

Diving accidents and the consequent fatalities are more often due to the failure of the diver than to the failure of his equipment. The factors contributing to an accident have been summarised by Stanley Miles in his equation :

$$A = C\,E\,\frac{p\,r\,f}{t\,m\,s}$$

(where C = Chance, E = Environment, p = accident proneness, r = risk acceptance, f = physical factors (alcohol, illness etc), t = training, m = maturity, s = safety measures)

However, the situation in which a diver finds himself completely without air is by no means unknown. Badly adjusted reserve systems and damaged or blocked demand valves may be the cause. The importance of a comprehensive pre-dive check of equipment cannot be over emphasised. A last minute examination of a companion's quick release system may help to save his life.

In the event of an air failure at depth, there are several ways in which a diver can return to the surface. One recommended method is known as Assisted Ascent. Its principal advantages being that the ascent rate is normal (20 metres/min), the technique may be practised beforehand, and decompression stops may be made if necessary.

Assisted Ascent Procedure

1 The 'distressed diver' attracts the attention of his companion by beckoning or banging on his cylinder. He makes the signal 'I have no more air'. He should then remain still and conserve any air that he has left.

2 The 'assisting diver' closes to him as quickly as possible.
If using a twin hose demand valve, he grips the 'distressed diver's' weight belt or harness and pushes him up to a position slightly above him.
If he has a single hose valve, he grasps the 'distressed diver's' straps and remains at the same level.

3 The 'assisting diver' takes a breath and quickly removes his mouthpiece passing it up to his companion and turning the aperture to enable him to breathe as soon as he drops his own mouthpiece. Both divers should be resting vertically in the water. A difference of approximately 10-20 centimetres in their level ensures that the 'distressed diver' receives a bubbling (twin hose) mouthpiece containing air and no water. This is essential as air failure is usually detected when trying to breathe in, and the diver in trouble may not have enough air to clear the tubes. The purge button may be used to expel water from single hose valves if necessary.

4 After taking his two breaths, the 'distressed diver' returns the mouthpiece down to the 'assisting diver' who also receives only air as it is higher than his demand valve. He then in turn takes two breaths.

5   When a steady rhythm has been established, the 'assisting diver' signals '(Let's) go up', and both divers start finning gently upwards, keeping the same relative position. During the ascent, each exhales slowly when not in possession of the mouthpiece to prevent any possibility of air embolism. The 'assisting diver' should check his rate of ascent, or at least that the small exhaust bubbles appear to remain stationary around his head, to make sure that the speed is not faster than 20 metres/min.

It is especially important that as the surface approaches, the 'assisting diver' should look out for obstacles and watch for bubbles from the 'distressed diver' to check that he is breathing out between inhalations. Gentle pressure on his stomach will remind him. He should also check that increasing buoyancy is not accelerating the ascent unduly, and hold the 'distressed diver' back if necessary. Stopping finning and breathing out will help to do this. The 'assisting diver' should hold his companion's weight belt or harness at all times.

In a real emergency, lack of air may give the 'distressed diver' a feeling of panic or breathlessness. The 'assisting diver' should then allow him to breathe three or four times to his own single breath on the bottom before indicating 'two breaths each' for the ascent. In extreme cases the mouthpiece may not be returned, and the 'assisting diver' will have to decide whether to forcefully retrieve it or to breathe out continually himself (see Free Ascent below) during their ascent.

Without doubt it is most important to *practise the technique regularly. This is ideally done by those who frequently dive together.* A diver cannot be expected to take the right actions in an emergency if he has never previously practised in open water.

Both divers should be well weighted for initial pool training. One sits on the bottom in the deep end and the other adopts a kneeling position facing him. The kneeling diver removes his mouthpiece and holds it against his chest. The sitting diver takes a deep breath, and then passes his mouthpiece up to his companion. Each in turn follows the breathing sequence : Exhale—Inhale—Exhale—Inhale—Hold.

Assisted Ascent forms part of the Second Class tests, and horizontal sharing is included in Third Class training (Group F3). When sharing horizontally and using twin hose valves, it should be remembered that the 'distressed diver' should swim on the side which keeps the exhaust tube below the inlet.

Free Ascent Procedure

Another way of regaining the surface quickly in emergency is by means of 'Free Ascent'. This method may be used when a diver cannot contact his companion or when he is untrained in Assisted Ascent or unwilling to take part. The risk of pulmonary barotrauma (see Burst-Lung and Ascent

Assisted Ascent

Photo: Mike Busuttili

*The 'assisting diver' should be 10-20 centimetres below the
'distressed diver' if a twin hose valve is being used.*

Assisted Ascent

Photo: Mike Busuttili

*At the beginning of the ascent both divers should be vertical.
The 'assisting diver' should be below the 'distressed diver' if he
has a twin hose valve.*

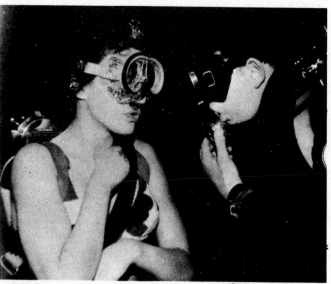

Assisted Ascent Photo: Mike Busuttili
When not breathing from the mouthpiece each diver exhales gently.

Hazards) may now be greater and success is dependent on a calm and controlled technique.

Immediately the diver finds himself without air, he fins steadily upwards. If the lack of air was discovered when he tried to breathe in, he will have a feeling of air starvation. This may be overcome by holding his breath *briefly* until the residual air in his lungs expands with the fall in the surrounding pressure.

The diver must then remove his mouthpiece and commence to exhale gently and continually through pursed lips. The rate of finning should be slowed as he ascends and he should try not to overtake his bubbles. A reasonable rate for free ascent is 30 metres/min. In low visibility he should watch his depth gauge to make sure that he is ascending, and if difficulty is experienced the weight belt should be jettisoned to lessen the load.

Most divers feel comfortable during this type of ascent and there is normally a desire to breathe out, rather than in. Enough partial pressure of oxygen exists, and carbon dioxide will be blown off as quickly as it is formed, providing little chance of CO_2 build up. The untrained free ascenter has most to fear from panic and over-exertion, both of which may use up precious oxygen.

As the surface approaches, the number and size of exhaled bubbles will increase and the diver should take the precaution of breathing out faster. He should remove his snorkel and have it ready before surfacing. If the diver does not get rid of the air continually during the ascent, he will suffer a serious accident through over-expansion or rupture of the lungs. Air embolism has occured in trainees holding their breath when returning from a depth of as little as 3 metres!

Current medical thinking is that free ascent should not be practised as a training drill in view of the dangers. It should be remembered that the Royal Navy training in the 30 metre escape tank involves different procedures, conditions and safety measures.

Buoyant Ascent

Finally, an alternative to 'Free Ascent' is provided by the use of an adjustable buoyancy lifejacket or 'ABLJ'.

Most types of 'ABLJ' (see Lifejackets) will bring a diver up at a rate of approximately 2 metres/sec with a consequent risk of embolism or explosive decompression, especially if the dive has been near to the maximum 'no stop' time. There is, however, a high degree of certainty of arriving at the surface.

This type of lifejacket is normally used by experienced divers who should be familiar with the mode of operation and the hazards. The drills listed on page 225 ought to have been carried out.

The diver does not release his weight belt before venting air into his lifejacket as it will keep his body in the correct position on the surface should he lose consciousness.

The sequence of actions should be as follows :

1   Open tap of 'ABLJ' bottle.
2   When starting to ascend, close tap.
3   Lean head back—breathe out—watch for surface.

During the whole of the emergency buoyant ascent the diver breathes out forcefully, keeping the volume of air in the lungs near the minimum to avoid distension of the chest. He should remain as relaxed as possible. Buoyant ascent should only be carried out in a real emergency.

If a diver has made a free or buoyant ascent which prevented him carrying out necessary decompression stops, he should get another aqualung immediately and return with the standby diver to a depth 10 metres deeper than his first planned stop. He should remain there for five minutes and then continue decompressing for a dive ten minutes longer than his original one.

If any symptoms appear after free or buoyant ascents, the diver should be taken immediately to the nearest operational recompression chamber. Although there is a natural tendency to take solo action when suddenly deprived of air, there is little doubt that the slow return to the surface characteristic of assisted ascent, makes it often less hazardous than free or buoyant ascent, and decompression stops may even be completed while sharing. Its practice gives greater confidence at depth, greater appreciation of the importance of diving as a team, and makes a diver more use to others in a real emergency.

READING AND REFERENCES

DAVIS, Sir Robert, 'Deep Diving and Submarine Operations' (Chessington, Siebe Gorman Ltd, Reprinted 1969) 273-274, 656-658, 661-662.

LEE, Owen, 'Snorkel and Deep Diving' (New York, Doubleday, 1963) 179-183.

MILES, Surgeon Rear Admiral, 'Underwater Medicine' (London, Staples, 1962) 76-77, 196, 302-303, 306-308.

'New Science of Skin and Scuba Diving' (New York, Association Press, 1962) 48-50, 52, 124.

OWEN, D M, 'A Manual for Free-Divers using Compressed Air' (London, Pergamon, 1955) 29-30, 43-46.

POULET, Guy, 'Connaissance et Technique de la Plongée' (London, Newnes, 1962) 146-147.

US Navy Diving Manual (Washington, Navy Department, 1963) 62-63, 134.

WALKER, Dr D, 'Scuba Diving Instructor's Handbook' (National Fitness Council of South Australia, 1970) 51-56.

SIGNALS

The normal methods of communication between human beings on land are by voice, touch, gesture and writing, and whilst they also apply underwater there are problems to be faced.

Vocal communication, for example, can be achieved, but the necessary equipment is expensive and at its best is still not ideal. A slate and pencil can be used for writing underwater, but this has limited application. Communication by touch is also not always practical.

The simple questions requiring simple answers, the urgent statements and the urgent orders, are, therefore, usually dealt with by the remaining method—hand signals—and these have proved to be adequate in almost every situation. It must not be assumed that underwater visibility will be good enough to enable hand signals to be used all the time, but it is imperative for all divers to understand the basic signals, for this method of communication is standard and the most common.

This and other practical methods of signalling are dealt with here, and it should be noted that they are all sub-divided into the following categories :

	Visual
Underwater	diver to diver
	diver to surface
Surface	surface to diver
Surface	diver on surface or boat, to boat or shore.

	Sound
Underwater	diver to diver
	diver to surface
Surface	surface to diver

	Rope
Underwater	diver to diver
	diver to surface
Surface	surface to diver

Visual signals underwater

On January 1, 1966, the British Sub Aqua Club changed over from its current signals to those more commonly used by member countries of the World Federation (CMAS). These signals are shown on the following pages, with full meanings alongside. However, before carrying out a dive, divers should never assume that everyone will use the same set of signals, no matter what the rules of the Club are. Always run through each signal with the group to determine exactly which signals are being used—and their meaning—for confusion may well arise now that changes have been made.

For example, one of the major changes in the Club signals was the complete reversal of the diver on surface to shore signal meaning 'I am all right' and 'I am in difficulties; please come and get me'. After several months—or even years—there may be a small group of divers who, for reasons known only to themselves, have stuck to the old system. If these groups are joined by other divers and the signals are not discussed beforehand, the ensuing mix-up could range from the embarrassment of saving a perfectly fit and capable diver to the tragedy of letting a man drown.

Although the example given above fits properly in the 'diver on surface or boat, to boat or shore' section, the importance of holding a pre-dive conference is illustrated.

When giving signals underwater, whether as a question, a request or an acknowledgement, the diver should remember the following points. The signals have been so devised that the diver does not need to wave his arms about like a bookmaker's tic-tac man at a racecourse, wasting energy and using up air. In other words, they should be given slowly, accurately and consciously exaggerated. Equally, the signals should each be acknowledged in the same manner, with, of course, the appropriate answer or reaction. If the signal is not understood the first time, the sequence is simple. The signaller repeats his signal until the other diver, or divers, acknowledge the signal with a correct reply, if not, he takes

Figure 1
You or me.
Diver points to himself or another diver indicating the person referred to in the signal which follows.

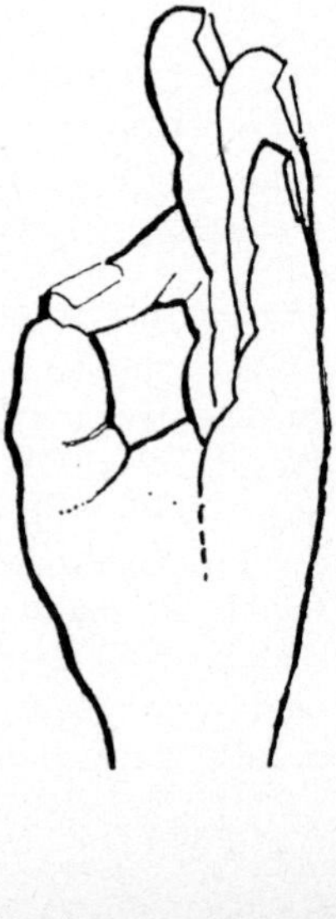

Figure 2
OK, all is well.
This can either be a question from one diver to another or an affirmative reply to this question.

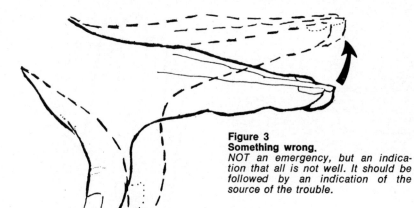

Figure 3
Something wrong.
NOT an emergency, but an indication that all is not well. It should be followed by an indication of the source of the trouble.

Figure 4
Go up, I am going up.
Command from dive leader to diver or indication from one diver to another, usually at end of dive.

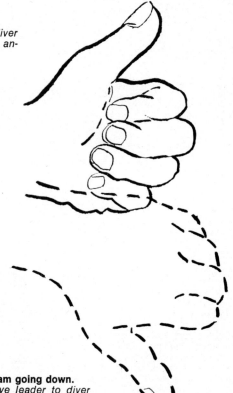

Figure 5
Go down (dive) I am going down.
Command from dive leader to diver or indication from one diver to another, beginning to dive.

259

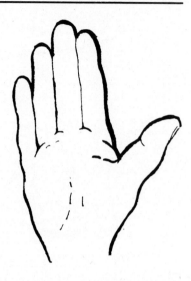

Figure 6
Stop, stay where you are.
A command from dive leader to diver to stay where he is. May be followed by an explanatory signal explaining the dive leader's next course of action.

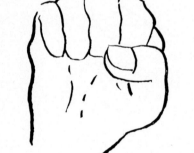

Figure 7
I am on reserve. I have 30ATS left in my set.
From diver to dive leader or diver to diver, indicates end of dive is near.

Figure 8
I cannot pull my reserve.
For divers with sets having a reserve system. Diver concerned makes sign to buddy diver or diver nearest him indicating that he requires assistance in operating his reserve lever manually, and if this is not successful he will require to share a set.

260

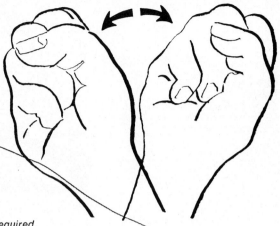

Figure 9
Distress.
Immediate assistance required.

Figure 10
I have no more air.
Diver repeatedly touches mouth-piece with cupped fingers.

Figure 11
I am out of breath.
From diver to dive leader or buddy diver. Indicates that he is out of breath from excessive swimming or work rate and wishes to stop or slow down so that he may regain his breathing rhythm. Important in avoiding exhaustion.

261

Figure 12
Danger.
Draw forefinger across throat, then
point to source or cause of danger.

appropriate action. It is also up to the diver at whom the signal is directed *not* to acknowledge the signal until he understands it. All these signals are officially approved by the BSAC. After studying them and what they mean, it is easy to understand how information can be exchanged underwater between divers.

Diver-to-surface and surface-to-diver

Snorkel divers, acting as surface cover—or safety-men—are considered necessary during many dives in British waters. The snorkel cover can aid the divers beneath him, provided they are within his free diving range or the visibility is ultra-good, so some means of communication must be set up between the diver on the bottom and the snorkeller on the surface. The snorkeller must, of course, be present when the dive is planned so that he knows whether two divers exchanging mouthpieces are doing it as part of the pre-arranged plan or are, in fact, in difficulties. The signals given by the diver, or divers, on the bottom to the snorkeller, and vice versa, will be standard signals, such as those shown above. The diver has the advantage in this situation because the snorkeller, by reason of his magnificent 'birds-eye view', will have no difficulty in noticing that he is being signalled to. The diver can also receive information from the snorkel cover, such as that concerning direction, merely by asking for it. It is simple to look up at the snorkeller, point around in various directions, shrug the shoulders and spread the arms wide in a supplicating gesture. Perhaps the latter is not a laid down signal, but it is one that can quickly be understood and answered by the snorkeller simply pointing.

Conversely, the method of contact between snorkeller and diver, with the snorkeller as instigator, poses a knotty problem if visual signals are being used. The diver will be swimming face downwards, and unless the snorkeller can free dive to the relevant depth and touch the diver the chances of instigating visual contact is small. Initial contact can, however, be made by the use of sound signals, which are discussed shortly.

Surface: diver on surface, or boat, to boat or shore

The diver underwater is in the element in which he has been trained to operate skilfully. When he surfaces, perhaps without air, the situation is different. No longer is he completely in control; he now has to cope with the effects of weather, tide, waves and currents as well as the problems of keeping his snorkel tube clear of the water. Therefore, signals are essential to let his shore and boat party know that he is all right.

Figure 13
OK at surface (Sig 2 with outstretched arm).
To be given by all divers on surfacing, should be held until acknowledged by surface or boat cover—by similar signal.

As soon as the diver surfaces, he must give the signal 'I am OK'. This is very simple; as shown in the illustration, the arm is held straight above the head with the fingers in the OK position. This indicates that the diver is in control of the situation, and it also lets the shore or boat party see exactly where the diver is. There may be a snorkel cover, but it is not 100 per cent certain that he will have stayed in contact with the underwater group, so this direct signal by the underwater party to their supporters is vital. As soon as the OK signal is received by the supporting party, it should immediately move to help the divers concerned. This is not because they will be desperately in need, but because

Figure 14
Distress at surface/come and get me (Sig 7 with arm outstretched).
To indicate that he wants to be picked up the diver waves his arm slowly and steadily from side to side. In an emergency he waves faster, perhaps uncontrollably, indicating that emergency action must be taken by the surface party.

a helping hand after a dive is just as important as the one before the diver goes in.

Other surface signals which should be used—and the need now is greater than before because of the increase in sea traffic—are flags to indicate that diving is in progress. The most noticeable and the one used to the best advantage in British waters, is the accepted 'Diver's Flag'. But it should be noted that this flag should only be flown *when divers are in the water*. It has become a flamboyant touch of many boat users to leave harbour with the Diver's Flag flying proudly at the masthead. Many small boat users—fishermen, speedboat drivers and water skiers—will later ignore the anchored boat with the Diver's Flag aloft if they have seen the vessel, flag bravely flying, steaming merrily through other boats half an hour before.

Sound signals

Diver to diver. When two divers are several metres apart, in good visibility water, one may want to contact his friend without leaving the precise spot he is at. The easiest method is to hit one's tank with some hard, preferably metallic object—a rock or stone found on the bottom, the handle of a knife, a torch, when carried. Whatever is used, the 'clang' carries some distance. For those divers who do not want to remove too much paint from their cylinders, the alternative is to bang two stones together, or a stone against a rock. This however, is not heard so far away.

Some types of breathing apparatus have a special diaphragm which enables the diver to speak underwater—not very clearly but, if the user talks slowly, clearly enough for his words to be quite understandable. The standard mouthpiece is not usually fitted with such a diaphragm, but the diver may make a succession of short 'toots' through his ordinary mouthpiece, and this can be heard quite a long way underwater. Sound signals are not effective with the beginner, as he is apt to confuse them with many other sounds in the so-called 'silent world'.

Diver to surface. To help a snorkel cover find his charges—pre-supposing that contact has been lost—the diver can keep making sound signals and the snorkel cover can home in on them. A suggestion will undoubtedly be put forward that all the snorkel cover has to do is to find the bubble stream, but in rough or low visibility water this is difficult.

Surface to diver. No signals are laid down for this as many clubs have their own systems. If the diving boat has a metal ladder, this can be 'clanged' an agreed number of times. This sound travels far. Also the motor can be started up and revved to a prearranged plan, and yet another system is to use small waterproofed fireworks—or thunderflashes —which can be heard some distance away. Another method is to use a waterproofed loudspeaker. If fireworks are used, the best and safest variety are those which are electrically ignited, a few feet underwater, by a small torch battery. Care must be taken with all fireworks as they explode powerfully and can cause great damage.

Surface to surface contact. Most communication between divers on the surface or in boats is done by shouting, but other aids are available such as whistles, transistorised loudhailers, wireless equipment and blank shots. Again, everyone should know what the various signals given mean.

ROPES AND ROPING

The purpose of any safety organisation is to keep all swimmers under observation, so that in the event of one of them getting into difficulty assistance can be rendered with sufficient speed to save life.

In calm, clear, still water there is usually sufficient safety in divers swimming together, with a safety boat attending in sight of the air bubbles.

It would be very pleasant if it were possible to swim in these conditions all the time. However, as soon as a diver wishes to carry out a useful underwater task, he finds he is frequently unable to choose optimum diving conditions. Diving will have to take place by day or night in tidal streams; in wrecks or among wreckage; in caverns or narrow clefts; in zero visibility on soft muddy bottoms; in rough weather; or, perhaps, when it is just generally cold, wet, and thoroughly miserable. This is to name but a few of the potentially hazardous conditions which exist.

When such conditions are experienced, a safety line of one sort or another will usually *have* to be used, with or without a surface marker, if the requirements of paragraph one are to be met.

The decision to use a safety line is the sole responsibility of the Dive Marshal, for it is he who will be held responsible for any accident in the eyes of the law. The Marshal's decision will, of course, take into account the type of underwater task on hand; the prevailing underwater conditions; the present and anticipated weather and tides; boat availability and engine reliability; number and experience of divers; depth of water; availability of a recompression chamber, and any other relevant local factors.

The different types of safety lines are as follows :

    a AS A LIFELINE—from diver to surface attendant.
    b AS A BUDDY LINE—from diver to diver.
    c AS A FLOAT LINE—from diver to surface float.

These three methods may be combined as necessary and a common combination is divers on a buddy line, with one of the pair on a float.

GENERAL RULES WHENEVER A SAFETY LINE IS USED

1 A safety boat should always be in attendance and this should contain :

    An anchor, with sufficient rope to reach the bottom in the deep expected diving depth;
    A large marker bouy;
    The diving flag;
    A diving ladder if access is difficult;
    A standby diver and an attendant.

If the safety boat is slow and clumsy, or if it is to be anchored and diving is to take place on float or buddy lines, then it should be backed up by a small powered craft.

2   A standby diver should be available at immediate notice, and immediate notice means : fins on, bottles switched on, sufficient air in bottles to work for 10 minutes at the maximum expected diving depth, mask to hand. A lifeline should also be worn.

It is good practice to exercise the standby diver occasionally and discover just how quickly he can enter the water.

3   All divers should carry a knife, and this must be sharp enough to cut the safety line with one blow when it is under tension. *Try it.*

4   All divers should wear lifejackets of either type, but it must be ascertained beforehand if the lifejacket could be inflated accidently owing to the nature of the work.

5   The lifeline signal code set out below should be known by heart. To avoid unnecessarily long signals, they comprise either *pulls* or *bells* or a combination of both. A *pull* is a steady single heave on the line. A *bell* is a sharp quick tug, always given in pairs as with a ship's bell, i.e. five bells is given as :

> two quick tugs *pause* two quick tugs *pause* one quick tug.

It should be noted that one bell does not exist as a signal on its own.

CLUB DIVER

These FIVE signals are those which are necessary for normal Club Diving and should be known and understood by all. The interpretation of rope signals has to be done with care and thought on the part of diver and surface tender. Varied shades of meaning can apply on successive dives : for this reason this short, basic table has the simplest interpretations indicated : for amplified meanings reference should be made to the complete table in which these five signals can be found marked*

Diver	Signal	Surface
Am O.K.	ONE PULL	Are you O.K.?
Am stationary	TWO PULLS	Stay put.
Going down	THREE PULLS	Go on down.
Coming up	FOUR PULLS	Come up.

(If you wish to stop the diver before he reaches the surface, give him two pulls.)

Emergency	CONTINUOUS PULLS	Emergency, bringing you to the surface.

The Lifeline Signal code is as follows :

SIGNALS—ATTENDANT TO DIVER

*a	1 pull	To call attention. Are you alright?
*b	2 pulls	Am sending down a rope's end, or as previously arranged.
*c	3 pulls	You have come up too far. Go down slowly till we stop you.
*d	4 pulls	Come up.
e	4 pulls followed by 2 bells	Come up, hurry up Come up, surface decompression.

Direction Signals

a	1 pull	Search where you are.
b	2 bells	Go to the end of distance line jackstay, or lifeline.
c	3 bells	Face shot lifeline then go right.
d	4 bells	Face shot lifeline then go left.
e	5 bells	Come into your shot, or turn back if on a jackstay.

SIGNALS—DIVER TO ATTENDANT
General Signals

a	1 pull	To call attention. Made bottom. Reached end of jackstay.
b	2 pulls	Send me down a rope's end, or as previously arranged.
c	3 pulls	I am going down again.
d	4 pulls	May I come up?
e	4 pulls followed by 2 bells	Assist me up. I want to come up.
*f	Succession of pulls (must be more than 4)	**EMERGENCY SIGNAL** (*ONLY* to be used in *GREAT EMERGENCY*.) Need not be answered but must be obeyed *IMMEDIATELY*.
g	succession of 2 bells	Am foul and need the assistance of another diver.
h	succession of 3 bells	Am foul but can clear myself if left alone.

These are the same as the signals required to be known by all Club divers.

268

Working Signals

a	1 pull	Hold on or stop.
b	2 bells	Pull up.
c	3 bells	Lower.
d	4 bells	Take up slack lifeline.
		You are holding me too tight.
e	5 bells	Have found, started, or completed work.

How to pass a signal.

A diver or attendant wishing to pass a signal should first give one pull to call attention, then wait for this to be answered. If the diver is engaged in a difficult task, the attendant must give him plenty of time to stop work, find his lifeline and answer the signal. If there is no answer within a reasonable time, the signal should be repeated. Of course, if no reply can be obtained at all the standby diver must be sent in without delay. When the attention signal is answered the diver/attendant passes his signal. He must then ensure that it is answered correctly. If it is not, it must be repeated until it is.

It is *not* necessary to call attention before giving the first three working signals, or the *emergency* signal.

Signals may also be passed on a float line or a buddy line, when the No 1 diver will act as the attendant.

These signals and techniques are also in common use in the Royal Navy.

THE LIFELINE

Material

2.5 centimetre circumference manilla or sisal, 3 centimetre plaited hemp, or 1 centimetre nylon, terylene, polypropylene, or polyethylene (courlene), are all suitable and have a breaking strain in excess of 450 kilograms. The larger vegetable fibres are more bulky but are easier to handle. However, they tend to become slippery when wet.

As the man-made fibres tend to twist very easily—although they are very light and have very little resistance in a tideway—they are best kept on reels.

The cable of an underwater telephone is also tested to double as a lifeline, as is the air hose for a hookah or surface demand breathing set.

Length

36 metres is a manageable length for a rope line. The cable for the underwater telephone is supplied as a made up length of 73 metres, and the surface demand hose line in 18 metre sections.

Fittings

No special fittings are required, but a rope line should be whipped at both ends. Surface demand and telephone cables are fitted by the makers.

Markings

Usual *standard* markings for a rope line are as in Figure one.

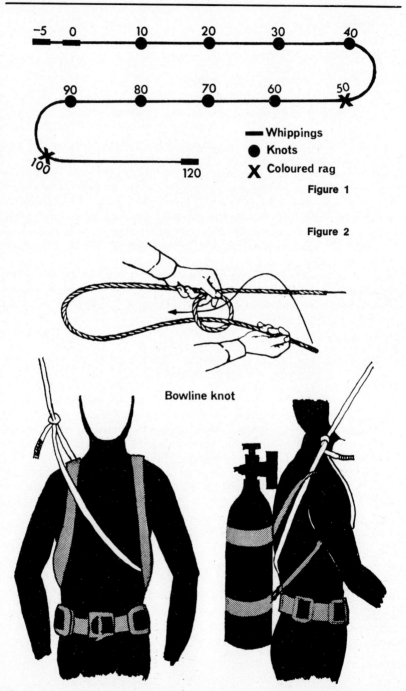

Figure 1

Figure 2

Bowline knot

Securing

The *zero* end is taken around the diver underneath his arm-pits and all equipment in such a way that if weight belt and set are jettisoned he is still held by the line. The line should then be tied with a bowline close to the body of the diver on the side of his useful arm.

The inboard end of the lifeline should always be securely tied to the diving platform; it cannot then be jerked from the attendant's hands.

The Attendant and the Art of Attending

The best attendant is another diver, for he will then be completely in sympathy with the diver and have an automatic knowledge of the diving signals.

His task is always to be aware of the diver's position and to keep the lifeline free of obstruction so that signals may be passed quickly and easily. The inboard end of the line in particular should be kept clear for there is nothing more infuriating to a diver than being held up purely because the attendant has got himself in a mix-up.

The attendant should be very careful in a tideway that the drag on the line does not mislead him into paying out too much—it is easy for a diver to give a signal on a taut line, but very difficult for him if he first has to take up yards of slack.

At the first sign of any difficulty, the attendant should inform the Dive Marshal who in turn should not hesitate to send in the standby diver. Trouble down below can be indicated in a number of ways : no sign of bubbles, signals unanswered, lifeline taut or slack, no movement felt when the diver should be working. Think twice, however, before hauling madly away on the lifeline; it may well be caught on a bottom obstruction and if the line is heaved the diver may well be hauled down.

If it is neccessary for the diver to swim to the end of his line or farther so that two lines have to be used, always make sure that the second line is either joined before the diver goes in or that it is readily available, again so that the diver is not held up by unnecessary delays.

At all costs the attendant must retain patience with the diver, giving him time to answer signals when working, repeating signals which are not understood. He should also always remember that the diver's safety and comfort are his responsibility. Avoid this : Figure four.

There are also a few points that the diver himself must bear in mind when working on a line.

If the line become too taut or too slack he should not swim against it, nor should he coil it up. He should pause and give the relevant signal (four bells) to his attendant and wait until the requisite action has been taken. It is particularly important not to swim against a taut line; inexperienced divers have been known to exhaust themselves by doing just this.

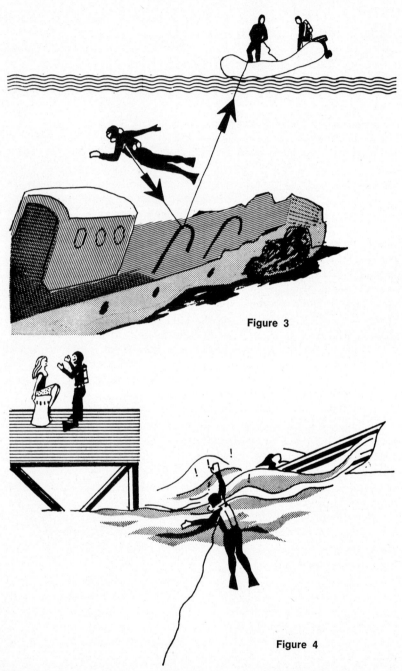

Figure 3

Figure 4

Resist the temptation to overrun the safety line when surfacing, as this will mean that signals will not get through, and an important one—perhaps ordering the diver to remain down because of boat's movements or similar events—may be missed with subsequent embarrassment. Finally, have patience with the lifeline and never hurry when you become mixed up with it. In an alien world of darkness and silence it is sometimes the only true friend.

THE BUDDY LINE

Signals

The lifeline signals set out in the preceding paragraphs may be used, with the lead diver acting as the attendant—only necessary, of course, when visibility is too low for otherwise divers can see one another.

The Dive Marshal in the safety boat should always carry a means of signalling to the divers when they are using buddy lines. The best noise signal is a small firework, preferably one which will sink before detonating. An explosion on the surface carries nothing like so far as one underneath.

Use of the Buddy Line

The Number Two diver should take station on the quarter of Number One, always keeping the line almost taut, so that it neither tangles with the Number One, nor does it drag on him.

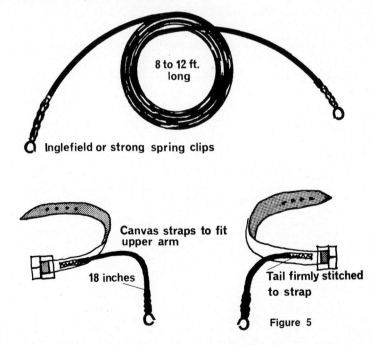

8 to 12 ft. long

Inglefield or strong spring clips

Canvas straps to fit upper arm

18 inches

Tail firmly stitched to strap

Figure 5

Always make sure that the clips are secured before leaving the surface. They should only be released in a case of dire necessity. To carry out a line abreast search, several divers may work together using buddy lines.

THE FLOAT LINE

Material

A float of sufficient size to carry the line to be used and of such colour and shape that it may be seen in the prevailing weather conditions should be used. The best type is a hollow plastic sphere, with the facility for a stick to be passed through its centre on which the line may be wound.

This kind of float produces a minimum drag and allows the line to unwind of its own accord as the diver descends. However, an oblong oil tin will do nearly as well, particularly if painted a bright colour.

The line should be in the order of 1.25 centimetres circumference and of sufficient length to reach the deepest diving depth plus 10%.

Signals

The normal signals set out in the table may be used from the safety boat on the float line.

Use

The float should be used to mark a single diver, a buddy line pair, or the end of a multiple diver search line.

It should *always* be secured to a diver, never held in the hand, as at the first sign of difficulty a diver may well let go and the whole purpose of the line is defeated.

When swimming in pairs or more, divers unmarked should remember that the float line may well reduce the swimming speed of the marked diver, and should reduce their own speed accordingly.

UNDERWATER NAVIGATION

A human being walking in dense fog loses his way in two dimensions. A free diver operating in conditions of poor, or nil, visibility and lacking firm ground under his feet is even more confused as he can easily lose his sense of direction in three dimensions. With no datum point for reference, and with no feeling of gravitational forces, he is often unable to distinguish up from down. The underwater environment is so different from the natural one that few of man's systems escape its influence and a close examination of these effects on the senses required for navigation is, therefore, necessary.

Vision

Without the aid of artificial light, vision is dependent on the clarity of the water and the penetration of daylight which, in turn, is dependent on the depth and the time of day. At midday in clear water it is only just possible to see what one is doing as deep as 75 metres. A considerable absorption of light by water is thus taking place, so much so that the intensity of daylight is reduced to $\frac{1}{4}$ at 4.5 metres and $\frac{1}{8}$ at 15 metres, the maximum penetration of sunlight being about 450 metres. Even at the best times, underwater visibility is very greatly limited (in the clearest water to 30 metres) but quite often suspended matter, such as stirred up mud, may reduce it almost to zero.

Colours, too, are deceptive, for the light is unevenly absorbed so that objects on the bottom may have quite a different colour when removed from the water. Blue light penetrates farther while red light is absorbed first, hence the reason for the diver who has the misfortune to cut himself at depth finding he has 'blue blood in his veins'.

In addition, due to refraction caused when light passes from air into water, and vice versa, it is found that objects underwater appear to be only about three quarters of their actual distance away and to be one third larger than their actual size. There is also a considerable restriction of the field of vision due to refraction as well as to the frame of the diver's face mask (see *Vision*).

Hearing

Sound in water travels much faster than its speed in air. In air, man is able to locate the direction from which the sound is coming. He does this by turning his head until both ears are equidistant from the source and the sound is synchronised in each. The increased speed of sound underwater makes this virtually impossible.

The sense of position

In water, no effort is required to maintain posture. Righting reflexes are not required and muscles which are normally responsible for posture

275

and balance are relaxed. When blindfolded and still, the sense of position is soon lost and disorientation, not unlike that experienced in extremely high altitude flying, develops. The same situation can easily occur in water of poor visibility.

The fact is that the underwater swimmer is largely dependent upon visual sensations for his navigation. The lighter wàter above him indicates the position of the surface and ascending bubbles give him a vertical. Take away these and he is soon lost. He may swim around in circles and he may unwittingly increase his depth or even turn over. Many occasions have been reported where a swimmer, even an experienced one, presuming to be travelling along an even course at steady depth has found himself on the bottom very many metres below his intended depth. This happens especially in the dark. Loss of direction can occur vertically and horizontally. Such loss of direction in three dimensions can be very dangerous, and this can occur not only in shallow, low visibility conditions, but in clear water, at a point where the surface disappears and the bottom is not yet in view. The visual world of the diver then appears as a blue globe, which due to the light-scattering effects of water, and reflection from the unseen bottom, shows no difference in light intensity to indicate the surface.

As an example, this phenomena occurs in the Mediterranean sea in depths of 48 metres at about the 24 metre level. It can be extremely confusing to the beginner and can cause attacks of vertigo due to a sense of unbalance. The experienced diver turns to his bubbles as a guide to the surface. In dirty water it may not be possible to utilise these, or to read instruments clearly.

Such conditions, when first met, can cause panic, and sufferers from claustrophobia are badly affected. The proficiency test of swimming in a pool with a blacked out mask was introduced to give pupils a foretaste of this experience and to guide instructors in detecting claustrophobia tendencies.

From the foregoing we see that the senses required for underwater navigation are seriously affected to different degrees according to the prevailing underwater conditions.

UNDERWATER NAVIGATION

Underwater navigation can be broadly divided into two sections. (a) Pilotage, where direction is found by use of topographical features such as rocks or ripple marks in sand, etc, and (b) Navigation, where the use of instruments such as compass and depth gauge are employed. Quite often a combination of both arts is utilised.

Pilotage

We have seen that the senses required for direction are impaired underwater and the first consideration should be to reduce the amount of direction-finding underwater to the absolute minimum. Thus, if one has some specific object to locate the maximum amount of information possible should be obtained in order to commence the dive as near as possible to the object. By the use of charts, fixes, information from local fishermen, landmarks, echo-sounders, sweeps, etc, it should be possible to eliminate much unnecessary searching underwater. The number of times divers are requested to recover some object of value which sank between here and there, an expanse of some square miles, are innumerable and usually impossible.

Having commenced the dive at the best possible position, the problem of navigating underwater therefore entails (a) the steering of a fairly accurate course on the bottom, (b) the ability to return to the point of departure, and (c) the ability to define the direction of the surface and to stop at the proper depths for decompression if necessary. It is obvious that different techniques will be required according to the condition of the water with regard to visibility and currents.

The golden rule in acquiring a sense of direction underwater is always to arrive on the bottom with a static reference point fixed clearly in the mind, be it the boat, the shore or another physical feature. If it is necessary to swim ' into the blue ' to reach the bottom or if the water is dirty, then a tangible datum such as an anchor chain, sinker line, or rope run out from the shore will have to be used. Once on the bottom with a sense of direction firmly established in the mind, it is then possible to swim over the floor picking out landmarks ahead, by which to steer a correct course, in the same way as a low flying airman flies by picking out objects on the horizon. In limited visibility even large pebbles will suffice. It is both necessary to remember the landmarks, and to remember the turns made, and at each turn the diver must re-orientate himself with his home base.

Other guides can be the luminous patches overhead caused by the sun (for corroboration only), wave ripples in the sand, or even the current itself if there is no fear of an immediate change of tide or current. A flat, featureless sand or mud bottom can be very confusing. Marks made are obliterated by the water almost immediately, but in conditions of good visibility, if the texture of the bottom permits, a track in the form of a dust cloud can be beaten up by the fins when swimming close to the bottom, to be used as a guide on the return. This track will only be used in comparatively still water, however, as otherwise the sand or mud haze is soon dispersed.

The worst type of sea floor to navigate over is one covered entirely by seaweed or similar vegetation, which soon causes confusion if no other visual aid is at hand. In shallow depths, where the vegetation is being swung to and fro rhythmically by wave or current conditions this can be a doubtful guide, and in this and similar conditions it is preferable to use a compass, or a guide line.

The use of a lifeline can be of great assistance in indicating direction underwater as one has only to pull the rope taut ensuring that it is not snagged around weeds or other obstructions, and face in the direction the rope is leading to discover the whereabouts of the boat and then obey rope signal. If one is facing away from direction of rope, a ' go left ' signal would be misinterpreted as a ' go right ' etc. A code of rope signals can be used in order that the surface attendant can direct the diver by indicating ' go right ', ' stop ', ' go left ', etc, and last but by no means least in a search the rope can be used to mark the object of the search, or to bring down a second line to mark it with. Many are the divers who have rushed to the surface in a blaze of success to tell of their find, only for it never to be located again. It is essential to mark the object temporarily by buoy or line, or even a companion diver and his telltale bubbles, before departing and making provision for permanent marking. Direction can also be ascertained by various types of rope or wire grids laid on the bottom (see grid search diagrams).

After some experience, a diver often develops a sixth sense with regard to direction underwater. He is guided subconsciously and reacts automatically to such pointers as increasing pressure on the ears and mask, the sound of exhaust bubbles, the sag of his weight belt or the gradient of a shelving sea bed indicating the shore. The ascending exhaust bubbles or a slight amount of water in a face mask will also indicate the surface direction.

In the limited visibility which often prevails in UK waters, it is advisable to send an inexperienced diver down with a guide or safety rope to ensure his safe return to the surface.

Navigation

Underwater navigation, utilising instruments such as the compass and depth gauge, is again subject to the same conditions as pilotage in commencing the dive at the nearest possible surface position.

Magnetic compass

Suitable compasses can be obtained for underwater work, adapted to resist the pressure of water and usually these are worn on the wrist. Cheap, poor-quality instruments are a bad buy, and liquid-filled compasses are preferred as being more sensitive and accurate. Being magnetic, they are badly affected by steel cylinders, the vicinity of metal boats and other metal objects above or below water, and give wide deviations on all headings, especially if the diver is keeping close formation with a companion, thus making it extremely difficult to steer an accurate course. Some idea of the amount of deviation to be expected can be gained by practising with the compass in a swimming pool and having a companion, also in an aqualung, finning alongside varying his position. It will be found that even the steel grating covering the pool drain will react on the instrument, as will metal steps and handrails. The compass should be strapped to a wrist by itself and not next to a watch or other ferrous instrument which will cause it to deviate.

Despite the disadvantage of metallic equipment causing deviation, the compass can be extremely useful underwater. When taking a magnetic compass reading always hold the compass in the same position, directly ahead of the centre line of travel at eye level (see Figure 1). When

Figure 1

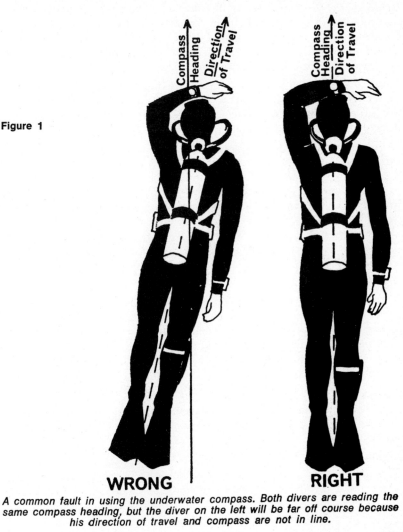

WRONG   **RIGHT**

A common fault in using the underwater compass. Both divers are reading the same compass heading, but the diver on the left will be far off course because his direction of travel and compass are not in line.

wearing a compass, always remember the bearing of the shore or boat before diving which will be a safeguard against travelling too far from the departure point is lost underwater. If in the vicinity of a metal boat it is advisable to swim well clear before taking a bearing. Once on the bottom with the course selected, it is only necessary to turn the course through 180 degrees in order to home on the point of departure, that is to swim on a reciprocal course.

To carry out a square search using a compass in conjunction with an underwater watch, swim at a constant speed for timed periods on four headings, eg, N—five minutes, E—five minutes, S—five minutes, W—five minutes, which should bring the diver within easy reach of the departure point. An alternative to the use of a watch can be to count a certain number of leg kicks for each side of the square providing they are consistent (see search pattern diagrams).

It is extremely useful both for direction finding and safety to use a snorkel cover overhead to follow the diver's bubbles. Should the diver lose his direction he can make contact with the snorkel cover who can direct him by pre-arranged signals.

If the diver has the slightest doubt about his correct position he should surface and pick up his bearings whilst he still has sufficient air in reserve to permit him to fin home underwater. To go inadvertently out to sea, or out of sight of the snorkel cover, and then to surface with little or no air leads to hazardous situations, especially in cold, tidal waters. A diver can, quite unknowingly, cover surprisingly long distances underwater, especially if swimming with a current. This may be dangerous if the correct procedure is not carried out—eg always commence the dive swimming against the prevailing current.

Depth gauge
The depth gauge is of great value for underwater navigation and is invaluable in water of limited visibility. In addition to indicating the ambient depth, it will also show whether one is ascending or descending and prevent the diver losing himself in a vertical direction. The depth gauge can become maladjusted through time and misuse and it is advisable to check it for accuracy periodically.

Divers watch
In addition to keeping a check on cylinder endurance and decompression times, the watch can be utilised for search schemes in calculating the length of side of the search.

Watertight torches
Though limited in their practical effectiveness in really low visibility water, they do provide sufficient light to examine objects and surroundings at close range, and do a great deal towards inspiring confidence in such adverse conditions.

Figure 2

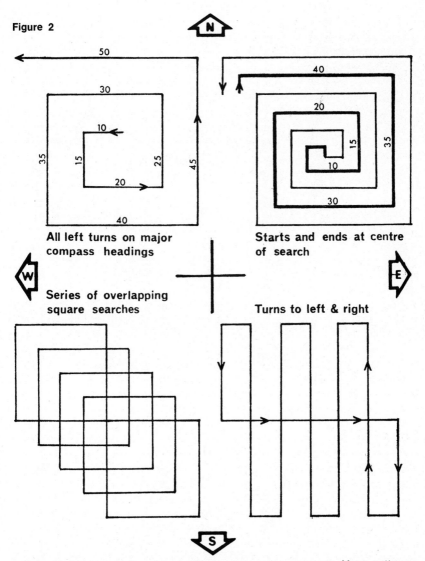

All left turns on major compass headings

Starts and ends at centre of search

Series of overlapping square searches

Turns to left & right

Some suggested search patterns with an underwater compass. Many patterns may be developed which will ensure maximum coverage, however simplicity is of major importance so that the diver will have minimum difficulty remembering the various headings; The cardinal points N, S, E, W; the length of side—one-minute intervals or, say, 50 fin strokes; and turning direction—all right turns. The search pattern should begin at the position where the object of the search is most likely to be.

281

Figure 3   GRID SEARCH PATTERNS

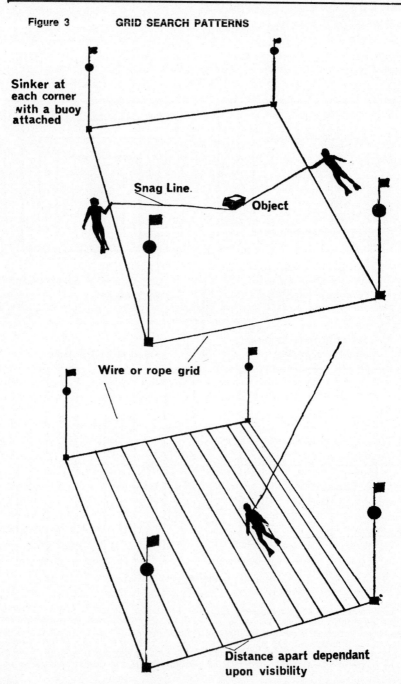

Sinker at each corner with a buoy attached

Snag Line.

Object

Wire or rope grid

Distance apart dependant upon visibility

Searching

In searching, accurate underwater navigation is of paramount importance if success is to be assured. Branches are often asked to carry out searches, and in the past have given valuable aid to authorities and others. It is a commendable feature of the club spirit, and deserves every encouragement. Diving officers are advised, however, not to undertake searches unless the branch is properly equipped with trained members, aqualungs, air supplies and the requisite ropes and marker buoys to cover the desired task with a reasonable chance of success.

Practice in underwater navigation and search schemes should be encouraged, firstly in the swimming bath and then in open water. Hit or miss or badly organised searches can only serve to bring the club into ill-repute, and perhaps cause unnecessary distress to bereaved relations if the search is for a drowning fatality. An efficient search ensures that every inch of the area is covered by sight, or touch in dirty water. Anything less just will not do. The methods of using ropes, grids, compass, watch and so on require ingenuity and practice. A diver's course may be traced by his bubbles, or better, by a surface marker and signals are more easily arranged with the latter.

What is often disregarded, however, is the need for proper preparation, surface direction, and an overall plan of the area to check coverage. In preparing for a search, obtain in advance details of water visibility and depth, area to be covered, the size of the lost object and, if possible, the type of bottom. In a sea search the time will have to be taken into account. From these details it is possible to anticipate the search methods required and the approximate coverage of a single diver. Thus, the number of divers and the air supply required may be calculated. Careful briefing of the divers, using a plan of the area plus teamwork, can save much misunderstanding and missed patches. Marker buoys (tin cans, empty bottles, etc), on pegs knocked into the bank-side, can be used to guide boats and divers and mark the limits of the sea area searched. Where a circular sweep is being made in dark water, on a featureless bottom, the diver's course may be traced by his bubbles and signals arranged to warn him on completion of a circle. Alternatively, he may make an artificial mark on the bottom with a stake, boulder or other substantial object.

Future

It is possible that research into the effects and possible uses underwater of supersonic and ultrasonic vibrations, and electro-magnetic devices, may bring about the development of further aids to navigation, detection and communication. Until then, we must rely on the aids that we have.

DECOMPRESSION IN PRACTICE

Safe Air Decompression is the use of knowledge found necessary for a compressed-air-breathing diver to return safely to the surface, following an exposure to pressure greater than twice normal atmospheric pressure, with practically no risk of Decompression Sickness.

An exposure begins when we leave the surface and ends when we begin the final ascent. The time of this exposure is known as the Bottom Time of the dive. This is normally recorded in minutes and is used in our calculations.

We must consider what happens in the human body during these exposures to depths below 10 metres. Nitrogen in the high-pressure air we breathe is dissolved and carried in solution in the bloodstream. This nitrogen is absorbed readily by fatty tissues and gradually by tissues like cartilage, in proportion to the partial pressure of the nitrogen in the breathing air at depth. The deeper the dive, the greater the pressure, then the more nitrogen the body will absorb. At depths below 25 metres, the presence of nitrogen alone has been known to produce a narcotic effect. This is considered to be dangerous as Nitrogen Narcosis, even in mild form, can lead to confusion in the mind and lack of co-ordination. It is therefore important that, as narcosis may not have been detected by the diver, no underwater calculations should be relied upon. Any calculations required during a dive should be done on the surface beforehand and the dive planned accordingly. One golden rule, often forgotten, is that having produced the dive plan—'Stick to it', even though you are still warm and may want to finish your air. The surface cover will be unaware of any changes in your plan and may raise the alarm unnecessarily.

We note the bottom time of the dive and as the ascent begins we enter the decompression phase. The compression phase is the dive duration until commencing ascent. The speed of the ascent should not exceed 18 metres per minute vertically. This rate will allow the pressure to be reduced under control. The tissues now begin to give up the stored nitrogen into the blood stream again as a liquid. This is returned to the lungs for exhaust as a gas via the demand valve to the sea. If, however, the ascent is made at an excessive rate, then the nitrogen will return to its normal gaseous state within the tissues and the blood, and in many cases this will give rise to decompression sickness. At this stage we must learn to appreciate that there is a difference between 'sickness', and decompression 'accidents' which are usually those caused by expanding air within the body, eg reversed ear, embolism, burst lung, divers colic, etc.

The circulation of the blood governs the rate at which the nitrogen can be eliminated; the less irrigated parts of the body, like cartilage, are the slowest to clear. Circulation rate is dependant on temperature, fitness, age, amount of work being done and emotional attitudes, like fear or anxiety. It takes up to 12 hours after a dive for the nitrogen to be eliminated completely.

As an analogy, we may shake a bottle of sparkling lemonade and wait for the gas to dissolve, when the liquid will appear quite still. This ' stillness ' would remain if it were possible to release the stopper slowly and the pressure within the bottle to be reduced under control. However, if the stopper is removed quickly, the liquid will take on its normal gaseous or fizzy state as the dissolved gas is given up, following the drop in pressure.

It is with the prevention of these bubbles, which would form in the body of a diver who has failed to execute the correct rate of ascent and other decompression procedures, that we must concern ourselves when considering safe decompression.

A great deal of research has been done since 1861 when Bucquoy published the first account of the hazards of working in compressed air, and the need to decompress slowly. The latest Royal Navy tables provide information for practical duration times for depths to 60 metres. We can also see that there is a time limit given in minutes for each depth increment of 5 metres below 10 metres; for example, 15 metres (80 minutes), 30 metres (20 minutes). These times are known as the Maximum No-Stop Times. By diving within these we satisfy the rules of decompression by ascending not faster than 18 metres per minute, the normal rate of ascent. If we dive beyond these limits, we can no longer return directly to the surface. We must pay certain time penalties according to the Decompression Tables at one or more stages. These penalties are known as Decompression Stops or Stages. They should ensure that the dangerous excess nitrogen has been given up by the body before returning to the normal pressure of the surface. Stops should be executed while the diver rests and maintains the correct depth with the aid of a weighted shot rope hanging below him, from the surface, and marked at the required depths. It is a wise precaution to attach a spare aqualung at the lower stop in case more air is needed during decompression. These stops are employed because it is not practical to slow the ascent sufficiently to take, for instance, 20 minutes to rise only 3 metres. The correct way of timing these stops is important. The time required at the first stop, which will be the deeper if more than one, is timed from beginning the ascent, as the decompression phase is entered. Therefore some time will have elapsed before reaching the depth of the stop, and it is only the balance of this time that must be spent there. The time to be spent at the next level will begin from leaving the previous one, and so on to the surface. The total time for decompression will therefore include the time taken for the actual ascent.

The correct use of Decompression Tables needs explanation. If the maximum depth of the dive falls between the depths shown in the tables, then the deeper one is used in the calculation even though this maximum may not be the depth at which most of the duration time was spent. Similarly for the time shown in minutes; for instance, a duration time of 66 minutes requires that the 70 minutes column is used in the table.

You will see that Limiting Lines appear on the RN Tables for each depth. Diving must not be attempted below these lines unless many other precautions have been made to ensure the divers' safety, a Compression Chamber is immediately available and manned under the supervision of a diving doctor. There must also be facilities for the correct execution of decompression stops during any weather conditions and wave height. Even so it is better to leave this type of diving to the professionals.

We must understand there is a large degree of biological variation between individuals and from day to day. Even very small changes in the atmospheric pressure have caused decompression sickness. A party of divers, having finished the day's diving, took a coach trip into the mountains and became ill. There is also a hazard in flying after a dive. The Royal Air Force limit flying to 600 metres for 48 hours after a dive. The reduced pressure at altitude can turn a No-stop dive into a decompression incident.

Cases have, however, been known of divers returning from as long as 720 minutes at 30 metres (NST 20 minutes!) without decompression stops with no ill effects. On the other hand, sickness has occurred after returning from as short a period as 4 minutes at 30 metres.

While it is possible to produce a graphical representation in the form of a curve for the No-stop times at each depth, it does not take all these variations into account. The No-stop curve represents the average from a collection of curves from different individuals, and does not guarantee safe diving for everyone. Cases of sickness even after correct decompression exist, but are few and far between. Resistance to sickness can be strengthened by working up to deep dives by a process of acclimatisation. If any alcohol is present in the system during a dive, it will serve only to aggravate an already complex problem, hence the divers' saying, ' The dive starts the night before '. This includes avoiding an excess of *anything*!

See also items following RN Air Decompression Tables.

LOW VISIBILITY DIVING

As a result of diving experience in murky waters it is apparent that some of the conceptions of true free diving must be amended to meet the typical conditions of low visibility so often encountered in both inland and coastal waters.

Conditions envisaged are :

1   Very low or nil visibility.
2   Confined diving area.
3   Underwater obstacles of largely unknown position.

To counter such conditions several adaptations of normal free diving techniques become necessary, viz :

1   In very low visibility, ie below 1 metre, a diver is often very much better off diving alone. Two divers in such conditions are liable to get in each other's way, get tangled up and probably displace equipment.

2   There must be a positive and reliable link between the diver and a surface tender, ie a signal rope.

3   A pre-arranged code of diver-surface tender signals must always be used.

4   The surface tender must be a responsible and experienced diver himself and in complete sympathy with his charge.

To the diver, groping along, blind, in mud and obstructions, it is a most comforting feeling to know that he is in the charge of an experienced and competent handler who appreciates his feelings.

A good standby diver should be ready, fully equipped, his mask on his forehead, really standing by and not laughing and joking with others of the surface party.

The standby diver should have a good knowledge of what could go wrong and have worked out his procedure for dealing with emergencies. He should also know that if the diver gives the emergency signal he should go down the SIGNAL line, so that he is sure of getting straight to the man in difficulties.

A spare breathing set should be kept at hand for a dire emergency when, for instance, a diver may be trapped under water and needs to be kept supplied with air whilst he is being freed.

A diver surfacing in a confined area, eg between boats, pontoons, or other surface obstructions, should always be hauled to the surface so that his surfacing position is controlled by his tender. It is unlikely that this type of diving would be undertaken in depths where considerations of decompression stops need be taken into account, but should this be the case the diver should be hauled up a a rate of 20 metres per minute and the necessary decompression stops strictly observed.

The question of whether or not to use a shot line in such conditions (in addition to the signal line) is largely dependent on the type of diving being done. If a definite object is being sought or a particular area being worked on, a semi-permanent mark of this type—or a long sounding pole—is definitely an asset. It provides a fixed datum point from which to work and saves much time in position fixing.

Divers should not discard their fins for this type of diving although they may be obliged to walk on the bottom rather than fin. The danger in diving without fins lies in the lack of positive control in free water and when on the surface.

The surface tender should keep a close and careful watch on the diver's exhaust bubbles. For his part the diver should keep up a steady, regular breathing rhythm.

All signals should be positive and distinctive with good, long rope travel and should invariably be answered—with the exception of the 'Emergency' signal, which should be acted on immediately. The failure by the diver to answer any other signal should be considered an emergency.

General Hints

Diving in really low visibilities can be thoroughly unnerving and must not be taken on lightly, or by inexperienced members. The possibilities of the development of claustrophobia are high, and the risk of sudden panic always present. Underwater movement should be slow, deliberate and exploratory.

With growing experience comes the ability to master the grave difficulties, and the technical ability to carry out quite comprehensive surveys and searches by touch alone or by the sight of only small sections of objects and surroundings.

An efficient knife must always be carried in an accessible place, and a torch is essential. It is probable that it will not be possible also to carry a snorkel tube, but it is reasonable to accept the risk of leaving it ashore, especially as the diver is roped, and can be hauled to the boat or bank on his back if exhausted.

Care must be taken to avoid fouling breathing tubes or other equipment on underwater obstructions. If such a thing does occur the diver should keep calm and try and disentangle himself in a slow and deliberate manner. He should always try to back out of such obstructions on the assumption that the way he went in was clear.

If, for considerations of decompression, it is necessary for the diver to make a slow ascent in water of such low visibility that the ascent rate cannot be accurately judged, he should overweight and allow his surface tender to control his rate of ascent by hauling him up against his weight.

DEEP DIVING

An obvious starting point for any consideration of the practice of deep diving is some attempt to define exactly what we mean by a ' deep dive '. A short answer could well be that it is a dive to depths twice that of one's previous dives on average. Thus, to the diver who has been content with depths of 9 to 12 metres a drop of 18 to 24 metres should be considered a deep dive; to the club diver who has made a number of dives to 18- and 21-metre level a descent to 36 metres is a major step and not to be undertaken lightly. However, the ' ton-up ' diver who frequents the 15 fathom mark should think seriously when contemplating the ' double-ton '. In general, then, depth is a matter of degree. But, for the purposes of sport diving, any dive in excess of 27 or 30 metres should be considered as a ' deeper dive ' and planned accordingly.

One further point : everything that follows is written on the assumption that the diver is physically fit, is in diving practice, without outside anxieties and not over-tired due to working strain or long distance driving. This man is in a position to plunge where he will—with due regard to all that is set out below—but the one who gives a doubtful ' yes ' to these requirements is well-advised to dive warily. Much enjoyment can be found at lesser depths—indeed, some say the greatest enjoyment and interest—and here should stay the diver who is slightly overweight, who has ' not yet had a dip this season ', who was late at the office yesterday, who found the traffic heavy or says that the ' last ten miles nearly killed me '. Let 15 to 18 metres be the limit for these people and they and their families and companions can enjoy their diving. A normal Branch or Club outing of members with varied experience, and probably even more varied equipment, would be well advised to limit themselves to 30 metres. If dives to greater depths are required then they should be meticulously planned and carefully manned, probably the joint effort of two, or even three, smaller branches. The 60 metre and 30 fathom mark should be sufficient for the depth-hounds who must get it out of their systems. Deeper dives no doubt are possible, sometimes may be necessary, but are hardly ever desirable for the sporting diver to undertake. The working diver rarely exceeds 15 metres, the experimental diver may not start till 60 metres, only the exhibitionist diver will wish to meet him there.

In considering the problems proper to deep diving, it is necessary to dispel the idea that the difficulties arise merely because there is a greater body of water than normal above the diver—like so many extra hurdles in a steeplechase. The problems increase in complexity and danger in greater proportion, in fact, than the mere accumulation of water, and for convenience we shall consider them under three headings : first, those which affect the diver physically; second, those which have a physiological effect; finally, the psychological aspects of increasing depth.

Elsewhere the facts and figures of increasing pressure with depth and of the general effects this increase has on the gases breathed by the diver and upon his body itself have been explained (*see Decompression*). Let these facts be reviewed in conjunction with what follows.

Physical effects

The primary factor here is to realise that by venturing deeper the diver is placing himself further than normal from his natural environment, from his bodily requirements and 'creature comforts'. Exposure and exhaustion are always to be considered by the diver, and as depth increases, added precautions must be taken. A base of operations which might be adequate for a dive to 12 to 18 metres will certainly not be so at greater depths and, again, pre-dive planning becomes not just desirable but essential.

The increasing pressures will affect the diver's buoyancy to a marked degree as he descends deeper. This is generally accepted but it is perhaps not appreciated that an average diver wearing a wet suit may well become negatively buoyant from 30 metres downwards and increasingly so as depth becomes greater. Further, the physical effort required increases just at the time buoyancy is lost and bodily reserves may be called upon in an emergency. The use of adjustable buoyancy lifejackets (ABLJ) (see *Lifejackets*), may assist at these times, but it must not be forgotten that they are primarily intended as a safety measure, not as a means of extending limits of safety. Coupled with the loss of buoyancy will come some loss of heat insulation due to the compression of the material of the suit ('wet' and 'dry' will both be affected here) and the lower levels of water are those having the lower temperatures. This is most marked in freshwater diving where the greater depths may well maintain a steady 4°C. As buoyancy and temperature decrease so will visibility, the water itself may be clear but light will become scarcer as the diver descends.

Physiological effects

Note should be taken of the purely physical action on the human frame of the 'weight' of water involved. The balancing of the pressures within the body cavities has already been noted and it can be argued that at the depths to which even the foolhardy might descend, the human frame is unaffected. But these cavities are surrounded by bone, muscle and other tissues which vary in condition from individual to individual, and from age group to age group. Movement under pressure calls for greater exertion of tissues which are already exerting themselves in their adaptation to the increased ambient pressure itself. Let the diver intending to go deep be very sure that his physical condition will match the burden he places on his frame. From 9 metres downwards, the diver becomes conscious of the 'weight' of water around him and is beginning to call upon his reserves of strength.

The rate of absorption of nitrogen depends upon a combination of time and depth. If the diver intends to descend to depths greater than 25 metres, he does so at the expense of the time factor and must watch very carefully the length of time of his dive, and before diving should carefully consult his dive-planning tables. At depths in excess of 35 metres he is almost certainly close to normal limits of nitrogen absorption. It must be remembered here that 'normality' applies to physically fit persons who are willing to accept some risk of decompression sickness only because there is the assured presence of full recompression facilities. 'Normality' does *not* apply to the run of sporting divers.

The toxic effects of oxygen under pressure occur as the oxygen content approaches two bars absolute pressure (10 metres) : but this, again, is an average figure and the individual diver may look for symptoms at lesser depths—from 7 metres onwards on occasion. Likewise a trace of carbon monoxide from a faulty compressor, barely discernible at the surface, may soon reach a partial pressure sufficient to affect the diver.

There may be academic argument that nitrogen under pressure is not narcotic, but there is no argument that depth has a narcotic effect and certain individuals may be affected from 20 metres onwards. Although these narcotic effects disappear on rising to lesser depths, this is no guarantee that the affected diver will be in a position to make the rise in time.

Psychological effects

These must vary with the individual and the practised diver may school himself to overcome many fears and inhibitions related to diving. Nevertheless it must be realised that any dive beyond normal limits will impose nervous strains not met before, whatever the mental capacity or endurance of the diver concerned. His own remoteness from base, low temperatures, low visibility, increased physical effort of movement and of breathing will all tend to impose nervous strain and bring nearer the onset of panic while making its control more difficult. Almost more to be feared is the frequent sense of well-being and supreme egoism which the more competent and practised diver may have at depth, and which can lead him to false decisions where only the one course of action can keep him alive.

If, then, the newly confident diver is proposing a deeper dive, let him first consider all these facts and then question himself—can he truthfully satisfy himself that he still considers the dive worth making?

Let him now find a more experienced diver to assist him in his project and make more certain the success of the venture. His chosen companion must be one who has been *beyond* the target depth on at least two or three occasions, thus fully understanding what is involved. What preparations should then be made?

Deep diving procedure

The following set of rules were printed in a past edition of *Triton* magazine. They were formulated by Dr N Flemming, the result of ten years of deep expedition diving. They are not offered as a set of inflexible cast-iron rules but rather as a guide to diving officers when preparing groups for deeper-than-usual dives.

1   Nobody should ever attempt to dive below 30 metres unless he is extremely fit, well rested, and has had a medical check and chest X-ray in the previous 12 months.

2   Nobody should ever attempt to dive to 30 metres or below unless he has dived to 15 metres for at least 15 minutes on the previous day, or to 30 metres for ten minutes in the previous week.

3   Nobody should ever dive to 30 metres or below unless he is a member of a team of at least four, and not more than ten, experienced divers.

4   Any dive to 30 metres or below should be from a large (10 metres +) powered vessel with an experienced boatman who has previously worked with divers, and is in addition to the minimum of four divers.

5   There should be no passengers of any sort on board. Photographers shouting ' hold that a minute ' cause frayed tempers, physical strain, and sweating. Surface photographs should be taken half an hour before or after the dive. Wives and girl-friends, whether divers or not, should not be on board unless they are actually on the deep-diving team. They cause anxiety, excitement, and can call forth unnecessary bravado, as well as taking up space.

6   A recompression chamber should be located before the dive, and means of getting there in a hurry arranged. There must be a car available, and someone to drive it, even if it's the car-owner that gets the bends.

7   There should be a dinghy with oars and outboard motor for picking up divers who surface away from the main boat.

8   If there is an appreciable current, a buoyant line can be streamed 100 metres or so over the stern, so that a drifting diver can swim to it and be hauled in.

9   A shot rope should be attached either to the moored boat, or to a buoy capable of supporting both divers in an emergency.

10   The shot weight should be at least 25 kilograms, and should be on the bottom.

11   If the divers are going to leave the shot they should use a distance line, follow a previously laid bottom line, or be attached to the surface by a life line.

12   The divers should descend in pairs, one diver definitely in charge, the other obeying all instructions. The standby diver should remain fully kitted up on the boat, and the fourth diver should be in charge on the surface, issuing instruction to the stand-by and boatman.

13   Both divers should wear adjustable buoyancy lifejackets, and be fully trained in their use.

14 The divers should carry depth gauges, watches, compasses, contents gauges, and knives. They should know their task on the bottom, and the decompression stages.

15 The descent should be by swimming or by electric tug. The divers should never descend by using excess weight. The buoyancy of the divers should be adjusted to allow for the loss of buoyancy of some 2 kilograms resulting from compression of wet suits at depth.

16 The divers should ascend at 18 metres per minute or slower, completely under control, and together.

17 Decompression should be carried out under relaxed conditions. If the divers are under weight, as they may be if they have used a lot of air and are wearing wet suits, keeping down to stops will be very exhausting.

18 The divers should be met at the first stop by the stand-by diver who keeps them under observation throughout decompression, either from beside them, or from the surface.

19 The ascent to the boat should be by way of a strong, safe ladder. Divers should immediately be de-kitted, warmed, dried, and de-briefed. Failure to make dives comfortable leads to anxiety and apprehension before subsequent dives.

20 No dive should ever be below 45 metres unless conditions are ideal and all members of the team have been gradually working up to this depth with daily dives for at least a week.

21 No dive should ever be below 60 metres on air. *Diving below 60 metres on air is like putting your head in a gas oven and asking a friend to time how long it takes for rigor mortis to set in.*

22 The discipline needed for diving must be impressed on the team before starting, and the organiser must have reason to believe that his instructions will be carried out promptly and accurately. Failure to come up to standard must result in dismissal from the team, not in lost tempers.

Personal equipment

This must be thoroughly checked. Demand valves which are satisfactory near the surface are not always so beyond 30 metres; harnesses must be well fitting; pressure gauges accurate and easily read; air should be of proven quality; weight belts must be faultless and adjusted for neutral buoyancy at the target depth; suits should be in good repair and well fitting with good overlaps at neck and ankles; ancillary equipment should be checked in good order and readily accessible—it should include knife, depth gauge, torch, compass and watch. An ABLJ is essential; it will raise the diver from depth, and may well save his life should he surface unconscious or uncontrolled.

Support party

This must be increased not only in number but in vigilance and quality. Standby divers must be equipped (one at least with experience at target depth) and have sufficient air for a full dive with a reserve set to take with them in emergency. One member should hold names, addresses, telephone numbers of any emergency services likely to be required and be able to initiate such services.

Surface cover, buoyancy and boats

These must be more than just adequate and must be completely reliable. Canoes and dinghies give way here to heavier, powered craft with no crowding and affording some protection.

If a shot rope is to be used, and it is highly desirable that it should be (the anchor chain is barely satisfactory), then it needs to be firmly anchored and positively buoyed—remember that it may well have to support the weight of two negatively buoyant divers endeavouring to pull themselves to the surface. Provision for a decompression stop may have to be made by marking the depth required—if a set is to be left for this purpose, see that its buoyancy is adjusted to be at least neutral, preferably slightly buoyant.

On making the descent

Make a thorough pre-dive check of your own and your companion's equipment—be thoroughly familiar with both. Is all equipment tightly secured—with compression of the body it will work loose and knife, watch, etc, may well slip round to an inaccessible position—and is it all there? As the descent is made, stop at your normal depth to check again that all is working correctly and equipment is to hand. Also check your buoyancy, you should still be positive. Check buoyancy again during the descent; it is better to drop and lose 2 kilograms of lead than to be negatively buoyant at target depth. If all reserve buoyancy is lost before the target depth is reached the descent should be halted and the dive re-planned.

AIR ENDURANCE

Air is needed to sustain life in all conditions and environments. For any given person the rate of breathing and the volume of air required for respiration is a *very variable* factor governed primarily by exertion, but also by nervous state, tension, cold, lung capacity, illness, age and other factors. It is obvious that it is impossible to lay down any hard and fast figure for an average consumption of air. Despite this, however, it is an advantage to establish with some degree of accuracy the quantity of air required for any given dive. For this purpose it is assumed that an experienced and relaxed diver under normal diving conditions will consume one cubic foot of air per minute at ambient pressure.

However, this figure is an assumption and the following points should be noted : to keep the consumption of air to this figure, or even improve upon it, it is important to have proper breathing control. A slow yet free breathing rhythm should be adopted and practised, and the degree of exertion controlled so that this rhythm is not disturbed. As a result of the slight restriction to breathing imposed by the aqualung when over-exerting or in a panic, the diver may commence taking rapid, deep breaths with the consequent possibility of over-breathing beyond the mechanical capabilities of the demand valve ('beating the lung'). This is very difficult nowadays, owing to the advanced design of valves. In such cases it is imperative to relax, remain calm and make conscious efforts to regain the normal breathing rhythm as quickly as possible. Lying in such a position in the water that the demand valve is below the level of the chest will assist this, as thereby air at slight positive pressure will be available. Lack of breathing control can easily reduce the duration of a dive by half through excessive air consumption.

It is important, however, not to attempt to prolong a dive by holding the breath, because if held too long it may cause anoxia; the risk of an air embolism if held on the ascent; or the possibility of a build-up of carbon dioxide if practised at the greater depths. A slow and steady breathing rhythm at all times will help to avoid most of the respiratory difficulties that may beset the free diver.

All dives should be planned; by this is meant that sufficient air should always be made available for the dive on hand. The factors influencing the air rate required are rate of consumption, depth and duration. In order to enable the diver to breathe, air is supplied by the demand valve at ambient pressure, ie at the pressure of the surrounding water. Thus, to maintain air at ambient pressure a larger mass of air is required at depth than at the surface. The mass required is directly proportional to the depth when measured in bars. Thus, twice the mass of air is used at 10 metres, where the pressure is two bars, than at the surface where the pressure is one bar, and the endurance of an air supply will be halved at this depth. From this fact one can work out a rough figure for a dive at a given depth, but there are so many variables that this calculation is seldom accurate.

Apart from careful dive planning, the diver has various ways of determining the quantity of air remaining in his cylinders and means of knowing when this supply is nearing exhaustion.

Some breathing sets are provided with a pressure gauge. This enables the diver to see at the commencement and at any time during the dive exactly how much air remains in the cylinders. Others incorporate a reserve device in the cylinder valve which curtails the air flow when a small pre-determined percentage remains in the cylinder. Operation of the reserve lever when a restriction to breathing is felt makes this air available. This is usually arranged to be sufficient to allow an ascent without stops at the normal rate of 18 metres per minute.

As a rough guide when using the above systems the diver should ascend when the pressure gauge falls to 30 bars, when the reserve lever is operated, or when half a cylinder of air remains when using a twin-bottle decanting system. In all cases the diver should commence the ascent with an adequate supply of air to reach the surface.

None of these systems is infallible, however. The divers should always take care to ascertain the quantity of air in their cylinders prior to the dive and to ensure that it is sufficient for the dive planned. If through carelessness or other reason the air supply is allowed to run out completely the breathing set should not be abandoned. At moderate depths the air supply does not fail abruptly, but a gradual increasing restriction to breathing is felt. The diver should fin up, but continue to draw what air he can from the cylinder, but at no time holding his breath. As depth decreases breathing becomes easier. This is due to the demand valve reacting to the reduced water pressure and releasing the low-pressure air remaining in the cylinder.

At depths in excess of 9 metres, due to the larger quantity of air required and the greater friction in the demand and cylinder valves, the failure of air supply is much more abrupt and very little warning is given. For the initial part of the ascent, therefore, it may be necessary to fin up, exhaling as necessary to avoid the risk of burst lung, but retaining the mouthpiece in position until air is again available from the cylinders, (see *Emergency Ascents*).

DIVING UNDER ICE

In common with night diving, diving under ice needs more than the usual amount of pre-dive planning. A diver lost under ice has only literally minutes of life left if not found. He cannot float for hours on the surface or call to the lookout. In fact he is lucky if he succumbs to the cold before his air gives out.

Planning items should include nylon rope and warm clothes, with hot drinks available at the surface. Also a heavy instrument capable of breaking the ice from above. And don't just assume that you have an instrument capable of doing this quickly—try it out on site. If it takes you ages to break an entry hole imagine how it would be with an air-starved diver underneath.

Cold is always a great danger, with the head and neck particularly vulnerable. Intense cold around the head or neck could easily lead to fainting. If a dry suit is worn, wear a 'wet' hood under the dry hood. Where a wet suit is worn, bring a large vacuum flask of very warm water with you and pour it into the suit before you get into the water. This applies particularly to the hands. If your hands are cold before you submerge, they will never get warm.

Much pre-dive planning depends upon the thickness of the ice, but always wear a knife with at least one serrated edge; and a compass; also, if the ice is not thicker than the length of the blade of your knife, a snorkel with a red or fluorescent pink tip. (If that last bit sounds peculiar, there is no point carrying a snorkel if your knife cannot chip a hole deep enough to reach the surface air.)

In general it is best for diving to be carried out in conjunction with a surface line, and the line should never be paid out more than 10 metres horizontally. It is better, and safer, to dive vertically down a shot line. And pay particular attention if there is a current of any sort. If a diver gets detached from the line in a current, he is as good as lost.

Always prepare for an emergency. The surface team should have a pre-arranged plan to swing into action in case a diver does not surface, or loses the line. And the diver(s) should be prepared for the eventuality of losing the line or direction of entry.

Always break the entry hole at the edge of the water. Thus if the diver does lose his way, or line, a compass will bring him back to a point where he can find his way out, or where the surface party can be of greatest assistance.

What if the diver does get lost? The simplest procedure, if the ice is thin enough, is to chip a hole for his snorkel and push this through. The lookout should easily be able to see the bright pink tip of the snorkel above the ice and race into action.

If the ice is too thick, or the lookout isn't looking out, scrape a rough square or circle under the ice with the serrated edge of your knife. Then swim in ever increasing 'circular sweep' circles, continually drawing a line under the ice with your knife, keeping the line you drew last time round always a few metres to your left (or to your right if you are left handed). In this way you can swing gradually away from your original point while searching for the exit without wasting time covering the same area.

The snorkel, if not attached to the mask, should be secured with a short length of line so that it cannot get lost. Likewise, a length of line should attach the knife to a secure point. The line could be tucked behind the sheath so that it is no encumbrance while not in use. You certainly don't want to lose your knife—and you've no time to start looking for it if you do.

It cannot be over emphasised—a lost diver is a dying diver. If the surface party are in any doubt whatever about events, the line should be hauled in, or the rescue team flung into operation.

NIGHT DIVING

Diving at night under ideal conditions can be a fascinating way to dive. The introduction of artificial light adds a new dimension to the underwater world. The diver can observe the quite different behaviour patterns of the underwater fauna and be enchanted at the apparent tameness of some species when mesmerised by a torch beam. On the other hand, night diving under conditions which are less than ideal can turn out to be a nerve-racking and extremely hazardous undertaking.

It is becoming increasingly popular with branches to incorporate a night dive with a beach barbecue, let us therefore study this type of dive in some detail. It would entail having a large number of divers in the water at one time to enable them to participate in the revelry and take advantage of the hot food and bonfire after the dive. The quality of this dive, in common with any large dive, would be in proportion to the organisation and prior preparation which had been put into it. The primary hazard which has to be countered is that of the diver becoming separated from the main party and being swept out to sea with no means of attracting attention to his plight. If this should happen it can be seen that rescue would be very unlikely until the following morning, by which time the diver would reckon himself lucky to be alive. It is clear therefore that the organisation must at all costs prevent this type of situation occurring. The dive marshal should choose his site very carefully, it should be well known to him under normal daylight diving conditions so that he can predict the type of bottom to be expected and the currents, if any, which will be encountered. The water should be sheltered, preferably by a headland or reef, etc and the boundaries of the diving site should be clearly defined. Natural boundaries should be utilised where they exist and these are linked up with artificial boundaries in the form of underwater guide lines. All diving should take place within this designated area, which may vary in size according to the natural conditions, the resources available and the number of divers being catered for, but should not exceed approximately a 100 metres square. The area should

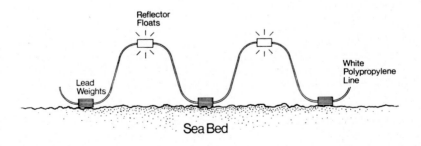

be buoyed so that it may be clearly identified by the surface cover. The siting of the barbecue bonfire is worth considering at this stage as it can **be a useful homing** beacon for the returning divers as well as possibly providing some illumination for the surface cover.

The dive marshal should ensure that his divers are competent and have logged several dives before attempting a night dive. There is a considerable psychological barrier to be overcome on entering the sea at night for the first time and a diver needs complete confidence in himself, his equipment and his partner if he is to overcome this handicap and enjoy the dive. It is, therefore, essential that a newcomer should be accompanied by a diver experienced in night diving from whom he can draw confidence. Divers should be paired off with buddy lines of some six to twelve feet in length, this minimises the danger of separation and aids communication between them. Each diver MUST have a torch and should be instructed that if one torch fails the pair should terminate the dive immediately, for if the second torch should fail the divers would have great difficulty attracting the attention of the surface cover if they are required.

A careful pre-dive briefing should be given to ensure that the divers understand how the dive area has been defined and that they do not wander out of it. They should be logged in and out of the water by a member of the shore party so that the marshal would know immediately if any one is overdue. Diver recall, if necessary, should be by means of a weighted thunderflash.

Surface cover should be provided in the form of a boat, preferably 4-5 metres long, either made fast to the down tide marker buoy or rowed along the down tide base line. The boat's motor should be used only for emergencies as the crew would have difficulty hearing a call for assistance and a rotating propeller would be very dangerous so close to the diving site. The divers could snorkel to the dive area or be ferried there by boats other than the rescue boat mentioned above. Unnecessary torch waving on the surface should be discouraged and a surface ' come and get me ' signal arranged, the recommended signal would be continually swinging the torch in a wide horizontal arc which includes the area you wish to attract.

Underwater signals can be made in the normal way providing the diver shines his torch onto HIS signal and not into his partner's face. This is a common fault and, of course, merely dazzles his partner who will be unable to see any signal for some considerable time afterwards.

Depths greater than 10-15 metres would not be expected with the type of enclosed site described above; it is possible to dive at greater depths if a vertical cliff face is used as the dive area and guide lines are run vertically down the cliff to define the horizontal limits of the site. This type of site is unlikely to be sufficiently sheltered around Britain, however, but can often be utilised in milder seas, eg the Mediterranean.

Drift diving at night is a further possibility, but only a very limited number of divers could be catered for and the hazards are greatly increased. It could be accomplished by the divers being attached to a normal drift line and buoy with the covering boat also firmly attached to the drift buoy with an extended painter. In this way the divers can drift in their desired direction and the boat can follow the buoy without the possibility of becoming separated from it. The boat should be rowed after the buoy or trouble will certainly be experienced with fouling the propeller on the long painter. Diver recall is easily accomplished, but is more likely to be required with this type of dive due to boat traffic. The surface boat should carry recognition lights to warn vessels not to approach too close, these are two red lights in a vertical line with a white light between them. This type of night dive is less likely to be as rewarding as a free dive in an enclosed area and carries a much greater risk if separation should occur, it is therefore not recommended except in exceptional circumstances.

Most satisfaction can be obtained from night diving by selecting a small area and studying it in detail. The underwater fauna will be found to behave quite differently when encountered at night time. Animals which normally ' hole up ' during the day, eg crabs, lobsters, conger, etc will often be found in the open. Normally timid fish can now be mesmerised by the torch beam and studied closely and even handled in some cases.

In addition to observing the new behaviour patterns of fish, etc we have the added benefit of colour. The light found underwater is unnatural to our eyes in that most of the visible spectrum has been filtered out and we are left with a predominantly blue-green illumination which distorts our conception of the colour of underwater objects. By introducing artificial light we can illuminate the underwater scene with a full spectrum and thus reveal the riot of colour which truely exists. Weeds and sponges which appear black by daylight are seen as bright scarlet and deep purple, etc in the beam of the torch. Contrast and shadows are restored and the shape of objects can be seen more readily in the directional beam of light. The diffuse daylight normally encountered hinders the recognition of objects, because of its lack of directionality.

The modelling effect and the complete colour spectrum of the artificial light is a boon to the underwater photographer. The full benefit of colour film can now be exploited with the subject standing out against a black background instead of being framed in the normal luminescent blue-green water.

As with any form of sport diving, night diving is pointless in poor visibility conditions, but the apparent visibility encountered at night can seem better than similar conditions by day due to the shorter range at which objects are studied. This is due to the limited range of the torch and the diver tends to look at objects much closer to him, a similar effect to the increase in apparent visibility experienced when diving under kelp. The range of a diver's vision is obviously linked to the power of the lamp he is using as well as the prevailing visibility, and generally the more powerful the lamp the better the diver is able to see. There is a limit, however, to the power available to a free diver without resorting to surface supply lines or underwater vehicles, this is around 50 watts with about an hour's duration—anything more than this tends to be very bulky and unmanageable—and expensive! There are a number of pressure-proofed hand lamps on the market with outputs of 5-10 watts, these are very easily handled underwater and give an adequate level of illumination for general sport diving, but they are still relatively expensive. A rather poor, but nevertheless cheaper, substitute is to purchase an expendable free flooding torch for the dive. Normal torches work quite reliably underwater when flooded, but the onset of rapid corrosion quickly renders them useless on returning to the surface. Thus for night diving addicts the most powerful pressure-proof model one can afford is recommended. The torch should be fitted with a lanyard and slipped over the diver's wrist as his torch is virtually his only means of attracting attention on the surface—he cannot afford to lose it.

After some time, when the divers have gained confidence in their surroundings, they should turn off their torches for a while and will be amazed at the quantity of natural light which exists underwater. Their every movement is accompanied by what appears to be a shower of sparks, but is phosphorescent-plankton which gives off a bright luminous glow when agitated. Many weeds, etc can be seen glowing quite strongly when the diver's eyes have become dark adapted. It is also surprising how much light from the moon and stars is transmitted below the surface on a clear night.

To conclude, a well organised night dive on a calm and warm summer's night with the promise of hot drinks and a large bonfire on returning to the shore can be the ultimate way of diving. There are many snags, however, which if not taken care of before the event could mar the proceedings and even have tragic consequences. It is essential, therefore, that night dives should be organised by experienced marshals on the lines explained above and novices should gain confidence and experience with a number of daytime dives before attempting this fascinating facet of the sport.

Suggested form of boundary marker/guide line

This pattern has been proved over a number of years and consists of a reel containing about 200 metres of 3 centimetre circumference white polypropylene line weighted at 2 metre intervals with a piece of sheet lead wrapped around the line. At points midway between the weights, wooden floats covered with 'Scotch' reflecting tape are attached. The weighted line thus lays along the sea floor in a series of loops and is clearly marked by the reflection from the floats. In relatively open terrain it is impossible to miss this form of boundary marker and if coloured reflector tape is used on the buoys the diver is made aware of his position in the designated area. This form of marker is of little use, however, in heavily weeded areas, eg kelp forests—this type of terrain is best avoided unless natural boundaries exist to prevent divers from wandering too far afield.

CAVE DIVING

Cave diving, usually with the aid of underwater breathing equipment, involves the penetration and exploration of submerged tubes, tunnels or passages in rock strata which are in the process of formation and subject to sudden and violent change. Ideally participants need certain attributes additional to those required by an open water diver. These additional attributes include an understanding and knowledge of caves which can only be gained by practical study of caves in various stages of formation prior to a continued study by means of diving of submerged sections, a greater degree of physical fitness and thorough theoretical and practical appreciation of diving equipment. The potential cave diver will also need an advanced level of diving expertise to allow the complex techniques of cave diving to be mastered, and a certain philosophy or attitude of mind to allow these techniques to be mastered in cave diving conditions.

Deficiencies in any or all of these ideal requirements are variously described as courageous, irresponsible or stupid. The object of this article is to indicate the situations which arise in cave diving, the techniques used, and to suggest a minimum standard of diving ability to cope with them. Attainment of this minimum standard does not imply capability to participate in cave diving.

One of the attributes of an experienced speleologist is a detailed experience of the possible body contortions, methods of controlled breathing and selective muscle relaxation, necessary to ease the body through passages of small cross section. In these situations temporary moments of panic, by the less experienced, manifest by jerky movements, usually of the head or limbs. In the cave diving situation where the cylinder may be jammed under the body and the air line stretched taut, such movements could wrench out the mouthpiece and prove fatal. An ability to complete these bodily contortions in a reverse direction is advantageous when further progress or turning round becomes impossible.

The open water diver does not usually encounter loose rocks on the under water sea cliffs or caves as the vigorous movement of the sea rolls them to the lowest position. However, in the gently flowing waters of submerged cave passages, it is possible for some parts of the roof and walls to be preferentially dissolved, leaving large pendants or flakes of rock so delicately secured, that even the movement of the water caused by the diver is sufficient to dislodge them. An experienced speleologist would be more likely to recognise passages of this type by sight and feel. Harmless clay banks can behave in a thixotropic manner when disturbed by a diver and flow across the passage as liquid mud. A firm shingle floor under flowing water can become quite mobile when a diver is forced by a low roof to squirm against it. The resulting debris can quickly consolidate the diver's position.

Visibility in syphons can vary from perfect clarity to the complete blackness at the bottom of a pool in a peat bog. An upstream dive into a large clean rock passage can in some instances remain absolutely clear from entry to return. However, emergence at an upstream end into a muddy stream bed could easily cloud the water for the return dive. At the other extreme when a small muddy downstream syphon is approached by walking down the muddy stream bed the visibility is zero when the dive commences. It is sometimes possible to swim faster than the flow of water in the passage and enter clear water on the inward journey but body and fins inevitably stir up the mud for the return journey.

In view of the foregoing it would be most unwise to proceed with any part of a cave dive in which the return journey depended on the assumption that the visibility would remain good. The significance of the loss of visibility will become apparent if you go to the middle of the swimming pool, close your eyes, do a few turns and somersaults and then, still with your eyes closed, try and swim back to a particular corner without touching the bottom. It would be possible perhaps to count the tiles on the way out and then return counting tiles by touch alone. The extent to which this technique can be used in a cave is limited by the fact that any irregularities on the bottom are not symetrically dispersed and the fingers can become numbed before the return journey. Obviously some form of guide line must be used to assist the return journey and the use of lines is probably one of the most important techniques to be learnt.

I will assume that the novice or trainee will use fins and first enter a syphon which is known to be simple and already has a guide line in place. A simple syphon is one without any awkward bends, tight sections or humanly impenetrable fissures, which the guide line can pull into. The guide line can be taut or slack, thick or thin, a floating line clinging to the roof or a heavy line lying on the bottom. Whatever kind of line, it is essential to treat it as a GUIDE line and not as a means of hauling yourself through syphons. There are rare exceptions where a line has been recently laid specifically for this latter purpose. The object is to swim along next to the line without disturbing its position. If the line is close to the roof, swim under it, if it presses against one wall and then the next, change sides, do not try to pull it away from the wall. Continuous contact with the line is made possible by passing it through a loose eye formed between the forefinger and thumb, the last three fingers are used to grip it lightly to assess actual rate of progress when ascending, descending, and going with or against the current. It is unwise to break contact with the line under any circumstances and particularly with a slack floating line when part of a coil of slack is observed through murky water because there is a good chance that you will grab the line back to front with the possibility of returning unwittingly towards the end which you have just left. It is also possible to grab a useless piece of abandoned line. Always note the colour and type of line and if you arrive at a knot, pass it close to your face mask and note what the next section of line looks like.

Use of non fixed lines

At first sight the most simple method of laying a line is to tie it round your arm just above the elbow and swim into the syphon whilst somebody pays it out from base. The fact that the line is tied above the elbow allows unrestricted movement of the hand without jerking on the rope. Indeed, for short simple syphons, this is a perfectly adequate method. Signals can be transmitted by a sequence of jerks on the rope to indicate whether more or less line is to be paid out. However, as the length of line paid out increases and the passage curves, it becomes more difficult for the diver to drag the line and signals become less distinct. Further, if the curves contain horizontal cracks or fissures it is possible that on the return journey the person at base will be pulling the the line through a fissure which the diver cannot enter.

Laying lines

Hence, as the length and complexity of the syphon increases, the diver has to secure the line at base and accept sole responsibility for the paying out and laying of the line during the inward journey in such a manner that it will assist him on the way out. The problems can be appreciated by imagining a wide cave passage one metre high with a maze fixed to the floor and a 15 cm gap between the top of the maze and the roof. The difficulties of finding the way in and out in zero visibility have already been outlined but it is also apparent that if a floating line was paid out in the above circumstances it could slip into the small gap between the top of the maze and the roof and be ineffective. To rely on the line completely would involve either tying it at each corner or securing it with a weight or peg. In practise, a combination of both the use of memory and securing the line is used. Most open water divers will have some experience of finding their way round the sea bed, in poor visibility, by memory but it is possible to develop the technique of using touch alone in open water by means of a blacked out mask.

Equally valuable practise can be obtained in open water in laying, following and recovering lines at night or with a blacked out mask. Experience in the above circumstances is unlikely to be a complete substitute for actual experience in cave diving conditions where the influence of roof and walls has to be considered.

The methods of paying out the line includes simply holding coils loosely in the hand and letting them slip through finger and thumb, a variety of simple reel mechanisms to a complicated device in which a line reel filled by means of a handle is fitted to a board containing a front searchlight and rear shielded light shining on to compass, depth gauge, writing cards, etc. The most beneficial innovation would be a method of reeling in the line one handed.

Equipment

Wet suits are used predominantly, and frequently they are worn for many hours and much arduous work before the dive commences, hence they should be well fitting and comfortable. One-piece suits avoid the discomfort of a crotch strap and additional layers of neoprene at the knees and elbows are useful. If a miner's helmet is not worn during the dive, extra layers of neoprene inside the skull of the hood are a useful but poor substitute. A helmet should have an adjustable headband in order to be functional with and without a hood.

The mask should be as small as possible and free from refinements. A knife is essential for cutting lines but sharpness is more important than size and if steel telephone cable is being used as a line, a pair of stainless steel pliers should be borrowed. The advantages of a quick release weight belt are debatable but it is essential that it cannot be inadvertently released and the open water reaction to pull the pin at the first sign of trouble must be suppressed. Weights that will stay in any given position are preferred.

Demand Valves

Twin hose valves are completely unsuitable for cave diving. On the other hand it should not be necessary to boost one's confidence by buying the most expensive or complicated single hose valve available. For cave diving purposes the two stage single hose varieties are inherently more suitable and the more simple ones are easier to service in the confines of a cave, should the need arise. The valve should have a small dead space in the mouthpiece so that it can be inserted into the mouth in the flooded condition and breathed from directly, without the need to purge and without the floodwater shooting to the back of the throat in a compact mass. The valve should be robust, and frequently a gauge high pressure tube is fitted instead of the normal low pressure tube to the mouthpiece as these latter, although more flexible, have been known to burst. It is possible on some valves to exchange the low pressure relief valve and the low pressure outlet to the mouthpiece so that the gauge high pressure tube and mouthpiece low pressure tube come off in the same direction and towards the body reducing the risk of an impact causing a fracture. Two layers of nylon stocking should be stretched over the breathing orifice before the rubber mouthpiece is pushed on to prevent grit entering and lodging in the exhaust valve. The most important feature of the valve should be the owner's confidence in it providing this has arisen from experience with the valve, complemented by an understanding of the principles and mechanism by which it functions.

TECHNIQUES

Pillar Valves

Two principles are used to connect the demand valve to the cylinder, an 'O' ring with a screw fitting and the more common 'A' clamp fitting. The former is extremely reliable but not very common, a factor which could be very important in an emergency where large quantities of air are required to search for a diver or a diver is stranded in an air bell with an empty cylinder. The 'A' clamp as presented by the manufacturer is an enigma of design which should not work and frequently does not in spite of the liberal use of spanners and tommy bars and as such cannot be recommended for cave diving. Fortunately most of the 'A' clamp fittings can be rendered equally as secure as the screw type fitting by a simple modification which causes a round cross section 'O' ring pressed into the pillar valve to be used under the approximate conditions for which it was designed. This modification to the 'A' clamp fitting is effected by loosening the large 'A' clamp securing nut until about 0.5 mm of the spigot which presses onto the pillar valve 'O' ring is left protruding. The 'A' clamp is then placed on the valve in the normal way with the demand valve pipes suitably orientated, and whilst the thumb-screw is screwed finger tight in a clockwise direction the clamp is turned as far as it will go in an anti-clockwise direction. This provides a metal to metal contact between the pillar valve and the demand valve with the 'O' ring suitably compressed and protected from any further stress other than that provided when the air is turned on, at which stage the whole assembly becomes rigidly and safely fixed in position.

Fins

The main consideration to give to the use of fins, is that it is frequently necessary to climb into or out of syphons wearing them, as well as full diving equipment. It is also necessary to negotiate quite long sections of cave between syphons, without the assistance of non-diving sherpas. The dual purpose fins are too rigid to climb in without the blades removed and the most simple method is to carry a pair of plimsoles tucked in your belt.

Cylinders

The cylinder, including the first stage of the demand valve, should be about neutrally buoyant so that it does not pull too strongly on the mouthpiece if you have to push the cylinder in front of yourself through a small opening and let go of it to use both hands for other purposes. Equally a diver relying on his cylinders to maintain neutral buoyancy would become non-neutral in the above circumstances and have more difficulty manoeuvring.

The necessary capacity of the cylinder depends on the intended dive. It is usual to plan to finish the dive with $\frac{1}{3}$ to $\frac{1}{2}$ of the air unused as a reserve for any unexpected contingencies which may arise on the return journey, further, in view of the serious consequences of a breathing valve failure, it is not uncommon to carry two completely separate sets of breathing equipment, one of which is for emergency use only.

The cylinders are mounted on the side of the body with the valve under the arm-pit : either one 17 cm cylinder on each side or two 14 cm cylinders on one side. Harnesses are invariably home made and should allow for the fact that they may have to be removed and refitted in zero visibility and restricted conditions. The harness should also allow reasonable mobility out of the water when climbing or negotiating passages between syphons.

Standard of diving required

This is of course indeterminate but a suitable minimum standard is desirable. Unfortuately at the moment The Cave Diving Group of Great Britain, which facilitates liaison between various cave divers, does not set a standard on a national basis and it is left to each diver or group of divers to formulate their own tests. These usually assume a diver has reached at least 3rd class BSAC standard with considerable caving and open water diving experience with the type of breathing equipment he intends to use, ie open circuit or rebreathing, and could well include : Swimming down a 7 metre line to breathing equipment, fitting it, laying and recovering a 100 m line around obstacles, releasing the equipment and returning to the surface. Sharing a lung whilst following a 100 m line round obstacles involving stages where one diver has to go backwards simulating passage through a constricted space. The completion of an underwater task involving the use or assembly of mixed positively and neutrally buoyant objects. All the above tests to be carried out in zero visibility. The divers should, during this period, reach 2nd class BSAC standard and the training and tests should be followed by a graded introduction to ten cave dives of increasing complexity.

The training and test should be carried out by a representative of the cave divers who will be involved in any future rescue or recovery attempt.

SPEARFISHING

The hunting of fish underwater is a major sport with many thousands of enthusiastic followers, especially in countries like the United States and Australia where, generally speaking, conditions are ideal. In the Mediterranean, birthplace of modern spearfishing as we know it today, activity is somewhat restricted by regulations concerning the use of underwater breathing apparatus while hunting fish, but this in no way affects the serious spearfisherman who relies purely on his own lung-power. The world authority on the sport, CMAS, has its headquarters in Paris and regulates the World Spearfishing Championships. The expense of promoting the latter has risen to such an extent that they now take place bi-annually.

In Great Britain, interest in spearfishing has risen considerably in the past few years, especially in the competitive field. Largely due to sea conditions, this interest has been mainly confined to the South and West of England, although competitions are held on the Yorkshire coast and Ireland has great prospects. To satisfy the demand for more competition, inter-regional events are being planned, culminating in the National Championships.

It may be of interest to branch committees, branch diving officers and members to study the sport of spearfishing, to learn a little of the techniques and equipment involved and to note the relevant safety precautions.

Harpoon and Spear Guns

The simplest and most primitive weapon is the metal hand spear. Many types are available with and without wooden handles, with single, double or triple-pronged head (the latter being, of course, the trident).

From the hand spear came the development of the catapult principle involving the use of a short, hollow, cylindrical wooden sleeve fitted with a length of rubber. The spear was inserted into the sleeve and its end drawn back against the rubber which, on release, shot the spear through the wooden sleeve. A short line was usually attached to the spear so that it could be recovered.

Many obvious developments of this principle can be made, and the inventive spearfisherman can very easily produce a reasonably effective catapult gun of this type with simple materials.

Modern spear guns have developed far from the simple catapult type. They are extremely powerful weapons designed specially for underwater hunting and they are dangerous in the hands of innocent, thoughtless and unskilled people. There have been nasty accidents with them and it is as well to learn the rules of handling them and apply these rules from the start (see *Safety Precautions,* later this chapter).

Basically they break down into three main groups, classified according to the method of driving the harpoon from the gun to its target. The three kinds of power are : rubber slings, springs, and air or other compressed gases.

Spear guns employing rubber sling propulsion are in the first category. The main advantages claimed for these guns are that they can be lighter in construction than other more complicated types, are cheaper to manufacture and to buy. They can be made quite small, yet they are very powerful and their power can be varied by the addition or reduction of the number of propulsive rubber bands. While the rubber will ultimately stretch and lose its elasticity, it can easily be replaced at small cost. This type of gun is also easier to load in the water than compressed coil spring guns. It is triggered in the usual way.

The first commercially marketed spear gun employing an alternative method of propulsion was produced in 1937. This was the compressed spring gun, a type that still is very popular. The advantages claimed for it are that it is sturdier and stronger in construction than other types, making for steadiness and accuracy in use. There is no ' whip ' on firing, as there is with rubber bands, and no worry about the failure of the gun through the perishing of the bands. The whole weapon is more robust and harder wearing.

Finally, we come to the guns powered by compressed air or carbon dioxide. These guns are silent in operation under water and easy to load. They are generally more powerful than either of the other types and, as they involve fewer delicate parts, such as mechanical trigger devices, are less liable to breakdown. In most of these guns the charge of gas does not escape free into the water and is not therefore wasted after each firing. Many of these guns are supplied with small hand pumps by which the pressure in the power cylinder is maintained, although it is usually not necessary to pump them up more than once per season. Underwater hunters of really big game usually employ this type of gun, particularly in national and international competitions.

In all the cases mentioned above, methods are employed for the recovery of the harpoon projectile usually by nylon line which may either be fixed under a clip on the barrel of the gun or carried on a reel attached to the gun. Different forms of detachable harpoon heads are often employed, dependent on the fish being hunted and general conditions.

When buying harpoon guns, whatever the type, make sure that all parts are rustless; that loading operations can easily be carried out in the water; that they are fitted with effective safety catches, and that the firing mechanism is simple but effective.

Ancillary equipment

Spare harpoon heads are necessary. It should be established that they are of the right size and thread to fit the harpoon. Spare harpoons should be carried in case one is lost or bent.

Next, there is the loader for your gun. This is a most useful piece of equipment, for many of the guns mentioned need considerable force to ram home the harpoon until it engages on the rear of the trigger. The loader is a piece of metal or plastic that fits over the harpoon point with a leg on each side for gripping. With your hand thus protected, you can draw the harpoon down into the gun barrel against the strongest resistance.

A knife is even more useful and essential to a spearfisherman than it is to an ordinary skin diver. When one considers the amount of line involved in spearfishing and the many tortuous routes it can take from man to harpooned fish, the need becomes apparent—it is certainly not unknown for a diver to become entangled in it. As with all diving knives they should be carried in a sheath, preferably on the leg and never attached to a weight belt or equipment likely to be jettisoned. Cork handled or other floating types of knife are often preferred.

To avoid the necessity of returning to the shore or the boat with each catch, a fish holder of some type is required. Many underwater fishermen prefer a simple wire ring, consisting merely of a circle of wire broken in one place with the ends bent back so that they will clip together. The wire is passed through the fish's gills and the ends clipped together, the whole being hung on the diver's belt. Another popular device to retain fish is simply a piece of cod line with a short length of heavy gauge brass wire attached at the end. The latter is passed through the fish's mouth and out at the gills and then turned laterally. It must be emphasised that all fish must be killed by knife before transferring from the harpoon to the retaining ring or cord.

For crabs and lobsters a heavy Courlene or Terylene net bag with a cod-line drawstring will be found most suitable. When searching for crabs, lobsters or crayfish it is advisable to wear some form of glove, either a stout pair of leather gardening gloves or the latest type of tough rubber glove. This is not so much a protection from their claws or pincers but more to save the skin from the sharp spines and rough shells of most crustaceans. Do not take crustacea with guns or spears or damage them in any way.

One more item of equipment which has reached prominence in competitive spearfishing in the past two years is a good underwater torch. Some form of artificial illumination was found necessary in the Mediterranean to locate cave fish, especially grouper, and members of a British Isles team competing in World events have found themselves at a serious disadvantage to be without a good waterproof torch. In this country, a torch has proved to be a great help for searching out conger eels and lobsters in dark holes and small caves. The lantern type are probably the most powerful but tend to be rather bulky, and the traditional torch shape with ordinary dry batteries gives out a useful light in practice.

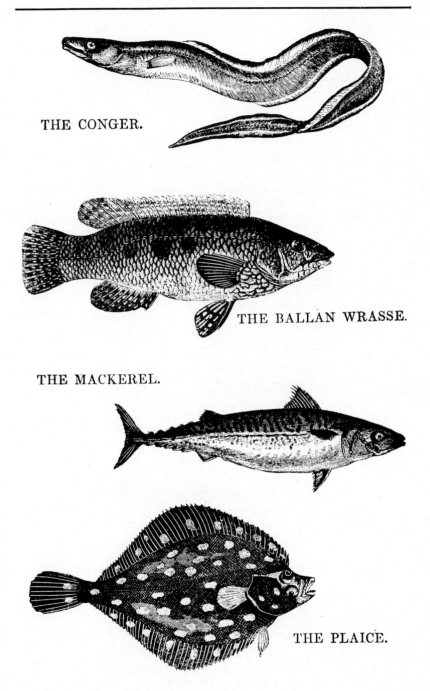

THE CONGER.

THE BALLAN WRASSE.

THE MACKEREL.

THE PLAICE.

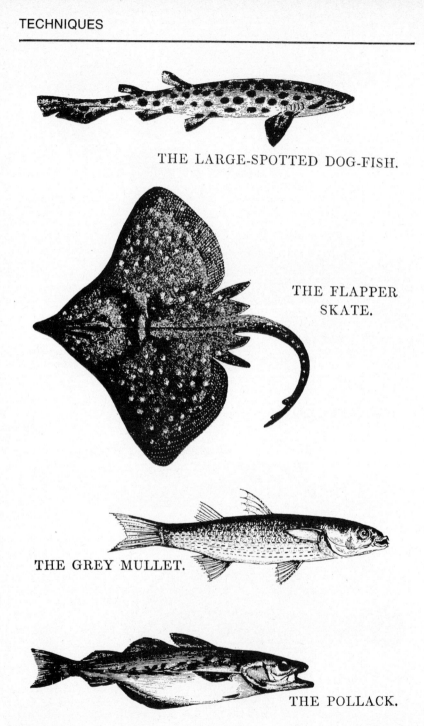

THE LARGE-SPOTTED DOG-FISH.

THE FLAPPER
SKATE.

THE GREY MULLET.

THE POLLACK.

An inflated inner tube can be used to carry a torch and spare harpoon heads or even food and drink in suitably sealed containers. These items can be carried in a net bag slung down between the centre of the tube. The latter can also be utilised as a resting place in between dives but it can prove a liability in a strong current or rough water and there is a tendency for the towing line to become fouled if working in shallow water around rocks.

In the past two years the paddle float has become very prominent with clubs. The main advantages are to combat the strong currents which exist, and most of the best fishing sites are between $\frac{3}{4}$ of a mile to two miles off shore; these can be reached without too much difficulty and without getting tired. Also with the increased speedboat traffic they are more easily seen than a rubber tyre or a small float. These floats are about 3 metres long, shaped as a conventional surf board but with increased depth up to 15 cm at the deepest part, and 90 cm wide at the centre. They are propelled by laying along the float and finning with the legs.

Equipment Maintenance

After use in sea water, spear guns should be carefully washed in fresh water and dried. Internal moving parts should be regularly inspected and lubricated. External parts should not be oiled otherwise they will collect sand and mud, but non-moving parts may be coated with a thin film of anti-corrosive compound of the type that forms a hard protective skin.

Rubber strands, if any, are highly susceptible to deterioration from sun, heat, salt water and oil. If detachable they should be removed from the gun after use, washed in fresh water and kept in a cool dark place.

Safety Precautions

A modern harpoon gun can be as fatal as a .22 rifle and must be handled with care and due regard for its dangerous potential. The following precautions should always be observed.

1 Never point a gun, loaded or unloaded, at anyone.
2 Never carry a loaded gun ashore.
3 Always load a gun in the water and unload it before leaving the water.
4 Never fire a gun towards the surface.
5 Never hunt within 30 metres of bathers or rod fishermen.
6 If the gun is fitted with a safety catch, use it—but don't rely on it.
7 Never trail a loaded gun in the water; always have it under positive control.

Spearfishing Techniques

It is of little use attempting to spearfish over flat, plain sandy bottoms for few, if any, fish will be present. They prefer rocks, ledges, wrecks, gullies and depressions that may afford them shelter and hideouts. Sandy plains are like deserts; rocks are like densely populated towns. Fish also prefer high and flooding tides and are always more active in the early morning or late in the evening.

Success in spearfishing depends first on the choices of site, and secondly on the technique of the dive. Swimming on the surface with fins flailing, followed by frantic exertion and splashing to submerge, will frighten away any fish in the area. The dive should be silent and controlled, as described in the first chapter of this book, and should be followed by easy fin strokes. If the fish has been spotted from the surface, it should be carefully watched and advantage taken of every natural cover and hunting aid, such as diving from the direction of the sun or greatest light, and making the approach from behind a rock or ledge. If the fish is frightened and swims off, it is little use attempting to chase it underwater. A fresh approach should be made from the surface.

The approach is of great importance. It should always be deliberate and controlled and the quarry stalked in the way that one would stalk game on land. It is usually necessary to use different tactics for different species. Some fish prefer rocks and gullies, others frequent thick seaweed growths. Only by experience and a study of the habits of the various species can success be gained.

The gun should always be held at the ready; some are better used held in one hand in the manner of a pistol, whilst others need the other hand for steadying the barrel. Aim should be taken along the line of the barrel at a point just behind the quarry's gills. The lower part of the belly is soft and the spear may not hold there. If the fish only presents its front to the gun, aim should be taken on the mouth but, if possible, a shot at right angles to the fore and aft line of the fish should be made. Glancing shots will very often bounce off, particularly in the case of scaleless fish. It is pointless to fire at too great a distance, as accuracy will be reduced and the fish will have ample time to escape during the actual travel of the spear. The ideal to aim for is to fire at a distance of not more than one spear's length away, to aim slightly high to allow for gravity and slightly in front of a swimming fish to compensate for its forward movement. Allowance should also be made for the magnifying effects of the water which will make the fish appear considerably closer than it actually is (approximately one-quarter).

Once the fish is impaled, the line should be held to prevent it swimming into a hole. Depending on the weight and size of the fish it may have to be played for some considerable time before it can be brought to the surface. It is unwise to attempt to spear a fish too large for the gear used or for the diver's experience and ability. For larger fish it is an advantage to have the spear line fixed to a surface float so that it can play itself out. The float will also act as a marker in following the fish.

A reliable knife should always be at hand to cut the line if necessary. This should be done without hesitation if the situation appears difficult and it should be borne in mind that it is better to lose a spear than a gun.

In order to prevent the fish flapping it should be kept under water until it can be landed, or put in a boat or float. Whilst removing the harpoon the fish should be grasped firmly in the gills by the thumb and forefinger.

Lobsters and crabs should be handled by the rear part of their bodies so that the claws cannot reach round and grasp the hand. They should not be picked up by the legs, as the leg joints are equipped with special muscles that enable them to snap off sections of the limbs at will. Apart from the danger of getting a severe nip from a crab's claws it is unwise to thrust a hand into any small hole in which it has hidden. If the hand is placed above the crab's shell it will instinctively brace its legs and exert upwards pressure, trapping the hand between its shell and the roof of the hole. Even a small crab is sufficiently powerful to resist the withdrawing of the hand.

The sport of underwater fishing is one that calls for stamina and ability. The use of a protective suit covering at least the trunk will conserve body heat and thereby increase the time that can be spent in the water. It permits an adequate rest of a minute or more to be made on the surface to regain energy between dives, without getting cold (see *Protective Clothing*).

Spearfishing, as with all sports, has its rules and etiquette. No underwater swimmer should interfere with nets, pots, traps or other fishing instruments used by commercial fishermen for the catching of fish or shellfish. They should not take crabs, lobsters or other shellfish by means of spears, tongs or other instruments which are liable to damage them. They should keep clear of other fishermen and anglers, buoys and nets. In Britain there is national legislation and local byelaws governing the sizes of fish and shellfish that may legally be taken; other countries impose similar restrictions (see Appendix). Otherwise, it is only necessary to apply common sense and ordinary courtesy in order to be able to enjoy this activity to the full.

RULES FOR COMPETING IN A BSAC OR NATIONAL SPEARFISHING COMPETITION IN GREAT BRITAIN

1   All Competitors must be over the age of 16 years.

2   All persons entering the competition individually will be grouped into teams of three. A team will be made up of three persons and there will be no replacements permitted after the start of the competition.

3   If the competition is interrupted by bad weather, or any other cause, the organising committee will adjudicate whether or not the time elapsed is sufficient to constitute a valid competition, but the time must be at least half that originally intended as the duration of this competition.

4   The competitors will all start from the place designated by the organising committee. No competitors will be allowed to commence from a boat or have the use of any boat other than that allowed by the competition organisers. All competitors must check in at the place designated by the competition organisers.

Penalties for late-comers will be :—

(a)   during the first ten minutes after the official end of the competition : HALF POINTS for the individual only.

(b) after the above ten minutes : DISQUALIFICATION for the individual competitor only.

(c)   any fish landed after the end of the competition will not be eligible for a trophy or prize.

5   It is not permitted to use any means to catch the fish other than a knife, handspear, spear expelled from a compressed air gun, or spring or rubber-powered gun, no cartridges or expellable gas guns of any description may be used. Guns must not be loaded on the beach or in a boat and all guns must be unloaded when leaving the water.

6   Whilst taking part in the competition all competitors are encouraged to use a lifejacket, or float attached to themselves whilst in the water.

7   The competitors must be in the water at the time of spearing the fish.

8   No breathing apparatus may be used by the competitors.

9   A competitor may come ashore as often as he wishes but cannot use any means of transport to get to another part of the competition area or back to the checking-in point, other than that provided by the competition organisers.

10   A competitor may not approach within an area of 7.5m of another or spear a fish within that area without the permission of the other competitor. If he helps the other competitor in any way to catch a fish then he will be entitled to 50% of that fish's points.

11   No lures of any description are permitted to attract the fish.

12   A competitor helping another in the case of injury or exhaustion is entitled to 50% of the other's total catch at that time.

13   The passing of fish in any way will disqualify the persons involved and their teams.

14 To qualify, a fish may be weighed in at any time with the official appointed to the duty within the competition time to limits and weigh over one pound. If the competitor then signs off after the end of the competition Rule 4 will apply.

15 Any competitor not being a current BSAC member or unable to produce proof of membership of a BSAC branch will be required to pay a 50p levy to the competition organisers who will pass it on to the National Spearfishing Committee.

16 No other equipment other than basic skin diving equipment may be used unless specified by the competition organisers.

17 The competition organisers may, with the approval of the National Spearfishing Committee, alter, change, or add to these rules/amendments if they feel it is necessary for the particular area where the competition is being held.

18 The point system for all BSAC and National Spearfishing Competitions is as the current list.

19 Any breach of the aforesaid rules will mean ABSOLUTE DISQUALIFICATION.

CHAPTER SEVEN

THE OPEN WATER

Open Water Diving : George F Brookes

Diving Expeditions : Derek M F Cockbill

Basic Seamanship : Lt Cdr Alan Bax RN

Basic Navigation : Lt Cdr Alan Bax RN

Charts and Tides: Vernon Knapper

Dive Reports and Log Books : George F Brookes

Scientific Expeditions : Dr N C Flemming

Exploration : George F Brookes

Wrecks and Salvage : Derek M F Cockbill

Safety : Brian Booth

OPEN WATER DIVING

In the planning and organisation of any open water dive, attention has to be paid to far more than the dive itself. Real success is achieved only by thoughtful preparation and no detail is too small to be ignored. For this reason, many points will be made here that may seem to be elementary. Planning, which involves anticipation, can also be very pleasant.

Appointment of leaders

It is of primary importance that all diving outings, whether large or small, should have a leader. Where only a few experienced divers are involved, the formal appointment of one may not be necessary if they all clearly understand one another's roles, but if this is not so, or if those concerned have not dived regularly together, it is always advisable.

Whatever the circumstances, there must always be an expedition leader on branch dives to comply with Club diving rules. The purpose of this regulation is to ensure that there should be no risk of accident because of uncertainty about who is in charge; confusion is likely to arise if several people are giving conflicting instructions at the same time. The rule is also made to avoid complications about payment of insurance under the Club's policy in the event of an accident or a claim for damages by a third party. So important is this matter that Club rules stipulate that, as far as diving conduct is concerned, the expedition leader has authority to exclude a member from diving if he will not obey diving instructions given to him.

Each dive should also be under the control of a dive leader whose instructions should be obeyed during the dive itself. The choice of a dive leader may be made in advance or immediately prior to diving, according to circumstances and the extent of preliminary planning. The dive leader is, of course, responsible to the expedition leader.

All this is not to say that jobs should be found for the sake of finding them. The purpose of planning is to guarantee a good dive, and diving is not arranged as an exercise in super organisation.

However, the spreading of the load of diving organisation has other advantages. Firstly, it gives the expedition leader more time to supervise overall conduct and actively to enjoy himself. Secondly, it enables members under training to take on diving duties and thus to increase their own competence. For this last reason, the appointment of diving marshalls and dive leaders need not be made from the most experienced members of the party. On dives involving training particularly, the expedition leader may well appoint a novice as dive leader with an experienced diver as his companion. In such cases, the experienced diver should obey the directions of the dive leader at all times short of actual emergency or danger when his greater experience would clearly indicate that he should take charge.

Preliminary planning

Everything possible should be prepared in advance of a dive. There will be so many aspects that can only be determined at the time—such as those caused by weather variations—that to encumber oneself on site with matters that could have been dealt with before will lead to delays, frustration and, possibly, a spoilt or cancelled dive. There is also the possibility of a dangerous situation developing, for if time is short and there is too much to do, safety precautions might be neglected.

Some preliminary planning can be completed well in advance, such as the selection of the diving area and a decision about the purpose of the dive. Often, the two points are correlated. For example, a dive to search for a sunken dinghy presupposes that its location is already fairly accurately known. For a dive of general interest, however, the choice of a site can make or mar the entire outing. A selection should be made in the light of all available knowledge of previous dives in the area, of accounts by other divers, and advice from local branches, seamen and information bureaux. If a sea dive is planned, the appropriate charts and coastal land maps should be studied for depths of water, reefs and rocky outcrops, which make the most interesting dives. Sandy sea beds are seldom interesting.

The choice of a time for the dive will frequently depend more on the availability of members rather than the best time to dive, but a decision should be made as much in advance as possible taking all factors into consideration. Accommodation should then be arranged, if necessary, together with transport for divers and equipment. Don't forget that permission to dive has sometimes to be obtained beforehand. Failure to do this may mean a refusal on the actual day.

Again, the hire of diving boats, if required, should be taken care of as early as possible, particularly if local facilities are unknown or if the area is popular. If cylinders are going to need recharging, arrangements should be made either for a supply of cylinders for decanting on site, the provision of a compressor or for the transport of empty cylinders to the nearest air station. All equipment, incidentally, should be checked a day or so before the expedition whether it is owned privately or by the Club. This should be done preferably by the person who is going to use or be responsible for it. Cylinders should, of course, be fully charged.

If it is necessary to dive at slack water, its time and duration should be established beforehand from charts and tide tables. Underwater visibility will usually be better on the flood tide rather than at low water slack, especially if there is a river in the vicinity. It is also better if out at sea to be clear of the shore wrack.

The weather conditions should be checked immediately before departure for sea diving if there is any likelihood of strong winds from an unfavourable direction, which may well render diving impossible. The conditions at sea in any specific area can be obtained by telephone from the local meterological office, who can also give a forecast for the next day. If the weather report is bad, it may not be worth setting out for the diving site at all.

Conduct of dive

Just as the amount and detail of advance planning depends on the complexity of the dive and the number of divers involved, so the degree of control and judgment that have to be exercised on the dive will depend on conditions at the diving site and on the experience of the divers. The expedition leader or his diving marshals will be responsible for this *conduct of the dive*.

It is impossible to lay down exact procedures to be followed for the circumstances of a dive—dependent as they are on the vagaries of personnel and weather—as each will in some way be different from the last, even if it is held at the same diving site with the same divers.

Although much of the diving arrangements may go according to plan, even to follow it out means that an assessment has to be made to do so. Any variation from the anticipated conditions on the dive will involve deviation to some degree, and this will depend on such things as changes in wind, rain, cloud, underwater conditions, tides, slack water, currents, cold, visibility, and many other things. All these factors will influence the conduct of the dive if a successful outcome is to be achieved.

One extremely important consideration is that diving should be cancelled either in advance, if conditions are unfavourable, or during the dive, if changing circumstances make prolonged diving unsafe or unsuitable. Many a dive is necessarily cancelled due to the passing of the time of slack water or the approach of evening. Frequently, this is due to un-necessary delays caused by inefficient organisation or divers taking excessive time in kitting up. Whatever the cause, the expedition leader should be firm in taking this decision so that it is carried out unquestioningly. Apart from the actual diving, there are matters of base organisation that require preparation and attention. Important among these is provision of creature comforts for both divers and attendants. Diving makes demands on the body's heat and energy resources. Food to replace these should be made available after a dive. Hot drinks, soup, and concentrated energy-giving foods such as chocolate, sugar, or glucose sweets should be made available after a dive, in preference to a full meal some considerable time afterwards. One should not sit about in wet clothing after a dive. Evaporation, which is accentuated by a wind, causes additional cooling and loss of heat. Put on dry clothes as soon as possible. The diving base should provide protection from inclement weather—rain, wind, cold or hot sun. Don't forget that rubber perishes in sunlight.

Charged cylinders should be protected from strong sun, if only by a towel or clothing, to prevent the heat causing an increase of pressure of air in the cylinder. Care should be taken that used equipment is not left about where it may be damaged; for example, demand valves lying loose in the sand or cylinders rolling about in a boat. Generally, little attention need be given to equipment on the dive if it has been properly looked after and prepared beforehand.

Apart from knowing in advance the location and telephone number of the nearest recompression chamber and such special services as helicopter sea rescue, the expedition leader should locate the nearest public or other telephone from which these services, and a doctor or coastguards, may be called. A simple first aid kit should be available at the diving base. In addition, inconvenience can often be avoided if toilet facilities are available or a public convenience is at hand.

On all diving expeditions care should be taken never to cause wilful or unnecessary damage to property, or to cause an inconvenience to the public, and diving sites should always be left clean and tidy on departure. At all times divers should adopt a code of conduct that has respect for other users of the sea or diving area.

Dive procedures

No hard and fast rules can be laid down for carrying out all the details of a dive. It is in this field that the diving marshal, as the person in charge, will use his judgment and leadership. There are, however, many factors that different dives have in common and for these general guidance can be given.

Each diver should be responsible for his own personal equipment. If all equipment is at the right place at the right time and functioning properly, this will contribute considerably to the success of the dive and there will be much less risk of failure or accidents. This can only be achieved by careful control and proper preparation in advance. In some cases it will be found advantageous for one member to be put in charge of all of certain items of equipment, such at aqualungs, particularly when these are commonly owned and used. In other cases where each diver has his own aqualung, it is preferable for him to be responsible for it also. When it comes to the actual dive, however, it is vital that the individual diver satisfies himself that his equipment, whether personally owned or borrowed, is in working order, ready to hand and not left behind when setting out for the diving site.

In order to assist the efficient conduct of the dive, the diving marshal should let all divers know in advance the diving order and dive leaders so that they may kit up and prepare in sufficient time to avoid delays or undue haste before their turn to enter the water. He should do this even if it becomes necessary for him to change the order as the dive proceeds.

Just before entering the water, each group should receive a pre-dive briefing from the dive marshal. During the dive, adequate records regarding the times the divers enter and leave the water should be taken, and further information regarding the depth and type of bottom, with particular emphasis on anything interesting. These records will prove invaluable to the branch in the future.

Immediately prior to entering the water, divers should carry out their pre-dive checks. These consist of proving the satisfactory functioning of their aqualung by turning on the air and taking a few breaths, checking they have all equipment on : fins, mask—duly rinsed out—snorkel tube, which should always be taken on every dive, weight belt and harness, correctly fitted and both with their quick-release in working order, lifejacket and any other special items being taken on the dive.

The dive leader should confirm that his group have carried out these checks and if necessary run over them himself. He should also give any last-minute instructions for the dive, including the signals to be used.

The method of entry into the water will depend on whether it is a shore or boat dive, the ease of access to the water, the sea and weather conditions and the experience of the divers. When in the water, divers should remain close to the point of entry until all those on the dive have come together and given an indication that they are ready to proceed, usually by means of the underwater OK signal.

To proceed with a dive if incorrectly weighted is unpleasant, an annoyance to other divers and possibly a danger. If in doubt, buoyancy should be checked at the start and any variations corrected by surfacing to remove or take on more weight as required. A member of the surface party should assist by passing the weights to the diver in the water. When all divers are ready, the dive leader should signal to descend.

The conduct of the dive will depend entirely on underwater conditions : the dive leader should observe, assess and act in accordance with them and the object of the dive. There are, however, five factors that influence every dive and should always be kept constantly in mind during it. These are :

1　The air supply remaining in the cylinders of all divers.
2　One's whereabouts relative to the surface party or point of entry.
3　The depth of the dive and the possible effects of nitrogen narcosis.
4　The depth and duration of the dive relative to the need for decompression stops.
5　The necessity to remain in constant contact with diving companions.

If the dive leader knows the amount of air carried by each diver in his team before entry, it should only be necessary to make a confirmatory check on reaching the bottom in case an excessive amount may have been used by any diver while waiting at the surface, checking buoyancy, or ear clearing on the way down. The air should then be checked periodically during the dive, but particularly towards the end so as to ensure that all divers surface in good time.

It is possible to travel quite considerable distances underwater during the progress of a dive, particularly if in shallow water where air consumption is relatively small. Usually it is desirable or necessary to complete the dive and surface near to some predetermined point, shore, surface party or boat. If the divers lose their way, or are uncertain of their position, they should surface to determine their whereabouts. There are sometimes exceptions to this rule such as when diving roped or when being given ensured surface cover. Methods of finding the way underwater are given in *Underwater Navigation*.

The causes and effects of nitrogen narcosis and the precautions and procedures to be followed on dives or repeat dives necessitating special decompression stops are dealt with separately. In respect of these matters, the dive leader should always bear in mind the experience and ability of his companion divers and preferably avoid dives involving nitrogen narcosis or decompression, particularly with novice divers.

Unless diving roped, diving should not be undertaken alone. Learning how to keep in constant contact with a companion diver without having to devote the whole attention to this one aspect of the dive is one of the first things to master. Visual contact will be more readily maintained if a pair of divers fin side by side sufficiently apart that should one lag slightly behind his companion he is not at once lost from view, yet always well within the limits of underwater visibility. If one diver pauses to look at something, the other should remain close at hand. Before moving off again they should glance towards one another to see that their movements and intentions are understood. With divers unaccustomed to diving together, or with beginners, the dive leader may positively have to signal each change of direction or activity.

If a diver loses his companion, he should set about finding him without delay. Firstly, look on either side, then turn slowly round looking both up and down as well as on the level. If he or his bubbles cannot be seen do not fin off in a probable direction in the hope of finding him, but after a short time, rarely more than half a minute, start out for the surface all the time circling slowly looking about for signs of the diver above or his bubbles rising from below.

The rule to be always observed is to *surface if separated*. If this is done, both divers should come to the surface within a short time of each other where they can come together again and recommence the dive.

Should a diver surface alone, he should remain where he is and turn around for signs of his companion, looking in the water for rising bubbles as far as visibility will allow and scanning the surface of the water for signs of the bubbles bursting. He should enlist the help of surface cover or lookout, who may aid in the search and who, from a higher vantage point, can frequently see bubbles which are obscured from a diver's view by waves.

If the surface cover is able to point out the direction of his companion's bubbles, the diver should fin on the surface towards them looking below for the rising bubbles. Only when he sees them should he dive to make contact with his companion, otherwise it is likely he will not be able to locate him due to changes in his companion's direction and the reduced visibility below water compared with that at the surface.

When the dive leader decides to terminate the dive, he should signal to his companion to commence the ascent. The correct procedure for surfacing and signals to be given to the surface party should always be carried out (see *Signals*). Particular care should be exercised to keep together throughout. If finning back to base on the surface is necessary, care should be taken not to outstrip the companion diver. Fin a foot or so apart in order to see each other easily, but if visibility through the water is poor, or in currents or rough water, it may be easier to hold hands, or to grasp the companion's harness.

Members of the surface party should always be ready to assist divers out of the water, particularly if the divers are likely to be cold or exhausted, have need to clamber over rocks or climb into a boat. In these cases, it is frequently an advantage to the diver to take off his aqualung and weights in the water and pass them to the surface party before getting out himself. Once out, the aqualung and other kit should be stowed or placed so that they are not in the way, where they may become damaged, hinder other divers, or even be used by them in error for a subsequent dive.

The first dive

A person who has had a thorough training on the aqualung in a swimming pool and been fully instructed on the techniques of diving will come adequately prepared to his first open water dive. Nevertheless, special attention should be given him because of the strangeness of his surroundings. His lack of experience in the new environment underwater may induce fear or foolish behaviour unless he is accompanied by another diver who can reassure him and direct his actions, and in whom he is willing to place his trust.

Only an experienced diver should take a member on his first dive. He should watch over him and give any necessary help while he is kitting up. He should not order him about, but render assistance in a confident and kindly way. The dive leader should either enter the water first or with the novice, never afterwards. He should check that he is correctly weighted and can clear his ears, give him frequent and precise indications and signals of what he should do, leading him on an easy and gentle dive. The first dive should never be in adverse conditions, even if the novice diver is roped, and it should be to a limited depth of 4-6 metres, not more. At first it may be a comfort to the novice if he is led by the hand. In order to divert his attention from preoccupation with his equipment, the dive leader should pause from time to time and point out some interesting plant, creature of aspect of undersea life. This will also start the novice early on along the road to acute observation and intelligent diving.

Afterwards the novice should be told of any interesting or significant aspects of the dive, instructed how to avoid any faults in the techniques or actions, but above all given encouragement and congratulations on his achievements.

DIVING EXPEDITIONS

This chapter, which could be sub-titled 'planning & organisation' is concerned with the general guidelines to be followed by those who may have the responsibility of running a branch diving expedition.

Obviously, these can vary from a small group on a day's dive from a local beach to a full-scale overseas scientific project lasting several weeks, and whilst the degree of planning, administration and organisation varies accordingly, the same basic problems need to be faced if a smooth, efficient operation is to be achieved, the hallmark of any successful expedition.

The particular problems of the larger scientific projects are dealt with elsewhere in this manual so this chapter will concentrate on the basic factors to be considered whatever the scope of the operation, although we must assume by definition that an 'expedition' is something a little more ambitious than a day's outing with no higher purpose than 'getting wet' with something for the 'pot' by way of a bonus. Any success, therefore, will depend entirely upon (a) pre-expedition organisation and (b) its efficient administration thereafter 'on site', so broadly speaking we can split the problems to be considered into these two categories.

Pre-Expedition Organisation

The purpose for and the decision to undertake any planned expedition will probably arise gradually from a great deal of informal discussion as a result of some experience or knowledge of an individual or group and although its purpose here is immaterial, the expedition exists only to pursue this particular objective which must be clearly defined and understood by all concerned so that all planning is directed towards successfully achieving this objective. It naturally follows, therefore, that the expedition leader on whom the ultimate responsibility must fall, will fully understand the nature of the undertaking as well as appreciating the particular diving problems which may also be encountered.

The next logical step is the selection of the team, who must combine an enthusiasm for the stated aims of the project with a willingness to accept responsibility for other routine duties and the ability to work as one of a group towards the common objective.

Whatever other particular skills may be required, the expedition must be organised initially as a diving team with the members accepting such duties as Dive Marshal; Dive Leader; Diving & Auxiliary Equipment Marshals; Log & Record Keeper; Safety Cover, etc. Other essential duties may also need to be covered for such matters as catering, treasurer, transport, boats, compressor operation and cylinder filling, and in some cases these may need to be duplicated or split in order to 'spread the load' of responsibility fairly throughout the group.

Having established the objective and selected the team the pre-expedition planning can now go forward in more detail and can be considered broadly under two headings :

1 The general logistics of any diving expedition and
2 The specific requirements for the particular project in hand.

In the first category the prime objective will be establishing and organising the operational base. Here there must be suitable accommodation with good food, facilities for washing, drying and maintaining diving gear, filling aqualungs using either a compressor or an air bank—the latter being quicker, quieter and more reliable. For maximum comfort, convenience and efficiency the need to carry gear should be reduced to the minimum either by having the base close to the boat or diving site or by laying on transport. Not only does this reduce the possibility of loss or breakage but there is nothing more tiring or frustrating at the end of a hard day's diving than lugging heavy gear unnecessarily.

If possible a visit to the proposed base should be made some weeks before the event to check on provisional arrangements made. This may reveal some unforeseen problems and it is also an opportunity of making a first personal contact with such local officials as the Harbourmaster, police, etc, and not the least of all with members of the local diving club whose particular knowledge of the area and their co-operation could be vital. Accommodation, food and ancillary facilities should be as good and convenient as one can afford. It is one thing to ' rough it ' for a weekend when there is nothing particularly at stake followed by a week at work to recover but another matter entirely if you are diving and working three or four times a day every day for a week or even longer.

If a boat is to be hired for the diving it is vital its essential facilities are checked and the Skipper briefed on what it expected of him and his craft. The chapter on boat diving elsewhere in the Manual covers this subject adequately, but the selection of a suitable vessel for your intended purpose and the need for it to be adequately equipped cannot be stressed too strongly.

The final consideration in this category is the personal fitness of the team members and their own equipment.

During an expedition the group must take full advantage of favourable diving conditions in order to achieve maximum effective bottom time and this may well imply repeat dives sustained over quite long periods, which can be extremely tiring. There is usually no time to get into ' diving trim ' once the expedition is under way, so the weeks before should be devoted to building up a high standard of physical and diving fitness so every member is in first class shape before departure. To this end a medical check may also be considered desirable.

Similarly personal diving gear should be thoroughly checked, overhauled and rechecked for maximum efficiency. A supply of repair materials, spares, and duplicate equipment for those items which are easily lost, damaged or can give trouble such as demand valves, masks, fins, etc should also be taken by each member or a pool of such items organised by the Equipment Marshal.

In the second category we are considering the means of achieving the purpose of the expedition and this being the whole object of the exercise, considerable thought, planning and discussion and, where possible, practice is essential. There is sometimes a tendency for the Expedition Leader to become so involved in the project himself that he may fail to keep the rest of the team fully informed, but this should be recognised and resisted as it is vital to the success of any expedition that as much basic research on the subject as possible from every conceivable source and angle should be undertaken and the results analysed and discussed by all members of the group at regular meetings. Not only does this cultivate a 'team spirit', stimulate and maintain interest but the significance of some seemingly irrelevant 'find' underwater may well be appreciated only because of some half-remembered fact gleaned from the pre-exped research.

With all the normal problems of open-water diving to contend with, tides, adverse weather, poor visibility etc, it must again be stated that maximum effective bottom time on site must be the aim of the pre-exped planning, so with some knowledge of the sort of tasks likely to be undertaken the necessary techniques should be practised and perfected as a group under easy diving conditions in local waters with the equipment you will be using. Some ancillary gear required for a specific task may need to be specially constructed so experiment and modification must be completed before departure. Ideas and equipment produced in theory do not necessarily work out in practice, so reduce your possible problems to the minimum beforehand—there will be plenty of unexpected ones to cope with on site!

'On-Site' Administration

Assuming now that all our pre-exped planning has gone as was hoped, the group has now arrived on site and all is ready to commence operations. The timing of the expedition will have been planned to take advantage of tides, good weather, location, etc and with time always at a premium the maximum amount of underwater work possible must be the aim of the exped leader. This will only be achieved by planning discipline and teamwork.

Although overall control would be effectively in his hands, the exped leader on site should concentrate on pursuing the main objective, assessing progress and varying the programme in the light of results obtained. The actual diving organisation should be delegated to the appointed Dive Marshal, whose responsibility would include the safe conduct of the diving operations taking all the factors involved into consideration as outlined in other chapters in this manual.

A routine of briefing and de-briefing each dive team should be developed to record information and impressions immediately on returning to the surface with the labelling and storing of 'finds' in an orderly fashion. A blackboard ruled to show the day's diving routine and the results, based on the diving log is an easy means of recording basic information and can be copied into a permanent log and individual log books before erasing.

If the operational base is a boat, space inevitably will be at a premium so orderly organisation both as individuals and as a group must be maintained. Team members not immediately involved should keep clear of the diving area and all gear should be stowed safely out of the way when not in use. Cleanliness is also important so the diving area should be regularly swilled and scrubbed down to prevent cut feet or slipping on the remains of some specimen.

Whilst continually stressing the need for effective organisation and planning, the possibility must be faced that factors beyond anyone's control can make the original objective abortive so a secondary alternative project should be planned to offset such a contingency. This can also be of benefit if the work goes better than anticipated on the original project and extra diving time becomes available which can then be usefully employed to give the expedition an unexpected bonus.

The expedition can only be considered successful if the objective is achieved and, dependent upon the type of operation, this may also imply a report in written form being made available, particularly if Sponsors have been involved. So to maintain interest to the end such a report should be presented at the earliest possible moment. Both in planning and conducting the expedition it is likely that a great deal of help, advice and co-operation of one sort or another will have been sought and freely given, and to all such people a letter of thanks with a copy of the results if relevant, a personal visit or even a telephone call will show at least their efforts were appreciated. Apart from being common courtesy it will also make it easier to ask again should the need arise.

In conclusion it must be stated that the organisation of a diving expedition should not be lightly undertaken involving as it does a great deal of painstaking research and arduous work. But a successful one is worth all the effort involved, giving a real purpose to diving and a deep feeling of personal satisfaction to all those involved.

BASIC SEAMANSHIP

SEAMANSHIP AND BOAT HANDLING

Just what is seamanship? I consider it to be a code of behaviour, much the same as say—'roadmanship' or even 'divemanship'. In other words just as it is wise to follow a number of common sense guidelines if you wish to work efficiently and safely underwater, the same is true above water. More than that, remember, boats are traditionally 'she's'—which means that their reaction in any given circumstances is not always quite what you expect . . . They need to be understood—caressed, not cuffed! First let's deal with something which is always with us in a boat.

ROPE

The main point to note, if I may quote Jerome K Jerome, is :— 'There is something very strange and unaccountable about rope. You roll it up with as much patience and care as you would take to fold up a new pair of trousers, and five minutes afterwards, when you pick it up, it is one ghastly, soul-revolting tangle.'

Rope can be made from various materials, either natural—manila, sisal, cotton, or man-made—nylon, terylene, Poly this and Poly that. Not forgetting that rope may also be made of wire, although as amateurs in small boats we are unlikely to come across it much except perhaps as the 'purchase' or lifting wire of a derrick.

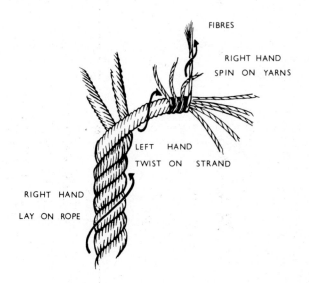

Figure 1: Make up of rope

Now, a few generalisations.

Measurement

With a few minor exceptions rope is traditionally measured by its circumference in the UK, and metrically by diameter in mm.

Composition

Spun or 'hawser laid' rope (Figure 1) is the more usual, and is made up of a number of thin 'yarns' spun into thicker 'strands', which are in turn laid out together to form the rope.

Most rope is three stranded, and the strands are laid up 'right handed', as shown in Figure 1.

The handling characteristics of rope are determined by its composition, and generally ropes whose yarns are made from short lengths of the basic material spun together, rather like wool, eg natural fibres . . . (man-made types), handle more easily than those whose strands are exuded as one continuous length.

Strength

National standards are set for the various types of rope, and samples are tested to destruction at the Factory. Manufacturers usually produce a table of strength for size.

It is obviously not sensible to work near this limit as the formulae are for new unworn rope. Before using a rope its SAFE WORKING LOAD (SWL) is required. This is found quite simply by dividing the Breaking Strength by a Safety Factor (SF) of 6 for natural and 4 for man-made ropes.

A knot reduces the strength of a rope by about 50 per cent, and a splice by 12 per cent. It is also of note that a natural fibre rope loses almost 50 per cent of its strength when saturated. Always be on the lookout, and watch for chafe or fraying over the whole of the rope's length—like chain, its strength is that of the weakest link.

HANDLING

The golden rule when using rope is 'tidiness', particularly when we remember the quote of Jerome K Jerome.

Tidiness in this sense means 'coiling'—either the whole of a rope when spare or the end which is not in use.

Coiling should be thought about, because that 'right hand lay' (Figure 1) is the cause of much twisting and tangling. Before coiling, tangled ropes are best laid out straight for their entire length on land, or streamed astern from a boat—even an inflatable. Once laid out on land give them a good stretch, this helps to remove final kinks, particularly in new natural fibre.

Then work as on Figure 2 starting with the end *which is secured* in the

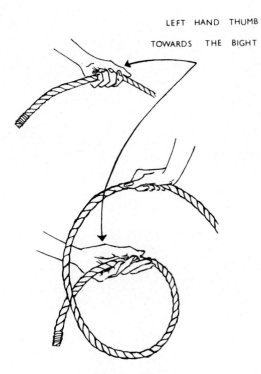

LEFT HAND THUMB

TOWARDS THE BIGHT

Figure 2: Coiling

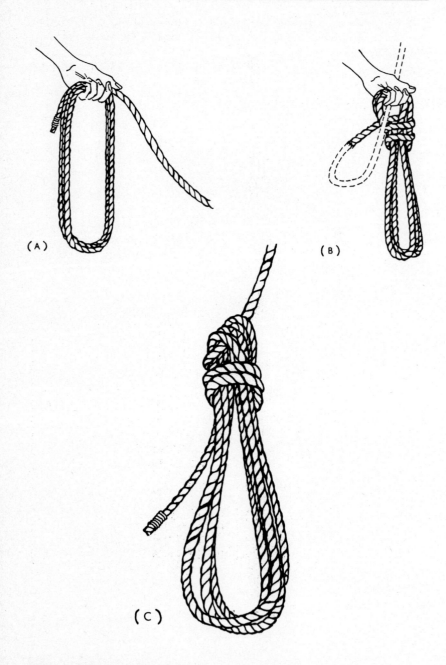

(A)

(B)

(C)

Figure 3: Stowing a small rope

left hand, and drawing in and coiling CLOCKWISE with the right. The whole secret is to twist the rope usually clockwise between thumb and forefinger of right hand before drawing it in to make each loop of the coil. This allows the rope to fall naturally, and neatly, on to the left hand. This 'twist' of the right hand will send the potentially tangly twists down the rope until they come out at the free end. The rope may well have to be shaken from time to time in order to clear them and prevent yet another tangle!

Having coiled them, stow. There are two ways, one as in Figure 3 where, having coiled as in Figure 2, you are left with—hopefully!—a neat coil in the left hand (Figure 3a). Wrap the end in the right hand round the coil about one-third from top (Figure 3b), then pass it through the top half and pull tight (Figure 3c). The coil may then be hung or thrown down with a reasonable chance of not tangling.

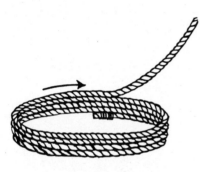

Figure 4: Coiling large rope

The second way is less often used but has a great deal to commend it, especially for larger ropes or those you need to use quickly, like that for the anchor.

Place the finished coil neatly on the ground—ropes too long or too heavy to be held in the hand may be coiled direct on to the ground (Figure 4). Simply take four short lengths of small unwanted line and tie them at 90° intervals round the coil with a bow—shoe lace type. The beauty of this method is that it provides an instant useable coil, just untie the bows—no knife required!—and there it is.

Finally there is one other method of stowing a rope. Just 'pour' it into a box or tub. As it goes in, so it should come out! and it works—providing you don't move or upset the box too much. If you do you will more than likely end up with a 'ghastly soul-revolting tangle'...

KNOTS AND SPLICES

So you leave shore on a nice flat sunny morning carefully placing your team for best water entry. Slowly as the dive progresses the wind blows, the sea height increases, until by the time all the divers have scrambled back on board it is really quite 'hilly'. On return the previously calm water at the harbour steps is now moving up and down quite alarmingly. Bill jumps ashore—hopefully without injury and holding the bow line—and finds that he can't hold the boat on his own, and in any case he must rush aft for the stern line in order to hold the boat so that someone else may leap out. Bill must tie a knot!

Figure 5   REEF   KNOT

Figure 7   CLOVE   HITCH

Figure 6   BOWLINE

OK, so he may be able to wind the line round and round a handy projection until something jams—but remember the infallible law of the Sea written by Murphy : ' You want a rope to jam? It won't ! ! '
It's so much simpler to tie a knot than try to jam it on purpose—it's also possible to untie it.

Now here are three of the basic knots which are easily learnt :

The Reef Knot	—	joins two ropes of equal thickness (Figure 5)
Bowline	—	a loop that will not slip (Figure 6)
Clove Hitch	—	for quickly securing a line (Figure 7)

Several of the man-made fibres are slippery and the conventional knots illustrated can work loose. The cure is to tuck the spare end between the strands of the rope (see Figure 8).

To move on to splicing, this is basically a stronger and tidier method of permanently joining or forming an eye in rope or wire.

However, rather than use the space which I have in describing the details of a splice, I would suggest that many knots would be much handier and last much longer if the ends were finished so that they would not fray.

In natural rope the answer is a whipping, as illustrated (Figure 9).

In man-made fibres the same effect can be more simply obtained by wrapping the end in Sellotape, cutting through it, then melting the neatly held strands together against a hot surface or flame. Even Sellotape need not be used, the ends may be sealed with a match and moulded together with fingers.

BLOCKS AND TACKLES

Blocks (Figure 10) have many functions, mainly concerned with leading a rope round a corner with a minimum of friction, and may be used with equal advantage above and below water.

Figure 8   KNOTTING SLIPPERY ROPE

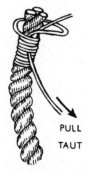

PULL
TAUT

Figure 9   COMMON   WHIPPING

There are two main pieces of information to find out about any block : its strength, and the size of rope it is meant to take. Normally a block is strong enough to cope with stresses above the breaking strength of the maximum size rope it will take, but beware, for some were made before the advent of man-made fibre with much greater working loads than natural rope of equal size.

The strength and maximum rope size of a block may usually be found in the manufacturer's catalogue.

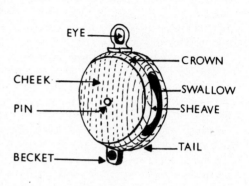

Figure 10: Parts of a Block

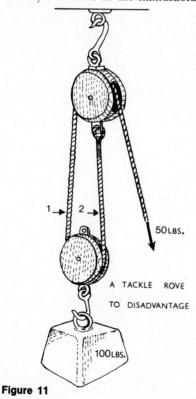

Figure 11

Tackles are two blocks used in such a way that they provide an increase in lifting, or shifting, power, rather like the gears of a car. For instance, if the blocks are rove as in Figure 11 and the resulting 'tackle' is used for lifting a 2 : 1 advantage is gained. However, a better advantage—3 : 1 —can be obtained when the tackle is used horizontally—for shifting rather than lifting—by placing the load on the other block (Figure 12). Incidentally 50 lbs is the sort of effort a 'normal' man can be relied upon to supply.

The tackle in Figure 12 is said to be rove to 'advantage' and the 3 : 1 increase in effort is simply calculated by counting the number of 'parts' of rope at the moving block (Figures 11 and 12).

In practice, friction reduces the theoretical advantage by one tenth for each sheave on the tackle.

Blocks can be single, double, or treble and tackles may be made up

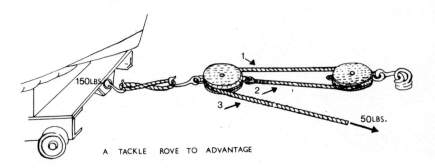

A TACKLE ROVE TO ADVANTAGE

Figure 12

with corresponding 'advantages' in effort. Treble blocks are not over common but similar advantages can be obtained by using two smaller tackles together (Figure 13).

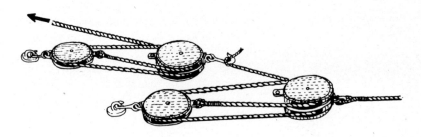

Figure 13: The use of two small tackles

As a final point, remember the efficiency of a block depends upon a free running sheave. Sea-water is the world's worst enemy when it comes to corrosion. Blocks need the odd spot of 'oily care', or consider investing in the modern type of stainless steel and fibre.

ANCHORS
There are various factors to consider when selecting an anchor and line :
Maximum weight of boat
Freeboard
Draught
Local seabed

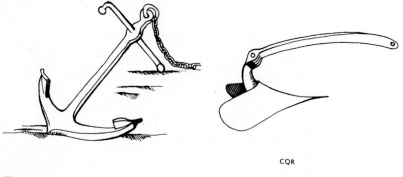

Figure 14 ADMIRALTY   PATTERN

CQR

Figure 15

from these, the

> Type and weight of anchor
> Size and length of line

must be determined.

There are four main types of small boat anchor from which to choose :

Admiralty Pattern (Figure 14)	Suitable for sand and mud bottoms, fair on rock—not good on shingle. Not readily available when stowed.
CQR (Figure 15)	Suitable for most seabeds, stows fairly well in all types of boat.
Danforth (Figure 16)	An excellent anchor. Not overgood on rock.
'Weight' (Figure 17)	Time honoured easy to stow and handle. Holds well in all types of seabed in low tidal streams and light winds.

The most useful of these types is the CQR.

Figure 16   DANFORTH

Figure 17   'WEIGHT'

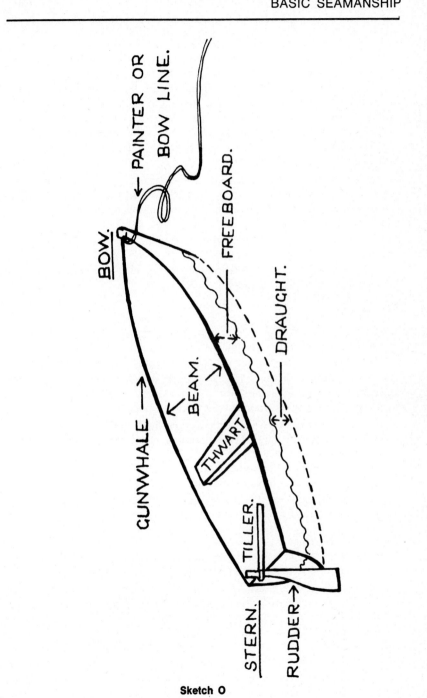

PAINTER OR BOW LINE.

BOW.

FREEBOARD.

DRAUGHT.

GUNWHALE

BEAM.

THWART

TILLER.

STERN.

RUDDER

Sketch O

Having chosen type, then to my mind size is most easily determined by having the maximum weight which can be conveniently handled and stowed, ie in an inflatable it is often difficult for one man to work very conveniently, perhaps a weight of 10 kg is enough, specially when it has to be stowed in a small space. On the other hand in a 10 m launch there is usually room for two men to work easily and weights of 25 kg can be considered. It may also be worth considering two anchors if there is space to stow them, one small, one large—for fair weather and foul.

As to line, a length of chain next to the anchor prevents chafe on the seabed, 5-8 metres with links, say, quarter of an inch diameter, is probably enough—again not so much that it cannot be reasonably handled and stowed.

For the rest, nylon or terylene rope is a *must,* because of its strength, elasticity and durability. It also handles easily and will stow neatly. It is not worth considering a size less than one inch as it will be difficult to grasp with wet, slippery hands.

Boat Handling

Boat handling is an aspect of seamanship and like it is best learned by experience, however it is never too late, and always best, to start with some theoretical background, otherwise it can be a little expensive!

As it is a practical activity it is subject to opinion and the aim of this section is to lay down some basic considerations which should be known by every cox'n and as many of his crew as possible.

The diver is most likely to be concerned with the following types of craft, each of which has its own handling characteristics :
Inflatable
Outboard engined conventional hull
Inboard engined conventional hull.

Before discussing their handling, however, there are some common points which are worth consideration.

Stability and Buoyancy

A diving boat needs to be stable and safe, for it is essentially a work boat—these requirements do not necessarily preclude speed.

Stability is needed so that fully kitted divers may enter the water or scramble back on board without causing the boat to heel so much that she is in danger of swamping. Safe, so that if for any reason she is swamped with a team of tired, cold, divers on board she will provide sufficient buoyancy to support them until the situation has been sorted out either by baling or rescue.

An inflatable craft fulfils these requirements admirably, as well as being light enough to carry in and out of the water fairly easily.

Sketch 1

Its buoyancy—will it float or sink when it is filled with divers?

Sketch 2

THE OPEN WATER

Small conventional craft vary enormously, and on the whole narrow shallow-draft craft are best avoided; something of the 'dory' type is probably best, with a blunt bow and plenty of beam, but make sure it has the necessary safe buoyancy.

As to larger vessels (say, over 6 metres), again I would look for a broad beam but not too shallow a draft, for such a boat must be seaworthy and requires the stability of a deepish keel.

Weather and Loading

Whatever the type of boat it will have a maximum load in calm weather, which will be determined by its physical dimensions, ie, just how many divers can acutally get in with all their kit!?

In my view a safe boat is one which when full of water will either support the weight of the *maximum* number of people it is expected to carry, or in the case of larger craft, carry liferafts capable of supporting the same maximum. Stability also matters, for a boat may be able to support a considerable weight but may then be so unstable that it is no longer able to right itself. This means that although the boat appears perfectly safe at the steps, out in the open water a violent helm movement will heel the boat such that she cannot recover, dip a gunwhale, and rapidly fill.

Now, having determined the maximum safe loading in calm water, what really matters is the *sea state* 'now' and, perhaps more important, what it is forecast to be at the end of the dive. A boat may be perfectly safe with her maximum load of fully kitted divers on board in calm weather, but the moment the *sea* begins to get up it is a very different matter. The load must be decreased to give manoeuvrability and prevent too much water being shipped; in small craft there must also be room to move the crew around in order to allow the boat to ride comfortably.

Too little crew weight can be as dangerous as too much, for the weight of the crew may be necessary to stabilise the boat. An inflatable which will carry seven should not reduce below three or certainly two, thereby giving the cox'n 'ballast' which he may move around the boat as he wishes. In particular it is possible for a strong wind to get under the bow of a light inflatable and turn it over. Ballast in the form of crew is needed to hold it down.

Before we go on to the practical aspects of boat handling, I would like to discuss the effect of the 'weather' in a little more detail. It is the sea state, not wind force, which really matters and this is dependant on:

Wind force
Surface and sub-surface topography
Distance offshore
Time
Tidal stream

348

Sketches 3 and 4

Let us take the bay illustrated in Figure A, which is typical of many round the UK. A Force 6 wind from the South East* is obviously ominous, the sea state will build up very quickly and diving will be impossible. However, if it is Force 3 it is a different matter. If it has only just started blowing the chances are that the sea height will not be enough to stop the dive. However, if it has been blowing for a day or two the sea height may well have built up to such an extent that the dive is no longer possible. In other words, time is more significant than the wind force.

Let us now take a south-westerly wind. In this case topography matters. In the lighter winds the whole of Biscuit Bay may be nicely sheltered, whereas at X diving is impossible. However, as the wind increases in strength the effect of the shelter from Heart Point diminishes and the sea at Flinders Bar may well be such that entry into harbour is impossible.

There is an additional complication here in that waves break at a given relationship between their height and the water depth. So that even if the wind force has only produced a relatively low sea in Biscuit Bay, at a certain tidal height this sea will break as it passes over the Bar and stop small craft entering or leaving the river. This effect will also occur on Smith's Shoal. At a given state of the tidal height, when the relationship of wave height to depth is right, the waves will literally stand up, walk across this shoal, and fall off the other side. This just might be dangerous in a gentle swell where conditions otherwise appear almost perfect.

Finally we are delighted when the wind blows northerly as we may dive certainly in Biscuit Bay in almost any wind force. Although just a thought . . . . . . north wind and ebb tide and engine failure might well bring an unexpected trip to distant shores! Do remember those Distress Flares—you never know, it might happen to you!

Handling

Whenever you handle a boat you cannot escape the influence of wind, tidal stream, rudder and screw, sea state, hull shape, and load—a formidable lot!

Their effect can be predetermined, to a greater or lesser extent. That their effect cannot be totally predicted is the reason why boat handling can only be completely learnt from experience.

Before we go on, let's just take a look at what we mean by 'boat handling'. It means the ability to control a boat in at least seven basic manoeuvres—and any others which crop up!

---

*Winds are named as coming FROM a direction.
Tides are named as going TO a direction.

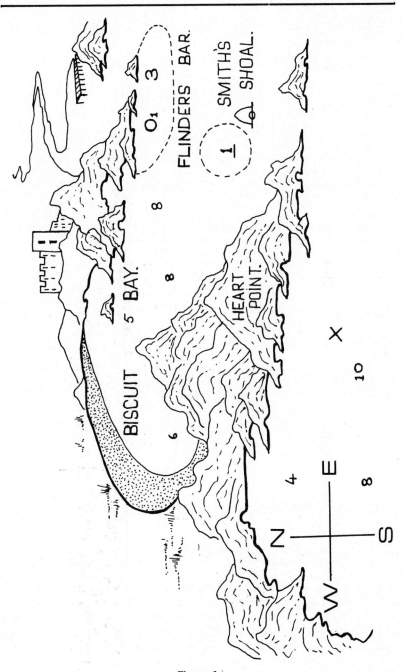

Figure A

Picking up a man
Anchoring
Berthing and Unberthing
Open Beach Work
Turning in a confined space
Towing
Securing to a buoy.

I hope these few sentences give some idea of the measure of the problem.

Let's now take a look at the factors which are reasonably consistent in each boat, but remember they may vary from boat to boat even in the same class because of minor variations in building.

Screw

A screw is termed as being ' right ' handed or ' left ' handed according to which way it turns when viewed from astern (Figure B).

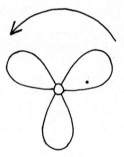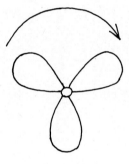

VIEWED FROM ASTERN.

Figure B

Left handed   Right handed

In an outboard this is of little consequence as the screw is so small that there is little differential water pressure between the top and the bottom. This is also true of smaller inboard engines. However, as screw size increases the pressure differential increases and the lower part of the blade, broadly speaking, ' bites ' the water more than the upper as the screw turns. This has the effect of ' walking ' the stern in the direction of rotation.

Underway this has little effect as it is overcome by the rudder. However, when moving off or going astern it must be taken into consideration. In the latter case it may well dominate all other effects until the boat has reached a reasonable stern speed.

Rudder
A rudder is only effective when there is a flow of water past it, either ahead or astern, therefore at slow speeds its effect will be dominated by the screw or one of the other effects, say, wind.

An outboard has no rudder, but the whole engine is turned, and so the stern will move as it is directed by the screw, either ahead or astern, irrespective of speed.

Hull shape
Above water this will determine the effect of the wind, and a cabin for'd will mean that the wind will have a greater effect on the front end.

Below water the difference between inflatable and conventional craft is most marked. An inflatable has a very shallow draft, almost the same for'd as aft, and little or no keel. Whereas a conventional hull has a keel and a greater draught aft.

The inflatable's direction of movement is determined by the direction in which the screw is pushing. The moment the screw stops the movement of the tiller has no effect, and the flat shallow-draught hull has little directional stability and will only *tend* to continue in one direction bow first; it will very easily skid sideways.

Conventional craft, on the other hand, have a fine underwater shape and a keel, which means that once the screw stops they will continue in the same direction for some distance, and the rudder will be effective so long as there is a reasonable flow of water past it.

Load
Like a car free-wheeling down a hill, a loaded boat will continue much farther than a light one when the engine is stopped. Due allowance for this must be made when manoeuvring.

Sea State
Apart from rolling the boat and making life thoroughly uncomfortable, waves have the effect of slowing down a boat. When the engine is stopped in a craft heading into the sea it will not 'free-wheel' as far as normal because of the waves 'smacking' against the bow. Another point to remember when manoeuvring.

Now let's consider the basic manoeuvres mentioned earlier in the light of these relatively consistent effects, coupled with those variables, wind and tide. Though perhaps wind and tide are not so much variable as extremely difficult to assess accurately without instruments.

Picking Up a Person from the Sea

As far as most fishermen, yachtsmen and boatmen are concerned, this is an emergency measure, whereas in diving it is an everyday occurrence. The helmsman of a diving boat must therefore be very well versed in this procedure.

One or two fundamentals first. Your only concerns are the wind and waves, the tidal stream is quite irrelevant as both man and boat are being moved in the same mass of water. It is the effect of the wind which is dominant, together with the thought that we wish to avoid damaging the person on the water with any part of the hull or the screw. The essence of the manoeuvre is to stop the boat at right-angles to, and up wind of, the man.

The boat is showing much more surface area to the wind than the man, and so will be blown down much faster.

This method ensures that the screw is stopped well clear of the man, and that the boat and the person in the water make contact at minimum speed!

Even when the wind is light it is remarkable how quickly boat and man separate, when the boat is stopped downwind.

Should the boat be rolling uncomfortably it may be worth stopping at 45° to the wind, but remember the boat will only hold this position for, say, half a minute; it will soon be blown broadside on to the wind. Finally, when this manoeuvre is a matter of emergency, there is one cardinal rule. One member of the crew *must* be detailed to *watch the man* and point at him until he is finally recovered. Preparations should also be made to help him inboard, and one of the crew should be ready WITH A SAFETY LINE to enter the water and assist him. These rules apply to all boats, although in small craft which are highly manoeuvrable and have low gunwhales it is unlikely a man will be required to enter the water. Nevertheless he should be ready.

Anchoring

A relatively simple manoeuvre? Yes, but you have two concerns: that the anchor is dropped in the right place and, that once dropped, it stays put!

It is probably best to drop the anchor when stopped heading into the wind or tidal stream, whichever is dominant. Then go astern gently and lay the anchor line out on the sea bed. A minimum of twice the water depth is necessary for the anchor line to hold a boat safely in good weather. This means quite a large coil when in, say, 50 metres of water.

To avoid tangles and this

Sketch 5

the line must be laid out.

In anything but calm weather you will need an anchor line of more than twice the water depth.

Consider the tidal stream, ie, will it run in the same direction throughout the dive? If so, it may be worth anchoring off site and allowing the boat to drop back over site. This will allow a nice long safe anchor line and at the same time allow divers to reach the site quickly. It is also the only method if any form of lifting is to take place.

It is possible to anchor with a short anchor line, ie, less than twice the water depth. If you do, remember the line must be strong and preferably nylon with its stretch capability, and the fittings on the boat must be equally strong to take the stress caused by the vertical movement of the boat.

Further, you *must* retain a competent cox'n in the boat and have total faith in the engine starting without difficulty. You believe?

If you have any thought of anchoring and leaving the boat unattended, may I advocate an anchor line at minimum three times water depth and that the cox'n never forgets the weather—actual and forecast.

Berthing and Unberthing

In this manoeuvre all the various influences must be considered, for the shore—be it jetty, wall, or whatever, is very solid and will not move, whereas the boat is subject to every whim of tidal stream and wind, relatively flimsy and 'bends' rather easily!

Tidal stream, if it exists, is often the dominant factor, and whenever possible berth heading into it. In fact because it is necessary to keep the screw turning to hold the boat stopped over the ground, there is a flow of water past the rudder, and so a tidal stream is quite useful in that the boat may be steered until the very last moment.

In all boats the safest method of berthing is to head slowly into the tidal stream, as near parallel to the jetty as possible, making due allowance for wind. Speed is often difficult to judge, and certainly in the larger conventional boats it is worth stopping short of the berth and then proceeding at slow speed up to it. Further, this manoeuvre will be much easier if bow and stern lines are neatly made up *before* arrival alongside. It is to say the least 'cross-making' when, after a 45-minute cold, wet, miserable passage back from the diving area, the bowline is found to be buried under four sets of tanks, three weight belts and two people. . . . With the wind blowing off an unsheltered berth the approach cannot be quite parallel and the boat will 'crab', ie, move slightly sideways (Figure C).

The important thing in this case is to secure the bowline. Once this is done, even if the boat 'weathervanes' onto the wind, the stern line can then be lead ashore over the bow and the stern pulled bodily alongside. An offshore wind such as this presents no unberthing problems, however an onshore wind is quite a different story. In an inflatable and the

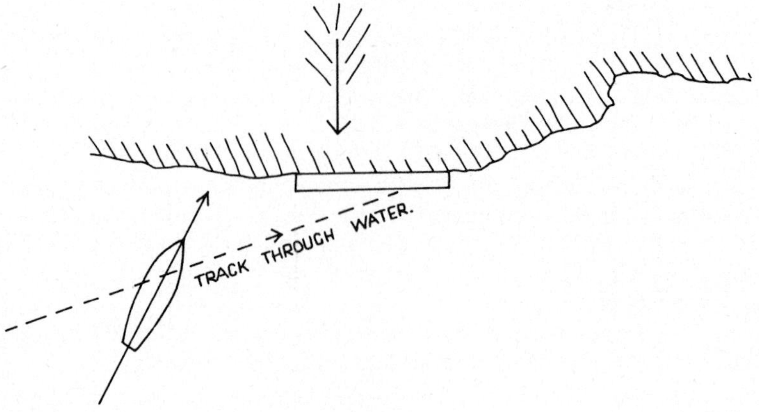

Figure C

smaller outboard engined boats it may well be best to leave the berth stern first, as going out ahead means brushing the side along the wall/ jetty until the boat has sufficient speed to head up into the wind.

Larger boats with inboard engines have even more of a problem, and here I have two suggestions. First, lead or secure the bowline as far forward as possible in the boat, then secure it on the shore at least as far aft as the stern. Cushion the bow well, hold the tiller or put the wheel over so as to head the boat into the jetty, then go ahead. Keep a careful eye on the bow, and increase speed smoothly, the stern will move out. When the boat has reached a minimum of a 45° angle with the wall, reverse the rudder, go full astern, and let go the bowline. The boat should move away from the jetty without damaging the bow. Now it may be that the effect of wind and tidal stream are such that the boat just will not reach 45° (Figure D). In this case try laying out the anchor at right-angles to the bow with a small boat. Then haul the bow off and go ahead, the tidal stream will help as soon as it is on the inboard bow. In this situation if an inflatable is available it may well be worth using it as a mini-tug on either bow or stern.

MINIMUM ANGLE
45 DEGREES. ———→

Figure D

Open Beach Work

Launch and Recovery from an open beach is a means of berthing used more frequently by the diver than any other sea user in these modern days.

I feel it should be appreciated that in anything but the lowest sea states this has never been and never will be a particularly simple or safe operation. Divers, however, have a bonus in that they are all wearing

—or have available—a warm buoyant wet suit and there should be no hesitation in entering the water.

As I mentioned earlier, waves break at a given ratio between their height and the water depth—roughly 3 :4. A steep shore may have only two or three rows of breakers, whereas on a shallow shore there may be a great many. It is the breaking waves which are the problem, as they break over and swamp a boat, rather than lift it up and down. Depending on the underwater terrain the situation may also be very different at high and low water. It is possible to leave shore at high water relatively simply only to return and find an impressive row of breakers although wind and sea remain unchanged—beware!

Whether beaching or launching a boat in surf, the essential requirement is patience. Watch the breakers for some time, note that they are not all of the same height or character. There are periods of relative calm—but don't depend on the mythical seventh or eleventh wave being larger than the rest.

When launching, have the boat with engine fitted ready on the beach, with enough men stationed round to lift it, and one ready to act as cox'n. Wait quietly for the moment when one wave has broken and another is not hard on its heels. Lift the boat onto the water quickly, and push/swim it as fast as possible through the breakers. As soon as the boat floats the cox'n must leap in and motor off clear of the crew, making sure they are not near the screw. He is then able to anchor, and drop back just clear of the breakers and wait for the others to join him with the rest of the gear. It may be worth launching without the engine and rely on clearing the breakers by straight pushing or use of oars or paddles. So much depends on water depth, the number and rows of breakers and, not least, crew experience.

Timing really is essential, and if there is any doubt—DON'T! Look for an alternative and more sheltered spot.

When landing, timing is equally important. Lie off and watch the waves for a while. In smaller breakers it may be possible to drive gently up to the beach—don't forget to unlock the outboard!—everyone leap out the moment the bow touches and quickly lift the boat ashore clear of the waves. In larger breakers there is little choice but to anchor off clear of the breakers, unload the boat, and swim or walk as much equipment as possible ashore. Then choosing the right moment of relative calm, pay out the anchor line rapidly until the crew can hold the boat, run it in stem first and lift it up the beach clear of the waves. If, whilst doing this manoeuvre, a breaker threatens to overtake the boat DON'T try to beat it ashore. Hold on to the anchor line, steady the boat, and wait for the wave or series of waves to pass.

Turning In a Confined Space

In the inflatable, outboard, or twin-screwed conventional hull this presents little problem. However, in a single-screwed conventional hull it requires some thought.

At slow speeds with little movement of water past the rudder the effect of the screw dominates. To manoeuvre your boat it is then necessary to know whether your screw is right or left handed (Figure B). Let

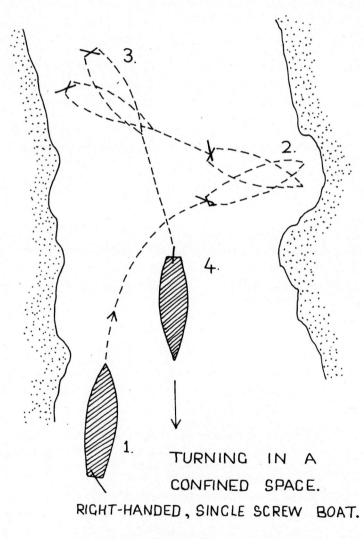

TURNING IN A CONFINED SPACE.

RIGHT-HANDED, SINGLE SCREW BOAT.

Figure E

us take a boat with a right handed screw at rest in a channel—position 1 Figure E.

1 Put the rudder to starboard, go half ahead for a few seconds, making sure the boat does not gather way. The stream of water past the rudder will kick the stern to port.

2 As soon as the boat is on the point of moving ahead, go half astern and put the rudder hard to port. The rudder is ineffective, and the screw turning left-handed astern will continue to 'walk' the stern to port.

3 As soon as the boat is on the point of moving astern, put the rudder hard to starboard and go half ahead. The stream of water past the rudder makes it effective and the stern continues to port.

4 Repeat actions 2 and 3 until the boat points in the required direction.

Theoretically, this is a beautifully simple manoeuvre, however in practice remember that the tidal stream may be moving the boat bodily towards a hazard although the manoeuvre appears to be going well. Further, the wind may distort the manoeuvre and if strong enough may well make it impossible, especially in boats with high superstructure for'd.

Towing

Sounds a simple manoeuvre, and certainly is in small boats and calm weather. However, as the sea state increases so do the problems, and I will list a few points.

1 Tow with your longest strongest rope—anchor line? It is then possible to adjust the length of tow until the boat being towed rides comfortably.

2 Towing points :
Boat Towed—Must be strong. The ring on the bow of an inflatable is probably not strong enough : consider the use of a yoke from the lifting handles. The thwarts of an open launch may well be stronger than the fittings on the bow.

Towing boat—In an inflatable consider a yoke from the transom either side of the engine, or the bottom boards or keel structure. Endeavour to get the point of tow as near the pivoting point as possible—about one-third from the bow.

3 Towing alongside—Good control possible, but of course there is the possibility of damage in any sea. The simplest method is to rig one line from bow to bow, another from stern to stern, and a third from the bow of the towing boat to the stern of the vessel

being towed. Try to adjust these so that the stern of the towing boat is behind that of the boat towed, this leaves the stern clear and permits greater manoeuvrability. This method is probably best used in sheltered waters or when manoeuvring the boat alongside after a sea tow.

4   If you are towing use ' his ' anchor line or painter—if he has one ! Because if your engine fails your anchor is the best remaining safety measure.

Securing to a Buoy

A fairly simple operation, especially when the buoy is small and the freeboard of the boat is low. Tide and wind matter as the buoy is fixed to the seabed. In the larger boats the cox'n may well be unable to see the buoy in the final stages of the approach; do help, and point it out to him. The cox'n in turn might well be advised to make his approach from the direction in which the other boats are lying—a simple method of observing if wind or tide has the major effect.

BASIC NAVIGATION

Let us for a few moments discuss why the ability to navigate might be of value to us as divers.

To begin with, it certainly isn't of any interest at all if we are always prepared to place ourselves in the hands of the local boatman, and are happy to dive roughly where the boat stops, purely for the enjoyment of being under water.

However, as soon as we have our own boat, or wish to visit and re-visit positions on the sea floor unknown to the boatman, ie, dive with a purpose, then some knowledge of navigation is required. For navigation is knowledge of position and as soon as our underwater interests mature and we take up say Biology, Archaeology, Wreck Exploration, Salvage, Geology or whatever, such knowledge is essential.

INSTRUMENT		COST		Accuracy * (Metres)		COMMENT
		New	2nd Hand	Good Weather	Bad Weather	
Our Eyes		?	Less	10	30	Used with transits.
SEXTANTS	Plastic	£4.50	don't	15	35	Robust, stands the wet.
	Conventional	£70 minimum	£30 to £40	10	35	Needs careful handling.
MAGNETIC COMPASS	Hand Bearing	£6.50 to £22	£6 to £10	50	200	Can be used for steering.
	Steering	£9.75 to £17.50	£6 to £10	Not applicable		Not usually fitted to take bearings in a small boat.
ECHO SOUNDER	Dial Read-out	£28	?	± 1% of recorded depth		Check that the recorder case is waterproof.
	Paper Read-out	£78	£30 to £40	better than ± 1% of recorded depth		Can be used from inflatables.

* The figures given are the radii of circles within which a position 'fixed' by the instrument concerned may be expected to lie.

We should also realise at this stage that our need for this knowledge to be accurate is much greater than that of the average yachtsman. In the UK, underwater vision is normally such that it is necessary to land a diver within, say, 30 m. of a target on the sea floor if he is to find it before his air supply is exhausted. Whereas the yachtsman in his surface travels only needs to know his position within 60-90 m. However you will be pleased to know that achieving such accuracy, and perhaps under some conditions—better, is not in any way impossible!! as I hope to explain in the remainder of the chapter. The method is usually simple even though it may be based on incomprehensible mathematics. The main requirements—as with most operations connected with the sea—are patience and determination.

As amateurs in small inflatables, or even in bigger boats, we cannot afford expensive equipment to help us find our way around. The table opposite sets out those that are available to us.

The first three may be used independently, but the Echo Sounder must be used with one of the others. In fact a more accurate result can often be obtained by using one instrument with another.

Note too, that to navigate accurately but cheaply we are limited to remaining in sight of land.

Now let's take a brief look at each of these instruments in turn.

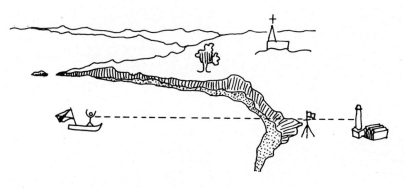

Figure 1: Transit

Eyes

By far the cheapest instrument and common to most of us! Can also be supplemented with binoculars. Their major navigational use is to observe what are known as 'transits' or fishermen's 'marks'.

If two objects, 'marks', on shore are lined up one behind the other they are in 'transit' and if the course of the boat is adjusted so as to keep them in this position it will proceed in a straight line.

Other 'transits' may then be used to give position, as I will discuss in a moment.

The magnetic compass

The earth acts as an enormous magnet. Invisible lines of magnetic force run from one end (pole) of it to the other, and a compass needle is so made that it will lie parallel to the lines.

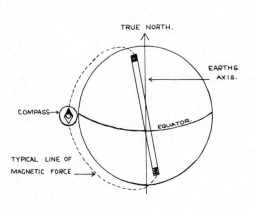

Figure 2

The lines of magnetic force really do act as in the diagram and so a magnetic compass will stand on its head in the Arctic or Antarctic and be of little use.

Now life would be relatively simple if the direction of this great imaginary magnet, and that of the axis about which the earth rotates—a direction used as the reference for all maps and charts—were the same.

Of course, nothing is ever that easy! and not only does this imaginary magnet point in a different direction, it also moves an appreciable amount each year.

Luckily it is possible to calculate the difference in direction—known as VARIATION—and predict the movement, and both values are shown on modern charts and maps.

It is also a regrettable fact of life that in addition to the difference between the direction of these two poles, the compass needle won't even point at the mag-

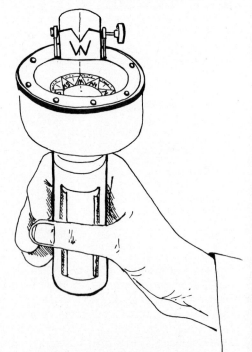

Figure 3: Handbearing compass

netic one! The metal parts of the boat, engine, and *people*! affect it, and worse, their effect varies with the direction the boat is pointing. Again we are lucky in that this effect may be measured and under some conditions even ignored. Lucky, too, that to make the measurement we don't require the services of a mathematician, we can with a little thought do it ourselves.

Figure 4: Steering compass

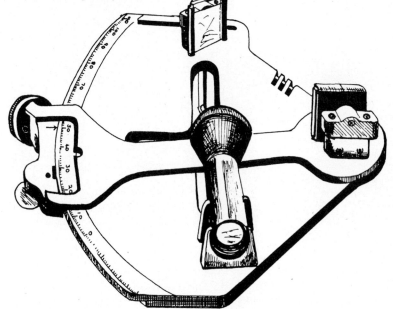

Figure 5: The Sextant

The sextant

This instrument is nothing more nor less than an accurate device for measuring angles, as shown in Figure 5.

The Echo Sounder

This device measures the distance from the transmitting head (transducer) to the sea bed. It does this by sending out frequent pulses of sound which travel through the water at a known speed, and measuring the time it takes for each one to reach the sea bed and return to the transducer. From this known time and speed it

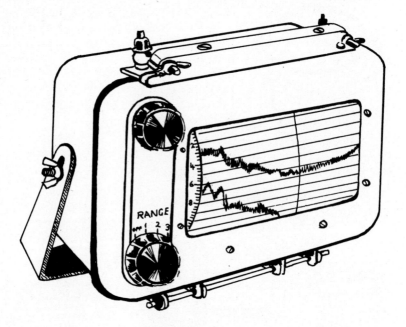

Figure 6: Echo Sounder

is then a relatively simple matter for the electronics to calculate depth, instantaneously for each pulse. It can then be displayed either on a dial or a paper trace.

Method

Coastal Navigation is position finding at sea, and in practice relies on similar rules to those used in land survey.

The chart or Ordnance Survey map provides us with an accurate plot of most of the conspicuous objects on shore visible from the sea. The simplest way to find our position is to work from these known positions with the instruments we have already discussed.

One way of looking at the problem is to consider that each instrument in conjunction with a shore mark or marks is capable of producing a 'POSITION LINE'. Where two such lines cross is then our position. I'll now go on to discuss how these lines may be extracted from each of the instruments we are likely to come across.

Eyes

If two objects marked on a chart are kept one behind the other, then we must be somewhere on the line. Two such lines as near as possible at right angles provide us with our position—figure 7.

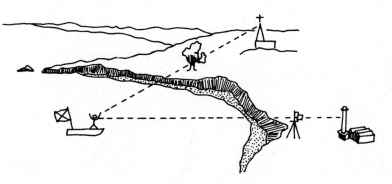

Figure 7: Position Lines—Transit

Magnetic Compass

The compass needle is set in a circular card marked clockwise in 360 degrees with zero at North (Figure 4). If a sighting device containing a prism is placed over the top of the compass (Figure 3) it is possible to look along a line from the centre of the needle to any chosen mark. By looking down through the prism the angle between this sighting line and North may be read. This angle is known as the 'Magnetic Bearing'—090° in Figure 8.

The sighting line may be reproduced on the chart of the area by adjusting a parallel ruler on the representation of the compass rose until it is lined up to the magnetic bearing. The ruler is then run over the chart until it passes through the mark, and a pencil line drawn along its edge.

The pencil line is our 'position line' for we know that at the time of the sight we were 'somewhere' on it.

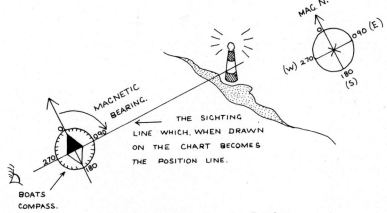

Figure 8: A Magnetic Compass Bearing

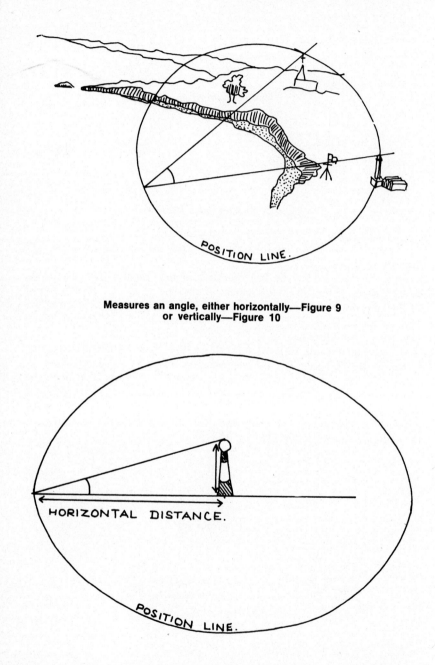

**Measures an angle, either horizontally—Figure 9
or vertically—Figure 10**

Sextant

In both cases this time the position lines are curved, but for different reasons.

Horizontally, we are governed by geometric principles, which say that any angle we measure between two marks can be represented by a circle of a given radius passing through those two marks. This circle is our position line.

Vertically from the angle we measure and the height of the target we are able to calculate or consult tables which give our horizontal distance. This distance is the radius of a circle and that circle becomes our position line.

Echo Sounder

The position line from an echo sounder is nothing more than a depth contour line taken from the chart. Providing you have a rough idea of position, and have made due allowance for tidal height, then a sharp contour may provide a position line.

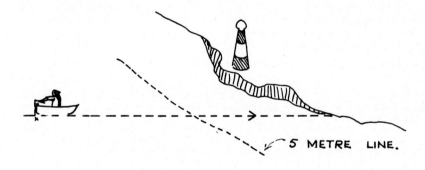

Figure 11: Contour line by echo sounder

For example, in Figure 11, when your sounder reads 5 metres + tidal height, you know that you are ' somewhere ' on that 5 metre line.

Practical notes

You're probably way ahead of me and have already sorted out that we are able to use our instruments either singly or in combination to produce position lines and where they cross is our position, or a navigational ' fix '. Both the position lines must also of course have been obtained at virtually the same time or else the boat will have travelled an appreciable distance between them and therefore the fix will be inaccurate.

It is also of particular note that a magnetic compass may be used to measure the angle between two marks simply by subtracting their bearings.

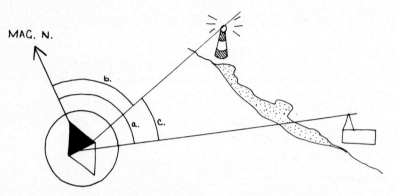

Figure 12: Angle measured by hand bearing compass

For example, in Figure 12, a−b=c. Provided the boat is kept on a steady course while the bearings are taken, in order that the deviation does not alter, then the direction of the compass needle is purely of value as a reference and the effect of variation, deviation, or anything else does not bother us at all, and the curved position line used just as one derived from a sextant.

Plotting the curved position lines obtained by a sextant or compass may seemingly be difficult, but this is not so, as an instrument known as a "Station Pointer" has been developed (Figure 13); for a purely sextant fix, three shore marks are needed so as to provide two angles (a and b in the Figure).

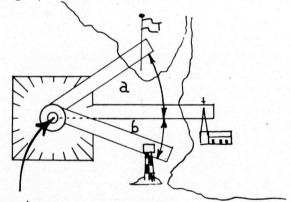

You are here.

Figure 13

The instrument consists of a protractor with one fixed and two moveable arms originating from the centre. The angles 'a' and 'b' are set between the arms, which are then locked in position. The protractor is then moved over the chart until the three arms pass through the chosen marks. Position is then simply marked through the centre with a pencil.

Echo Sounder

The pulses of sound are not terribly strong and if a small boat travels at speed or even slowly in rough water the turbulence around the transducer will destroy them, and no depth will be recorded. Care must be taken to site the transducer on a part of the hull where the water flow is smooth. If the transducer is portable—lashed to a broomstick!— as it is almost bound to be in an inflatable, the same rule applies and the best spot found by experience.

If you are literally using a broomstick, do make sure that it is lashed so that it points vertically downwards, otherwise you will get a reading which is too deep. Thought might also be given to mounting the transducer in a streamlined block of wood which may reduce turbulence and permit readings at a higher speed.

A reasonable idea of the likely error from any is given by the fact that an angle of one degree subtends an arc of 30 m at one nautical mile. If we sight with our magnetic compass and the needle is swinging about three degrees either side of the mark, as it will from a small boat on a choppy day, then we can expect an error in our position of between say 90 and 180 m at one nautical mile, and more, of course, the farther away we get.

A sextant is much more accurate all the time, until the sea or rain is such that the marks cannot be lined up in the mirrors.

For maximum accuracy, try to combine as many of these factors as possible :

Calm day

Stable boat

Minimum time between observing position lines

Minimum boatspeed

Marks at same height

Marks with good vertical edges.

Finally, we have talked so far of two position lines as being enough to 'fix' our whereabouts. Two lines cross, great, we know just where we are . . . . . or do we? As your experience improves, try to obtain a third—remembering to keep the boat's speed at a minimum as they are taken. The result will probably be surprising, for instead of all the lines crossing at a nice neat point they're much more likely to produce a peculiar picture. Then where are we? Conventionally when navigating the point of the triangle—known as a 'cocked hat'—nearest danger is chosen, but for our purposes choose the centre. The size of the cocked hat also gives a very clear indication of the error of the fix, which is of course most useful. If it is too big, forget it and quickly take another round of position lines.

This chapter is intended to give a broad picture of the various aspects of navigation.

Plotting a Course

The diver, having decided where he wants to go by inspection of the chart and when he wants to arrive by investigation of the tables, must plot a course in soft pencil on the chart from the point of departure to the desired diving site.

Remembering to allow some time for finding the site after the believed area has been reached. Unless the diver is unbelievably lucky he will not drop straight on top of the wreck, especially navigating from a small boat. Time will have to be spent making an organised search once the approximate position has been verified. On a site undived before and without the help of local knowledge on board, too much time can't be allowed, two or three hours is not out of the way and in extreme cases even a period of days is involved. It is surprising how long it can take to find a particular hump on the bottom. This must be taken into account when plotting the course so that the arrival at the site will be well within the time desired.

First draw a line from the departure point to the site on the chart (line AB in Figure 1). Then inspect the chart to see which of the tidal diamonds are being passed on the trip (see Figure 1).

The diver, already knowing the desired time of arrival and allowing search time if necessary, must estimate the time to be taken for the trip so that an approximate departure time can be found. This is done by setting the dividers on the latitudinal scale and adjusting them for one minute, then step off the distance of the line AB (assuming the scale is one inch to the nautical mile and the course line is five inches long, then the distance from A to B will be five nautical miles). With a boat making five knots the distance would be covered in approximately one hour. Therefore assuming the dive should begin two hours before high water, an hour was allowed for search time and the voyage was going to take approximately one hour, then the time for departure would be four hours before high water.

Having found the relevant tidal information diamond which affects the planned course (A in Figure 1), the tidal stream panel on the side of the chart is examined for the corresponding symbol. A tidal rate and direction can then be extracted for four hours before high water.

Now, using the parallel rules, set them on the nearest compass rose to the departure point—courses in degrees are given for the direction in which the tidal flow is going, as with a boat for the direction that it is heading; values for wind are always given for the direction from which it is blowing—lay them through the centre point and to the value given in degrees for the flow of the tide marked on the outside circle of the rose. Then move the parallel rules across the chart to the departure point (A) and draw a line from that point in the direction of the flow (along the line AC). Then with a compass measure the rate given for the flow against the latitudinal scale and then from the departure point (A) mark (C). Again with the compass adjusted to the speed of the boat against the latitudinal—one minute for each nautical mile of speed— with the compass point at (C) mark off point (D) on the course line.

Using the parallel rules the line (CD) is moved across the chart to the compass rose and the true course in degrees can be read off to which must be applied the Variation for a Magnetic course to steer. This course then allows for the way the flow of tide is setting the boat back. The distance (AD) on Figure 1 will be the actual distance made good along the course. It will be found that the boat will make greater or lesser speed through the water depending on whether the flow is with or against the boat. The magnetic course may be adjusted to take account of the deviation factor which is an additional error to the compass due to the magnetic effect of iron/steel in the boat itself.

Note that if the course takes more than an hour to cover it will be necessary to draw as above hourly for each successive change in rate and direction of the tide from the last point reached, as in description above at point (D).

If the chart is large scale, then the distance on the latitudinal scale may become cumbersome, in which case work it out for half the rate of flow and half the speed of the boat.

Leeway. Attention when making the course must be paid to the wind. This can be allowed for, when plotting the course on the chart, if the force and direction of the wind and the action of the boat as a result are known.

However, it tends to be more of a seamanship factor—the helmsman allowing a little for the wind as he is making his course. No two boats react the same, the effect depends on the draught, freeboard and (with sailing boats) the amount of sail and how close to the wind.

The reaction for a particular boat can be found by sailing a previously plotted course towards a fixed point ashore to see how much the boat is being pushed to leeward. Alternatively a magnetic bearing of the farthest part of the wake can be reversed by adding or subtracting 180 degrees and comparing the result with the boat's magnetic course.

Information on Laying a Course and Leeway :
  Reeds Nautical Almanac   Page 265.
  Coastwise Navigation   Page 46.

Fixing a Position

Having arrived where the diving site is supposed to be, it is doubtful an obliging funnel will be sitting clear of the water to mark the position of the wreck. It is necessary therefore to prove that the boat has in fact arrived in the vicinity of the proposed dive and this can be done in three ways : horizontal sextant angles, compass bearings and cross transits.

Compass Bearings. Compass bearings of prominent marks on the coastline from the boat must be taken and plotted on the chart. Two are sufficient to obtain an approximate fix, the angle between them not being less than 30 degrees. However, a much more accurate fix will be obtained if three bearings are taken, these when plotted will make a small triangle on the chart, the centre of which can be assumed to be the position of the boat.

Before plotting on the chart don't forget to allow for variation on the compass bearing. It is difficult, if not impossible, to allow for deviation for a small boat carrying diving gear. Deviation is the local magnet effect that a boat will have on a particular compass, a factor that can be calculated and allowed for in larger boats.

Horizontal Sextant Angles. A sextant and a station pointer are necessary for this operation, although it is possible to plot the angles on the chart with only the use of a compass and a protractor. Obviously a knowledge of the sextant is necessary and practise is needed in becoming quick and efficient in its use.

This method has an advantage over compass bearings because it is not affected by either variation or deviation, therefore eliminating a source of some considerable error if the allowances are not calculated properly. Again I must stress that unless much practise is done with the sextant errors will quickly be made in the angles observed. However, in the absence of a sextant an uncorrected compass could be used to fix the angles, eg bearing of A=030 degrees; bearing of B=060 degrees; bearing of C=100 degrees : then the angle A-8=030-060=30 degrees and angle B-C=060-100=40 degrees.

When two suitable features can be observed on either side of a central point at angles of greater than 30 degrees, the angles the outside ones make with centre one can be measured by holding the sextant along the horizontal plane with the index bar uppermost, the angles obtained can then be plotted on the chart.

Transits. This is a particularly good fix if two points in a line can be seen and recognised. For instance a flag staff in the foreground with a church steeple in the background, or a headland in line with something in the distance. It is unlikely that two separate transits could be found to fix a position. However, one will give a definite line of position and a compass bearing will fix it pretty closely. It should be pointed out that a double transit fix is extremely accurate.

Due to the fact that diving is usually done from small boats it is as well to work out what the compass bearings (magnetic) or horizontal angles should be from the seaward at the diving site, of prominent features shown on the chart before the dive. Then they can be compared with those obtained in practice, the boat being moved until the predetermined factors are found. This will certainly save a lot of difficulty trying to plot things on a chart in difficult conditions. Don't forget that once the position has been fixed that it is desirable to anchor, or, more important if a search is to be made with the boat from this point, a buoy should be put down, otherwise a point from which the search should relate will not be available.

Use of a Station Pointer. A thorough explanation of their use is given in the instructions at purchase. They are made in both steel and plastic. The plastic ones are extremely effective and inexpensive. The use is quite simple, setting the movable arms against the fixed central arm to imitate the angles found either from the compass or horizontal sextant angles. Fixing a Position :

The Mariner's Handbook	Page	16,
Coastwise Navigation	Page	49.
Reed's Nautical Almanac	Pages	263.
		267B, 316.

How to Plot Horizontal Sextant Angles with Compass and Protractor

Join points A to B and to C the observed horizontal angle between A and B is 42 degrees : subtract this from 90 degrees

$$90 - 42 = 48 \text{ degrees}$$

Lay off angles of 48 degrees from A and from B, to intersect at X, making an isosceles triangle.

Using X as a centre, and with the compass radius XB, draw a circle over the seaward area. This circle will pass through A.

The horizontal angle between B and C was observed to be 57 degrees.

$$90 - 57 = 33 \text{ degrees}$$

Construct angles of 33 degrees at B and C to intersect at Y. Using Y as a centre and compass with radius YC cut circle already drawn at P on the seaward part of the chart. This is the observed position.

Pencils—Hexagonal, grade B.

Soft Rubbers.

Dividers—Large (say 7") most suitable.

A pair of Compasses—Ordinary school brass type compasses are adequate. However, one with an extending arm is sometimes more convenient, giving a larger reach.

Parallel Rules—Roller type are easily moved across the chart. Sliding type are made in either wood or plastic, the latter are inexpensive, the best length about 15 inches.

Douglas combined protractor and parallel rule—Cheaper and smaller than a parallel rule of the conventional type, with more functions but a little more difficult to use initially.

Recommended Reading:

Admiral Manual of Navigation, Vols. 1 & 2: Published by H.M.S.O. (chart agents) cost similar to Seamanship.

Admiralty Manual of Seamanship, Vols. 1 & 2: Published by H.M.S.O. (chart agents).

Marine Chart Work and Navaids: Published by Kandy Publications. Author D. A. Moore.

The Mariner's Highway Code: Published by The Maritime Press. Author Capt. D. P. Derret.

Outlook (Weather maps and elementary forecasting): Published by Kandy Publications. Author W. W. White.

Reed's Nautical Almanac: Published Annually. Wonderful value for money. A wealth of information clearly set out with examples. Obtainable at most chart agents and book shops.

The Mariner's Handbook: Published by the Hydrographic Department. Thorough information about charts clearly set out, symbols, buoyage systems and the weather. Obtainable at chart agents.

Coastwise Navigation: Published by Kandy Publications. Author C. G. Watkins. This little book can't be spoken of too highly. Simple, clear and easy to understand.

Admiralty Tide Tables Vol. 1: Published by the Hydrographers Department. Obtainable from chart agents.

Admiralty Chart No. 5011: Contains information on chart symbols.

Catalogue of Admiralty Charts: Published by the Hydrographers Department. Obtainable from chart agents. Contains list of chart agents, list of charts available for the British Isles and some Continental countries, and showing map sections of the relevant parts.

Met. Office Leaflet No. 1: Obtainable from the weather centre, 284-286, High Holborn Road, London W.C.1. A mine of information.

CHARTS & TIDES

Chartwork

The best charts made are Admiralty Charts which are published by the Hydrographers Office. They are printed in three main scales. At one inch to the nautical mile for Ocean Charts, three inches to the nautical mile for Coastal Charts and six inches to ten inches to the nautical mile for harbours and entrances. The actual scale of the chart is stated on it; the larger the scale of the chart the more precise the information on it. The charts are available from chart agents, a list of whom are published in the *Catalogue of Admiralty Charts,* published by the Hydrographers Office.

The charts are continuously being brought up to date as new information is received, the Hydrographers Office publishing regular statements called 'Notices to Mariners' which are numbered. It is possible by looking at the bottom left-hand corner of the chart to see how recent and accurate the particular chart is. Written in small italics are the words 'Small Corrections' and immediately afterwards, yearly dates with numbers printed after them. These corrections have been made since the first date shown and relate to alterations made to the particular chart, the numbers identifying the specific Notice. Corrections will often be seen on charts obtained from chart agents in purple ink and are corrections done by them to the stock of charts they have in hand from the latest Notices.

At the bottom right and top left hand corners of the chart will be found the number of the particular chart.

Along the top and bottom of the chart runs the longitudinal scale and at the sides, the latitudinal scale, which are marked off in degrees and minutes. Positions on the chart are related to these two scales. Distance is found from the latitudinal scale, one minute always being equal to one nautical mile.

When courses are plotted on the chart they should always be true courses. On the chart will be found two or three circles marked off in degrees. These are called Compass Roses and are used for laying courses onto the chart. Each Rose is marked with an outer and inner circle. The outer marked in True bearings and the inner in Magnetic. Along the diameter on an East to West line will be found in bold print the words and figures—Variation so many degrees and so many minutes, East or West and a date in brackets; afterwards in italics will be found a note saying decreasing so many minutes annually. To find Magnetic North this decreasing value must be calculated from the year shown to the present one and then applied to True North.

When this Variation is applied to a True course plotted on the chart then a Magnetic course is found. There is also a factor called

Deviation which is local magnetic effect of the boat on the compass on a particular heading. When Variation and Deviation are applied to the True course a Compass or Steering course is obtained. If there is no Deviation then the Magnetic course would also be the Compass course.

Courses written in degrees on the chart should carry a letter after them to designate their type. T = True course, M = Magnetic course and C = Compass course.

On the chart in one area will be found a section usually comprising a series of boxes giving information which relates to the chart.

There is usually one box for the conversion of fathoms and feet to metres. All charts that are being made now are being changed over to the metric system.

A scale of latitude and distance.

A tidal information box relating to chart datum. The Lowest Astronomical Tide is the lowest level which can be predicted to occur under (a) average meteorological conditions and (b) any combination of astronomical conditions. The level of LAT is reached only occasionally and not every year. Lower levels than this can occur with particular meteorological conditions (see page 433 *Reed's Nautical Almanac*). Mean Low Water Springs will usually be about two feet above this level.

Panels marked Tidal Streams are of particular use and importance. At various points on the chart will be found diamonds with a capital letter in them. These relate to sections in the panel and give information of the rate and directions of the Tidal Streams hourly before and after high water at the point marked on the chart. Latitude and longitude of the sites of tide measurement are given at the top of the section. At the side of the panel will be found the name of a standard port to which these facts relate.

Attention should be paid to the cautionary notes that are marked on the chart.

Much can be learned about charts and symbol recognition by the individual by references to and study of the keys that are to be found in several publications. Much rewarding time can be spent going over a chart with one of these keys as a reference, it is quite surprising the diverse amount of information that can be obtained.

For an explanation of the use of charts refer to :

Admiralty Manual of Navigation Vol I (and II)

Reed's Nautical Almanac

Coastwise Navigation   Pages 3 and 26.

The Mariners' Handbook   Page 11.

For an explanation of chart symbols :

Admiralty Manual of Navigation Vol. I (and II)

Admiralty Chart No 5011

Reed's Nautical Almanac   Page 270.

The Mariners' Handbook   Page 50.

Tides

The diver usually knows the site at which he is planning to dive and would normally want the best conditions if his dive is to centre round a specific site. He would of course look for swifter moving water if he were planning a drift dive or hoped to see surface disturbance on a calm day caused by an obstruction on the bottom.

Firstly, the site must be identified on the chart and the latitude and longitude references determined. Then the nearest diamond with a capital letter in it must be found, which will refer to a corresponding symbol in the panel marked 'Tidal Streams' indicating a particular section. On inspection there will be found a list of tidal directions and rates, for both before and after high water, referring to the site but relating to a specified standard port.

On examination it will quickly be seen when the slackest currents are available, there will quite possibly, in some cases, be one or two consecutive hours when the current will be reasonable or even low. The rates will always be slower at Neaps. Having found the current suitable note the times before or after high water as the case may be.

Then with this information go to the tide tables in either *Reed's Nautical Almanac* or the *Admiralty Tides Tables Vol I*. Turn up the index and look for the name on the port given in the 'Tidal Stream' panel on the chart. On turning to the page indicated, the times for high water and the height of the water (which must be added to chart datum if the depth of water is required, for instance if an echo sounder is to be used in combination with charted depths) will be found set out for each day of the year. The Admiralty Tide Tables give low water heights and times as well.

Then add or subtract from the time given in the tables, the time before or after high water found on the chart. For example if it was necessary to commence diving two hours before high water and the times given for high water at the standard port were 02.00 or 14.00, then the diving time would be 02.00 less two hours—00.00 or midnight. 14.00 less two hours 12.00 or mid-day.

Tidal stream atlases are also available to show the general direction of the tide before or after high water, the rate of the tide being shown above the arrows. They again relate to a standard port. Twelve pocket atlases are published by the Hydrographers Office covering the British Isles and some are reproduced in *Reed's Nautical Almanac.*

Sometimes the diver may want to know the height of the tide at a given time, this can be calculated by a fairly satisfactory rule of thumb method. As long as the range of the tide is known, that is the difference in height from high to low water, the problem is easy. The range is divided into twelve parts and the time which is approximately six hours into six parts. Then the height is said to change one-twelfth in the first sixth, two-twelfths in the second sixth, three-twelfths in the third sixth, three-twelfths in the fourth sixth, two-twelfths in the fifth sixth and finally one-twelfth in the sixth sixth.

Don't forget that the tables whilst being substantially accurate are still approximations. Local knowledge from, for instance, fishermen is invaluable for specific sites as well as general information.

Range of tides : *Reed's Nautical Almanac*   Page 436.

Coastal Navigation   Page 26.

Tides :   *Reed's Nautical Almanac*   Page 421.

Coastal Navigation   Page 21.

DIVE REPORTS & LOG BOOKS

The keeping of logbooks and dive reports is as necessary in diving as in any other activity requiring careful supervision. They fulfil two basic purposes: the control of a dive and its permanent record.

Control of dive

On a small diving party there is probably no need for a written record of the progress of the dive, although frequently the expedition leaders will jot down the order of diving—the names of dive leaders and companions—on a piece of paper. This is a rudimentary form of dive log.

On full scale expeditions far more detail needs to be recorded. There may be many divers, different parties—such as snorkel, aqualung, photography—specific underwater exercises, or diving over several days. Certain parts of the log should be prepared in advance where these are known, such as the names of divers. These parts can be used to control the conduct of the dive. Other parts of the log will be filled in as the dive proceeds, such as the duration of divers underwater, cylinders used and those still available for use, progress or need of decompression. Logs for this purpose should be drawn up to suit the particular dive or expedition in hand, and filled in at the time by the diving marshal or someone specially appointed to be in charge of these records. A suggested diving log is shown on the following page.

In this specimen log, the wind force should be noted in terms of the Beaufort wind scale (see Appendix) and it should be remembered that the wind direction is that from which the wind comes. In the case of swell direction, it is that towards which the swell is travelling.

In order to provide some measure of standardisation, it is recommended that the state of the sea and swell is noted in accordance with the sea and swell scales listed in the appendix.

Tides should be noted as ebbing, flooding or slack, ie, at high or low water. Spring tides are exceptionally high and low tides that occur with new and full moons. Neap tides are tides with the smallest water movement, or 'tidal range', and occur midway between spring tides. Tidal streams are measured in knots, (see Appendix) and so are currents. Their strength and 'set', or direction, can be different at depth than at the surface. In this respect, a check should be made on the bottom by comparing the lie of the anchor line or a compass reading against the lie of seaweed, movement of disturbed sand, or merely by relaxing to observe the effects of the current on the body. In the sea or open water, the set is the direction in which the current is going. In rivers the direction of the current is usually of great importance.

Weather may be described as seen without resorting to the standard meteorological terms by the uninformed. Surface visibility is expressed in

Diving Log

Date ....Location ....Diving Marshal...................

Purpose .... Equipment...

....

....

....

Nearest Doctor .... Nearest Coastguard...........................

Nearest recompression Chamber ....

Nearest First Aid ....

Weather.................. Wind.................. Visibility.................. Air Temp..................

Current.................. Sea........................ Tide........................ Swell..................

Underwater visibility .... Surface Water Temp...........................

1st Dive   Start................. Finish.................

	Air Supply			Time		Dura-tion	Depth
	Bottle Cap.	Bars In	Bars Out	In	Out		
Dive Leader							
Diver							
Diver							
Diver							
Diver							

Safety Party

Boat .... Special Features ....

Shore ....

Snorkel Cover ....

General Remarks ....

....

....

2nd Dive   Start................. Finish.................

*(Details of subsequent dives to be recorded
similarly to those of the first dive)*

kilometres or metres from the height of 2 metres above water level; underwater visibility is unfortunately limited to feet and sometimes inches and should be measured with a standard secchi disc. This is a round, white disc 22 cm in diameter. It is lowered on a line into the water and the visibility is the depth measured by the line at which the edge of the disc is just discernible. Alternatively, the estimated horizontal underwater visibility may be recorded.

Expedition records

From the logs used on a dive, and from personal accounts, a permanent record can be kept of all branch expeditions. These are useful for planning future dives, recording useful and important details of dive conduct, findings or research carried out, and for listing the extent of individual members' participation in branch activities.

As well as dive details, factors affecting base organisation, air charging stations, boat hire, and so on should be recorded. In this way, a complete account of all factors affecting diving will be built up for future reference.

Branch records

A branch log is very well worthwhile. It should detail the experience of each member, his diving training qualifications and experience. The names of expedition leaders, diving marshals and dive leaders should be kept together with a list of other branch diving officials. It is also useful to record the names of those members who are qualified and suitable to give lectures and instruction or to train and test members on behalf of the branch diving officer.

Another purpose of a branch log is to list all branch-owned equipment, where it is kept, who is authorised to use it, and when it is, or is due to be, overhauled, or tested.

A divers' logbook

From the official Club point of view, a member's Diving Qualifications Logbook is an essential record of his training, progress and qualifications, and should always be treated as a valuable document.

Accordingly, members should see that details of training, tests, lectures and dives are filled in as soon as possible, not left until later when memory of details has become blurred, dates forgotten and signatures of instructors or companion divers unobtainable.

An accurate and carefully completed logbook will also recall to mind many enjoyable dives and interesting facts that might otherwise be forgotten.

Apart from being of interest to a diver himself, his personal logbook is evidence of his diving experience and standard. Within the Club, and for many other bodies also, the Qualifications logbook is the primary record of a diver's ability, and it enables him to take part in dives of other branches, among people until then unknown, without having specially to prove his diving standard or to undergo renewed tests.

Additionally, the record of dives may be drawn upon as a reference book for such purposes as Club surveys of national diving performances, scientific investigations of conditions prevailing at different sites or times of year, or for medical checks relating to problems of decompression.

The members' logbooks provided by the Club contain all the essential elements for a record of dives.

A tidy and complete logbook is the hallmark of a thorough and competent diver. It reflects both pride and interest.

SCIENTIFIC EXPEDITIONS

There are fundamental differences between a diving expedition over a weekend—usually undertaken for pleasure and virtually no more than an outing—and one that is mounted for a specific purpose and likely to last for a longer period of time.

Weekend outings that are loosely termed 'expeditions' have been dealt with competently elsewhere in this book, so it is unnecessary to draw comparisons here. What must be done, however, is to give detailed guidance about full-scale diving expeditions for there is a great deal to be taken into consideration if they are to be both successful and enjoyable. For convenience, I have broken down the various sections as follows :

1 Definition, planning, flexibility.
2 Background, literature, charts, special maps.
3 Time, place, season, weather, type of diving, special equipment.
4 Personal logistics, team selection, training, official bodies, banking, insurance.
5 Material logistics, boat, store, filling, fresh water, workshop, transport, accommodation.
6 Records, echo-sounding, fixing, dive-logging, photography, diary.
7 Special equipment.
8 Fitness, psychology, sleep, food, drink.
9 Writing up and publication.

1 The principal aim of a diving expedition cannot be decided overnight or fabricated after gathering together a jolly team and choosing a nice diving site. The aim must arise naturally out of the developments in a sphere of knowledge, and plans for the project must be made in the context of previous work on the subject. In general it is never worth just 'searching for something'. Discoveries of underwater features are usually accidental, and the discoverer is seldom qualified to take the work to completion. Conversely, to deploy an experienced diving team for many days in a search and then wind up the project without applying expertise to the discovery is a waste of effort. In any case, if nothing turns up within a few days, the search is extremely tedious.

A working expedition will consist of between four and ten experienced divers. Since diving efficiency increases rapidly during the settling in period of about one week, it is not worth considering working periods of less than two weeks. On the other hand, working periods of more than three months are unlikely because of variable seasonal conditions. Planning period for an expedition varies from a *minimum* of six months for a four-man two-week job to two years for a ten-man three-month one.

385

In spite of the scale of planning, the precision with which the aim must be defined, and the detailed calculations as to working methods, it is essential to preserve flexibility. This in fact arises naturally from thorough planning, since it will pinpoint the problems likely to arise, and the points at which discoveries during work will influence the future programme. Thus it is essential to anticipate the different courses along which the project may develop on the site, the events which may cause plans to be curtailed or altered, and to provide alternative minor projects if part of the main programme has to be abandoned.

2   An operational diving project is aimed at solving a problem, and the expedition will only be a success if the project leader becomes an expert in that subject. It is not adequate simply to be a good diver : whether the project is scientific or industrial, the dive leader will have to take decisions relating to the basic problem as well as the diving. This means that preparation must include considerable reading and effort devoted to finding people who are already familiar with the topic. The urge to be first, to *discover* things, leads many divers to neglect wilfully this search for other people who may have tackled the problem before them, and yet only by doing this, and laying one's plans so as to build on other people's work, can you hope to avoid duplication and the rediscovery of old facts.

The necessity is for thorough reading, plenty of contacts and plenty of time. The popular and semi-popular diving and underwater books contain reading lists of a more specialised nature, and these in turn contain references to original research papers, with names of research workers, institutes and companies. These lines of inquiry must be followed up.

When the work site has been selected (see item 3), further reading may have to be done on the special conditions of the area, geology, biology, weather, water movements, and so on. In addition Admiralty charts, large scale Ordnance Survey maps and possibly Geological Survey maps and other specialised maps should be purchased well in advance (Stanfords; Admiralty Chart Agents). Always write in advance to local contacts, marine research stations, coastguards, harbour-master, boat owners, and any other officials you may have to deal with. Get from them information about local conditions, tides, weather, local diving regulations and laws. Remember that some countries regard diving as a menace to security, possibly the economy, and probably morals.

3   Projects can be classified as *systematic* and *regional*. A *regional* project is concerned with a specific problem in a specific area : is there tin off Cornwall; is the rock under the English Channel suitable for a tunnel; what kinds of coral grow off Gibraltar and why? A *systematic* project is concerned with more general problems : what is the relation

between waves on the surface and waves on thermoclines; what is the relation between concentration of heavy minerals and wave patterns; what is the relation between light intensity, depth, and rate of growth of algae?

If you select a regional problem, your working site is obviously narrowly defined, and you have only to choose the exact harbour to work from, and the precise diving point. Nevertheless, it is often worth travelling to the site many months in advance for a 'recce', and to make yourself known to the locals. A pint of beer or a glass of wine will often work wonders with a contact who had previously not bothered to answer letters. If your project is systematic, the question becomes 'where in the world is the phenomenon most clearly manifested in such a way that you can get at it within reasonable limits of time and money?' Because good diving conditions are an important consideration, the answer to this question is often the Mediterranean. But these good conditions are equivalent to stating that the Med does not display a wide range of problems which the diver might tackle; there is relatively little fauna and flora, no tides, few currents, little erosion, little sediment transport, little mixing of waters.

When your project area has been tentatively decided upon you still may not feel inclined to plunge in with all your eggs in one basket. The solution to this is the pilot project. Plan a mini-expedition with about three members drawn from the final project team, for a week or so, to test the feasibility of your plans and working methods, and modify your final project accordingly.

It is often convenient to stage the pilot project about Easter for a main project in the summer. During the pilot project you should test the methods and equipment you intend to use, estimate rate of work, daily gas consumption, and cost in terms of man-days. Special equipment may have to be developed, and this is dealt with in section 7. If your study is systematic, the pilot project will not need to be in the same area as the main project, but if your study is regional, then one of the essential points at issue is that of suiting the methods to the precise study area.

The time required for the project must be estimated. Consider how much can be achieved by one man in one dive, calculate how many man-dives can be made in a day, estimate the number of man-dives required in the project, and assess the optimum balance of team size and time on site to suit overall budget and time available. In England between April and September one can reckon on at least 30 per cent of days lost through bad weather. If planning has been flexible (see item 1) the work schedule can be compressed to allow for unexpected time lost and, conversely, if the weather is surprisingly good secondary projects can be attempted without undue improvisation. It is worth noting that from May to August the visibility off many parts of the British coast is reduced by the bloom of plankton. Weather records and wind directions can be obtained from the Admiralty Pilot, with further details from the Meteorological Office. Tidal currents are indicated on charts, and times of tides in the Admiralty Almanac.

The rate of work will obviously depend on the type of work and the depth of water. Daily work rate slows down dramatically as depth increases, not just because of decompression, but because everything to do with the dive takes longer. In shallow water several divers can be working on different tasks in the water at one time, whereas in deep water only one pair can be working while the rest of the team are involved fully in safety precautions. You must assess what type of equipment is most suitable for the task : aqualung surface demand, semi closed circuit; whether diving will be done in pairs or singly, roped or unroped, swimming or with an electric tug, from a boat or from the shore. Estimate the amount of surface work connected with each dive, and from this arrive at your overall efficiency. Never underestimate the time required in paper work, record keeping, preserving samples, filling cylinders, charging batteries, and just plain thinking. It is useful in pre-planning to divide the project up into parts involving spot or bounce dives, linear searches horizontally or vertically, and area searches horizontally or vertically. These factors, combined with the depth and distance from shore, determine the required equipment.

4 The team should meet and work together many months before the main project, but it is unlikely that a group of amateurs who habitually dive together will possess all the skills required for a successful expedition. It is probable that a team will have to be selected. The project leader is ultimately responsible for everything, but his second in command should be of equivalent diving experience since, if the project leader is to dive, he must leave somebody in charge on the surface. This rule will not apply so strongly where all diving is shallow and divers may work singly, but even here the project leader may wish to spend a day or two on administration. Depending on the type of project, the remaining members should have the special skills concerned with the object of the expedition, plus ability for engineering and maintenance, boat-handling, surveying, cooking, first aid, and possibly languages.

The team should work together on the planning, each taking responsibility for an aspect of fund-raising, equipment, transport, and the separate research programmes. Where the project requires new or complex techniques, the proposed methods should be practised and snags ironed out in shallow water or during the pilot project. Teamwork is vital, and the more the working methods are practised in advance the less time will be wasted on the site.

Before going to work in a strange area, make sure that you have notified tactfully those official bodies who, at the very least, might be offended if you did not. For a foreign country get the necessary visas, if any; work permits if you are staying a long time; excavation permit if you are archaeological, and notify the official bodies concerned with the subject which you are studying. On site, get on good terms with the harbour-master, police, secretary of the nearest diving club, and the director of the local museum, etc. This may sound pompous and old-fashioned, but if you run into any trouble later, such as a breakdown of compressor or transport, or illness, the goodwill of these officials will make the difference between a trivial inconvenience and disaster.

Make sure that you have plenty of cash or banking facilities close to the site. Although all your equipment must be specially insured and you should have full accident insurance, lost or damaged equipment will have to be replaced immediately if work is not to be held up, and you only get the money back later. Similarly with the costs of an accident.

5 We now consider the basic on-site logistics. The dive site, the boat quay, equipment store and filling station, and the accommodation, are the four fixed points in the work area. On a light mobile project they may be effectively united with a vehicle and trailer carrying gear, compressor, dinghy, and sleeping bags. On a large project the points must be chosen carefully. Since carrying heavy gear on land is the most tiresome activity the key step is to get the equipment store, the filling point, and the boat quay as close together as possible—say within 150 metres of each other. This minimises the delay caused if people forget bits of gear. Ideally accommodation should be within 200 metres of the jetty as this minimises the chore of working on the equipment late at night.

The distance of the dive site from the jetty determines the type of boat required, and separation of the jetty from the accommodation determines the type of land transport. (I am assuming that the question of transport to the work area has been solved by buying a ticket—by far the quickest and often cheapest way; let's have no mock heroics.) A good boat and good land transport save time and boost morale. If you are working a 12-hour day six days a week (see item 8) a loss of two hours a day travelling is exactly equal to a lost day's work each week. The basic requirements of a boat are obvious, but it pays always to have plenty of deck space, to consider the difficulty and time taken in anchoring in the working depth, and to assess the loss of dive-site mobility if the boat is very large—over 20 metres. In this case take an extra dinghy.

Accommodation must be good—again, no heroics. It is possible to run a three-week trip on the assumption that everybody can afford to lose a stone or two and go without sleep, but diving efficiency drops rapidly during the second week and may become positively dangerous. If you are to work well for several weeks, this means at least lilos and sleeping bags, and preferably digs with bed and breakfast.

Remember that although a compressor is necessary in the wilds, a bank of supply cylinders is quicker, quieter, and more reliable. There are equivalent companies to BOC in most countries who will deliver gas. Ensure sufficient fresh water to wash all gear every day, especially in a hot climate, and find out in advance where the nearest workshop facilities are. If you are diving deep, below 30 metres, lay on emergency decompression facilities.

6 A fundamental part of most projects is position fixing or mapping. Depending on the size of the area and distance form the shore, you can use Decca Hi Fix, horizontal sextant angles, theodolite, or alidade, for surface plotting. When underwater use echo-sounding equipment, a compass, depth gauge, lines, tapes, and a rule.

Anticipate the form in which you wish to record standard data and prepare duplicated sheets with slots for each item of information. On shallow diving projects a record should be kept at least of the number of man-hours in the water each day so that a watch can be kept on efficiency; if diving is regularly below 15 metres, a detailed log should be kept of every dive. In any case, an overall diary should be kept, as well as the special scientific reports.

7 A random selection of the odd things which may be needed on an expedition might include the following special items : electric tug, battery charger, distilled water, electronic communications, soldering iron, acoustic positioning equipment, sediment corers, hundreds of polythene bags and labels, fish-traps, clinometer, chemicals and preservatives, plastic resin, ropes and tapes, floats, lifting bags, Dan-buoys, decompression stage, derricks and winches, aquarium tanks, colour filters, stopwatch, books, and duplicated forms.

8 All members should be free of physical ailment, and in addition should be actively fit either as a result of frequent diving or from some other sport. Although an unfit person can dive, in regular diving fitness prevents deterioration of efficiency and gets you out of emergencies.

During the project you will probably work a 12-14-hour day, but everybody must get at least 8 hours sleep a night, including the project leader. At least one day per week must be total rest without any diving or swimming at all. If any individual gets run down and starts making more mistakes than usual he should be given the day off; similarly if the whole team gets tired and inefficient a whole day's rest usually cures it.

Good food is as important as plenty of sleep. Try not to live out of tins, it's boring and not particularly nutritious. Steak, milk, eggs, cheese, green vegetables and fruit are obtainable almost everywhere.

In many parts of the south and east Mediterranean and points east, it is advisable to treat water with Halazone 24 hours before drinking it. The addition of fresh crushed lemons removes the chlorine taste and adds vitamins. If you must drink alcohol, indulge on the evening before your rest day.

Take plenty of sticking plaster, bandages, aspirin, codeine, enterovioform, kaolin, charcoal, mercurochrome, Halazone, and tweezers. If you are going to be really isolated, have a doctor on the team and morphia.

An essential part of the pre-project training should be a personality shake-down. This does not mean that every man must be a life-and-soul-of-the-party-good-mixer but simply that people should get used to each other so that, under the stress of work and confined living space, personal idiosyncrasies do not seem intolerable. Although it takes all sorts to make a team, the obvious source of splinter groups, factions, rows, and recriminations, must be dropped before the team is finalised.

9   The expedition is not complete until every person or official body who helped the project has been thanked and provided with a brief report on results, and the full results have been published. This is liable to take at least six months, since different people require different sorts of reports. The simplest report is that which simply states that the project is completed successfully, and gives a brief idea of the results. This is sufficient to accompany thanks to a general sponsor, and the critical factor here is to get the report out quickly. Next come the specialised reports for sponsors interested in a limited part of the work. This might be a report on the performance of an outboard motor, usefulness of a type of medicine or first aid, reliability of a flare after immersion to 50 metres, or reliability of a new decompression table. Depending on the nature of the problem, these reports may vary from ' yes, it worked ', to 20 pages of closely typed foolscap.

The project leader may or may not be involved in writing up the scientific results of the expedition. In any case he should collect all the records of the expedition and prepare a general report on progress, diving efficiency, health, finances, usefulness of different methods, and such other matters. This document is of vital importance when planning future expeditions.

The last reports to see the light of day are usually the scientific or technical papers describing the complete results of the site work and subsequent analysis. An expedition often has to be followed by several months of laboratory or paper research, and this should never be skimped.

Remember that your sponsors never see how hard you work on the site, and probably never see the film and slides you shot. Their assessment of the value of your work is based solely on the written information they receive afterwards, and it is this which will influence their decision to support you again.

EXPLORATION

There are some people who take up diving for a specific purpose, such as spearfishing, underwater photography, serious scientific investigation, or salvage for trophies or gain. The first approach of by far the greater number of sports divers, however, is for the thrill of exploring a new, alien and—from all reports they have probably received—fascinating world. In this they will not be disappointed.

Diving for pleasure
The pleasures of diving are many-sided, as diverse as the feelings of those taking part, but as all derive from entry into a new environment they have first to be anticipated, experienced, assimilated and understood before they can become fully enjoyed.

Some aspects of enjoyment spring from the different-from-normal experiences that the human senses encounter underwater. Each time a diver sinks below the surface, his whole world changes. The light dims and colours fade as the sun's rays are rapidly absorbed by the water. Normal hearing ceases, to be replaced by the vague awareness that only comes from long familiarity with slight sounds whose direction cannot be located—sounds of sea creatures, stones rattling in the waves' thrust and surge, the gurgle of a demand valve. Taste and smell are virtually non-existent, while the feel of water is all encompassing. The surrounding water imposes its presence in many ways : its cold and wetness in direct contact with the skin, the increasing pressure as the diver descends, the weightlessness when properly neutral buoyant and the irritating, sometimes panicky, fight against it if grossly too light or too heavy.

The experienced diver who is at home in the water has learned to understand these once unaccustomed and frightening perversions of his senses. He has come to recognise the features of living underwater : the silence, the calm, the caress of the water, and its support for his weight-laden body. No longer are his senses distressed. They have reawakened in a new world with a new set of values and expressions and they have engendered a self reliance, an awareness of things and their significance. The diver has become one with the underwater world and learned to love it.

On every dive, whether in the sea, rivers or quarries, whether the visibility be good or bad and the currents fast or slack, the experienced diver makes renewed contact with a world he has made, in part, his own. But there is one thing on every dive that stands out above all others. This is the sublime joy that comes at the instant of breaking surface. The shades of the underwater world are gone, light bursts in on the senses, hearing returns and the wonder, perhaps awe, that compelled the emergence of creatures from the seas millions of years ago to make a life for themselves on the land is experienced.

The pleasures of diving are therefore two-fold : to explore and uncover the unknown, and then to return to the familiar with an added appreciation of its beauties.

Diving ability

In order that a diver may immerse himself in this new environment, and for a time become part of it, he must have previously rid himself of cares and worries about the functioning of his diving equipment, or of his personal ability to use it. Of course, the problems of diving and the fundamental need eventually to return to the surface to breathe when the air supply is exhausted can never be forgotten. What is required is a complete self assurance to the extent that the use of the aqualung and any actions underwater have become instinctive. Thought, time and energy spent on the technicalities of diving are then reduced to a minimum, in consequence of which the diver can devote himself towards other ends.

Elsewhere, this Manual is devoted to achieving a mastery of diving equipment, installing a knowledge of the physical factors involved and an understanding of the reactions of the human body and mind to them. These are the passports for entry into the underwater world, and with them the diver can make contact with his new environment. A broadening of his knowledge and an understanding of it will only come from personal experience and intelligent observation. It cannot be achieved otherwise, however extensively he may read about the subject or practise with his equipment in a swimming pool.

Observation

Especially underwater it is easy to look at something yet not to see it, or to see it yet not understand its significance or what it is because of the strangeness of its surroundings or its camouflage. Unless the diver makes a conscious effort at observation and identification, his dives will lack interest and become a series without variety. The art of intelligent observation needs to be acquired.

To set about this, look definitely at things as you come upon them and do not let your eye move idly from one thing to another as you fin along. Take note deliberately of the shape, size and colour of some facet of undersea life, plant, creature. Establish the circumstances surrounding it, whether it is among rocks, on sandy sea bed, or in open water, hidden in dark holes or beneath overhanging ledges, its depth and movement or any other feature peculiar to it.

Give it a name if you can as this is a sure way of fixing in your mind what you have seen. You can also discuss it sensibly afterwards with other people. If you do not know what it is you have seen, remember its characteristic features so that you can find out what it was after the dive by asking another diver or by using books of reference, invaluable for such occasions (see Appendix).

There are so many new things to be seen underwater that, for the beginner, it is an advantage to set out on a dive looking for one or a few specific things—the amount of seaweed, the type of rocks or the number of crabs—to the exclusion of all else. This will avoid becoming overwhelmed with too great a number and variety of facts to carry in the mind. In making a dive in a familiar area, remember previous dives there and look out especially for similar conditions and specific differences. This quickly builds up experience in knowing what to expect and a keen observation of anything unusual, which may well be of particular interest. When diving in the same place a number of times, you can get to know not only the shape of the sea bed, the location of rocks, gullies and patches of seaweed, but also the creatures living in the area, sea anemones, crabs and even individual fish. Then you know that place underwater and can return to it with a friendly familiarity just as you would if visiting again the fields, woods or village on a country walk that you have made sometime previously.

Never forget a dive the moment you have finished it. Go over it in your mind at leisure when you have returned home. Picture the underwater scene, recall the significant things, try to account for the unexpected happenings. The more you ponder on it the more you will be able to resolve and learn.

The one outstanding advantage that a diver has is to see plants and creatures in their natural surroundings. Much can be learnt by careful study of fish in an aquarium, just as from animals in a zoo, but in both cases the environment is unnatural and the creatures' actions and reactions are quite likely to be radically different from those of wild life. Ecology is the study of creatures in their natural surroundings, and this is the one thing that divers alone can do in the underwater world as they become part of it themselves.

The greatest satisfaction can be obtained from a dive if such a study is carried out. Observe how plants and animals live, their interdependence upon one another, where they grow or are to be found, the effects of different types of sea bed, rocks or flat bottoms, why some areas are empty and devoid of life—all intricate and fascinating aspects of undersea life. The genuine explorer goes out from the normal world to bring back and record sights and experiences from an unknown or unfamiliar one. To seek the pleasures of underwater exploration is truly an end in itself.

The seascape
The first time that a novice diver glances through a reference book on undersea life he may well become confused at the welter of different

forms of species. These books are invaluable later on in diving, but it is a great help to know a few of the more common plants and animals that a diver may expect to see in his home waters. In British waters the exotic shaped and coloured creatures of the tropical seas are not to be found, but nevertheless there is a profusion of varieties and an abundance of life not to be found in many other coastal waters anywhere in the world.

Plant life is limited to the depth at which the sun's light can penetrate. The British diver will see three main classes of seaweed : green coloured, close to the surface and on rocks around the seashore, red in a little deeper water, but, by far the most noticeable, the brown seaweeds that grow from a few feet below the surface down to about 10 metres. The most significant of these is kelp, which spreads its broad fronds outwards from the top of a thick stem as much as 2 metres tall. Below 15 metres there is usually very little plant life to be seen.

An interesting seaweed is called *Chondrus Crispus*. This is a common tiny brown weed growing on rocks near to the surface. When the sun's light strikes the bunching tips of its new shoots it causes them to glow with a blue irridescence which vanishes quickly when the plant dies if it is picked from its holdfast on the rock and removed from the water. To see this below water is a good example of the advantage a diver has over his land-based fellows.

It is often difficult for a diver to recognise the difference between animal and plant as many animals give up the life of free movement and fix themselves, at least for some stage of their development, to a rock, seaweed or sea bed.

Unlike seaweeds, animals are to be found in the sea at any depth because they feed either off the weed or off one another. Thus anything below 15 metres, although fixed to a rock and looking very much like a plant or flower, is more likely than not a member of the animal kingdom. Common among these are the sea anemones, of which there are many varieties found from the surface downwards. All of them have tentacles which wave around attempting to catch food which they pass to the mouth in their centre.

Other normally-fixed creatures are the shell fish. A diver will see many varieties of these, the most common type depending largely on the area in which he is diving. Periwinkles browse on weed-covered rocks, while the empty shells of the common cockle may often be found on flat sandy sea beds.

Prominent among the legged animals are the many varieties of crab, including the edible one, the spider crab and the little hermit, scurrying over the sea bed in his borrowed shell which he uses to protect his soft body. Also noticeable because of their distinctive features are the lobsters usually found hiding in a well chosen rock hole.

Starfish and sea urchins walk slowly on a multitude of tiny suckers. There are many varieties of each, but the starfish can be recognised by the radial arms and the sea urchins by their hard shell, often spine covered.

Among the free swimming fish there are two main types : the flat fish, such as the plaice or ray, which are found close to the bottom on flat, sandy sea beds, and others that live among rocks like the gregarious wrasse. Of the fish that swim in the open sea, the diver less frequently sees them and when he does they are usually very timid and keep their distance.

Conservation

These creatures and plants are the diver's companions and seeing them forms the main pleasures of his diving. A dive devoid of them lacks interest, which is why diving in fresh water, where there is generally less underwater life than in the sea, is less popular. The balance of nature and creatures in their environment is sometimes very delicate, and the intrusion of man may easily disturb it. This applies particularly to hunting such fish as wrasse or collecting creatures, such as sea urchins, where a whole area can be denuded by extensive and indiscriminate removal from the sea.

Another way of adversely affecting the profusion of undersea life is by disturbing the environment : moving stones which provide shelter, or destroying seaweed patches on which animals feed, or in which they hide.

It has long been known that thoughtless actions of destruction can damage and spoil the countryside. Laws and public opinions have succeeded in reducing such acts of vandalism to a reasonable minimum. Undersea, however, it is sometimes not realised that considerations of this kind have equal force. Divers should take particular care that they do not destroy some species of underwater life, for the sake of the creatures themselves, for the contribution they make to the life of the sea and for the pleasure their presence there gives to other divers. The true underwater explorer looks and records; he does not wantonly destroy the things he sees.

This does not mean, of course, that divers should never remove anything from the sea. Within limits, a trophy of some unusual or interesting specimen, or a lobster, crab or fish for the pot, is a legitimate prize and one which adds spice to the dive, gives a sense of achievement and provides pleasant memories afterwards.

Dangerous creatures

In British coastal waters there are no creatures that are a real danger to the diver and none which can even cause him discomfort or harm which he cannot avoid by knowledge and reasonable care.

The most frequent cause of hurt to a diver is cuts and abrasions, caused by contact with barnacle- or mussel-encrusted rocks or supports of piers and jetties. The skin becomes soft and easily damaged by submersion in water, while pain, usually associated with a cut in the open air, is frequently not present when it occurs in water. Consequently, the diver may be unaware of the danger and only see the results of his actions when returned to the surface.

By comparison with the vast majority of sea creatures, man is a large animal. Few would attack him willingly and most that are able to do so will keep their distance or retreat in flight. Moreover, he is unknown in their environment and sea creatures are ill-equipped to face the new intruder. However, should man attack or disturb any that are able to defend themselves, most will usually do so—sometimes to good effect. A crab or lobster may make a tasty meal, but to take one the diver must beware of its claws for a pinch can not only be painful but, from a large specimen, quite serious. Even to thrust an inquiring hand into a rock hole or crevice may be inviting trouble. Other types of creature can inflict pain by stings. Those of the jelly fish, particularly the Portuguese Man-o'-War, which floats along the surface trailing long thread-like tentacles, may be quite unpleasant. Sensitive skins may even have a rash brought up by contact with the small tentacles of the snakelocks anemone.

Fish such as the stingray and weaver can inflict nasty wounds if trodden on, but this is unlikely to occur even when entering the water from a beach.

Unlike the relatively safe British waters, in the tropics there are undoubtedly some creatures that must be treated with respect, such as the shark and stinging coral. A diver should always take heed of local conditions, where the advice and experience of fellow divers in the area is the surest guide. If any harm befalls him from attack or contact with a dangerous undersea creature it is most probably caused mainly by his own folly.

WRECKS AND SALVAGE

Although the Diving Manual is directed mainly towards the amateur diver and salvage, in the accepted sense, is usually beyond the scope of his normal diving activities, it is almost inevitable that sooner or later the opportunity to carry out some form of salvage will arise.

The basic problems of locating, raising and transporting salvage to shore, which is basically what all salvaging is about, will be considered here, bearing in mind the limitations of equipment and resources which would normally confront the average diver in these circumstances.

Although salvaging may be undertaken in a variety of circumstances, with each operation presenting its own particular problem, the sort of underwater work to come under the broad heading of salvage most likely to be encountered is as follows :

1 Small valuable items dropped into the sea, lost anchors, cables, moorings, etc.

2 Small boats sunk in relatively shallow water.

3 Non-ferrous metal, cargo and other items from wrecks going ashore and breaking up.

4 Non-ferrous metal, cargo and other items from wrecks in deeper water.

Group 1   Locating and raising small objects in restricted areas
Although often a long and tedious business, the location of small objects in relatively shallow water in a restricted non-tidal area presents few problems, except that of time, if procedures are carried out properly, and the search techniques as described are usually successful. If a line with a small buoy is carried, it is a simple matter when the object of the search is located to attach the line and then surface, the buoy and line acting as a marker to which one can return directly with a heavier line and/or buoyancy bag for lifting purposes.

Points worth bearing in mind under these circumstances are :

a   The object to be located is seldom where the loser imagines it to be and one should be prepared to search a relatively large area.

b   A search, more often than not, is useless unless carried out systematically and thoroughly.

c   In non-tidal waters, the longer the search the poorer the visibility becomes. Arrange the search so the ground is covered only once.

Group 2   Raising small boats
As with any salvage operation, the raising of sunken craft will present particular problems with each case; for instance, whether it is on a hard or soft bottom, upright, upside down or on its side. The method adopted

will also depend upon the design and size of the boat, whether it is open or partially decked, the number and position of its compartments, and so on.

In the case of small dinghies, it is usually possible to raise these by securing a line to the first thwart or the ring in the stem and then tow it, using a boat with sufficient power. If the line is kept as short as possible, the dinghy will come to the surface under tow and most of the water will be spilled out over the stern; the remaining water can then be baled out by hand. If the dinghy is holed, it will still come to the surface but it would be necessary to beach her in order to bale her out and effect repairs. If this is done at high water the falling tide will leave her high and dry for this to be done.

With larger boats, when lifting barges and/or block and tackle are not available, salvage may be carried out using buoyancy bags which can be installed inside compartments and inflated by air cylinders. In order to raise the craft on an even keel it may also be necessary to attach buoyancy bags externally but these should be secured by slinging lifting ropes under the keel in order to cradle the weight.

The amount of buoyancy required can be calculated and if the operation warrants the effort, it might also be worthwhile to construct a model in order to plan salvage procedure in a tank.

If the buoyancy method is adopted care should be taken to ensure the lift is equally balanced so the vessel is raised on an even keel and the bags are adequately vented so that any excess air is expelled during the lift. An alternative to bags for this sort of operation are 40-gallon oil drums, which have the advantage of being both cheap and expendable. If the boat is lying on a soft bottom it may also be necessary to break the suction effect of the mud using high pressure hoses or ' rocking '.

Group 3 Wrecks broken up in shallow water

Wrecks which have gone ashore and are lying in shallow water are quickly broken up and dispersed by gales, often in a matter of days. Even a wreck sheltered from heavy seas will disintegrate rapidly if lying in tidal waters from the ' wetting and drying action ' of the tide. They are also a relatively easy salvage proposition so there is usually little left after the sea and salvage have taken their toll.

Most of the older wrecks, however, have continued to break up and lie forgotten along the shore, and this continuing sea action might well reveal material or cargo left because it was uneconomic to salvage or was unknown to the earlier salvors.

Enquiries from local sources, such as coastguards, local fishermen and in Lifeboat Institution records, will usually give a clue to wrecks lost in the area and then it is a matter of systematically searching that part of the coastline. These wrecks are not always easy to find as they quickly become encrusted with marine growth and are almost indistinguishable from their surrounding terrain. The secret is to look for regular shapes such as the straight lines and holes cast into the basic structure, ribs and ships' plates, these parts usually being too heavy to have moved far from the original site of the disaster. It is then a question of properly combing the area for anything that might be of value.

Group 4   Wrecks sunk in deeper water

This last group offers the greatest scope for anyone considering serious salvage operations. Many are wartime casualties, others the result of collision or some unusual accident. Even though they may be charted they are often of unknown origin, virtually forgotten, lying on the seabed undisturbed since disappearing beneath the waves except perhaps to have had their superstructure dispersed by post-war wreck clearance teams to reduce them as a hazard to navigation.

Research

Obtaining information on wrecks usually involves a great deal of research and correspondence. A beginning can be made at any or all of the following sources :

For wrecks that are charted, some information will be available from The Hydrographer of the Navy, if only the reports from the various surveys carried out over the years which give position, depth, height above seabed, name if known, together with other relevant information available. A charge is levied for each item of information supplied.

All British losses during the second World War and those after the 20th August, 1917, were either wholly or partly underwritten by the Government, and information on those which may come into this category can be obtained from The Secretary, Minister of Transport, St Christopher House, Southwark Street, London, SE1.

If you have the name of the wreck and other information to assist identification, particularly the date of its sinking, the Shipping Editor, Lloyds, London, EC3, should have some information.

In the case of wrecks under the jurisdiction of Trinity House, write to The Secretary, Trinity House, Tower Hill, London, EC3.

Identification

The positive identification of a wreck is often a most difficult task, so many of them being officially unknown so that it then becomes a matter of patient detective work and a great deal of luck. Quite often it is the apparently insignificant clue which builds up the picture and finally leads you to the answer. During exploration it is well worthwhile looking for items which might possibly bear manufacturers' names or the steamship company's crest. Crockery, cutlery, the ship's bell and various other non-ferrous fittings used in the ship construction are items well worth searching for.

Diving conditions

Wrecks in deeper water unfortunately present the added difficulties of awkward currents and/or poor visibility. If a wreck is lying on a hard sand or gravel bottom which will give good light reflection and in an area subject to medium tidal streams, these conditions will give certain advantages. One can expect good visibility during slack water periods and the wreck to be relatively free from long weed and the sponge types of marine growth, with little fine silt to be stirred up except in confined spaces. On the other hand if the bottom is mud or very fine sand, even slight tidal streams stir this up to give poor visibility near the bottom from which there is little light reflection. The wreck is invariably covered in a thick layer of 'dust' which is easily disturbed when finning and is slow to clear. If the tidal streams are normally slight in the area, the wreck may well be covered by sponges and marine growth to such an extent it may be almost impossible to distinguish its shape apart from the main structure, and cutting away the growth immediately reduces the visibility to that of a London pea-souper.

An assessment of the strength and state of tidal streams and type of bottom taken from the Admiralty chart for the area, together with prevailing weather conditions, will allow a fair appraisal of what you are likely to encounter at any particular site, but, ideally, diving is best undertaken during a calm weather spell at slack water, neap tides. High slack water generally gives better visibility than low, though low water may give a longer slack water period than high. Because of air endurance, decompression problems and lack of light, even under ideal conditions, 180 ft is the maximum practical depth for this type of operation in British waters and then only for experienced divers.

Wreck location

Except for those wrecks buoyed by Trinity House as a hazard to navigation, the location of wrecks can be a long, tedious and frustrating business so the various methods one can adopt must be considered.

The basic difficulties are time, opportunity and the facilities necessary to devote to searching for what is virtually a needle in a haystack, and the greatest single asset is probably the goodwill of local fishermen who can be of inestimable value. The thought to bear constantly in mind is that although you might be within a yard of your objective, a miss is as good as a mile.

The simplest method of accurately pinpointing a position at sea assuming you are in sight of land is by the use of *marks,* ie, geographical features, which are used to give transit bearings (see figure 1). These can

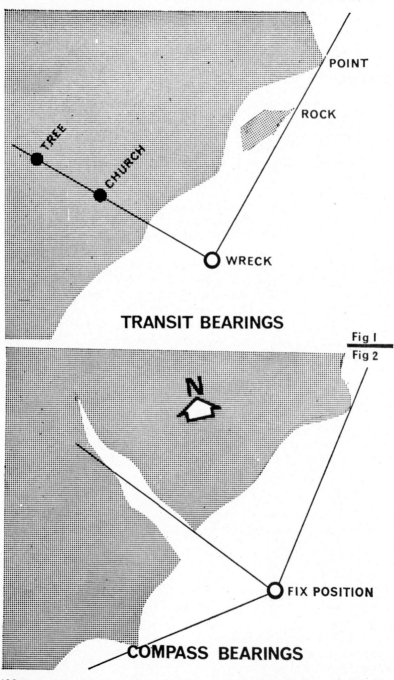

POINT

ROCK

TREE

CHURCH

WRECK

TRANSIT BEARINGS

Fig 1
Fig 2

N

FIX POSITION

COMPASS BEARINGS

be incredibly accurate, and a good set of *marks* can not only pinpoint the wreck but put you over a particular part of it, although for this sort of accuracy it is essential the bearings are as near to forming a right angle as possible. Good *marks* are usually known to local fishermen who may use them for laying crab and lobster pots, but it is also worth bearing in mind that so-called wreck marks used by trawlermen are often for trawling on a line in order to miss the wreck and may be of little use for actually locating it. Hiring the services of a local boatman is probably the best way of ensuring success as he may not only be able to locate the wreck quickly and accurately but his knowledge of local conditions is invaluable in ensuring a safe operation. An apparently calm and harmless looking stretch of water can be treacherous at certain states of the tide.

An extremely useful piece of equipment and a great help in finally pinpointing a wreck is a portable echo meter, preferably the paper recording type. This is particularly the case when your marks may not be as accurate or as clear as you could wish, due perhaps to mist or summer heat haze. If you are working to a set of marks given verbally, it is even more important as often the phrase used is ' with such-and-such a landmark just open '. This rather vague phrase ' just open ' can vary from person to person and can be very misleading if misinterpreted. A sketch can be of help in cases like this.

If you are working from a chart taking compass bearings (see Figure 2) from prominent landmarks, you will most certainly need an echo meter as this method will only give a rough location.

When using either method you will be extremely lucky to pick up the wreck straight away and usually it will be necessary to search the area. This is invariably a waste of time unless tackled systematically and the easiest method is to drop a small buoy and sinker where you think the wreck should be, to use as a datum point, and using the echo meter steam round the buoy in increasing circles or in parallel lines as in Figures 3 and 4. In this way the whole area is covered thoroughly.

If you have no echo meter available and the sea bed is sand or shingle an alternative is to search the area by dragging a weighted anchor or *creep* astern on a length of chain or wire, tracing the same pattern as before in the hope of fouling the wreck. This is a slow business as the anchor will leave the bottom if towed too quickly. It is also possible to drag over a wreck without hooking into it, misleading you into continuing the search in the surrounding area without success. It is therefore necessary to have someone holding or pressing on the towing line in order to *feel* the progress of the anchor over the bottom. Should the anchor then come in contact with the wreck it will be felt and the skipper warned to ease up to prevent the line parting should the anchor foul as is hoped.

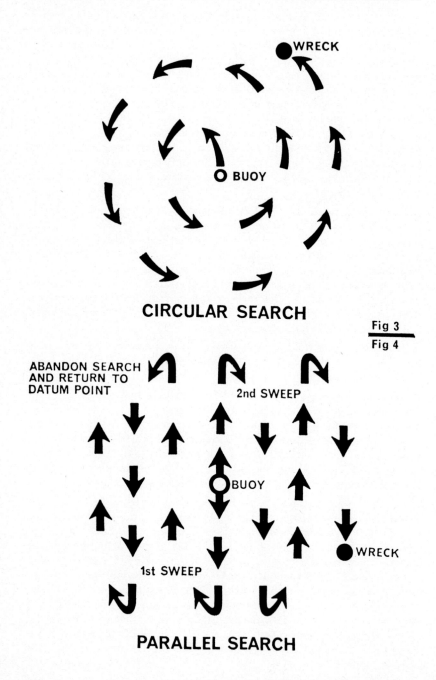

CIRCULAR SEARCH

Fig 3
Fig 4

ABANDON SEARCH AND RETURN TO DATUM POINT

2nd SWEEP

BUOY

WRECK

1st SWEEP

PARALLEL SEARCH

If you can persuade a fisherman with trawling gear to co-operate, a variation on this system is to put down trawl boards and the connecting ground chain but without the trawl attached. This enables a much broader path to be swept, but obviously it would be necessary to convince the trawlerman you will recover his gear or compensate him for any loss or damage, which could be expensive.

Decca navigation equipment will give an accurate fix to within 15 metres and used in conjunction with an echo meter is probably the ultimate in wreck location if you are fortunate enough to obtain the services of a skipper whose vessel is fitted with this equipment. If it is not possible to hire and dive from such a boat, it may be possible to persuade the skipper to drop a buoy supplied by you into the wreck during the course of his normal fishing activities. Generally speaking, most fishermen are not only willing but most interested to co-operate in the hope of learning more of their local hazards. Once having got a buoy on the wreck it is then only a matter of locating it at a later date, bearing in mind that even this can be difficult to find from a small boat in a choppy sea with a tide running. It is still necessary to have reliable marks to put you in the vicinity.

Another indication of a wreck's position in calm conditions with a tide running, particularly if the wreck is lying across the tidal stream, is a surface disturbance caused by the current being diverted over and around the obstruction.

The co-operation and goodwill of local fishermen is probably an amateur diver's greatest single asset in the location of wrecks in any particular area. Their knowledge may also include the many uncharted and, for the most part, unknown wrecks with which our coastline abounds, and knowing the area, they can also be invaluable in recommending the most favourable diving conditions. In any case, the amateur diving group is largely dependent upon such men for boat hire as vessels suitable for salvage operations, even on a small scale, are usually too costly to own and maintain for private purposes only.

Anchoring in position

If a wreck is in water unaffected by tide and wind, it is a simple matter of steaming ahead of the wreck, dropping the anchor and then, paying out the anchor rope, go-astern until you are directly over the wreck again, when it is then possible to drop a shot line directly into the wreck. Unfortunately, most wrecks lie in tidal streams of varying strength and often the current is too strong to dive at all states of the tide. One is therefore obliged to wait until the tide slackens sufficiently to permit safe diving. Quite often the tide changes direction before the dive is completed or the wind may alter the lie of the boat so that if a shot rope is dropped in these conditions, it can easily be dragged out of the wreck or the line parted. Under these conditions, it is best to arrive at the site before slack tide and having located the wreck, steam against the tidal stream and drop the anchor, which should be on a stout wire or a sufficiently long length of chain so the anchor rope cannot chafe on the wreck. If the length of wire paid out is only a little more than the total depth of the water, this will prevent the anchor holding in the bottom and if the boat is then allowed to drift with the tide, with any luck the anchor will foul as it is dragged across the wreck by the boat. If unsuccessful the first time, the procedure can be repeated until the boat is firmly anchored in the wreck, when more wire should be paid out to ensure a good hold. The descent via the anchor rope is necessarily longer than by shot rope but it is the more practical method. The first two divers down should check the position of the anchor (and as a precaution, all subsequent divers) to ensure it cannot drag free from any position in which the boat may eventually lie. The anchor rope should be buoyed in case it becomes necessary to move the boat quickly and another buoy on as long a length of floating line as possible should be streamed out astern. Any diver surfacing away from the boat can then fin for the line and, if tired, be hauled in.

Preliminary Survey

Although normal safety precautions, dive planning and equipment are required, there are some points which should be stressed when diving on wrecks, being of particular importance and not encountered with other forms of diving.

A knife, of course, is essential, and no wreck diving should be undertaken without one. A torch is also a *must* and particularly useful for illuminating the confined spaces within the hull and attracting the attention of other divers. The hands more than anything can suffer a great deal of damage from rusting metal work, frayed wire hawsers, and so on, so gloves should be worn; a metal hook is also a useful tool for pulling yourself along and for general use in place of your hand. A non-floating line, a small bag and a small hacksaw are most valuable for collecting small items. As diving will, of course, be conducted in pairs, the gear can be split between the two divers, a companion being one's greatest single safety factor. Diving on wrecks should never be attempted alone.

Although diving is best undertaken at slack water, it may be necessary to dive whilst there is still some tide in order to have the benefit of slack water when resurfacing. If this is the case it is important to ensure mask straps are secure and your mouthpiece in good condition as you will be descending the anchor rope against the tide and these items are under a much greater strain than normal due to the pressure of the water. Make sure, too, that your snorkel is secure and readily available.

It is also worth remembering that the tide is generally stronger on the surface than the bottom due to the surface drag of the sea bed and in the lee of the wreck there is little, if any, tide at all.

Arriving on the wreck it is important first of all to orientate yourself. Some divers have a natural sense of direction whilst others move a dozen yards and have no idea where they are. If the type of vessel and something of its construction is known beforehand, a study of this before the dive will help you to recognise that part of the wreck into which you are anchored and what to expect as you investigate further. Unless a real effort is made to remember your point of departure in relation to the rest of the wreck, you may not be able to relocate the anchor rope, which may, of course, be lying in a different direction on your return, and this means surfacing free. This could entail a long surface swim against the current, perhaps at a time when you are tired. In any case, a controlled ascent up the anchor rope is infinitely preferable. For the preliminary survey and a quick overall impression, it is best to start on the lee side of the wreck, sheltering you from any tide, and in sight of the bottom. Working your way round will give an idea of its size, design and general condition and the disposition of any superstructure lying on the sea bed. Particular care should be taken when rounding the extremities and when coming over the ship's side where tidal streams are strongest. It is easy to be taken off your guard and swept away, and in poor visibility you can lose sight of the wreck altogether.

Inside the wreck it is best where possible to fin well clear of the deck as the fine silt which has settled inside is easily disturbed and being sheltered, is slow to clear. Move with caution to avoid damage to gear and person; rusting plates are often reduced to paper thickness and will leave a bad gash in your suit, or you.

When exploring the interior, extreme caution is of paramount importance. A guide line should be rigged and a torch carried as visibility can be quickly reduced to zero as you move in a confined space. It is in conditions such as these that panic can result very easily.

Many well-known wrecks are extensively fished by anglers whose tackle is frequently snagged and broken. Nylon line can be floating free, virtually invisible and can become entangled in your gear. Should this happen, don't attempt to break the line by pulling yourself free as this may result in the hook becoming embedded in you or your suit. Instead, use your knife or get your companion to free you.

Trawls lost by fishermen are also a very real hazard, particularly if diving is attempted in poor visibility. With the extensive use of man-made fibres, which are virtually unaffected by salt water, they are likely to be an increasing menace on wrecks in trawling areas. Caution, a sharp lookout with good visibility, and a reliable companion, are your safeguards.

It will be appreciated that wreck diving, particularly where salvage work is to be carried out, is a more hazardous form of diving than usual, so particular attention must be paid to dive planning, ie, depth time, cylinder contents and, where applicable, decompression stops. During the dive a regular check should be made on these points so the return to the surface can be controlled and unhurried with air and time in hand to allow for the unforeseen which could delay surfacing, resulting in the need to decompress. On the surface, divers should be timed in and out of the water and a shot rope with the decompression stops marked hung over the side with a spare aqulung(s) rigged ready for any diver surfacing without air and requiring to decompress.

Permanent buoying prior to salvaging

If a salvage operation is intended then it is obviously desirable to buoy the wreck permanently with at least one buoy. This will avoid the wasted effort of relocation with each visit and the descent via the buoy wire puts you on the same part of the wreck each time. Wire rather than rope should be used for this purpose, securely attached to a solid high point on the wreck with a small non-collapsible buoy fixed to the wire so as to be permanently under the water at all states of the tide and capable of supporting the lower end of the wire.

In this way, the wire below this supporting buoy is kept taut and clear of the wreck so preventing it becoming entangled at slack low water. In order to avoid trouble with HM Coastguards, the main buoy should not be of metal but preferably the inflatable orange plastic type or similar which is easy to see and will not damage a small craft should one hit the buoy in the dark.

If the salvage vessel is required to be moored directly over a particular part of the wreck then at least two buoys need to be positioned, preferably on the extremities of the wreck, so that by picking up both buoys and adjusting the length of the mooring lines at the bow and stern, the salvage vessel can take up any position between them. If a cross current or wind should affect this positioning, then two further moorings would need to be placed to port and starboard, thereby mooring the salvage vessel between four positions. Mooring in this way allows the use of a shot rope for a direct descent to the working area.

Salvage

It is not possible to lay down hard and fast methods of salvage as so much depends on the particular problems each operation presents together with the patience, skill, ingenuity and persistence of those involved. By comparison with the professional salvor, the amateur diver is limited in time, equipment and experience, and any success will depend entirely upon the best use that can be made of those resources available to him. On the other hand, the amateur diver can afford to attempt operations which would be uneconomic for a salvage company whose overheads are inevitably higher. Because of these considerations and the limitations of space, it is only possible here to outline the fundamental principles involved and give a brief description of materials and apparatus available and cost commonly used. For more detailed information it will be necessary to make reference to the various publications dealing specifically with particular subjects, the most comprehensive being *Deep Diving and Submarine Operations—Parts I & II,* by Robert H Davis, late Principal and Managing Director of Siebe, Gorman & Co Ltd, which covers all aspects of underwater work. Siebe Gorman also offer courses of instruction in the use of underwater tools, underwater cutting and welding, etc, in the tanks at their works in Chessington. Details are available on application.

The first essential is, of course, a boat which must be large enough to accommodate the divers and their gear and equipped with a well constructed diving ladder, a derrick and/or winch(s) for lifting purposes. Various ropes, buoys, shackles, wire, block and tackle, engineers' tools and the like will also be required, dependent upon the undertaking.

Underwater cutting apparatus
If it is intended to salvage parts of a wreck, it will first be necessary to free the material before lifting. This can be done either by underwater cutting apparatus, by explosives or by hand. The oxy-hydrogen underwater gas cutting torch or oxy-arc electric cutter are in common use. Training and experience are essential to be successful.

Explosives
The selection of the type of explosive most suitable for a specific job, the amount required, its positioning and type of detonation are a matter of experience although the basic principles involved are covered by the pamphlet *Underwater Blasting* by R Westwater and R Haslam, published by the Nobel Division, ICI Ltd Glasgow. And Underwater Swimming—an Advanced Handbook (Kaye Ward).* It will be appreciated that there is also the problem of obtaining explosives, which require a police permit both to buy and use. With the exception of very small quantities, explosives must be stored in specially constructed buildings, but if the necessary experience is available and police permission is granted it may be possible to arrange storage with a local quarry where such facilities are usually available.

Other underwater cutting appliances
Underwater wire-rope and chain cutting machines and various other pneumatic tools for drilling and cutting rock, wood and steel are avail-

---

*And *Underwater Swimming—an Advanced Handbook* (Kaye Ward).

able, but these tools are normally the province of the professional salvor and would not normally be readily available to the amateur diver.

Raising and transporting salvage to shore
The basic methods here are either direct winching, buoyancy or tidal lift.

Winching
If the boat is equipped with a winch or derrick and the material to be lifted is within the capacity of the apparatus then direct lifting is possible either into the boat or an attendant barge. If the weight is beyond the capacity of the winch but the boat is capable of supporting the weight involved, then it may be possible to incorporate the use of block and tackle, preferably lifting on the bow. This would allow much greater weights to be raised and conveyed whilst slung under the lifting vessel.

Buoyancy
A submerged body in the sea displaces a weight of water equal to its cubic capacity. Therefore, if a hollow container of known capacity is filled with water, submerged and attached to the object to be lifted, the water can then be expelled, using compressed air, resulting in a lifting force being exerted equal to the amount of water displaced, less the weight of the container. Points to bear in mind when using this method are : (1) the buoyancy container must be adequately vented to allow excess air to escape; (2) if the container is sufficiently buoyant to raise the object before all the water has been displaced, the air will expand, so increasing the speed of the ascent as more water is displaced by the expanding air as it approaches the surface due to lessening pressure; (3) the weight in water of the object to be raised is less than its weight in air by an amount equal to the weight of water it displaces. This difference can therefore be calculated if its volume is known; (4) if it is intended to use a buoyancy bag to assist in moving heavy items from one point to another, eg, to a central collecting point prior to lifting, it is virtually impossible to unfasten or 'spill out' the air from a buoyancy bag under load unless prior provision is made for this purpose. Cutting it free will only send it straight to the surface.

Tidal lift
This method also employs buoyancy but it is that of the salvage vessel itself or a pontoon. Wires are slung under the salvage to be raised and attached to the lifting vessel or pontoon so that the load will be evenly distributed. Some means must also be arranged for the wires to be drawn as taut as possible at low water. As the tide rises the burden is also raised and it is then possible to steam to shallower water until grounding occurs. The process is then repeated with successive tides until the salvage can be dropped in the shallowest water.

The law of wreck and salvage

The law on this subject is largely contained in part 9 Merchant Shipping Act 1894, which enlarges upon the Old Common Law principles. The Act defines 'Wreck' and 'Salvage' and it clearly includes any vessel, part of a vessel, cargo, fittings or equipment, anchors and fishing gear— in fact, anything which might be found on a wrecked vessel or in tidal water. The law as applied to ships is now applied to aircraft by virtue of the Civil Aviation Act 1949.

Any object which comes within the definition of 'Wreck' remains the property of its lawful owner; beware the object that apparently has no connection with ships or aircraft. Any person who takes any such object commits a criminal offence. Any person who steals any object belonging to a 'Wreck' can be imprisoned for up to 14 years under Section 15 (3) Larceny Act (1916). There will be no offence if the owner has expressly given his permission to take the 'Wreck' or anything to do with it.

The Minister of Transport has appointed Receivers of Wreck around the coast of the UK, who are usually Customs Officers or Coast Guards.

Summarising the law of 'Wreck' and 'Salvage', any article which is brought into the UK shall be delivered to the Receiver of Wreck; if the article is unclaimed at the end of one year, it becomes Crown property and the Receiver sells the article deducting his fees and expenses and also the salvage claim upon the Ministry of Transport scale. There are instances where the Receiver may sell the article immediately, but he then retains the proceeds of sale for one year.

Where the owner or his Agent brings the 'Wreck' or article into the UK, he need only declare it to the Receiver of Wreck. Customs Duty may be payable upon certain goods but that is another matter.

It is an offence to take any 'Wreck' which is within UK territorial waters to a foreign port; the offender is liable to imprisonment for three to five years. Anyone who fails to comply with the Merchant Shipping Act can be fined up to £100, and if he is not the owner of the 'Wreck', he loses his right to claim salvage and will be liable to pay double the value of the article to its owner.

Divers wishing to enter the realms of salvage should make a serious attempt to discover the ownership of the wreck concerned, when he can either act as the owner's Agent for the purposes of salvage, agreeing to accept a percentage of the value of the goods recovered. He might be able to purchase the wreck from the owner, thus being entitled to the full value of anything salvaged. The owner of a 'Wreck' is responsible to Trinity House for ensuring that the wreck does not become a hazard to navigation.

SAFETY

The object of this section is to describe the principal physical diving hazards which a sports diver may encounter from time to time.

Without a wide appreciation of the hazards of diving there are pitfalls for the unwary diver and there is no other field in which a limited knowledge may prove so dangerous.

It should also be remembered that any mishap, no matter how small, could be serious. For example in a non fatal accident on land the victim may lie around until help arrives, but in the water if help is not immediately available the victim may well drown. That underwater accidents are not always fatal depends not so much on the nature of the accident but on whether there is someone available at the time to effect a rescue. These points must be thoroughly emphasised during training, and not until the trainee has achieved a high degree of confidence and efficiency should he be allowed to venture out of easy reach.

Hazardous diving through lack of experience or insufficient training

The majority of people do not find it unduly difficult to learn to use diving equipment and this in itself constitutes a hazard, for inexperienced divers often attempt foolhardy dives far beyond their capabilities. Even experienced divers will sometimes attempt dives which are fraught with danger.

In pre-dive planning, the dive should be considered from every possible angle and should only be carried out by those considered capable enough for the particular dive in question. Many diving accidents are caused by poor judgement, failure to recognise potentially dangerous situations, the inability to recognise one's own limitations or inadequate training.

Equipment

Adequate equipment for the proposed dive should be available, and it should be checked thoroughly before use to ensure correct functioning.

Many divers expose themselves to unnecessary hazards by operating with insufficient or inadequate equipment.

Shore diving

Quite a large number of trainee divers, having completed their swimming pool training, take their first dive from some convenient beach. By necessity, many newly-formed diving clubs restrict their activities to shore diving until available funds justify the purchase of a boat.

Quite often the success of a particular shore dive depends on the height of water and tide tables should be consulted in advance to obtain the appropriate time for diving. It can be extremely embarrassing for the dive-leader if the dive requires a half-mile knee-deep wade out to sea before obtaining sufficient water to dive into. On the other hand, it can be dangerous on a steeply sloping beach to take trainee divers straight into deep water. Dangerous currents are often associated with rise and fall of tide and local boatmen can often provide the best information about these and many other local hazards to the diver.

Dive planning should provide for the usual lookout system from shore to snorkel covers for divers. Shore lookouts should be provided with appropriate safety items such as throwing lines, whistles and flags. Snorkel covers should have an inflated inner tube if a surface cover boat is not being used. There should be one shore lookout and at least one snorkel cover to each group of divers. This is extremely important because of the increasing use of power-boats, especially fast outboards. These constitute a major danger to divers and the number of near misses and accidents reported from this source is increasing. A snorkel cover with a large inner tube with a diving flag attached to it floating over the divers' exhaust bubble can protect them from the very real danger of boats and propellors. Boat's engines are usually heard clearly underwater and divers should look and listen around 360° and should do the same again after surfacing. They should surface with hands held overhead for protection and give the appropriate signal clearly to snorkel cover or shore party.

The use of propellor driven boats by divers is increasing. In addition to being an asset they can also be a hazard if not handled safely. The propellor should not be turning whilst divers are down if possible. It should be noted that putting the engine in neutral does not necessarily mean the propellers are not turning as they sometimes 'creep' with sufficient rotation to injure a diver.

Having gained permission and ascertained that an area is safe to dive in, the entry to the water can prove dangerous, especially for the inexperienced. Clambering over slippery rocks, weighted down by an aqualung, has proved many a diver's literal downfall for the additional weight can convert a simple slip into a serious accident. It is an advantage to wear some gripping footwear to the water edge as it is not practical to walk any distance in fins. In shallow water it usually proves easier to wade backwards with fins on. Every assistance should be given to divers in order to save them unnecessary exertion before they enter the water and again when they land. It is essential to see that the entry point is also an easy exit point.

On first entering the water a final briefing, check of equipment and buoyancy check should be made before proceeding with the dive. Whilst in the water it is quite easy to cut oneself sometimes without even realising it. Shellfish are generally razor sharp and to grasp a jetty pile for support or to be dragged across a barnacle encrusted rock, usually results in a lacerated hand. The edge of the shore can also be the dumping ground for every unwanted item, and jagged, rusted metal and broken glass is sure to exist.

Incidentally, it is not uncommon to find some object which could be a mine or a bomb and for obvious reasons these should not be disturbed. An accurate fix on the position should be reported to the police, if possible mark an adjacent position with buoyed line and sinker.

The sea itself is far more powerful than the best of divers, and the strength of the sea, swell, currents, tidal flow, rip currents, and breaking water should be considered before diving. Heavy seas can seriously injure a diver by flattening him against rocks. Breaking waves are an indication that the water is shallow, or that a bank reef or other obstruction exists a short depth below the surface. Rip currents which often run from shallow water out to sea may be recognised by their flattening effect on incoming waves in their path, the waves being larger on either side of the current. Rip water is often muddy and discoloured. If caught in a strong tidal stream or rip current, always fin across its direction of flow, never against it, which is a useless waste of energy. If diving is necessary in lesser currents, the dive is always commenced swimming against the current.

Fishing nets and lines can be a real source of danger and divers should avoid them; apart from incurring the wrath of angry fishermen, a diver can be caught on hook or line or become enmeshed in nets. For this reason, he should always carry a knife.

A shore dive should not be carried out with the intention of travelling as far as possible from the shore. When in the depth appropriate to conditions and experience, a course parallel to shore should be set. It is very unwise to travel too far into deep water and away from shore assistance, especially with trainee divers. The dive should be planned so that the return to shore can be carried out on air, not with empty cylinders.

Sea diving
Sea diving is probably the next step a diving club takes after shore diving. Diving from shore has perhaps lost some of its attraction, and though funds are not available to purchase a boat the urge to explore new regions exist. So a compromise is made and a boat hired.

Many of the points raised in shore and boat diving are also appropriate to sea diving. The dive should be planned to coincide with suitable conditions, taking into account weather, currents, state of tide, and such other factors. The boat should be suitable for diving, preferably with a boatman who has experience of divers' requirements.

Although currents and tidal streams may be encountered in diving from shore they will be more likely out at sea. The strongest swimmer cannot achieve a speed much in excess of two mph, but currents frequently exceed this speed and even in still water they can commence with extreme rapidity. Diving in strong currents should be avoided by planning the dive for the correct time. Again, fishermen can usually provide excellent information on currents in their area. Charts, nautical almanacs and seaside publicity and entertainments offices can be used for obtaining such information. It should be noted that slack water does not necessarily coincide with the times of high and low water. If it is necessary to dive in a current, the cardinal rule is to commence the dive swimming against the current; the return journey can then be carried out with the assistance of the current.

Current diving techniques have been devised which require the use of lifelines, cover-boats, marker buoys attached to the divers, and buoyed lines floated from the boat. These techniques are for the experienced divers; the inexperienced should not dive in any current at all.

Some final points on this subject :

Diving should not be carried out in fairways or shipping channels due to the danger from collision, and the diving flag should be always displayed throughout diving operations.

Some seaweeds can prove extremely difficult to negotiate and divers should avoid weeds that could cause entanglement with equipment.

Divers should not enter unknown underwater caves due to the risk of becoming lost or getting trapped.

Spearfishing should not be allowed in the vicinity of other divers or bathers.

Divers should keep away from sewage outfall to avoid possibly polluted waters and risk to health.

A check on divers entering the water and times should be recorded; It has been known for boats to return to shore leaving a diver still underwater and a long swim back.

Boat diving

It is the aim of most diving clubs to acquire a boat of their own once they are firmly established, and although a boat is invaluable to divers, certain hazards can arise from its use if the rules of diving and seamanship are not observed.

It is prudent before setting out to sea to leave a message ashore giving full information on the proposed trip. All diving and boat equipment should be fully checked before sailing and every single item should be taken along; it is usually the items left ashore which are the first required at sea.

Rig lines in loops, life-boat fashion, along the sides for divers to rest on. Rope ladders are inadequate and a fixed ladder should be placed well clear of the propeller and extend well below the surface.

On arrival at the diving site take compass bearings of the shore and log the position of the boat. This will give a steering bearing if blanketed by fog and also record the area for future reference should any interesting find be made.

Further safety precautions mentioned in another chapter with regard to running the propeller, harpoon guns, lookouts, signals, diving flag and safety lines must be strictly observed.

In order not to upset the stability of small boats, entry to the water should be done by falling backwards in pairs (one from each side) at a given signal. To re-enter small boats it is generally necessary to remove aqualung and weight belt in the water before the diver is brought inboard. It may be possible to bring a diver over the bow or stem without upsetting the stability of some small boats.

No hard and fast rules can be laid down for the actual dives as this will depend on water conditions, but some basic principles will help in determining procedure. Even if the visibility permits large group dives, divers should pair off; the leader cannot watch everyone. Never put three divers in a team unless the visibility is at least 5 metres, otherwise one is bound to be continually on the fringe of visibility and will eventually lose his companions. Make a note of the entry time of each diver as a check against air supply, and in a current or tideway use a safety line. If divers keep in contact with one another at all times and the surface cover is rigidly maintained, the possibility of accidents is greatly reduced. When diving from a boat, always swim upstream on the outward run using the anchor rope as a guide; the assistance from the current will then be gained for the return journey. A badly planned dive could well place the diver downstream of the boat when he surfaces, which should not be allowed to occur. Remember that a current may first appear or increase in strength during a dive. If a large boat is used stream the safety dinghy well aft as in a tideway or current it is here where it will be needed most. A roped inner-tube will serve the same purpose in smaller craft.

With these precautions there is less likelihood of a diver drifting away from the boat after surfacing but rather that he will be swept towards it by the current.

Inland water

In general, inland waters are less affected by weather conditions than coastal waters and thus provide fewer threats from tide and current, but other threats not generally found in sea diving may be found and the following should be borne in mind.

> Inland water is usually fresh and the diver will require less weight to achieve neutral buoyancy than in the sea.

The thermal inertia of fresh water, particularly small pools, is much less than sea water. Consequently water temperature, especially near the surface, responds much quicker to good and bad weather. Such fresh water pools heat up quickly at the first signs of warm weather but cool rapidly at the first sign of autumn temperatures, while the sea often maintains a reasonably comfortable temperature even during winter (March is the coldest sea temperature). Inland water can include very cold water and adequate precautions must be taken.

Swift flowing rivers should be avoided by divers who stand the risk of being battered against rocks and other obstructions.

Old quarries, flooded valleys, dams and reservoirs may be liable to poor visibility and many obstructions.

Permission is usually required to dive in many inland waters and diving is not generally allowed in reservoirs.

Diving should not be carried out near lock or sluice gates, valves, or anywhere where a suction drag may exist. A diver can be held by the suction even if a valve has a protective cage over it.

Spearfishing should not be carried out in inland waters without special permission.

Visibility in inland waters can rapidly deteriorate by disturbing the bottom, sending clouds of mud or other sediment into suspension.

Canals usually have poor visibility, thick weed and many obstructions. Inland waters are generally the happy dumping ground for most unwanted objects and everything from old bicycles to weapons dumped after the last amnesty may be encountered. Ammunition and explosives should be left well alone, but reported to the police. The risk of underwater or above-water landslides exists in quarries and divers should avoid areas of possible rock fall.

Polluted inland waters should be avoided unless the appropriate injections have been given.

Diving under ice is extremely dangerous. If, as can occur in very cold water, the demand valve freezes up with the diver some distance from his entrance hole, even a lifeline will not save him. The chances of getting lost and of suffering from exposure also exist. Very deep and cold water can be found in some lakes and flooded quarries and divers should not be tempted to dive to undue depths without adequate precautions (see *Deep diving* later in this section). Cave diving is fraught with difficulty and danger and should be confined to highly experienced cave-diving groups on organised expeditions.

Wreck diving

Wrecks provide some of the most interesting dives as there is usually an abundance of life to see as well as providing excitement of diving on a sunken ship. However, wreck diving is not without risk for the unwary diver. The maritime law with regard to wrecks, by the way, is rather involved, but if the wreck is a modern one it usually belongs to someone, if only the insurance company, and permission may be required to dive on it.

Wrecks abound in sharp objects such as jagged steel plates, razor sharp shell fish and stranded wire ropes, and severe wounds can be incurred especially if any swell or sea movement is apparent on the wreck. The wreck diver is advised to wear a full diving suit including gloves for protection. He should be constantly aware that aqualung breathing tubes can easily snag on sharp projections and that a cylinder on the back is not ideal for squeezing through narrow openings. Some wrecks may also be festooned with fishing nets, lines and ropes and there are then even greater possibilities of the diver becoming caught in them. The danger of the collapse of corroded steel decks and rotten timber is ever present, especially if the diving boat is secured to some part of the wreck in a swell. Entering a wreck has its own special risks for a diver may lose himself and run out of air, or propped hatches may be closed by the movement of the sea. It is usual for a second diver to tend a diver entering a wreck on a lifeline.

Again, it is possible that large pockets of gas may be trapped in parts of the wreck and it is very unwise for a diver to remove his mouthpiece to breathe in these pockets. Poisonous or inflammable gas may be given off from rotting cargo (this rule also applies to gas pockets in underwater caves). Many wrecks met their fate in times of war and could be carrying explosives which should not be tampered with. Often also they have settled on the bottom at some precarious degree of list, and it may be quite easy to dislodge some heavy object, which has been hanging in balance till disturbed, injuring the diver or blocking his exit.

Wreck diving may thus prove to have unhappy consequences for the incautious diver, but for those who are not it is both safe and exciting (see also section on Salvage).

Harbour or ship diving, or underwater work

Diving clubs may occasionally be requested to carry out some underwater task by a commercial organisation or local authority. The first point to be considered should be whether the dive comes within the jurisdiction of the Factories Act, Diving Operations Special Regulations, 1960, and if so are the appropriate regulations contained in the Act fully covered? Secondly, one should consider the question of insurance and whether one is still covered whilst carrying out the work.

In general, any underwater task should be commenced with the object of reducing the work underwater to a minimum, which will obviously also reduce the hazards to the minimum. For example, in removing a wire from around a propellor shaft, hours may be spent underwater with hacksaw, hammer and chisel. On the other hand, a thoughtful diver may spend a few minutes in the water securing a rope to the end of the wire which is taken to the barrel of a winch, and by turning the propellor in hand-turning gear and heaving at the winch the wire is unwound.

Work on ships. The following safety precautions must be considered:

Inform all concerned of diving activities, especially engine room staff, if diving around propellors or inlets.

Shut off all dangerous inlets and outlets.

Fly the diving-flag from the masthead and above the position where diving is taking place to keep other vessels away and their speed down. The wash from a fast boat can be dangerous.

Take adequate precautions to prevent the diver getting fouled by mooring the diving vessel in the best position, and rig bottom lines to guide the diver to his task and to facilitate hanging on.

Use lifelines where required. It is possible for a diver to lose himself under a large flat bottomed vessel and run out of air before regaining the surface.

Harbour diving

Appropriate lock and sluice gates, inlets, outlets and valves should be shut down as required.

If working around electricity cables, current should be switched off.

If diving in polluted water the appropriate injections should be given.

Diving near underwater submarine detection devices (Asdic and Sonar) can be hazardous to the diver.

Deep diving

Many fatalities to amateur divers can be attributed to deep diving, a subject that is dealt with in detail in *Deep diving*. The process appears to be that a diver or group of divers are trained to use the aqualung until they are competent and confident, and after numerous dives to moderate depths the urge to 'do the ton' and more grips them.

The rapture-of-the-depth-guage is just as big a hazard to the diver as 'rapture of the deep' (nitrogen narcosis). With inadequate equipment, insufficient experience, very little planning and organisation, and total disregard for safety, deep dives are carried out which result in a number of near misses at first and a fatality at last.

It is calculated that at the pressure acting on the body of a diver at 30 metre depth, it is certain that he cannot sustain tremendous pressure increases without many changes. Some of these changes become obvious when a deep dive is carried out in the comparative safety of a re-compression chamber. This experience would tend to make the prospective deep-diver think again. As the air pressure increases over the equivalent 30 metre depth the change of voice to something akin to Donald Duck gives a positive indication of the increased density of the air. The metallic taste of the air, the feeling of light headedness and the giggling of one's companions indicates nitrogen narcosis. In water these warning signs are not as obvious and are consequently ignored, sometimes with fatal results.

It cannot be stressed too heavily that deep dives require immense planning and massive safety measures.

CHAPTER EIGHT

UNDERWATER ACTIVITIES

Archaeology : Joan du Plat Taylor

Biology : Drs Norman and Joanna Jones

Geology : Major Hume Wallace

Photography : Dr Horace E Dobbs

ARCHAEOLOGY

There will always be those divers who get sufficient satisfaction from the act of diving itself to keep them contented. Many more, however, will want to occupy their time underwater more profitably once the skills of diving have been mastered.

The British Sub Aqua Club is producing separate publications on marine archaeology, biology, geology, and underwater photography, so the following material is in the form of a basic guide to sources from which the enthusiast can develop his or her interest.

The modern archaeologist is a detective searching for every minute clue that will help to fill in the detail in the story of man. Underwater archaeology was a part of this detective story which had been largely ignored until recent developments in diving—and the finds made by aqualung divers—drew attention to the vast potential of this field. It is now clear that archaeological techniques can be adapted to furnish as accurate a record underwater as on land. The pioneer work was done in the clear waters of the Mediterranean and this undoubtedly made such work easier. But British waters did not prove the obstacle to serious work that such lack of visibility might have been expected to be. In fact in Britain now serious underwater archaeology has only just started and the first results, in many cases done entirely by amateurs under the guidance of qualified archaeologists, have been startlingly good.

In fact this co-operation between divers, both professional and amateur, and archaeologists is proving to be the keystone of success. The Committee for Nautical Archaeology was formed specifically to assist this co-operation. Its aims are to co-ordinate the work of divers and archaeologists, to gather information on all aspects of nautical archaeology, and to act as an advisory body in matters of policy and special work. Represented on the Committee are : The BSAC, The British Museum, The Council for British Archaeology, London University, the Institute of Archaeology, the National Maritime Museum, the Science Museum, and the Society for Nautical Research.

In fact if you have any problem about underwater archaeology, need guidance or assistance, contact the Committee through the Institute of Archaeology in London.

You'll find that the experts in this field prefer to talk of *nautical* archaeology rather than underwater archaeology, in other words the archaeology of the sea and inland waters. They divide nautical archaeology into three main sections :

a   ships

b   harbours, anchorages and submerged sites

c   Inland waters, lakes and rivers.

So, taking them in that order, we'll deal first with ships. .

Wrecks, whether ancient or modern, undersea or silted up in creeks, rivers or ancient harbours, have all something to contribute to the archaeological record. Most in-shore ships have been broken up by storms, and it is probable that only in deeper water will they survive more or less intact.

Photo—P. Gill

The diver's first view of a typical Mediterranean wreck. This wreck situated off Capo Graziano, Filicudi, Aeolian Islands has had a large proportion of its cargo lifted for the Museum in Lipari.

Seventeenth and eighteenth century ships are mostly recognised first by their guns and divers are finding more and more cannon on the seabed. Earlier ships, such as the amphora-carriers of the Mediterranean, have yet to be found in British waters, but recent clues, including the neck of an amphora found by divers off the Sussex coast, indicate that this discovery will not be long delayed.

And do not scorn the wreckage that comes from a ship running ashore. Such broken material can tell a dramatic story if every tiny clue is collected. It is a sad thought that a single souvenir on someone's mantelpiece—if not reported and shown to the archaeologists at the time of discovery—is another clue lost in the detective story of man. And an even sadder thought is that such a souvenir will, sooner or later, find its way into a dustbin or rubbish dump.

The Hydrographic Department of the Admiralty, maintains files of wrecks. This Department is anxious to receive reports of modern wrecks and aircraft lost at sea. Many of those lost during the war have never been identified, as well as others sunk without trace. Apart from inspecting wrecks for navigational hazards, they require data on how fast wrecks break up. This information must be available in many branch logbooks, where the members dive regularly on known wrecks.

The Hydrographic Department's files carry information on many wrecks in British waters, ancient or modern, and it is glad to receive reports of visits to known wrecks. Its files may be consulted for a modest fee. The Committee for Nautical Archaeology is also opening its own records for ships up to the 18th century, both at home and abroad, from which it hopes to build a solid foundation for research on ancient ships. Report forms for these files may be obtained on application.

Apart from wrecks themselves, one would like to know how many have piled up on specific coasts and how long the places have been a hazard. Changes in coast line could be indicated by losses in deeper water, or where time has removed the hazard. Other groups of losses may be due to battles or to particular storms. The amassing of such information forms the tool of archaeology from which the story of a particular coast may be reconstructed. This might well form part of a branch project working on a specific piece of coast, and the CNA would gladly advise on how this might be carried out.

Harbours, anchorages and submerged sites

British harbours are for the most part silted up. Nevertheless, British divers have reported submerged blocks and structures in the muddy estuaries of our coasts; these could well be recorded on charts for consideration in connection with neighbouring Roman or mediaeval sites. The approaches to these sites would also be worth examining in conjunction with any land exploration which may be taking place. Divers may be reminded that the foreshore is usually someone's property and should take care to see there is no trespassing.

As has been said, little is known of early harbours or landing places, but roadsteads could give the archaeologist a useful clue as to what parts of the coast were used as trade routes and at what periods. These off-shore moorings may have marked places where sailing ships waited for a favourable change of wind to enable them to proceed; they may also have marked fishing grounds. If these sites were charted and lost anchors dated, we would learn something of early sea lanes and methods of navigation.

Other types of roadstead are the temporary shelter in a bay, or an off-shore position to await the turn of the tide before entering a river estuary or harbour. On these roadsteads not only may there be anchors, but there will be much refuse thrown overboard.

To chart these roadsteads would be a useful and interesting branch project. The information could be supplemented by local lore from old inhabitants and fishermen who know the coast better than anyone. A look-out should be kept, too, for changes in coastline or direction of current, and also for erosion and other geological phenomena.

Submerged city sites are worth exploring and planning to find the old coastline and where the harbour was, if any, but in themselves they are unlikely to yield information which cannot be better studied on land.

Inland waters, lakes and rivers. Gravel pits and sand pits are a frequent source of Stone Age implements and their position in the gravel beds is important for chronology. Any implements found should be reported to the local museum.

And if you should make an archaeological discovery during the course of one of your dives, here is what you should do :

1 Make a good note of the position of the object so that you can find it again.

2 Make sure that you can describe the object when you return to the surface—measure it with your hand span, your snorkel, your own body length or that of your diving partner.

3 If you have a camera with you, photograph the object against some object which can be measured again on the surface.

4 Report the find as soon as possible, through your branch, to your local museum or direct to the CNA Institute of Archaeology, 31-34 Gordon Square, London, WC1.

Some further reading:

Bass, G.	*Underwater Archaeology*, Thames & Hudson, 1966.
Birley, A.	*Life in Roman Britain*, Batsford, 1964.
Blair, Clay.	*Diving for Treasure*, Barker, 1961.
Clark, G.	*Prehistoric England*, Ed. Batsford, 1948.
Crawford, O. G. S.	*Archaeology in the Field*, Phoenix House, 1953.
du Plat Taylor, J. (Ed.)	*Marine Archaeology*, Hutchinson, 1965.
Dumas, F.	*Deepwater Archaeology*, Routledge & Kegan Paul, 1963.
Franzen, Anders	*The Warship Vasa*, Stockholm, 1960.
Frost, H.	*Under the Mediterranean*, Routledge & Kegan Paul, 1963.
Kenyon, K. M.	*Beginning in Archaeology*, 2nd Edn. Phoenix House, 1961.
Ordnance Survey	*Field Archaeology* (Some notes for beginners), HMSO, 1963.
Throckmorton, P.	*The Lost Ships*, Cape, 1965.
Webster, G.	*Practical Archaeology*, Black, 1963.
Wood, E. S.	*Field Guide to Archaeology*, Collins, 1963.

BIOLOGY

Many Club divers will have had some experience of biology thanks to their co-operation on marine pollution with Durham University and Dr. David Bellamy on such major tasks as 'Operation Kelp' and 'Project Starfish'.

And, as in nautical archaeology, they will have realised that the key to success in marine biology as in other skilled fields is co-operation with the experts. If divers, who are not trained marine biologists, want to undertake a project that will add to scientific knowledge they will need guidance from a trained scientist.

But first of all the diver who wants to become involved in marine biology should read some of the books listed at the end of this section. He can then examine plants and animals underwater and collect them to identify later. If our diver wants to go further in the field then he must look for some specially arranged course or find an extra-mural course at a suitable university. In fact the Field Studies Council and the BSAC are combining to run a series of courses in marine biology for divers. Applications to Club HQ.

Another way that divers can become involved in biology is by collecting for non-diving scientists.

The most generally useful fluid for preserving animals is a 5% solution of formalin in sea water. Strong formalin is normally sold as a 40% solution of formaldehyde and one part of this should be added to 19 parts of sea water to make 5% formalin. For preservation of shells and other calcareous material the formalin should be neutralised with calcium carbonate. For initial fixing or killing, stronger solutions may be needed. Formalin is poisonous and its vapour is unpleasant but with care it is not dangerous to handle. For long term preservation 70% alcohol is most often used but it evaporates rapidly and any vessel holding it should have a good seal. Even so the addition of a small quantity of glycerine is advisable and may prevent specimens being ruined through drying out. When nothing else is available methylated or other spirits may be used to preserve small specimens.

Soft-bodied and fragile animals may need to be narcotized before killing as they would contract or break up if placed straight into the preservative. Magnesium chloride or sulphate or ether solution added slowly to sea water, or menthol crystals sprinkled on the surface of water in a dish, may be used to narcotize marine animals. When the specimen no longer contracts on touching it may be plunged into the fixative or preserving fluid. For subsequent microscopical examination of tissues

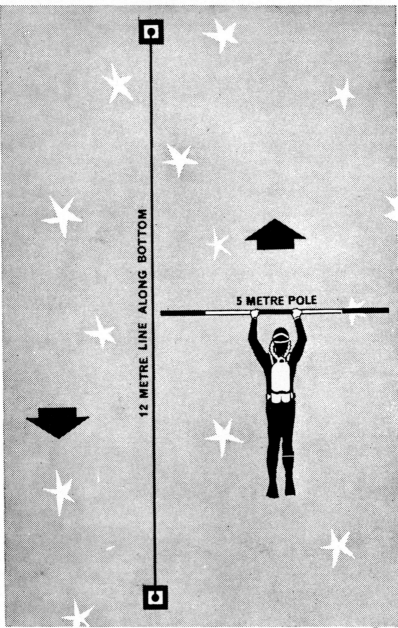

Fig I

Counting starfish or other large specimens. Using this method the diver will cover an area of 120 square metres and be able to calculate the number per square metre.

or for preserving specially fragile animals special methods of killing and preserving must be used for which a textbook or an expert should be consulted.

Seaweeds can also be preserved in 5% formalin in sea water and in 70% alcohol with 5% or so of glycerine added. For more delicate microscopical work they should first be fixed in one part of formalin to 19 parts of 70% alcohol. Unless kept in the dark, most seaweeds quickly lose their colour when preserved in liquids, particularly in alcohol.

In many ways a more useful way of preserving seaweeds is to dry them on paper. A sheet of cartridge (not glossy) paper is put in the bottom of a shallow dish of *fresh* water and the specimen spread out in the water over it, with suitable pruning if it is bushy. The paper is slid or lifted out gently, with the plant spread out on it. After a little draining, a piece of muslin is spread over the plant and the paper and plant pressed between blotting or newspaper, with changes as necessary until dry. The muslin can then be drawn off gently, in most cases leaving the seaweed stuck to the paper. Specimens can thus be preserved in a very pleasing way.

A diver's observations of the way fish behave is valuable provided the observations are reported correctly to scientists. The observations may well start scientists on a new train of thought. On the whole, diving has not often been a means of discovering new species of animals or plants—almost all were known to exist previously. But it has altered ideas about the abundance of certain forms. Some thought to be extremely rare have been found to be quite common. And on-the-spot observation has revealed important aspects of ecology.

Photography by divers is valuable in this field. Divers can take much better, more informed photographs, than can be obtained by cameras lowered from the surface.

Barnes, H.	*Oceanography and Marine Biology*, Allen & Unwin, 1959.
Barrett, J. H. & Yonge, C. M.	*Collins Pocket Guide to the Sea Shore*, Collins, 1958.
Carson, Rachel	*The Sea Around Us*, Staples Press, 1951.
Clegg J.	*The Freshwater Life of the British Isles*, 1952.
Colman, J. S.	*The Sea and its Mysteries*, Bell, 1950.
Dickinson, Carola I.	*British Seaweeds*, Eyre & Spottiswoode, 1963.
Eales, N. B.	*The Littoral Fauna of Great Britain*, Cambridge Unversity Press, 1939.
Hardy, A. C.	*The Open Sea (Vols. I & II)*, Collins, 1956 & 1959.
Hedgpeth, J. W. (Ed.)	*Treatise on Marine Ecology and Paleoecology (Vol. I)*, Geological Society of America, 1957.
Hill, M. N. (Ed.)	*The Sea (Vol. II)*, John Wiley, 1963.
Jenkins, J. T.	*The Fishes of the British Isles (2nd Edn.)*, Warne, 1936.
Kennedy, M.	*The Sea Angler's Fishes*, Hutchinson, 1954.
Luther, W. & Fiedler, K.	*Die Unterwasserfauna der Mittelmeerküsten*, Parey, Hamburg, 1961.
Macan, T. T. & Worthington, E. B.	*Life in Lakes and Rivers*, Collins, 1951.
Marshall, N. B.	*Aspects of Deep Sea Biology*, Hutchinson, 1954.
Newton, L.	*A Handbook of the British Seaweeds*, British Museum, Natural History, 1931.
Norman, J. R. & Greenwood, P.	*A History of Fishes*, Benn, 1963.
Ray, C. & Ciampi, E.	*The Underwater Guide to Marine Life*, Nicholas Kaye, 1956.
Riedl, R.	*Fauna und Flora der Adria*, Parey, Hamburg, 1963.
Russell. F. S. & Yonge C. M.	*The Seas (3rd Edn.)*, Warne, 1963.
Yonge, C. M.	*The Sea Shore*, Collins, 1949.

GEOLOGY

The study of the rocks of the continental shelf in no way differs from the study of similar rocks of the adjacent continent, except that the raw materials, rock samples and observations of the way in which the rocks lie, are more difficult to obtain. This has the great advantage that, unlike terrestrial biologists, the terrestrial geologist who learns to dive can immediately apply his geological knowledge without additional study; and the non-geologist diver who wishes to take up the subject to give additional interest to his diving can easily acquire sufficient knowledge for the purpose by reading the books or attending the evening classes intended for the far more numerous dry land students of the subject.

Figure 1

At the end of the day and before memory fades, write up your notes and replace the scratches made underwater to record the orientation of the rock samples by more visible marks. A small tin of quick drying enamel is excellent for this purpose.

There is the further great advantage for those now going into the submarine branch of the study that until recently it just was not possible to obtain rock samples below the low tide mark except by the use of very inefficient grabs, and though the diver now has a competitor in the corer, a weighted sharp tube let down with considerable force, this instrument can only deal with harder rocks with great difficulty, and is at all times cumbersome and expensive to operate. For this reason, much of the greater part of the continental shelves of the world are geologically virgin territory and any diver can make a useful contribution to knowledge merely by going down and bringing up bits of them provided that he can say exactly where the pieces came from and swear that he detached them from the bedrock and did not just pick up some odd bit transported to where he found it by seaweed, ice or a fisherman's trawl. It is better still if the sample can be orientated with regard to direction and the horizontal, but this is not essential.

> Kingston Branch 24 Sept 63
> Rock SAMPLE C
> Approx 100yds in from N.E edge of
> HAND DEEPS - By to Eddystone ⦿
> Light 135° Mag - Depth - 30 ft
> Mag. EAST-WEST line marked
> on TOP surface of sample
> Dip-Nil as cleavage almost horiz.

Equipment. The equipment required by the diver-geologist, in addition to normal diving equipment, is simple and similar to that used by his dry land colleague : hammer, chisel, magnetic compass for orientations, collecting bag and something on which to take notes. However, the hammer should be lighter since a diver being weightless cannot strike hard blows with a heavy hammer without propelling himself violently in the opposite direction, which usually results in him missing what he is aiming at. It is, therefore, better, where the nature of the rocks will allow it, to work a chisel into any natural crevices with a light hammer. Once the chisel is embedded one can secure oneself to it with one hand and strike it with the hammer in the other.

Observations. In making his observations of the rocks and how the strata lie the diver is often up against the difficulty of poor visibility which only allows him to see a very small section of the picture at a time, and in areas of complicated folding this can make things very confusing indeed. The only remedy is to take things calmly and methodically and using a compass carry out a series of observations, if possible at right angles to the apparent strike, but if the current just will not allow this, in a straight line in some direction, carefully noting all changes in the nature and dip of the rocks. It is a help here if the diver has previously ascertained approximately how far he swims in full equipment with a certain number of finbeats.

Use mode of information. As with all scientific work, there is little point in gathering samples and taking observations and then doing nothing with either, and it is just in this matter of directing his work

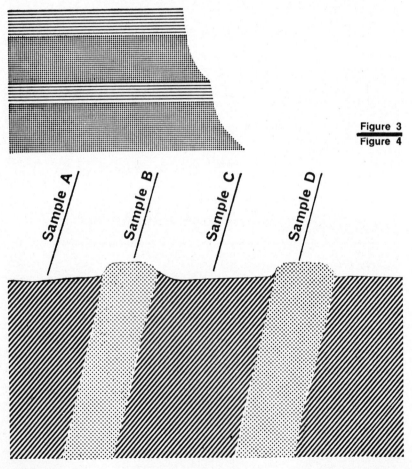

Figure 3
Figure 4

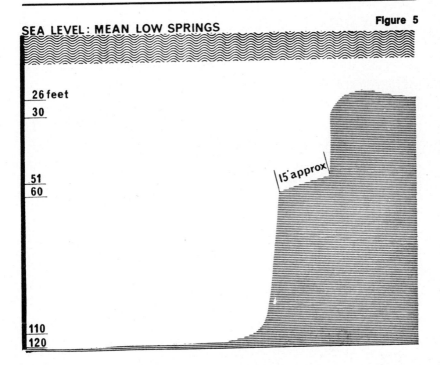

SEA LEVEL: MEAN LOW SPRINGS

Figure 5

26 feet

30

51

60

15' approx

110

120

to the most useful project and seeing that the information he gathers gets to the right quarters that the amateur most needs direction and advice from the established geologist. A group of divers who are thinking of taking up the subject should therefore make every effort to get a competent geologist, amateur or professional, to direct their work. If they know none, a visit to the local museum or college may produce the necessary introductions to the local learned society. With luck, one may even be able to find a geologist prepared to take up diving, but even without this it should be possible to establish a sound working partnership between a group of divers who regularly dive in a certain area and a geologist interested in the adjacent coast who will usually jump at the chance to extend his knowledge outward from it, and in return can guide and direct the studies of the group.

Also, in Great Britain at any rate, divers without their own geologist adviser, or diving outside the area in which he is interested, can still do useful work since the Geological Survey are now anxious to obtain rock samples from anywhere more than half a mile off the British Coasts provided that they are from the bedrock and the place whence they came can be accurately located. BSAC members who are doubtful as to presentation and the way the accompanying notes should be written up should send their samples to Major Hume Wallace at 25, Orchard Place, Kingston-on-Thames, Surrey, who will then pass them on to the Geological Survey.

For further reading:

Elementary
Ager, D. V.   *Introducing Geology*, Faber & Faber, 1961.

More advanced
Holmes, Arthur   *Principles of Physical Geology.* A new and fully revised edition. Nelson, 1965.
Shepard, Francis P.   *Submarine Geology.* A revised second edition. Harper & Row, 1963.
Steers, James A.   *The Coastline of England & Wales.* A new and enlarged edition. Cambridge University Press, 1964.

Papers describing techniques of underwater geology
Graindor, M. J.   Revue de Geographie Physique et de Geologie Dynamique Vol 2, fasc 1, p 29. Paris, 1959.
Dill, R. F. and   Geologic use of self-contained Diving Apparatus. American Associa-
   Shumway, George   tion of Petroleum Geologists, Vol. 38, p 148, 1954.

PHOTOGRAPHY

One of the most satisfying and rewarding of underwater activities is the recording of pictures of underwater scenes and life. The diver-photographer, whether he be snorkel or free diving is however, faced with a number of problems peculiar to the environment. It is these special aspects of photography that are considered here.

Underwater visibility is stated to be extremely good if it reaches 30 metres. Under such conditions—equal to a fog on dry land—the difficulties of obtaining clear photographs are legion. Add to this the fact that the photographer himself is probably moving, drifting up and down, swaying with the movement of the water, and the necessity of taking special precautions and adopting specialised techniques can readily be understood.

Physical factors involved

Light is absorbed in its passage through water, the intensity decreasing rapidly with increased depth. At the same time a process of selective colour filtration takes place, the red colours being absorbed much more rapidly than the greens and blues.

When rays of light strike the water a certain percentage of them are reflected from the surface and do not penetrate below surface level. This percentage is least when the sun is high in the sky, and increases as the sun sinks and the angle of the rays becomes more oblique to the water. If there is a wind or rough sea running, the waves break up the surface of the water and less light penetrates.

Reflection also takes place under water. Particles of organic and inorganic matter suspended in the water diffuse and scatter the light, reducing the visibility in good conditions to rarely more than 30 metres—but more often to 5 metres in British waters—down to absolute zero. All these influences combine to produce pictures of low contrast—the definition falling off rapidly with increasing separation of the camera and the subject. Under the conditions prevalent in most British waters, clear bright pictures can only be obtained in relatively close-up shots.

Poor lighting conditions are thus a severe drawback to underwater photography. The best conditions are obtained in clear water, just below the surface, in calm weather, in the summer, between the hours of 10 am and 4 pm, with bright sunlight overhead.

The different refractive indices of air and water make underwater objects appear bigger and closer to the diver. They also affect a camera when it is used underwater, resulting in a reduction of the acceptance angle of the lens, ie, the camera records a smaller field of view than normal, and requiring that the lens is focused at a shorter distance than the actual separation of the subject and the camera.

435

The same difficulties of taking moving subjects are present as on land, but they are intensified due to the apparent reduction of distance, angle of view, and the diminished visibility.

Cameras

Normal camera lenses are designed for use in air. To use them in direct contact with water would result in the formation of blurred images similar to those seen by an unmasked diver. Although it is possible to design lenses for use in direct contact with water, most commercially available cameras made specifically for underwater use do not incorporate them, but utilise instead standard camera lenses, hermetically sealed behind flat glass windows. This enables the cameras to be used above and below water without modification. The bodies of these cameras are made of pressure and corrosion resistant materials, the controls operating through watertight seals.

The use of special underwater cameras, such as the Calypso-phot and the Nikonos, undoubtedly greatly simplifies underwater photography. The camera controls are reliable and easy to operate underwater. Film changing is no more difficult than it is with conventional 35mm cameras. These underwater cameras are very compact. They can be regarded as part of the normal diving equipment, and the diver can adopt the same attitude to photography as his above-water counterpart, that is, if an interesting subject is encountered during a dive it can easily be photographed. If no photogenic subjects present themselves then the camera is no more of an encumbrance to the diver than a similar camera would be to a climber, say. The same cannot be said of a camera housed in a bulky underwater case.

The number of cameras designed specifically for underwater use is, as yet, extremely limited. The photographer who wishes to use a particular conventional camera, or requires to use a camera with a format for which there is no truly underwater camera available, must resort to housing a standard above-water camera in some form of watertight case. When a range of cameras are available, there are a number of factors that should be borne in mind when making the selection. The first is that ultimately the camera is to be put in a housing and the camera controls operated by remote control. A camera should therefore be chosen in which the movements of the various working components can easily be actuated by control rods with simple rotary, or to-and-fro, motions. Without doubt the fewer controls there are the better. All external controls are possible sources of failure and potential leakage points in the underwater housing. Thus a camera with a 'magic eye' which automatically alters the setting of the iris diaphragm, is to be preferred to a camera which requires a manual manipulation for this operation. However, an automatic camera will not give the correct setting for flash photography. If you intend to use flash, the camera will need to have a manual over-ride, ie a calibration in 'f-numbers'.

Another feature which is of paramount importance for cameras that are to be used in Britain's none-too-clear waters is the acceptance angle of the lens. The field view should be as wide as possible in order that the cameraman can get close to his subject. This reduces the loss in contrast and definition, due to suspended matter between the lens and the subject, to a minimum. A lens with a wide maximum aperture is also advantageous in poor lighting conditions. Fast shutter speeds (1/250th - 1/1000th sec) are usually precluded because of the reduced light intensity underwater. However, shutter speeds in excess of 1/50th sec are desirable because many of the subjects photographed underwater are mobile.

Camera Housings

There are three basic types of underwater camera housing. The simplest of these, known as the compensating type, has a section made of rubber or soft plastic. This enables the air enclosed in the case to compress with increasing water pressure, thereby equalising the pressure inside and outside the housing. The simplest form of this type of case consists of a plastic bag fitted with a glass or Perspex window. The camera is placed inside the bag and the controls manipulated from the outside through the plastic. In more elaborate designs the camera is mounted on a rigid frame and the controls operated through a rubber glove. The depth to which this type of housing can be used is limited by the elasticity of the rubber sections and the volume of the free air space inside the case. The reduction of volume with increasing depth results in a variation in buoyancy of the complete unit.

The type of housing most commonly used by underwater photographers, however, consists of a rigid box capable of withstanding the considerable pressures encountered underwater. The camera controls are operated via control rods passing through waterproof seals in the housing. Metal, wood, plastic and glass fibre can be used for their construction, which is generally for a specific make of camera so that the various controls can be accurately coupled to it. General purpose housings are also available that can be modified to suit most types of camera.

Most photographers who build their own camera cases construct the rigid type. A host of materials can be used for this purpose. Sheet Perspex is a popular starting material. Alternatively, pre-formed objects can be used. Many suitably shaped metal containers, such as pressure cookers and fuse boxes, have been ingeniously transformed into first class camera housings.

Another type of housing, usually restricted for use with large, or very expensive cameras, incorporates an automatic internal pressurisation system. The camera is enclosed in a rigid box fitted with a small compressed air cylinder and demand valve similar to those used with aqualungs, which maintains the air pressure in the case a little higher than the external water pressure.

The type of viewfinder employed with many housings is of some consequence. The normal type fitted in the camera can rarely be employed as it is either too small to be placed to the eye with the mask intervening, will not admit sufficient light, or is obstructed by the case.

An external double-frame viewfinder is, therefore, usually used. The dimensions of this must be such that the field of view sighted through the two frames corresponds to the reduced field of the camera under water. Increasing the separation of the axis of the lens and the viewfinder enhances parallax effects. This can be corrected by making the back sight adjustable.

For reflex cameras an aperture in the case to permit direct viewing of the screen allows accurate composition of the picture, but this method fails in poor lighting conditions, particularly when flash has to be used.

When rigid housings are taken to great depths, they must be robustly made to withstand the pressure of the water. Pressure resistant housings are sometimes equipped with a valve that enables the case to be pressurised with a bicycle pump. Pressurising serves the double purpose of counterbalancing to some extent the external water pressure, and of enabling the diver to check if there are any leaks by looking for an escape of bubbles when the case is first lowered into the water. Some sealing devices work only one way, however, and may be damaged if the pressure is reversed. It is advisable, therefore, to check the seals before fitting a valve to a housing.

The number of controls fitted will affect the versatility of the unit. Shutter release and film wind controls are essential. The addition of an aperture control is of considerable advantage as it enables the diver to vary the exposure according to the light intensity, which changes continuously with varying depth. A focus control is useful if the photographer wants to record a variety of subjects on a single dive. The speed setting is usually limited in one direction by the movement of the subject, and in the other by the lack of sufficient light, to one of the medium speeds. It is therefore rarely altered underwater and is the least important of the controls fitted to a housing.

When taking a camera and case below water, allowance has often to be made for its buoyancy. The underwater camera should not be so heavy that it materially affects the diver's buoyancy nor should it float upwards on the strap hung round his neck. The ideal is that it should have 1 kilo negative buoyancy. It should not encumber the diver and should be so retained that it will not get lost, but it should be considered as one of the jettisonable items of equipment. A simple method of support is by means of a cord round the neck so that the case hangs low upon the chest. In this position it will not get in the way of the weight-belt and can readily be brought up to eye level for use.

Some cases are fitted with stabilising fins or other means of preventing unwanted movement. These have only a limited use, mainly when swimming in the water or when using cine.

If there is a choice of colours for the case it should be black and white, as these are the most easily seen colours underwater and may assist in the recovery of the camera if lost there.

Techniques

As explained, one important factor is to avoid movement of the camera when taking the photo. Slight negative buoyancy assists this, but the main consideration is shutter speed, which should rarely be less than 1/60th sec and preferably 1/125th sec. All camera controls available should be used to the maximum efficiency. Do not wait until the subject looms into view before getting the camera ready. Keep all the controls set in advance, including cocking the shutter. Fish may be frightened away by the sound of triggering and often a good shot is lost for this reason. Assess the lighting conditions and set the speed and aperture.

While swimming, get into the habit of altering the aperture and focus controls as lighting and subject conditions change, so that when the time comes to take a photo everything has been set in advance. It will not then be necessary to spend time estimating exposure and adjusting controls when a suitable subject appears, but possible at once to concentrate on composing and centring the picture before firing the release. Bearing in mind that the eye and camera both see objects under water in the same perspective, the easiest method of judging distance is to estimate the distance as seen and set the camera accordingly. For distances of more than three feet, the depth of field of the lens usually extends beyond any inaccuracies of the visual assessment of the distance by the diver. When the subject is close to the lens the depth of field is greatly reduced and distances must be more accurately determined. One method of achieving an accurate assessment is to use a focusing stick. This consists of a stick marked out in a 4/3 scale, ie, a stick four measures long represents three underwater.

Colour pictures using daylight film can be effectively taken underwater. The high speed films that are now available are ideally suited for such use, although they usually record the scenes in slightly more pastel shades than slower films. As the red colours are rapidly absorbed, at depths below 6 metres flash should be used. In depths of less than 6 metres, colour correction filters can be used to compensate for the colour modifying effect of the water. Without flash, the overall monotone green hue at 10 metres might equally well have been reproduced in black and white.

Photos taken with flash, however, show up the splendid colours that otherwise go unseen, even by the diver himself. Flash bulbs are fitted to an external reflector, where they can easily be changed by hand, and the electrical components of the flash unit are located inside the camera housing. Clear flashbulbs should be used for both colour and black-and-white photography, if the subject is more than three feet away. For close-ups, use blue bulbs. When electronic flash is used as the light source, the entire unit, including the flash tube, must be housed in a waterproof case.

Due to the fact that sediment reflects the flash light back into the camera, flash pictures should not be attempted at a distance greater than a quarter of the visibility.

Cine, either black-and-white, or colour, brings to life the underwater world. It is often possible to produce a good cine film under conditions in which it would be impossible to take really acceptable still photographs. For this work it is essential to keep the camera steady. Swimming with the camera in front, in line with the eyes, produces good sequences as seen by the diver.

Exposure and Development

The diffuse lighting usually encountered underwater gives pictures that lack the sparkle produced by more intense and directional illumination. This effect can be partially overcome in black-and-white photography by the choice of suitable film and printing paper. As a general rule slow films have a higher contrast than fast films, and are therefore to be preferred. Unfortunately the use of the slowest films is precluded because of the reduced light intensity underwater. The photographer must, therefore, select a fairly fast film. Nonetheless, he should choose a film with the lowest speed commensurate with the lighting conditions he expects to prevail when taking the pictures.

The film should be developed to a high contrast (to a gamma of 0.8, say) and printed on high contrast paper.

The best method to determine the correct exposure underwater is to use a light meter. If the camera housing is made of Perspex, the meter can be positioned alongside the camera. Alternatively, the exposure meter can be accommodated in its own waterproof case. It can be used in the same manner as a meter above water. As there is little directional light, it is best used as a reflectance meter, ie, the reading is taken when the meter is directed towards the subject.

The light intensity underwater depends upon such a vast number of variables that it is virtually impossible to tabulate a comprehensive exposure guide. The following table can be used as a basis for experiment, but should not be regarded as an absolute guide.

**Comparative Exposure Guide for
Colour and Panchromatic Films
with a Speed of Approximately 50 ASA**

Depth	Water visibility			
	Very clear		Average clarity	Slightly murky
	Calm water	Ruffled water		
Above surface	f16	f16	f16	f16
Below surface	f11	f8	f5.6	f4
5 mtrs. ...	f8	f5.6	f4	f2.8
10 mtrs. ...	f5.6	f4	f2.8	—
20 mtrs. ...	f4	f2.8	—	—
30 mtrs. ...	f2.8	—	—	—

Sun overhead—shutter speed 1/60 sec

If flash is used, the contribution of the natural lighting to the total illumination may have to be taken into account. However, this is only normally necessary for distant subjects. For close-ups and flash can usually be regarded as the sole source of illumination. As with natural lighting the determination of the correct aperture to use with flash depends upon a variety of factors. These can be determined by a process of trial and error. As a general rule, however, dividing the above water flash factor by four or five gives a reasonable correction.

When a camera case is taken underwater, the reduction in temperature may cause water to condense on the inside. If this results in the window in front of the camera misting up, it will cause a loss in picture quality. Condensation can be greatly reduced by loading the camera into its housing at night when the air temperature is low. Alternatively, a fresh bag of a moisture-absorbent material, such as silica gel, can be put in the case with the camera. If, however, you have a flash battery in with the camera, it is not advisable to use a desiccant. Also, very low humidities achieved by silica gel can give rise to film problems such as static and brittleness. The camera and the desiccant should not, therefore, be left in a sealed case for protracted periods.

A leak of salt water into the case will rapidly corrode the camera. In such circumstances remove the camera from the case as soon as possible. If the camera is flooded rinse it thoroughly in fresh water and dry out, using warm air if available. It should then be taken to a repairer for attention as soon as possible.

CHAPTER NINE

PUBLIC RELATIONS

Public Relations and You : Michael Treloar

PUBLIC RELATIONS

It is not uncommon in this day and age to pick up a newspaper or to see an item on a TV news bulletin and to learn that amateur divers have been involved in a police operation of one kind or another.

Sooner or later many other branches are likely to be dealing with this kind of activity, and it is important for members to know the mechanics of co-operation with the police. The situation is as follows :

In the British Isles, the police are organised into a fairly complex and de-centralised network. Some counties, cities and boroughs have their own forces, although the modern trend is to have larger forces covering bigger areas, brought about by the amalgamation of groups of smaller ones. This is a movement towards Regional Forces and, perhaps, an eventual National Force. Each Police Force is commanded by a Chief Constable who, generally speaking, is reponsible to his police authority.

This authority is made up of local councillors and magistrates who largely allocate the finances available to run their forces. This often means that the police are not able to equip themselves as they might wish. For this reason, there is a wide variation in the way in which one force is equipped as compared with a near neighbour.

Underwater units in the police have only come into promi..ence in the last five to ten years. In fact, ten years ago there were only about three forces which had their own divers. The situation now is that a gradual acceleration is taking place, and more and more police authorities are making the funds available to train and equip teams, as the interest stems from the various Chief Constables because of the obvious value of such units.

Now, for many years Club divers have carried out various voluntary duties for their local police forces. In many cases policemen themselves have been introduced to diving through the Club and carried their interest into their work, eventually to form official teams. Is there, therefore, still room for BSAC participation? The answer is yes. Despite the fact that police underwater units are becoming more commonplace, there remains a place for the interested and proficient amateur to give valuable assistance in the spirit of public service. This is particularly so in areas where the local police do not have their own units, and even where they do there are occasions where their resources are insufficient to perform all the work that has to be done. There are times when 20 or more divers can usefully be employed, and police units do not run to this size.

However, before an amateur diver undertakes work for the police he should understand several facts. To start with he must be fully competent to carry out the type of work for which he has offered his services; well meaning but incompetent helpers can get in the way of success. The senior police officer must have the confidence to trust the word of the divers regarding what they have, or have not, found, and nothing will instil confidence more than previous success.

The diver must also put aside any idea of glamour seeking. Such work as he is likely to be involved in is very often tragic, and sometimes sordid. Frequently it has to be carried out in very unpleasant water conditions, and certainly at any time of the year. There is also the added nervous strain that such affairs as body searches can produce, and the would-be volunteer must ask himself, and answer realistically, if he could face up to such tasks. It may be that he will recognise that in such things he has limitations and restrict himself to the less arduous task of searching for lost or abandoned property.

Another question which must be answered concerns insurance. Care should be exercised to examine the terms of any life insurance he may have; such work as he may be offering to undertake may place himself outside the terms of its coverage. He may not be insured in any case, and the police may not cover him. Previous research into the true position should be made, and some agreement reached. More often than not you will dive entirely at your own risk, with no redress for your dependents in the event of an accident.

There is also the risk of damage to any of the equipment used, or its actual loss. Puncturing of suits, and the tearing of hoods or wrist seals in the case of dry suits, may be experienced. This sort of thing is much more likely in police type diving, due to the litter-laden waters in which such searches are usually required. Fins are frequently lost through standing on slippery muddy banks. Minor injuries such as cut hands from broken glass and old tins can become infected, particularly if not promptly treated, through exposure to contaminated water. All these things must be considered beforehand, and the branch or individual diver prepared to cover losses or to ensure that the police themselves will be prepared to look after them. The latter eventuality is not automatic as there may not be any funds available for this purpose; and something may have to be arranged between the police and the local authority concerned.

These things have, of course, been recognised before, and Club divers have tended to treat such searches as normal training dives. Quite probably they are in waters that they normally use anyway.

In any Club, or branch of the Club, that has an interest in this type of work, there must be formed a team of suitable diver volunteers. It normally follows that such people are the cream of that particular group, and wish to turn their talents to some useful purpose apart from pure leisure. Preferably, they should be prepared to be called out at any time, even during normal working hours. It may be that employers will be prepared to release them on continued payment in view of the reason for their work, and this should be arranged beforehand. Certainly it would not be safe to assume that the police would be able to make up for any salary lost.

Contact can be made with the police in a variety of ways, but perhaps the best is to write to the local Superintendent of Police in the case of county areas, and the Chief Constable for cities and boroughs. Details of the availability of the team, and whom to call on for their services, can be furnished. It may be that before any concrete offer of assistance is made, preliminary enquiries are put in hand to obtain answers to some of the questions raised earlier in this article.

The type of work which amateur divers can undertake is the search for and recovery of drowned persons, known to be in a particular stretch of water, or the general search of perhaps larger areas of water for missing persons who may have been suicides or the victims of murder, and property which has been stolen and thrown into rivers. In this category one can include safes, bicycles, motor cycles and even cars. Sometimes there is the need to search for lost property, particularly when it has some value, although this is more likely to be at the request of an insurance company and will then border on commercial diving, for which there will probably be some form of reward.

To do this sort of work efficiently one must obviously have some form of training, although it is fair to say that training to 2nd class diver standard will provide a good foundation. The diver must be at home in dark water, and well able to plan and execute various types of search techniques, in particular the grid and circular methods. Merely having passed the third class certificate is not enough, although such a person could join in as a junior member of the team. However, the diving marshal must be able to feel that the diver has made a thorough search, and not spent most of his time groping along the search line unable to concentrate on anything else.

Diving for the police is never likely to bring much in the way of financial reward, more often than not it will bring about financial loss, but the one thing that it does earn is a sense of satisfaction through having done a worthwhile job of work. It also is good from the public relations point of view, for press publicity usually follows, inaccurate and lurid though this sometimes is. Nevertheless, it is read eagerly by many people and stands to enhance the reputation of the branch or Club, and perhaps attract the attention of new members.

Public relations
This term is not readily understood by very many people, but it simply concerns the relationships between people. There are good public relations

and bad public relations, and there is no doubt about which it is best to have.

By and large, the relations between divers and some sections of the public have not been good, and it is only in recent times that divers have really begun to break down the core of resentment and antipathy directed towards them by many other users of the sea and the water.

There are various reasons for these ill feelings, some acceptable, some not. Certainly, in the beginning there were quite a few divers who trod with colossal lack of tact upon the susceptibilities of fishermen and others, and since one black-suited diver looks much like another we all get the blame.

Though the situation has been improving for several years, it is still far from ideal, and much is made in some quarters about the deterioration of relations between divers and local fishermen in various parts of the country.

No one is entirely blameless in this kind of situation, but let us as a group be sensible about the matter. The fact is that we are fully entitled to our pleasures as long as we do not interfere with those of other people. They may even be the very people involved in our rescue if we happen to get into difficulties, which is a disquieting thought.

At any rate, one meets all kinds of people in the diving world, ranging from the highly responsible to the complete opposite, and it is the last group that causes most of the trouble. Difficulty was at one time created at a diving site in the West Country by parties of Club members visiting the popular local, drinking more than they could hold and launching into bawdy sing-songs. Good fun maybe, but not for all the people there. For quite a time all divers were shunned at this place and the reputation of the Club was at a pretty low ebb.

This is just one example among many, but poor behaviour has a wider range than this: it extends from the disregard of other people's property right up to the stage of actually stealing it, and it takes in discourtesy in general on the way.

Fortunately, all such incidents are rare compared with the vast number of divers operating up and down the country each year and no doubt most of the trouble stems from sheer thoughtlessness. For this reason, it is worth stressing that there are basic rules of adult behaviour and if they are followed an atmosphere is created in which we are welcomed back time and time again.

Inland waters very often present different problems from the coast. For example, that attractive-looking lake must belong to somebody, and that river must run through privately-owned land. The smart diving group is the one that takes the trouble to find out who is the owner and ask permission to use, or have access to, the water. This kind of approach

BSAC members assisting the police in a search for a missing person.

15

almost always brings success, whereas no approach at all can be followed by an argument and a complete ban coupled with ill feeling.

Diving in rivers involves other problems. If they carry much traffic, antagonism is likely to be provoked unless divers are specially careful, quite apart from the obvious dangers of being run down. This also goes for fairways and estuaries, and many boatmen have in the past complained bitterly at having to make emergency alterations to course when a round black head bobs up under the bow. Fishermen on the banks will also not take kindly to divers surfacing nearby, possibly tangled in their lines. And, finally, gates left open, cars driven where they ought not to be, and litter and debris left about are killers of good relations.

In respect of the sea, keep the harbour authorities happy. It always pays to let the harbourmaster—and the coastguard—know where you are going. Also, never fool around in the sea giving rise to suspicion that you are in trouble. There is the story of the boy who cried ' wolf '! It goes without saying that a diver's flag should always be flown when diving is in progress, but not before or after.

It is also a good idea to contact the local diving club. Though this is not absolutely necessary if only a day's outing is involved, it is vital if any sort of expedition or research is planned for the area. There have been cases where violent rows have developed between branches because this has not been done, and almost always it is the visiting group that suffers : the locals know the waters and have all the other relevant information.

If you happen to be planning an interesting dive or expedition that is likely to be newsworthy, don't forget the local newspaper. Some good publicity could result, and both you and the Club might benefit in one way or another.

A few last words about fishermen. They are particularly touchy about divers, sometimes without good reason, but don't forget that their livelihood is at stake and a hard one it can be. They are not impressed when skin divers appear on the quay laden with crabs and lobsters, especially if diving has taken place close to where their pots have been laid, and they get positively angry if those concerned then begin to hawk these wares around at well below their market value. In some places now they will not have anything to do with divers, although in the past they often took parties out at very low cost.

Those diving groups who do have good relations with fishermen are usually on the winning end. Help in the recovery of lost nets, pots, anchors and the like, works wonders.

I am sorry if there has been a predominance of ' don'ts ' in this section but I think you will agree that they are all relevant and really do not involve much sacrifice. We all want to go diving and we all want to be welcomed when we go. The fact that one does not intend to return to a diving site often results in less effort being made to stick to the rules, but remember that there may well be another diving group in the same frame of mind elsewhere, and unknown to one another each crosses over to the other's past ground, both to be made unwelcome.

Generally speaking, a consistently good standard of courtesy pays handsome dividends, and it considerably enhances the fun aspects of our sport.

To turn finally to a few positive aspects of public relations. If you want to do your branch and your Club some good—and speed up recruiting—you can certainly do so by becoming publicity and promotion minded. If there is a nearby yacht club, contact them and offer your help whenever it is needed. Volunteer to train members of the local Boy Scouts Troop for skin diving proficiency awards and other young people for the Duke of Edinburgh Award. Offer assistance in the form of speeches, film shows and so on, to local political parties, youth clubs and other organisations. Think of organising some diving event, perhaps only once a year, and contact your local authority for help. If there is a film concerning diving at a local cinema, mount an exhibition in the foyer. If a branch activity is mentioned in *Triton,* get some additional copies and send them off, with the relevant items ringed, to people of importance in the town. And keep on good terms with your local newspaper; they will probably use items about you from time to time.

All these things, and many others, can improve your image and make life much more interesting. Try it and see.

CHAPTER TEN

BSAC ENDORSEMENTS

The Sub Aqua Bronze Medallion: G T Skuse

The Deep Rescue Test: National Diving
Committee

THE SUB AQUA BRONZE MEDALLION

Conditions

For the Examination the candidate must supply a suitable subject. Forms must be filled in and fees paid before the start of the exam. A minimum of fourteen days' notice should be given to the Branch Secretary, or RLSS Headquarters. Examinations may only be conducted by authorised Examiners, each of whom will carry a current (annual) card of authority signed by the Branch Secretary or the Chief Examiner.

Examinations will be conducted in accordance with the *current* edition of the handbook. The numbered sections of each exam may be taken in any order, but in the water tests the individual tests must be taken in the order given. The primary requirement is for the candidate to prove his ability in the Society's methods of life-saving and resuscitation : a candidate who shows an acceptable standard of life-saving proficiency and speed will not be failed solely on imperfection of swimming strokes or diving technique.

Candidates are not permitted to refer to the handbook or other aids to memory during the Examination.

Recommended Reading

1 Life Saving and Water Safety 1969, 25p. ⎱ Both from
2 Emergency Resuscitation 1970, 15p ⎰ The RLSS
3 First Aid 1965, 30p. The St. John Ambulance Association.
4 Underwater Medicine, Stanley Miles, £3.75, 1970.

1(a) Water Test with Full Diving Gear

Equipment. Wet-suit jacket and trousers. (A dry-suit is an alternative.) Inflatable lifejacket with full cylinder. Full aqualung.

Weight belt with quick-release buckle.

Mask, fins and snorkel.

Shallow Forward Entry. Holding mask to face with one hand, and aqualung harness at the waist with the other the diver steps forward off the side and enters vertically, feet first, breathing from the aqualung.

Neutral Buoyancy. The diver should lie prone in the water, and he should sink when he exhales, and rise again when he inhales. The fact that he sinks on exhalation is more important than rising by inhalation.

Fin 50 Yards. The use of fins only is mandatory—no overarm strokes. A reasonable speed must be maintained. The rescuer may breathe from his aqualung although it is more usual to use the snorkel when swimming on the surface.

Surface Dive. Head-first. Without pausing from the swim the rescuer should change from snorkel to aqualung just prior to diving.

The subject should be waiting on the bottom of the deep-end.

Remove Subject's Weight Belt. Very important, he may also remove his own if he wishes, placing them carefully on the pool bottom.

It is most important that the rescuer retains firm hold on the subject or the subject will float free to the surface.

Owing to this increase in buoyancy, and the lack of real depth he may be unable to carry out the following hold, but he should be able to describe it fully later.

Retain hold of the subject from the back or side with the right hand. With the left hand grip the subject's chin and ensure his mouthpiece is held in position. Extend the subject's neck to enable air in the lungs to escape as it expands, and the head is in the right position to give immediate EAR on the surface.

Inflate Subject's Lifejacket. One of two actions may be undertaken here, chosen according to the equipment worn.

(a) He immediately inflates the subject's lifejacket by use of the inflating cylinder, in which case the rescue can proceed, or

(b) he raises his arm indicating ' I would normally inflate the lifejacket '. The subject then inflates his own lifejacket by mouth. This is to avoid the expense (up to £1.00) of a replacement CO_2 cylinder. The rescue then continues.

NB. The lifejacket must *not* be inflated until both divers have surfaced.

Remove Subject's Mask and Snorkel and remove the subject's mouthpiece. (The subject may wish to secure his own air tubes during the tow to avoid excessive loss of air.) The rescuer lifts his own mask and snorkel and removes his aqualung mouthpiece. (The rescuer's mask and snorkel may be needed for further rescue work and should not be discarded, unless by accident.)

EAR Four Cycles. See notes on ' Deep-water EAR '. NOTE : The subject will have a tendency to lie flat on the surface of the water with an inflated lifejacket. One solution to this is to remove the right hand from the nape of the neck and use the arm to press down on the life-jacket.

The left arm must then be ' crooked ' and the rescuer moves round to the ' wrong ' side of the subject to give mouth-to-nose EAR, holding the subject's mouth closed with his left hand.

Tow 20 Yards. Use the extended tow. See notes ' Deep-water EAR '. Give two to three breaths every 15 to 20 seconds.

EAR While Walking to the Side. This must be at least five yards. When the rescuer is able to feel the bottom of the pool he may then use the foothold to get his subject to the side, continuing to give EAR on the way. He then hands the subject over to the Examiner on instruction.

Explain the Use of Another Lifesaver. This may be now, or during the oral exam later; ie, ensure the continuance of EAR by the people to whom he hands the subject, checking it is effective. See to the removal of the subject's equipment when satisfied, and get him into the boat or onto the pier/shore as appropriate.

1(b) Water Test with Basic Equipment only

Equipment. Swimming costume, mask, fins and open-ended snorkel.

Entry for Unknown Water. The rescuer should slide into the water carefully.

50 Yards Overarm. The rescuer approaches the subject in deep water at the end of the swim, and just before contact stops and gives instructions to the subject on the lines ' take your snorkel out of your mouth, stretch out your arms towards me with your hands together and lie back '. Note the subject may be allowed to raise his mask or retain it in place, but his snorkel mouthpiece *must* be removed. The rescuer retains both.

25 Yards No. 2 Method. Remember that the subject is supposed to be co-operative.

25 Yards No. 1 Method. There should be no pause when changing methods, and no loss of contact. There must be no deliberate contact with the pool side or bottom. (This change of method of tow could occur in a real rescue should the subject cease to co-operate.)
The subject's mask *must* now be raised onto the forehead, or removed completely. The rescuer has a choice depending on his own position when towing, but it is usual to remove the snorkel mouthpiece from the mouth. The essential factor is that the rescuer should not limit his own access to air while towing. If he gets swamped through retaining either mask or snorkel, he has made an error of judgement.

Land Subject Unaided. The crossed-arm method is required, taking care to lift the subject well clear of the water. The rescuer does not need to remove his own fins before carrying out the removal. No assistance is permitted.
(The straight-arm method is needed when the subject is wearing an aqualung which for some reason cannot be jettisoned.)

Coma Position. Ensure the rescuer protects the subject's head and face as he rolls him over, and there is reasonable extension of the neck.

2 Water Test Without Diving Gear
(a) Deep Water (Ideally will not take longer than 4½ minutes)

Straddle Jump. Forward motion and the use of the arms should ideally prevent the rescuer's head sinking below the surface of the water. Splash may well make this difficult to judge.

50 Yards Swim. The rescuer should not dawdle on the way. He may swim any style, but back-stroke should not be used unless the rescuer does not have another strong stroke. The final few yards must be made head up, eg, breast stroke.

Reverse. The basic defensive technique to reverse the position of the body with rapidity and ease. Contact with the subject in any way is a failure of technique.

Approach from Behind. The rescuer must avoid contact until he is in position.

50 Yards Chin Tow with Restraints. (See RLSS handbook.) During the tow the subject will struggle twice, as briefed by the Examiner. The rescuer must show ability to control the subject.

Support Position. Used to secure the subject in a position of safety against a firm support with his face out of water.

(b) Shallow Water

Shallow Water Entry. A shallow dive is permitted, or a jump. Approach the subject on the surface, swimming at least 10 yards.

Extended Tow. Cup the subject's chin or grip his hair. Use side stroke or life-saving back stroke. The subject must be taken to the nearest deep water support.

EAR Three Cycles. The subject is held supported with one arm behind his head, gripping the bar or side. The other hand holds his mouth shut and head tilted, being cupped beneath his chin ready for EAR.

Releases. Demonstrate in the water a release specified by the Examiner from each of three types of clutch. Take any approved towing position after each release. In all cases care should be taken to maintain control of and *contact with* the subject. The moment of contact between the rescuer and the victim is the most dangerous part of any rescue. The rescuer must immediately seize the initiative in gaining control of the victim.

3 On Dry Land

(a) Resuscitation

Demonstrate EAR for a period of 3-6 minutes at the Examiner's discretion, to show :

(i)   the mouth to nose method

(ii)   the mouth to mouth method

(iii)   the action for vomit.

Following each explain the techniques involved. NOTE : The candidate must pay special attention to the following : obstruction, extension, seals and rhythm. The action for vomit requires the subject's head to be low for natural drainage.

Clearance of vomit must be seen to be made.

(b) Oral

Answer two questions on respiration and blood circulation.

4 Assessment of an Emergency Situation

The Examiner will describe a typical open-water emergency. The candidate will be required to explain the action he would take. The situation will apply to diving, and more than one correct solution may be possible.

DEEP RESCUE TEST

Introduction

It has been of considerable concern to the National Diving Committee that a number of incidents have been recorded in recent years in which rescue attempts of companion divers, at depth, have resulted in failure.

These failures, on the whole, were due to a lack of appreciation of the finning effort involved in ascending with a fully kitted diver.

To this effect this test, culminating in a log book endorsement, has been formulated. *The main purpose of this test is not necessarily a ' pass ' standard*—although this is desirable—*it is designed to acquaint divers with the difficulties of extreme conditions.* Thus, divers who find that they are physically unable to lift a victim in full kit to the 15 metre mark will at least appreciate that in such circumstances they will have to ensure that at least one weight belt is jettisoned.

The test will be conducted by divers who have a minimum qualification of 2nd Class and who have had considerable experience of deep (30 metres) diving. In view of the fact that this test can be quite exhausting, divers taking the test should be of at least an advanced 3rd Class, with at least seven dives to the 30 metre mark.

Successful completion of the test can be endorsed by the appropriate D.O. in the log book.

Points for Examiners

Mainly, the average diver at a depth of, or in excess of, 30 metres will be severely overweight and his ascent from these depths requires a much more vigorous finning action than usual. When a rescue is involved including one unconscious diver the rescuer—who, in panic, usually finds difficulty in releasing a weight belt—will have to ascend with two full sets of equipment. The degree of effort required to overcome the inertia of such a weight is not generally realized; and this is the main point to impress.

For this reason it is essential to guard against fatigue on the part of the rescuer. If the rescuer is seen labouring heavily against the task of ascending with the victim, the supervising diver should terminate the test.

The reason for leaving both weight belts on is to stimulate the worst possible conditions.

460

General Notes

a   Lifejackets should not be inflated in practise rescues.

b   The dangers of embolism should always be borne in mind.

c   Brief thoroughly prior to descent and arrange distinct signals.

d   Be aware that it is EASILY possible in practises for the rescuer to exert himself to the point where dangerous distress can occur.

TEST CONDITIONS

Minimum number of participants will be : Victim, Rescuer, Supervising Diver, Standby Diver, Snorkel Cover.

Victim and Rescuer will be weighted for Neutral Surface Buoyancy.

The test will commence at a depth of 30 metres, the Rescuer will close on the Victim and, using a recognised ascent procedure, without releasing weight belts, lift Victim to within 15 metres of the surface; here the test will terminate and the divers will ascend normally to the surface where the test will be completed. The Supervising Diver must see that the first part of the test ceases at or near the 15 metre mark.

Either the Rescuer or Victim must wear a ABLJ (lifejacket) although this will not be used on the test.

The test will take place in the immediate presence of a heavily weighted shot line marked at the 15 metre level.

TEST PROCEDURE

1   At a signal from Supervising Diver, Rescuer grasps Victim in an approved manner.

2   Rescuer ascends with Victim to the 15 metre mark.

3   Terminating at 15 metre mark, Rescuer and Victim ascend normally to the surface.

4   At the surface Rescuer must achieve maximum buoyancy. Inflate victim's lifejacket or pass a weight belt to snorkel cover.

5   Signal for assistance.

6   Remove Victim's breathing tubes and face mask.

7   Simulate Expired Air Resuscitation.

8   Tow Victim to safety (at least 45 metres) stopping half way to repeat EAR (7).

9   On reaching shallow water, boat or shore, Victim should be landed (with assistance) and simulated EAR given until the examiner gives order to stop.

General Training

(Not specifically for the test, but for rescue conditions in most cases)
Training should include swimming pool practise in weight belt release
WHILE FULLY KITTED FOR DIVING. It is no use practising in
swimming trunks, the drill is only of value when trainees are fully
equipped in bulky suits, snaggable accessories and gloves.

Divers should be thoroughly acquainted with the rules of ascent procedure; this is particularly important in view of the lack of practical
experience.

Divers should be able to quote the procedure for all types of ascent on
request.

CHAPTER ELEVEN

APPENDICES

BSAC & How It Works
The Divers' Code
Training & Diving Organisation
Baths Discipline
Diving Flags
Weather
Tidal Constants
Recompression Chambers
Distress Signals at Sea
Coastguard Stations
Fish Law
Conversion Tables
Bibliography
Underwater Films
Diving Operations, Special Regulations
Beaufort Wind Scale
Decompression Tables
Metrication
BSAC Club Tests and Qualifications

APPENDICES

APPENDIX 1—THE BRITISH SUB AQUA CLUB—ITS ADMINISTRATION AND WORKINGS

The administration of the British Sub Aqua Club is the responsibility of the General Committee which is elected by a ballot of all members each year. The Club Officers are the Chairman, Vice-Chairman, Secretary, Treasurer and National Diving Officer, and they normally hold office for a period of three years.

Day to day administration, planning and liaison are handled by the Club's full-time Director, and his office forms the headquarters of the Club.

The General Committee meets quarterly to discuss policy and new activities and to hear reports from its members. Besides the Officers, the Director and elected members, meetings are attended by the National Coach, the editor of 'Triton' and representatives from the CCPR. The minutes of meetings are circulated to all branches of the Club.

The elected members of the committee are in most cases responsible for different aspects of Club activities—scientific, films and photography, spearfishing, competitions and holidays. Other members of the General Committee chair their own sub-committees such as the Medical Committee and Publications Committee.

The largest and most important sub-committee is the National Diving Committee ('NDC') which is presided over by the National Diving Officer. The NDC, besides its elected members who are Diving Officers of branches, includes representatives from the Royal Navy, the British Association of Lecturers in Physical Education and the Club's regional and Service federations.

The NDC deals with all practical diving matters and arranges the annual Diving Officers' Conference. Its members organise BSAC Instructor Examinations, First Class Diver Examinations and National Boathandling Courses. The National Equipment Officer and the Accident and Incident Officer are also present.

The Director and the National Coach attend NDC meetings and form a link between the Club's ten regional coaches and headquarters. These honorary part-time coaches are the Club's official representatives in each region and, besides organising courses and coaching, represent the sport at Regional Sports Council level.

The backbone of the Club is undoubtedly formed by its branches. There are now over 450 of these in Britain and overseas and they have made the British Sub Aqua Club the largest diving Club in the world. Each branch is run by a committee which, besides a Chairman, Secretary and Treasurer, has its own Branch Diving Officer. These committees run branches in accordance with the Club rules and contribute to the expenses of the Club by sending membership dues in respect of each member.

The Club in return provides each member with a copy of this Manual, six issues of the Club magazine each year, public liability insurance and a large number of services including coaching, courses, conferences, visits, holiday information, book and film libraries and a bookshop. In the future the Club expects to have a headquarters building and national diving boat.

All questions on matters other than routine branch administration are dealt with by the Director and his staff at BSAC Headquarters, 160 Great Portland Street, London W1N 5TB. Matters for the attention of Club officers and members of committees may also be sent to headquarters.

Questions regarding the renewal of subscriptions, distribution of the Manual and 'Triton' and changes of address should be sent to the Club Administrative Agent who deals with these matters from 25 Orchard Road, Kingston-upon-Thames, Surrey.

Technical advice of all kinds is available from the Regional Coaches whose addresses are listed in the BSAC Year Book.

APPENDIX 2—THE DIVERS' CODE

1. Before diving within harbour limits, or in private water, or where access is over private land, obtain permission. Inform the owner when you leave.

2. Consult the local branch about diving conditions—particularly before using a new site. Avoid overcrowding.

3. Do not let your vehicles obstruct highways, or damage land or verges.

4. Pick up litter, close gates, guard against fire risk. Do not damage land or crops—take particular care where entering the water.

5. Fly the 'Divers Flag' when diving in tidal waters to warn shipping that divers are down.

6. Avoid diving in fairways or areas of heavy surface traffic. Remember that large ships cannot alter course or speed quickly and must keep to recognised channels.

7. Only use a boat that is both adequate for the dive planned and is in competent hands.

8. Do not interfere with fisherman's lines, nets or pots, or with activities of other users of the diving area.

9. Never use a spear gun or harpoon in the vicinity of swimmers or bathers, or line or net fishermen.

10. Do not spear fish in fresh water.

11. Do not take 'berried' crabs or lobsters, or fish or shellfish below the minimum permitted sizes.

12. Do not remove articles from wrecks without permission. Avoid damage, pillage or disturbance to underwater plants, creatures or to the seabed.

13. Remember the reputation of the Club depends on your diving efficiency and good conduct.

APPENDIX 3—POSSIBLE DEVELOPMENT OF TRAINING AND DIVING ORGANISATION IN A LARGE BRANCH

The scheme outlined below is based on an analysis of the operations necessary to ensure safe diving. It is emphasised that all of these operations are in the proper field of the Diving Officer. This appendix therefore reduces to a list of sections of the Diving Officer's job which it has been found in practice can be delegated as more or less self-contained units. The Diving Officer, while maintaining his personal responsibility and authority for ensuring safe diving, tends to assume a more general co-ordinating role in the environment of the large branch and his delegates, so long as they carry out their jobs effectively, are more or less autonomous.

In the operation of this system it must be borne in mind that under varying local conditions some jobs will become redundant, a member may handle a number of jobs, or on the other hand may require assistance in order to cope with a single job.

The first stage in the analysis is the separation of the organisation into two distinct parts—different in both function and nature—Base and Expedition organisation.

(a) The Base Organisation

This will be characterised by sub-committees and conferences—there is time to think, talk, hatch new ideas, and thrash out problems while at base. The main function will be to produce disciplined, technically competent members who have the right club spirit and whose abilities are very accurately known to the Diving Officer. The organisation may be represented diagrammatically as follows:—

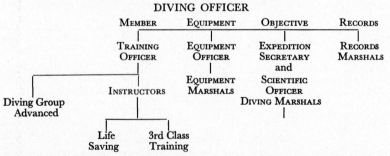

Those members of the organisation bearing the title 'Officer' should be selected from the Branch Committee or co-opted to it. This is not essential for the other positions although it is found in practice that about half of them are filled by Committee members.

(1) *The Training Officer*

Appointed by the Diving Officer to be responsible for the administration of swimming-pool training.

(2) *Instructors*

Appointed by the Diving Officer to instruct and examine for the individual items of the various Certificates and to be responsible for maintaining bath discipline. The existence of a strong, well-run team of Instructors should be the first aim of any Diving Officer. The appointments, if made by the branch committee, of the Training Officer and Instructors, should be on the recommendation of the Diving Officer, since he will generally have to rely absolutely on the signatures of these members as witnessing the ability of the novice.

(3) *Records Marshals*

Appointed by the Diving Officer to keep records and minutes and to handle the correspondence appropriate to this part of the organisation.

The posts (1-3) can be formed into a very effective sub-committee for pooling ideas on training and technique.

(4) *The Equipment Officer*

Appointed by the branch committee to be responsible for maintaining the branch equipment in a state fit to be used for training and diving and for the provision of adequate supplies of air for these activities. It has also been found to be convenient for the Equipment Officer to act as the buyer for new gear on behalf of the branch.

(5) *Equipment Marshals*

Appointed by the Equipment Officer to assist in decanting and other aspects of his job.

(6) *The Expedition Officer*

Appointed by the branch committee to be responsible for the base administration of expeditions, eg arranging camp sites, transport, the delivery of air, and the collection of money. He should also keep the Diving Officer posted on new sites and would be in touch with neighbouring and coastal branches.

(7) *The Scientific Officer*

Appointed by the branch committee to deal with Headquarter information and to be responsible for keeping the Diving Officer informed of scientific projects, current and potential, so that Diving Officer can decide which, if any, the branch has the ability to tackle.

(8) *The Senior Training Group*

This will consist of the keen divers in the branch who wish to maintain sea-diving fitness. Given a separate bath meeting from the general training they would practice search techniques, test gear, and generally prepare themselves for useful open-water work.

(b) The Expedition Organisation

This will be characterised by full authority and responsibility being in the hands of one person for the duration of the expedition. The main function of this part of the organisation will be to continue the training of members from the previous stages and also to procure safe and, it is hoped, enjoyable and useful diving.

EXPEDITION LEADER

This member will be appointed by the branch committee in accordance with club rules to be in complete charge of a diving activity.

The expedition leader will normally be the Diving Officer, or a Diving Marshal recommended by the Diving Officer.

EXPEDITION LEADER
(The Diving Officer or a Diving Marshal)

SAFETY COVER	LOGKEEPER	DIVE LEADER	EXPEDITION ASSISTANT	EQUIPMENT MARSHAL

The various positions in this organisation are filled for a single expedition only and all appointments are made by the Expedition Leader.

(1) *The Diving Marshal*

The Diving Marshal will be the personal delegate of the Diving Officer and may be the leader of the expedition or in charge of a section or particular phase of the expedition. His main responsibility will be the safety of the members and he will also endeavour to achieve the predetermined object of the activity, whether this is general training with novices or special training and work with more experienced divers.

APPENDICES

(2) The Safety Cover
His ONLY activity will be to take charge of surface arrangements and warning devices and to monitor the snorkel cover. He will normally be changed at frequent intervals during the day and during his tenure of office will take no part in any other activity.

(3) The Logkeeper
He will take charge of the diving rota set out by the Diving Marshal at the beginning of operations and, using this as a basis, will maintain adequate records of dives and gear used. The log should at all times be available to the Diving Marshal so that he can give the divers adequate warning of the approach of their turn.

(4) Dive Leader
He will be the senior diver on the dive and is in absolute charge underwater. In the event of an emergency it is the responsibility of the Dive Leader to get all divers to the surface, particularly when the accident has happened to himself.

(5) Equipment Marshal
He will maintain, fit, and check club equipment although this in no way relieves the Dive Leader from the responsibility of rechecking his own and his divers' gear before diving. He should also have at least one complete spare set of gear ready for use at all times and should notify the logkeeper of any defective gear.

(6) Expedition Assistant
He is responsible for the smooth organisation of transport, acts as treasurer to the expedition and, most important, chases up the member who is always late for the boat.

APPENDIX 4—BATHS DISCIPLINE

Behaviour at 'wet' meetings is most important: if it isn't good, you may lose the best baths in your area. It has happened to others, don't let it happen in your branch.

Bath Regulations
(1) Members are to observe and obey the rules and regulations of the swimming baths as laid down by the owners, the bath superintendent or relevant authority.
(2) While responsibility for the organisation of instruction and direct training discipline is in the hands of the relevant branch diving officer of the British Sub Aqua Club, and his assistants, the swimming baths are at all times in the charge of the bath superintendent, whose ultimate authority must be unquestioned.
(3) Payment for the use of the swimming baths must be made to the relevant authority, as arranged and stipulated in the terms of hire.
(4) Where necessary, arrangements must be made for the collection of payments from the members present at the training sessions, preferably at the door, by a responsible member of the British Sub Aqua Club properly appointed for that duty.
(5) The swimming baths must be vacated at the time stipulated and on the instruction of the bath superintendent.
(6) Any mishap resulting in physical injury to any person, whether a member of the British Sub Aqua Club or not, or any damage to any property of the swimming bath authorities must be reported immediately to the instructor in charge, and, by him, to the bath superindendent.

British Sub Aqua Club Regulations
(1) All instruction in swimming baths must be under the authority of the branch diving officer, who may delegate his authority to bath marshals, suitably qualified to take charge of training sessions.
(2) Such bath marshals are to be responsible for the enforcement of bath rules and regulations, the maintenance of bath discipline and for the proper conduct of training.
(3) No 'mixed' swimming may take place, ie some members with and others without underwater swimming equipment, unless in separate sections of the bath.
(4) It is recommended that bath marshals wear red skull caps, armbands, or other distinguishing marks when on duty at training sessions.

Bath Discipline
(1) No interference with other swimmers using the bath.
(2) No jumping or diving into the water. *You run the risk of hurting others and damaging equipment.*

468

(3) No overarm strokes except when taking swimming tests, in approved free swimming sessions, or in parts of baths distinctively set aside for free swimming only. *You might impede others, and you are wasting vital energy.*

(4) Move quietly and calmly in the water. *That is good diving.*

(5) No splashing with fins. *That is bad diving.*

(6) No racing or underwater endurance contests. *Exhaustion and anoxia can kill.*

(7) Always look down before diving, up before surfacing. *Remember the other bath users.*

(8) All equipment must be in sound condition and of high standard. *Faulty and shoddy equipment is inefficient and dangerous.*

(9) Never drop heavy equipment either in the bath or on the surrounds. *It can cause considerable damage.*

(10) Equipment is always to be worn in the water, except under certain circumstances of controlled instruction.

(11) No running round bath sides in equipment. *Fins can easily trip you and others: masks fall off.*

(12) No shouting or rowdyism. *You might divert attention from an emergency.*

(13) It is recommended that skull caps or helmets be worn. *For identification, hygiene and prevention of heat loss.*

(14) Never enter the water with a cold, catarrh or other infection. *It is dangerous to swim in such circumstances.*

(15) Never enter the water with an open wound, or when wearing a bandage or plaster. *It is unhygienic and inconsiderate.*

(16) Obey the instructions of the bath marshals. *Non-compliance may result in exclusion from bath training sessions.*

(*Approved in principle by the Institute of Baths Management*).

APPENDIX 5—DIVING FLAGS

Flag signals are used to give warning that diving is in progress. Their use is two-fold: (a) to give an indication so that vessels may keep clear of divers; (b) to inform vessels that there may be ropes or other obstructions in the vicinity, on or below the water, which may foul their propellors or rudders.

The diving flag recognised by the BSAC is the International Code of Signals letter 'A' which indicates 'I have a diver down; keep well clear at slow speed'.

Although naval and ocean-going vessels and fishing vessels are required to know the International Code, many small coastal vessels and pleasure craft do not. Branches of the Club are advised to use flag 'A' and to inform all fishermen, yachting clubs and other small craft users in their diving localities that the branch will display this flag when diving.

Flags should be displayed clearly. They should be hoisted when diving commences and kept flying during the whole time of diving. It is useless to run them up at the last moment as many ships require considerable time and sea room to alter course and speed.

Masters of large vessels or strangers to a neighbourhood must keep to recognised channels if they are not to hazard their ships, and they are not always able to alter course to give wide clearance.

Reliance should not be placed on flags alone, particularly where small craft operate. A good lookout who is prepared to give warning by other signals should be used.

There are two other flags used around the world as diving flags, although they are not internationally recognised shipping flags. They are NATO 4 and the American Divers' Flag. It is well to make note of them as they may be encountered when abroad.

A plain red flag has sometimes been used as a general danger flag or to indicate diving. This is not a recognised signal and gives no indication that diving is in progress.

N.B. Information on the use of the International Code of Signals can be obtained from the following books: Brown's Signalling (Brown, Son & Ferguson); International Code of Signals (H.M. Stationery Office).

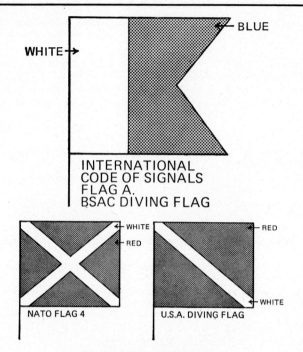

INTERNATIONAL
CODE OF SIGNALS
FLAG A.
BSAC DIVING FLAG

NATO FLAG 4

U.S.A. DIVING FLAG

APPENDIX 6—WEATHER

Gales and weather can wipe out a dive—so can a light wind from the wrong direction. Too many checks on the weather cannot be made before a dive.

Details of weather services in the British Isles via Press, Radio, Television, Coastal Stations and Telephones are given in MO Leaflet No 1, obtainable free of charge from the Senior Meteorological Officer, London Weather Centre, 284 High Holborn, London WC1. Telephone 01-836 4311.

BBC Shipping Forecasts are given on Radio 2 (1500 metres only). As they sometimes show some variance they are not listed here as they might be incorrect by the time they are in print. Full details of current times are given in the Radio Times.

SEA AND SWELL

Sea is defined as the waves caused by wind at a given place.

Swell is caused by waves formed by past wind, or wind at a distance.

Short swell: where the length or distance between each successive top of the swell is small.

Long swell: where the length or distance as above is large.

Low swell: where the height between the lowest and highest part of the swell is small.

Heavy swell: where the height as above is great.

INTERNATIONAL SEA SCALE

Scale No.	Description					Height of waves—crest to trough
0	Calm ...	...	...	...	...	0 feet
1	Smooth	...	...	...	...	0–$\frac{1}{2}$ feet
2	Light ...	...	...	...	...	$\frac{1}{2}$–2 feet
3	Moderate	...	...	...	...	2–5 feet
4	Rough	...	...	...	...	5–9 feet
5	Very Rough	...	...	...	...	9–15 feet
6	High ...	...	...	...	...	15–24 feet
7	Very High	...	...	...	...	24–36 feet
8	Precipitous	...	...	...	...	over 36 feet

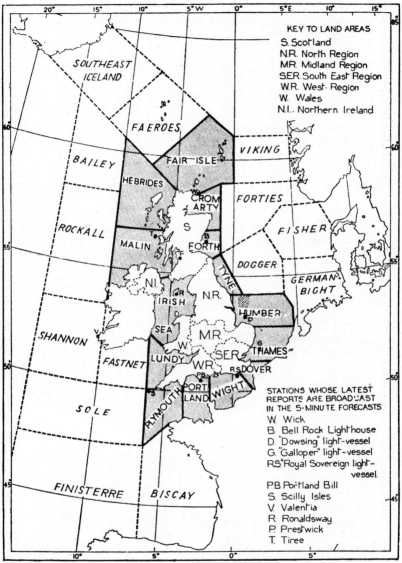

KEY TO LAND AREAS
S. Scotland
N.R. North Region
M.R. Midland Region
S.E.R. South East Region
W.R. West Region
W. Wales
N.I. Northern Ireland

STATIONS WHOSE LATEST
REPORTS ARE BROADCAST
IN THE 5-MINUTE FORECASTS
W. Wick
B. Bell Rock Lighthouse
D. "Dowsing" light-vessel
G. "Galloper" light-vessel
R.S. "Royal Sovereign light-
vessel.
P.B. Portland Bill
S. Scilly Isles
V. Valentia
R. Ronaldsway
P. Prestwick
T. Tiree

Meteorological Office, January, 1958

Boundaries of Sea and Land Areas.
as used in BBC and GPO Weather Forecasts.

Weather within an estuary, and particularly the visibility there, may often be expected to differ from that forecast for the coastal sea area in which the estuary lies, though this will not necessarily be mentioned in the forecast.

The tinted sea areas are those for which visual gale warnings are displayed.

471

INTERNATIONAL SWELL SCALE

Code figure	State of the swell in the open sea	
0	None	
1	Short or average length	Low
2	Long	
3	Short	
4	Average length	Moderate height
5	Long	
6	Short	
7	Average length	Heavy
8	Long	
9	Confused	

FOG AND VISIBILITY SCALE FOR SHIPS AT SEA

Code No.	Description	Definition	
0	Dense fog	Objects not visible at	50 yards
1	Thick fog	,, ,, ,, ,,	1 cable
2	Fog	,, ,, ,, ,,	2 cables
3	Moderate fog	,, ,, ,, ,,	½ mile
4	Mist or haze or very poor visibility	,, ,, ,, ,,	1 mile
5	Poor visibility	,, ,, ,, ,,	2 miles
6	Moderate visibility	,, ,, ,, ,,	5 miles
7	Good visibility	,, ,, ,, ,,	10 miles
8	Very good visibility	,, ,, ,, ,,	30 miles
9	Excellent visibility	Objects visible more than	30 miles

APPENDIX 7—WHEN IS IT HIGH TIDE?
Table of Tidal Constants Relative to High Water at London Bridge
Add +, or Subtract —, to time at London Bridge

Place	hr. min	Place	hr. min
Southend	—1.25	Portpatrick	—2.38
Clacton	—2.11	Balcary Point	—2.12
Felixstowe	—2.18	Annan	—2.2
Aldeburgh	—3.23	Whitehaven	—2.35
Lowestoft	—4.26	Barrow-in-Furness	—2.46
Gt. Yarmouth	—4.55	Morecambe	—2.36
Wells-next-the-sea	+5.11	Blackpool	—2.41
Skegness	+4.25	Wallasey	—2.37
Grimsby	+4.2	Llandudno	—3.18
Bridlington	+3.11	Holyhead	—3.32
Scarborough	+2.43	Nefyn	—4.30
Whitby	+2.19	Barmouth	—5.47
W. Harlepool	+2.5	Aberystwyth	—6.12
Sunderland	+2.0	Cardigan	+5.40
Alnmouth	+1.22	Skomer	+4.28
Berwick-upon-Tweed	+0.55	Tenby	+4.28
Dunbar	+0.33	Llanelly	+4.32
Leith	+0.41	Swansea	+4.33
Kirkcaldy	+0.38	Porthcawl	+4.40
Fife Ness	+0.20	Barry	+5.13
Dundee	+1.11	Clevedon	+5.18
Montrose	+0.30	Burnham-on-Sea	+5.17
Aberdeen	—0.20	Ilfracombe	+4.28
Fraserburgh	—1.25	Padstow	+4.8
Lossiemouth	—2.0	St. Ives	+3.43
Inverness	—1.38	Lizard	+3.20
Dornoch	—1.40	Falmouth	+3.36
Golspie	—2.14	Plymouth	+3.54
Wick	—2.28	Salcombe	+4.6

Tidal Constants (continued)

Thurso	−5.31	Torquay	+4.39
Tongue	−6.6	Lyme Regis	+4.46
Kylesku	+5.39	Weymouth	+5.5
Ullapool	+5.29	Swanage	−3.23
Portree	+4.59	Cowes	−2.30
Plockton	+5.9	Ventnor	−2.50
Mallaig	+4.26	Southsea	−2.28
Tobermory	+4.23	Bognor Regis	−2.28
Oban	+4.13	Brighton	−2.38
Crinan	+3.33	Hastings	−2.47
Greenock	−1.32	Dover	−2.42
Ayr	−1.52	Margate	−2.1
		Sheerness	−1.19

Printed by permission of the
Liverpool Observatory and Tidal Institute.

N.B.—The times of High Water at London Bridge may be obtained from the newspapers each day, from the current Automobile Association Handbook, and from various almanacs and other publications.

The places given in the table are listed anticlockwise, starting from the Thames Estuary.

APPENDIX 8—RECOMPRESSION CHAMBERS

In all cases where decompression sickness is suspected, the nearest compression chamber should be contacted. A list of all chambers which may be available is maintained at HMS Vernon, Portsmouth. Phone calls in an emergency should be made to the Superintendent of Diving, or his deputy, (telephone: 07 05-22351 extension 72375) during working hours and to the Officer of the Watch (extension 72588) outside of working hours. It is advisable to make long distance calls as a 'Personal Call' made via the telephone operator.

Where the nearest chamber is some distance away the Police may be able to assist with transport cases.

APPENDIX 9—IN TROUBLE AT SEA

DISTRESS SIGNALS

The following distress signals can be used from ship to ship and from ship to shore:—
Red Roman candles.
Red flare rockets fired one at a time.
International Code signal flags N.C.
A square flag with a ball—or anything resembling a ball—either above or below it.
Morse letters S O S sent by lamp, flag or sound.
Flames, eg burning oil-saturated waste.
A coat or other article of clothing fastened to an oar.

APPENDIX 10—COASTGUARD STATIONS

Here is a list of coastguard stations and telephone numbers (which may change from time to time). The stations are listed anti-clockwise round the coast.

Walton District	Southend	Shoeburyness 2611
	Walton-on-Naze	Walton-on-Naze 148
Gorleston District	Lowestoft	Lowestoft 365
	Gorleston	Gorleston 420
Cromer District	Cromer	Cromer 2417
Flamborough District	Spurn Head	Spurn Point 222
	Flamborough	Flamborough 285
Whitby District	Whitby	Whitby 285
Tynemouth District	Tynemouth	North Shields 72681
Seahouses District	Seahouses	Seahouses 437
Fifeness District	Fifeness	Elie 337

Coastguard Stations (continued)

Aberdeen District	Aberdeen	Aberdeen 29264
	Belhelvie	Balmedie 202
Peterhead District	Peterhead	Peterhead 3592
	Fraserburgh	Fraserburgh 74
Lerwick District	Lerwick	Lerwick 115
Wick District	Wick	Wick (Caithness) 333
Stornoway District	Stornoway	Stornoway 134
Portpatrick District	Portpatrick	Portpatrick 217
Formby District	Formby	Formby 2902
Ballycastle District	Ballycastle	Ballycastle 246
Bangor District	Bangor	Bangor (Co. Down) 60055
Ramsey District	Ramsey	Ramsey 3136
Holyhead District	Holyhead	Holyhead 2262
St. Davids District	St. Davids	St. Davids 244
Mumbles District	Mumbles	Swansea 66253
	Nell's Point	Barry 5016
St. Just District	St. Just	St. Just 208
	St. Mary's (Scilly)	Scillonia 51
	Tol-Pedn-Penwith	Sennen 219
Falmouth District	Lizard	Lizard 244
	Falmouth	Falmouth 4269
Hartland District	Hartland	Hartland 235
Brixham District	Brixham	Brixham 3110
Wyke District	Wyke	Weymouth 169
	Portland Bill	Portland 3100
	St. Albans	Worth Matravers 220
Needles District	Needles	Freshwater 120
Shoreham District	Shoreham	Shoreham-by-Sea 3883
Deal District	Deal	Deal 1296
	Margate	Thanet 24241

APPENDIX 11—FISH LAW

There are laws about practically everything found in or taken from the sea. Fish and shellfish are not exceptions, and here is a guide to those laws. There may be local restrictions as well, and this should be checked.

Sea Fishing Industry (Immature Sea Fish) Orders 1961

These orders prohibit the landing, sale or possession for sale in Great Britain of certain species of fish below the following minimum sizes:—

COD	30 cm.	11.8 in.
HADDOCK	27 cm.	10.6 in.
HAKE	30 cm.	11.8 in.
PLAICE	25 cm.	9.8 in.
WITCHES	28 cm.	11.0 in.
LEMON SOLES	25 cm.	9.8 in.
SOLES	24 cm.	9.4 in.
TURBOT	30 cm.	11.8 in.
BRILL	30 cm.	11.8 in.
MEGRIMS	25 cm.	9.8 in.
WHITINGS	25 cm.	9.8 in.
DABS	20 cm.	7.9 in.

Any fish below the minimum size which may be taken in the course of fishing operations must be returned to the sea forthwith.

SHELLFISH

The Sea-Fishing Industry (Crabs and Lobsters) Order 1966
Sea Fisheries (Shellfish) Act 1967

This legislation prohibits the landing, sale or possession for sale in Great Britain of crabs measuring less than 4½ inches in breadth and of lobsters measuring less than 9 inches in length; and of 'berried' lobsters and 'berried' or soft crabs (ie lobsters or crabs in spawn).

FRESH WATER FISH
Salmon and Freshwater Fisheries Act 1923 (Section 1)
This act prohibits the use of a spear or like instrument for the purpose of taking salmon, trout or freshwater fish.

There are laws, too, that govern the spearfisherman through his possession of a harpoon gun, and the following should be noted:—
The spearfisherman may be affected by both the Gun Licence Act of 1870 and the Firearms Act of 1937. An inquiry about previous confusion over whether or not spearguns came under these Acts brought the following reply from Scotland Yard:—

'All types of spearguns need a gun licence, that is a licence obtained from the Post Office as for shotguns, etc.

'But certain of the types of spearguns require a firearms licence which must be obtained from the Police as for revolvers, etc.

'It is suggested that the owner of such a weapon should ask the advice of the police locally about his particular speargun.'

APPENDIX 12—CONVERSIONS

At some time or other, divers will find themselves struggling to convert cubic feet into cubic centimetres or something equally as irritating. The following figures will help you:—

Length
1 inch	=	2.540 centimetres
1 foot	=	0.304 metres
1 yard	=	0.914 metres
1 fathom	=	1.828 metres
1 statute mile (5280 feet)	=	1.609 kilometres
1 nautical mile (6080 feet)	=	1.853 kilometres
1 centimetre	=	0.393 inches
1 metre	=	3.280 feet
1 metre	=	1.093 yards
1 metre	=	0.546 fathoms
1 kilometre	=	0.621 statute miles
1 kilometre	=	0.539 nautical miles

Cubic and Capacity
1 cubic inch	=	16.378 cubic centimetres
1 cubic foot	=	0.028 cubic metres
1 cubic foot	=	28.317 litres
1 cubic yard	=	0.764 cubic metres
1 pint	=	0.568 litres
1 gallon	=	4.546 litres
1 cubic centimetre	=	0.061 cubic feet
1 cubic metre	=	35.314 cubic feet
1 cubic metre	=	1.308 cubic yards
1 litre (1,000 c.c.	=	0.035 cubic feet
1 litre	=	0.220 gallons
1 litre	=	1.760 pints

Weight
1 lb	=	0.454 kilograms
1 long ton	=	1.016 metric tons
		1,016 kilograms
1 kilogram	=	2.205 pounds
1 metric ton	=	0.984 long tons
		2,205 pounds

Pressure
1 pound per square inch = 0.073 kilograms per square centimetre.
1 kilogram per square centimetre = 14.223 pounds per square inch.

Water
1 cubic foot of fresh water weighs 62.5 pounds approx.
1 cubic foot of average salt water weighs 64 pounds approx.

TEMPERATURE

To convert degrees Fahrenheit to degrees Centigrade: deduct 32 and muliply by 5/9.
To convert degrees Centigrade to degrees Fahrenheit: multiply by 9/5 and add 32.

CONVERSIONS (APPROXIMATE)

Miles to kilometres	multiply by 8/5
Kilometres to miles	multiply by 5/8
Statute miles to nautical miles	deduct 1/8
Nautical miles to statute miles	add 1/7
Pounds per square inch (p.s.i.) to atmospheres	divide by 14.7
Atmospheres or bars to kilos per square centimetre	nearly the same
Water depth (feet) to bars absolute ...	divide by 33 and add 1 bar
Water depth (metres) to bars absolute ...	divide by 10 and add 1 bar
Bars absolute to feet of water depth ...	subtract 1 bar and multiply by 33
Bars absolute to metres of water depth ...	subtract 1 bar and multiply by 10

NAUTICAL DEFINITIONS

Nautical Mile At any place on the earth's surface is the length of one minute of arc measured along the meridian through that place. It varies in different latitudes owing to the irregular shape of the earth. In practice, it is taken to be 6,080 feet, which is its value in latitude 40 degrees.

Knot In navigation the unit of speed is a Knot, which is a speed of one nautical mile per hour.

Cable A Cable is one tenth of a nautical mile; in practice it is taken as 200 yards.

Fathom A Fathom is a unit of six feet used in sounding and recording depths of water. It is not generally used for fresh water soundings.

Shackle A Shackle is the amount of cable between shackles in an anchor cable. As a measure it is taken to be 15 fathoms.

WIND—DIRECTION, SPEED AND MEASUREMENT

Direction Wind direction is always specified as the direction from which the wind blows.

Speed Wind speed is expressed in: knots by mariners and airmen; miles per hour by landsmen and coastal navigators.

Conversions
1 knot	= 1.7 feet per second approx.
	= 0.51 metres per second approx.
1 mile per hour	= 1½ feet per second approx.
	= 1.609 kilometres per hour approx.
1 foot per second	= 2/3 miles per hour approx.
	= 0.3 metres per second approx.
1 kilometre per hour	= 5/8 miles per hour approx.
1 metre per second	= 3⅓ feet per second approx.

Conversion Tables for, and Approximate Values of, Depths

Feet	Fathoms	Metres	Feet	Fathoms	Metres
1	—	0.3048	59.1	9.8	18
1½	¼	0.4572	60	10	18.3
2	—	0.6096	62.3	10.4	19
3	½	0.9144	65.6	10.9	20
3.2808	0.5486	1	70	11.7	21.3
4	—	1.2192	80	13.3	24.4
4½	¾	1.3716	90	15	27.4
5	—	1.5240	98.4	16.4	30
6	1	1.8288	100	16.7	30.5
6.5616	1.0936	2	120	20	36.6
7	—	2.1336	131.2	21.9	40
8	—	2.4384	164.0	27.3	50
9	1½	2.7432	180	30	54.9
9.8424	1.6304	3	196.8	32.8	60
10	—	3.048	200	33.3	61.0

Conversion Tables (continued)

12	**2**	3.7	229.7	38.3	**70**
13.1	2.2	**4**	**240**	**40**	73.2
16.4	2.7	**5**	262.5	43.7	**80**
18	**3**	5.5	295.3	49.2	**90**
19.6	3.3	**6**	**300**	**50**	91.5
20	3.3	6.1	328.1	54.7	**100**
23.0	3.8	**7**	**360**	**60**	109.8
24	**4**	7.3	360.9	60.1	**110**
26.2	4.4	**8**	393.7	65.6	**120**
29.5	4.9	**9**	**400**	66.7	121.9
30	**5**	9.1	**420**	**70**	128.1
32.8	5.5	**10**	426.5	71.1	**130**
36	**6**	**11**	459.3	76.6	**140**
39.4	6.6	**12**	**480**	**80**	146.4
40	6.7	12.2	492.1	82.0	**150**
42	7	12.8	**500**	83.3	152.4
42.7	7.1	**13**	524.9	87.5	**160**
45.9	7.7	**14**	**540**	**90**	164.7
48	**8**	14.6	557.7	93.0	**170**
49.2	8.2	**15**	590.5	98.4	**180**
50	8.3	15.2	**600**	**100**	183.0
52.5	8.7	**16**	623.4	103.9	**190**
54	**9**	16.5	656.2	109.4	**200**
55.8	9.3	**17**			

And for sorting out those little arguments, here are a few facts and figures:-

Ocean Data

Gross area of oceans	139,000,000 square miles or 72 per cent. of the earth's surface.
Gross volume of oceans	330,000,000 cubic miles.
Gross volume of land above sea level	23,000,000 cubic miles.
Average depth of oceans	2,070 fathoms (12,420 feet).
Average height of land above sea level	2,300 feet.
Pacific Ocean: largest	69,000,000 square miles with its adjacent seas.
deepest	a sounding of 5,940 fathoms was recorded in the Marianas Trench by H.M. Survey Ship 'Challenger' in 1951.
average depth: ...	2,200 fathoms.
Atlantic Ocean: 2nd largest ...	31,530,000 square miles.
2nd deepest	the deepest sounding was in the Puerto Rico Trench where a depth of 4,750 fathoms was recorded.
average depth ...	1,820 fathoms.
Indian Ocean: 3rd largest	28,350,000 square miles.
3rd deepest	the deepest recording was from the Sunda Trench where a sounding of 4,060 fathoms was made.
average depth ...	2,120 fathoms.

Mean Sphere Level. If all the land masses were pushed into the ocean basins and the sea floors levelled off, the average depth of water ('mean sphere level') would be 1,700 fathoms.

Salinity. The salinity of ocean water is fairly consistent at depth, but there are broad variations at the surface from 41 parts in a 1,000 in the Red Sea, where the evaporation exceeds the rainfall and the river flow, to 30 parts in 1,000 off Calcutta, off N.W. Siam and in the Yellow Sea, where rainfall and river flows exceed the evaporation.

Mineral Contents. Most common are chlorine (1.9 per cent.) and sodium (1.05 per cent.) found in combination as common salt.

Mean Annual Surface Temperatures. These vary from 28.5° Fahrenheit in the Polar Regions to 85° Fahrenheit in the equatorial parts of the Pacific and Indian Oceans.

Certain land-locked seas, eg Persian Gulf, have surface temperatures of up to 90° Fahrenheit.

Topography. The floor of the seas may be divided into three: the continental shelf, the continental slope and the abyss. The division between the shelf and the slope is known as the continental edge. From the tidelines the floor of the seas and oceans slopes gently across the shelf until the edge is reached at about 60 to 80 fathoms. The gradient then sharply increases down the slope to depths of between 1,500 and 2,000 fathoms where the ocean floors tend to level off into the abyssal plain.

These divisions are very pronounced in the Atlantic Ocean, and on its continental shelf, with its average gradient of 1 in 520, are deposited the heavier material residues washed down by rivers and eroded from the coastlines. On the continental slopes, with gradients of 1 in 20 to 1 in 10, the finer deposits come to rest. The abyssal plain, deeply covered—in some places as deep as 12,000 feet—with deposits of oozes, largely consisting of the skeletal remains of planktonic creatures, together with meteoric and volcanic dusts and such organic remains as shells, minute teeth, earbones, etc, is not so level as its name suggests. The Atlantic Ocean has a submarine mountain range running almost its entire length from north to south—its rising peaks forming the Azores and St. Paul's Rocks—and its entire bed is cut and slashed by precipitous trenches and canyons.

In the Indian Ocean the continental shelf is almost non-existent, and its continental slope fairly steep. In general, however, the definitions of 'shelf,' 'slope' and 'abyss' remain valid over the world's off-shore areas.

APPENDIX 13—BIBLIOGRAPHY

The following books will be of interest to any diver. Though you may find that some of them are out of print, this does not mean that they are out-of-date and any good library should be able to obtain them for you. Often copies can be bought at secondhand book shops for a few shillings.

INSTRUCTIONAL

Admiralty Diving Manual BR 155/43 (H.M.S.O.).
Manual of Seamanship, Vols. 1 & 2, Admiralty (H.M.S.O.).
Ship Salvage, G. R. Critchley.
Caisson Sickness, Sir Leonard E. Hill (Edward Arnold).
Diving, Cutting and Welding in Underwater Salvage Operations, Frank E. Thompson, Jr. (U.S.A.).
Underwater Blasting, R. Westwater and Haslam. I.C.I. Nobel Division.
Deep Sea Salvage, A. G. Whyte and Hadfield (Sampson Low), 1933.
Respiration, Prof. J. S. Haldane and J. G. Priestly (Clarendon Press).
Breathing in Irrespirable Atmospheres, Sir Robert H. Davis.
Deep Sea Diving and Submarine Operations, Sir Robert H. Davis (St. Catherine's Press).
Life at High Pressures, Prof. J. B. S. Haldane (Penguin Science).
Manual for Free Divers, D. M. Owen (Pergamon Press), 1955.
Dive, R. and B. Carrier (Nicholas Kaye).
Free Diving, Demitri Rebikoff (Sidgwick & Jackson), 1955.
The Art of the Aqualung, Robert Gruss (MacGibbon), London.
The Master Diver and Underwater Sportsman, Captain Hampton, 1956.
Shallow Water Diving and Spearfishing, Hilbert Schenck, etc., 1954.
The Royal Life Saving Society Handbook of Instruction, London.
Your Guide to Underwater Adventure, Peter Small, Lutterworth Press, 1957.
Underwater Swimming, Brennan (ARCO), 1962.
Underwater Navigation, Glatt (Sea-well Engineering Co.), 1960.
Discovering the Undersea World, Kenyon (University of London Press), 1961.
Snorkel Diver, Matkin & Brookes (Macdonald), 1961.
Scuba Diver, Matkin & Brookes (Macdonald).
Skin Diving, Jack Atkinson (Foulsham), 1962.
Mask and Flippers, Lloyd Bridges (W. H. Allen), 1961.
The Complete Manual of Free Diving, Talliez, Dumas, Cousteau (Putnam), 1957.
Skin Diving and Exploring Underwater, Sweeney (Muller), 1956.
Underwater Work, Cayford (Cornell Maritime Press), 1959.
Skin Diving for Boys, Wyndham Davies (Scout Shop), 1959.
The New Science of Skin and Scuba Diving, (Darton, Longman & Todd).

Underwater Swimming—Know the Game Series, Brookes (Educational Productions), 1962.
Venture Underwater, Wyndham Davies (Faber & Faber).
Underwater Sport on a Small Income, Barry J. Kimmins (Hutchinson).
The Master Diver and Underwater Sportsman, T. Hampton (Adlard Coles).
Skin Diving, Elgin Ciampi.
U.S. Navy Diving Manual (U.S. Navy).
Underwater Medicine, Sgn Rear Admiral Stanley Miles (Staples).
The Skin Divers' Handbook (Muller).
The Underwater Handbook, Burke (Muller).
Complete Guide to Underwater Swimming, Poulet (Newnes).
Underwater Swimming, Dobbs (Collins).
Teach Yourself Underwater Swimming, Zanelli (EUP).
Principles of Diving, Terrell (Stanley Paul). .
Underwater Swimming—an Advanced Handbook, Leo Zanelli (Kaye & Ward).
Coastwise Navigation, G. G. Watkins (Kandy Publications).

SCIENTIFIC INTEREST

Sea Shore Life of Britain, L. R. Brightwell (Batsford), 1947.
Science of the Sea, Challenger Society, Ed. E. J. Allen, 1928.
The Freshwater Life of the British Isles, J. Clegg, 1952.
The Sea and its Mysteries, J. S. Colman, 1950.
The Floor of the Ocean, R. A. Daly, 1942.
Life in Ponds and Streams, W. S. Furneaux, 1906.
Life in Lakes and Rivers, T. T. Macan and E. B. Worthington, 1951.
Aspects of Deep Sea Biology, N. B. Marshall, 1954.
The Ocean, Sir J. Murray (Home University Library), 1913.
The Depths of the Ocean, Sir J. Murray and J. Hjort.
The Ocean Floor, Hans Petterson, 1954.
Wonders of the Sea, Adolph Portman.
Dynamical Oceanography, J. Proudman, 1953.
The Seas, F. S. Russell and C. M. Yonge (Fredk. Waine & Co.), 1947.
The Origin of Continents and Oceans, A. Wagener, 1924.
The Sea Shore, C. M. Yonge.
The Sea Around Us, Rachel Carson (Staples Press), 1951.
The Edge of the Sea, Rachel Carson (Staples Press), 1955.
The Open Sea, Alister C. Hardy (Collins), 1956; (News, No. 4).
The Problem of the Deep Sea, T. H. Huxley (Collected Essays), Vol. 8, 1894.
The Life of Inland Waters, J. G. Needham, etc., 1916.
The History of Fishes, J. R. Norman (Ernest Benn), 1947.
The Ocean, F. D. Ommaney (Oxford University Press), 1949.
The Depths of the Sea, Sir C. W. Thompson, 1873.
The Open Sea, (Vol. 2), Sir Alister Hardy (Collins), 1959.
Underwater Guide to Marine Life, Ray & Ciampi (Nicholas Kaye), 1958.
Amphoras and the Ancient Wine Trade, Virginia Grace (American School of Classical Studies, Princeton, New Jersey), 1961.
Underwater Naturalist, Latil (Jarrolds), 1954.
Underwater Life of the British Isles, Darnell (Ward & Lock), 1960.
A Biography of the Sea, Carrington (Chatto & Windus), 1960.
Pocket Guide to the Seashore, John Barrett & C. M. Yonge (Collins), 1960.
Pocket Guide to the Undersea World, Ley Kenyon (Collins), 1956.
The Fishes of the British Isles, J. Travis Jenkins (Warne), 1958.
Die Unterwasser Fauna de Mittelmeerkusten (Underwater Life of the Mediterranean), German text, W. Luther K. Fielder (Paul Pavey), 1961.
Life of the Shore and Shallow Sea, D. P. Wilson (Nicholson & Watson), 1935.
A Complete Guide to the Fishes of Malta (Central Mediterranean), G. G. Lanfranco (Malta), 1960.
4,000 Years Under the Sea, Diole (Sidgwick & Jackson), 1954.
Under the Deep Oceans, Gaskell (Eyre & Spottiswoode), 1960.
Seven Miles Down, Piccard and Dietz (Longmans), 1962.
Observers' Book of Fresh Water Fishes, Wells (Warne), 1959.
Observers' Book of Sea Fishes, Wells (Warne), 1958.
Seaweeds and their Uses, (Methuen), 1950.

APPENDICES

The Standard Natural History, A. Laurence Wells (Warne).
Littoral Fauna of Great Britain, Eales (Cambridge University Press).
Handbook of British Sea-Weeds, Newton (British Museum).
Marine Geology, Kuenen (John Wiley), 1960.
The Impenetrable Sea, A. Constance (Oldbourne), 1958.
The Galathea Deep Sea Expedition, Bruunetal (Allen & Unwin), 1956.
Deep-Water Archaeology, Dumas (Routledge & Kegan Paul).
Under the Mediterranean, Honor Frost (Routledge & Kegan Paul).
Marine Aquaria, Jackman (Cassell).
Shell Life, Step (Warne).
Shadows in the Sea, The Sharks, Skates and Rays, McCormick (Sidgwick & Jackson).
Mediterranee Vivante, Theodor, French text (Librairie Payot).
Coquillages Marins, Arrecgros, French text (Librairie Payot).
Marine Archaeology, Joan du Plat Taylor (Hutchinson).
The Coastline of England and Wales, J. A. Steers (Cambridge University Press).
Archaeology Under Water, Bass (Thames and Hudson).
The Plankton of the Sea, Wimpenny (Faber).
Farming the Sea, McKee (Souvenir Press).
The Ecology of Rocky Shores, Lewis (English Universities Press).
Great Waters, Hardy (Collins).
History Under the Sea, Peterson (Smithsonian Institute, U.S.A.).
The Deepest Days, Stenuit (Hodder & Stoughton).
Freshwater Life of the British Isles, Clegg (Warne).
The Life of Fishes, Marshall (Weidenfeld and Nicolson).
Marine Life, Haas and Knorr (Burke).
Seashore, Kosch, Frieling and Janus (Burke).
British Seaweeds, Dickinson (Eyre & Spottiswoode).
History Under the Sea, A. McKee (Hutchinson).
The Coral Reef, A. Butterfield (Hamlyn).
The Fishes (Life Nature Series).
Sea Shells of the World (Hamlyn).
British Shells (Warne).
Collecting Sea Shells, F. D. Ommaney (Arco).
Abyss, C. P. Idyll (Constable).
Living Underwater, F. Hussein (Studio Vista).
The Physiology and Medicine of Diving and Compressed Air Work, P. B. Bennett and D. H. Elliott (Balliere, Tindall & Cassell).
The Fishes of the British Isles and North West Europe, Alwyne Wheeler (Macmillan).
Dolphins, Antony Alpers (John Murray).
Shipwrecks and Archaeology, The Unharvested Sea, Peter Throckmorton (Gollancz).
Natural History of Sharks, H. Lineaweaver and R. H. Backus (Andre Deutsch).
The Shark: Splendid Savage of the Sea, Jacques-Yves and Philippe Cousteau (Cassell).

PHOTOGRAPHY

A Guide to Underwater Photography, Rebikoff & Cherney (Greenberg).
Underwater Photography Simplified, J. Greenberg (Seahawk Products).
I Photographed Under the Seven Seas, Hass (Jarrolds), 1956.
Underwater Photography, Schenk & Kendall (Cornell Maritime Press).
Underwater Photography and Television, Cross (Exposition Press).
Camera Underwater—A Practical Guide to Underwater Photography, Dobbs (Focal Press), 1962.
Photography on Expeditions, D. H. O. John (Focal Press).
A Film Maker's Guide, Brian Branston (Allen & Unwin).
Camera Below, Frey and Tzimoulis (Association Press of New York).

SPEARFISHING

Spearfishing in Britain, Kendall McDonald and Phil Smith (Stanley Paul).
Shark Hunters, Ben Cropp (Angus and Robertson).
Lord of the Sharks, Prosperi (Hutchinson), 1955.
Underwater Hunting, Doukan (Allen & Unwin), 1953.
Mediterranean Hunter, Gorsky (Souvenir Press), 1954.
Modern Spearfishing, Vane Ivanovic (Nicholas Kay), 1954.
Hunting Big Fish, Isy-Schwart (Burke), 1954.

Moana, Gorsky (Elek), 1956.
Lady with a Spear, Clark (Heinemann), 1954.
Guide to Underwater Hunting, Codrington (Adlard Coles), 1954.
My Adventures Under the Sea, Jean Foucher-Creteau (Muller), 1957.
Undersea Hunting for Inexperienced Englishmen, Aldridge (Allen & Unwin).
Shallow Water Diving and Spearfishing, Schenk & Kendall.

GENERAL INTEREST

The Silent World, J. Y. Cousteau (Hamilton), 1953.
Diving to Adventure, Hans Hass (Jarrolds), 1953.
Under the Red Sea, Hans Hass (Jarrolds), 1952.
To Hidden Depths, Phillipe Taillez (William Kimber), 1954.
The Undersea Adventure, Phillipe Diole, 1953.
Underwater Exploration—a History, Phillipe Diole (Elek), 1954.
Man and the Underwater World, Pierre de Latil, etc. (Jarrolds), 1956.
The Naked Warriors, Douglas H. (Wingate), 1957.
Man and Dolphin, Lilly (Gollancz), 1961.
Captain Cousteau's Underwater Treasury, (Hamilton), 1960.
The Lost Land, John Dunbar (Collins), 1958.
The Coast of Coral, Clarke (Muller), 1954.
We Come from the Sea, Hans Hass (Jarrolds), 1958.
The Marvellous Kingdom, Pierre Labat (Odhams), 1956.
Diving for Treasure, Clay Blair (Barker), 1961.
Skin Diving in Australia, Du Cros (Angus & Robertson), 1960.
My Adventures Under the Sea, Foucher-Creteau (Muller), 1957.
The Seas of Sicily, Diole (Sidgwick & Jackson).
The Ancient Mariners, Casson (Gollancz), 1960.
Down to the Ships in the Sea, H. Grosset (Hutchinson).
The Underwater World, J. Tassos.
The Complete Goggler, Guy Gilpatrick (Skin Diver Magazine).
Skin Diving Annual, Bill Barada (Skin Diver Magazine).
Epics of Salvage, D. Masters (Cassell), 1953.
Subsunk, Capt. W. O. Shelford (Harrap), 1961.
The Blue Continent, F. Quilice, 1956. (Weidenfeld & Nicolson), 1954.
Holidays Under the Sea, W. Roy Midwinter.
The Pearl Seekers, N. Bartlett (Arrow).
The Frogmen, Waldron & Gleeson (Evans), 1950. (Pan), 1954.
Man Explores the Sea, Dugan (Hamish Hamilton), 1956. (Pelican), 1961.
Underwater Exploration, H. Culpin (Muller).
Sixteen Hundred Years Under the Sea, Falcon-Barker (Muller).
Roman Galley Beneath the Sea, Falcon-Barker (Brockhampton Press).
The Living Sea, Cousteau (Hamish Hamilton).
The Lost Ships, Throckmorton (Jonathan Cape).
Expedition into the Unknown, Hass (Hodder).
Navy Diver, Karneke (Hale).
The Treasure of the Great Reef, Clarke (Arthur Barker).
Aquarius, Tailliez (Harrap).
Exploring Under the Sea, Cook (Abelard-Schuman).
World Without Sun, Cousteau (Heinemann).
The Wreck Hunters, Jefferis and McDonald (Harrap).
Pieces of Eight, Wagner (Longmans).
Islands of Angry Ghosts, Edwards (Hodder and Stoughton).
Sinkings, Salvages & Shipwrecks, R. F. Burgess (American Heritage).
Diving Around Britain and Ireland, Leo Zanelli (Aquaphone).
Finders Losers, Jack Slack (Hutchinson).
They Dared the Deep, Robert F. Marx (Pelham).
Commander Crabb Is Alive, B. Hutton (Library 33).
The Underwater Book, Kendall McDonald (Pelham).
Cornish Shipwrecks, The South Coast, R. Larn and Clive Carter (David Charles).
Cornish Shipwrecks, The North Coast, Clive Carter (David Charles).
Whale of a Shark, Ben Cropp (Angus and Robertson).
Oil and Water, Edward Cowan (Kimber).

The Realm of the Submarine, Paul Cohen (Collier-Macmillan).
The Frogmen of Burma, B. S. Wright (Kimber).
The Second Underwater Book, Kendall McDonald (Pelham).
How To Get More Fun From Your Boat, Kendall McDonald (Pelham).
Shipwrecks Around Britain; A Diver's Guide, Leo Zanelli (Kaye & Ward).
Cornish Shipwrecks, Isles of Scilly, R. Larn (David & Charles).
The Man in the Helmet, D. Young (Cassell).
Deep-Salvage, White & Hadfield (Sampson Low).
Twenty Years Under The Ocean, H. J. Bruce (Stanley Paul).

APPENDIX 14—BSAC FILM LIBRARY

The objective of the BSAC Film Library is to provide a specialist film service for all those interested in underwater activities.

The organisation and content of the BSAC Film Library is the responsibility of the BSAC Films and Photographic Officer, who reports to the General Committee. The day to day running of the Film Library is in the hands of a professional organisation which specialises in this type of service.

Each film is given a computer code. Applications for film hire are fed to the computer which immediately registers the booking. If the film is already booked, alternative dates are printed out. The applicant is then notified accordingly. The film is despatched, by post, to the borrower several days before the showing date. All films are cleaned, inspected and if necessary, repaired upon return to the Film Library. The Film Library is responsible for the collection of hire fees from borrowers and makes a monthly return to the Honorary Club Treasurer within 8 weeks of the end of each month.

Each film title in the library is negotiated separately. Some films are purchased outright. Others are purchased at print costs and copyright holders receive royalties on a per showing basis. Some films have been donated to the Film Library.

Sponsors are being sought to help defray the costs of setting up this film service and buying new titles. Films may therefore carry the name of a sponsor and/or a short advertisement.

The films are available for hire to all organisations interested in underwater activities.

All branches of the BSAC are entitled to 10% discount on hire fees over £10. As the Film Library will have no method of determining if an applicant is a bona fide member of the BSAC, the full fee should be paid to the Film Library. Receipts, which can come from several bookings as long as they total more than £10, should be sent to the Honorary Treasurer with a note requesting the 10% refund.

Customs and postal difficulties make it necessary to restrict hire mainly to borrowers in the British Isles. However, special arrangements can be made for special showings overseas.

An up-to-date list of films is available from BSAC headquarters or from the Film Library.

All applications for film hire should be made to:
British Sub Aqua Club Film Library,
Guild Sound & Vision Ltd.,
Sponsored Sales Division,
85–129 Oundle Road, Peterborough PE2 9EY. Tel. 0733 63122.

APPENDIX 15—THE DIVING OPERATIONS SPECIAL REGULATIONS, 1960
EXPLANATORY NOTE
(This Note is not part of the Regulations, but is intended to indicate their general purport.)

These Regulations impose requirements for the safety and health of persons employed in diving operations in any place to which the Factories Act, 1937, applies.

The Minister of Labour by virtue of the powers conferred on him by section 60 of the Factories Act, 1937(†), section 8 of the Factories Act, 1948(*), and of all other powers enabling him in that behalf, hereby makes the following Special Regulations:—

Citation and commencement

1. These Regulations may be cited as the Diving Operations Special Regulations, 1960, and shall come into operation on the first day of July, 1960.

(†) 1 Edw. 8 & 1 Geo. 6. c. 67.   (*) 11 & 12 Geo. 6. c. 55.

Application of Regulations

2.—(1) These Regulations shall apply as respects diving operations carried out therein—

(*a*) to all factories; and

(*b*) to all premises, places, processes, operations and works to which the provisions of Part IV of the principal Act with respect to special regulations for safety and health are applied by sections 105 to 108 of that Act.

(2) The chief inspector may (subject to such conditions, if any, as may be specified therein) by certificate in writing (which he may in his discretion revoke at any time) exempt from any or all of the requirements of these Regulations—

(*a*) any particular plant or equipment or any class or description of plant or equipment; or

(*b*) any particular work or any class or description of work

if he is satisfied that the requirements in respect of which the exemption is granted are not necessary for the protection of persons employed or not reasonably practicable.

(3) The provisions of these Regulations shall be in addition to and not in substitution for or in diminution of other requirements imposed by or under the principal Act.

Interpretation

3.—(1) The Interpretation Act, 1889(†), shall apply to the interpretation of these Regulations as it applies to the interpretation of an Act of Parliament.

(2) In these Regulations, unless the context otherwise requires, the following expressions have the meaning hereby assigned to them respectively, that is to say:—

'air' includes any gas suitable for breathing at the depth at which the diver is to operate;

'appointed doctor' means any appointed factory doctor appointed under section 126 of the principal Act for a district or any duly qualified medical practitioner approved for all or any of the purposes of these Regulations;

'the principal Act' means the Factories Act, 1937, as amended by or under any other Act;

'plant or equipment' means plant or equipment intended to ensure the safety of persons working under water and includes any plant, equipment, machinery, apparatus or appliance, or any part thereof;

'self-contained' in relation to any diving plant or equipment means diving plant or equipment in which the supply of air is carried by the diver independently of any other source.

Obligations under Regulations

4.—(1) It shall be the duty of every contractor and employer of workmen who is undertaking any diving operation to which these Regulations apply, to comply with the requirements of Regulations 5 to 9 insofar as they may affect any workman employed by him:

Provided that the requirements of the said Regulations shall be deemed not to affect any workman if and so long as his presence in any place is not in the course of performing any work on behalf of his employer or is not expressly or impliedly authorised or permitted by his employer.

(2) It shall be the duty of every person employed to comply with such of the requirements of these Regulations as relate to the doing of or abstaining from an act by him and to co-operate in carrying out these Regulations and if he discovers any defect in the plant or equipment, to report such defect without unreasonable delay to his employer or foreman, or to a person appointed by the employer to supervise the safe conduct of the operations.

(3) No person shall be held not to have complied with a requirement of any of these Regulations by reason of any matter proved to have been due to causes over which he had no control against the happening of which it was not reasonably practicable for him to make provision, including (without prejudice to the generality of the foregoing) physical conditions which were unknown and which could not have been reasonably foreseen by a person experienced in the operations or in the use of any plant or equipment involved.

(†) 52 & 53 Vict. c. 63

Employment of qualified persons as divers

5. No person shall be employed under water as a diver unless—

(*a*) he has previous experience and a knowledge of diving practice (including decompression procedure) to the depth at which he is to operate and has a full understanding of the operation both of the diving apparatus in use and of the apparatus which may be available in an emergency: or

(*b*) he is undergoing training under the immediate supervision of a diver who has such experience, knowledge and understanding.

Diving plant or equipment

6.—(1) No person shall be employed under water as a diver unless he is provided with diving plant or equipment (including means of access to and from the water) which is sufficient and suitable for the operations and properly maintained.

(2) Whilst any person is employed under water as a diver he shall be supplied with air which is fit for respiration, is adequate in quantity, and of suitable pressure for the plant or equipment with which and in the circumstances in which he is working.

(3) In the case of diving plant or equipment which includes an air pipeline through which air is supplied from the surface, such plant or equipment shall include air pumps or air compressors or air cylinders; and where use is made of air compressors, a sufficient reserve of air shall be provided to allow the diver to reach the surface if the compressors fail.

(4) No self-contained diving plant or equipment shall be used which is regenerative and operates on a closed circuit.

Safeguards during work

7.—Where any person is employed under water as a diver—

(*a*) a sufficient number of suitable and competent persons shall be employed in attendance upon him with a view to ensuring his safety; and

(*b*) save where the nature of the operations to be undertaken renders it either undesirable or not reasonably practicable to do so

    (i) a lifeline shall be provided for and used by the diver, and

    (ii) arrangements shall be made for a suitable signalling system between the diver and persons on the surface; and

(*c*) save where neither the diver under water nor his plant or equipment is likely to become jammed, entangled or trapped, another diver provided with sufficient suitable plant or equipment shall be available to go to the other diver's assistance in an emergency:

    Provided that, if in an emergency, a spare diver goes to assist another diver, the temporary absence of another spare diver shall not be a contravention of this sub-paragraph while an additional diver cannot reasonably be made readily available.

Tests and examinations of plant or equipment

8.—(1) No diving plant or equipment shall be used unless—

(*a*) before being brought into use for the first time on operations to which these regulations apply it has been tested and thoroughly examined by the manufacturer, supplier or other competent person and there has been obtained a certificate of such test and examination signed by the person making or responsible for the carrying out of the test and examination; and

(*b*) it has been thoroughly examined by a competent person at least once within the preceding three months and a report of the results of such examination signed by the person making or responsible for the examination has been obtained.

Every such certificate and report shall within fourteen days be entered in or attached to the general register.

(2) No air pump, air compressor or air cylinder and no air pipeline shall be used on any day in a diving operation unless within the preceding twenty-four hours the pump, the compressor or the cylinder and the whole of the air pipeline have been tested for leakage by the diver or other competent person to determine that a pressure in excess of that at which the diver has to descend is maintained for a sufficient period when the pump or compressor is not operating.

(3) No diving plant or equipment shall be used on any day unless any inlet and outlet valves on the diver's dress, and any regulator or demand valve on the plant or equipment

have been examined within the preceding twenty-four hours by the diver or other competent person and found by him to be in efficient working order.

(4) No self-contained diving plant or equipment shall be used on any day unless it has been tested for efficient functioning by the diver or other competent person within the preceding twenty-four hours.

Medical examination and diver's fitness register

9.—(1) In this Regulation the expression 'certified' means certified by an appointed doctor by certificate in the prescribed form in the diver's fitness register; the expression 'diver's fitness register' means a diver's fitness register in the prescribed form; and the expression 'medical examination' means a medical examination by an appointed doctor, except that the appointed doctor need not himself carry out any radiographical examination.

(2) No person shall be employed under water as a diver unless—

(a) there has been issued in respect of him a diver's fitness register in which, following a medical examination which includes a chest examination by radiography, he is certified as fit for that employment; and

(b) within the previous six months he has undergone a medical examination and has been certified as fit for that employment.

(3) If by reason of disease or bodily injury a person is incapacitated for employment under water as a diver for a continuous period exceeding fourteen days, he shall not work under water as a diver until—

(a) he has furnished his employer with a medical certificate showing the nature of the disease or injury, which certificate, together with the diver's fitness register shall be sent by the employer to an appointed doctor; and

(b) he has thereafter been certified fit for that employment. Before certifying a person's fitness in pursuance of this sub-paragraph the appointed doctor may require that person to submit himself for medical examination.

(4) It shall be the duty of the employer to arrange for any medical examination required by sub-paragraph (a) or (b) of paragraph (2) of this Regulation and the duty of every person employed or proposed to be employed as a diver under water to submit himself for examination accordingly. Any such medical examination may, if the appointed doctor so decides, include a chest examination by radiography.

(5) The diver's fitness register shall be kept by the employer or his representative whilst the diver is in his employment except at times when it is required by the diver, or by the appointed doctor for purposes of these Regulations, and shall be handed to the diver on the termination of such employment. When an employer proposes to employ a diver and is not already in possession of a current diver's fitness register for him, the diver shall produce his diver's fitness register (if any) to the employer and if the diver is unable or fails to produce the said register, the employer shall supply a fresh form of register and shall not employ him under water as a diver until a certificate of fitness for such employment is entered therein in accordance with these Regulations. The employer shall also supply a fresh form of register when an existing register has become full and a further entry is required.

(6) Where diving operations are urgently required to be done before it is reasonably practicable, because of the inaccessibility of an appointed doctor, to arrange for any examination or obtain any certificate required by the foregoing provisions of this Regulation, any examination so required of a person proposed to be employed on such work and any certificate so required in relation to any such person may be made or given by any duly qualified medical practitioner who in that behalf shall have all the powers of an appointed doctor. The employer shall notify a superintending inspector of factories as soon as practicable whenever any diving operations are carried out in reliance on the provisions of this paragraph.

Dated this 5th day of April, 1960.

Edward Heath,

Minister of Labour

APPENDIX 16—THE BEAUFORT WIND SCALE

NOTE: Mariners never use the term 'Gale' for winds of less than Force 8. Gale warnings are only issued and cones hoisted for winds of Force 8 upwards.

Beaufort International Number	As used by Mariners				As used by Landsmen		
	Wind	Nautical miles per hours (knots)	Feet per second	Indications at sea	Wind	Statute m.p.h. recorded at 33 ft. above ground level	Indications on land
0	Calm	Less than 1	Less than 2	Sea mirror smooth	Calm	Less than 1	Smoke rises vertically.
1	Light air	1-3	2-5	Small wavelets like scales, no foam crests	Light air	1-3	Direction shown by smoke but not by wind vanes.
2	Light breeze	4-6	6-11	Waves short and more pronounced; crests begin to break; foam has glassy appearance—not yet white	Light breeze	4-7	Wind felt on face; leaves rustle, ordinary vanes moved by wind.
3	Gentle breeze	7-10	12-18	Waves are longer; many white horses	Gentle breeze	8-12	Leaves and small twigs in constant motion; wind extends light flag.
4	Moderate breeze	11-16	19-27	Waves now pronounced and long; white foam crests everywhere	Moderate breeze	13-18	Raises dust and waste paper; small branches are moved.
5	Fresh breeze	17-21	28-36	Larger waves form; white foam crests more extensive	Fresh breeze	19-24	Small trees in leaf begin to sway; crested wavelets form on inland waters.
6	Strong breeze	22-27	37-46	Sea heaps up; wind starts to blow the foam in streaks	Strong breeze	25-31	Large branches in motion; whistling heard in telegraph wires; umbrellas used with difficulty.
7	Strong wind	28-33	47-56	Height of waves increases visibly; also height of crests; much foam is blown in dense streaks	Moderate gale (see note)	32-38	Whole trees in motion; inconvenience felt when walking against wind.
8	Fresh gale	34-40	57-68		Fresh gale	39-46	Breaks twigs off trees; greatly impedes progress.
9	Strong gale	41-47	69-80		Strong gale	47-54	Slight structural damage occurs (chimney pots and slates removed).
10	Whole gale	48-55	81-93	High waves with long overhanging crests; great foam patches	Whole gale	55-63	Seldom experienced inland; trees uprooted; considerable structural damage occurs.
11	Storm	56-65	94-110	Waves so high that ships within sight are hidden in the troughs; sea covered with streaky foam; air filled with spray.	Storm	64-75	Very rarely experienced; accompanied by widespread damage.
12	Hurricane	Above 65	Above 110		Hurricane	Above 75	—

APPENDIX 17—DECOMPRESSION TABLES

Introduction

The following metricated decompression tables are a necessary part of the metrication of the Diving Manual; and it is recommended that divers, whenever possible, should use them. Branches should also encourage the use of 'metricated decompression' so that the changeover to the new units is as swift as possible.

However, it is recognised that some divers already practising decompression diving may find some difficulty in effecting a smooth transition. In some circumstances to do so too quickly could even be dangerous. For this reason the metricated tables are followed by tables in the old units, but it must be stressed that future editions of this manual will include only metricated tables.

DECOMPRESSION

SECOND AND SUBSEQUENT DIVES WITHIN 12 HOURS. A diver carrying out a dive on Table 1 above the limiting line, may carry out a second and subsequent dives to depths not greater than 9 m, without time restriction or further decompression. If, however, he is required to dive again to a depth exceeding 9 m within 4 hours of a previous dive to 9 m or less, or within 12 hours of a previous dive to more than 9 m, he may do so only if he is given the stops for a combined dive. A diver who has carried out a dive below the limiting line is not to carry out a further dive within 12 hours.

STOPS FOR A COMBINED DIVE. The stops for a combined dive are obtained by adding together the duration of the first and each subsequent dive to obtain a Total Time for the combined dives. This total time and the depth of the deepest dive made are used to obtain the stops in the relevant table as for a single dive. The total time of the combined dives, except that dives carried out using pure oxygen should not be considered for calculation of a combined dive, is to be limited so that the Total Time for Decompression (column 4 or 6 as applicable to the table in use) does not exceed 75 minutes.

PROCEDURE AFTER DIVING TO 37 M OR MORE. Any man who has carried out a dive to a depth of 37 m or more for a period above the limiting line in Table 1, is to remain within 4 hours travelling time of a compression chamber for 12 hours after completing the dive.

Any man who has carried out a dive of 37 m or more for a period below the limiting line in Table 1 must remain in the immediate vicinity (i.e. on board) of a compression chamber for a period of 4 hours after completing the dive, and within 4 hours travelling time of a chamber for a further 12 hours.

TERMS USED AND METHODS AVAILABLE

1. Definition of Terms

STOPPAGE. A calculated pause at a specific depth in the diver's ascent to allow the dispersion of excess nitrogen absorbed by the body.

DECOMPRESSION. A series of stoppages and decrease in pressure to allow the diver to surface safely.

2. Methods Available. The following methods of decompression are available:

AIR DECOMPRESSION. Decompression carried out—

While the diver is in the water breathing air and being surfaced in accordance with Table 1.

SURFACE DECOMPRESSION. Decompression carried out in a compression chamber on the surface—

With the diver breathing air and being surfaced in accordance with Table 1.

THERAPEUTIC DECOMPRESSION. The recompression of a diver suffering from decompression sickness and his subsequent decompression at a slower rate than normal.

GENERAL INSTRUCTIONS. Any diver who dives to a depth and to a period covered by the decompression tables is to carry out decompression strictly in accordance with the appropriate decompression table, except on the advice of a trained diving Medical Officer or in extreme emergency.

Maximum Depth of Dive. The decompression tables in this Chapter provide for a maximum dive of 61 m, but the present maximum permissible depth of dive is 55 m.

Hard Work—Use of Decompression Tables. When a diver exerts himself unduly, his body absorbs more gas than usual and he will require a longer period of decompression to eliminate this gas. *On all occasions when hard physical work is carried out by a diver the decompression routine for the dive is to be taken as that for the next longer time increment for the dive.* Fin-swimming is rated as "Hard Physical Work".

AIR DECOMPRESSION—TABLE 1. Table 1 is used to obtain the times for the diver's stops in water.

DEPTH IN METRES (COLUMN 1). This column is entered with—
When breathing air, the actual deepest depth of dive.

Column 1 of Table 1 is divided into sections which contain increments of 3 m. The section used is that which immediately exceeds the depth obtained, but if there is any doubt about the accuracy of this figure, the next deeper section is to be used, e.g. if the depth obtained was 14 m and the accuracy of this depth was in doubt, the 18 m section would be used.

DURATION (COLUMN 2). This is the interval of time in minutes between the time of the diver leaving the surface and the time that he leaves the bottom to commence the ascent. Where the actual duration does not coincide with one of the figures in the table, the nearest higher figure is to be taken, e.g. if the actual duration was 27 min. at 43 m, the stops would be taken for 30 min. Where there is any doubt about the accuracy of the duration, the next higher figure is to be taken and in the example quoted would be 35 min.

LIMITING LINE. The part of each depth section above the limiting line is the ordinary working table where the risk of decompression sickness is negligible; diving for periods below the line carries a greater risk of decompression sickness and this risk increases with an increase of duration below the line. Intentional diving below the limiting line should only be undertaken when a compression chamber is immediately available on the site and then only when circumstances justify the risk.

RATE OF ASCENT. The rate of ascent from the bottom to the first stop, between stops, and from the last stop to surface should be as near as possible (18 m per minute), a steady rate of ascent is however more important than the precise time taken to complete it. Where the diver's exhaust bubbles can be seen the correct speed of ascent is best obtained by keeping pace with the smaller bubbles.

METHOD OF TIMING STOPS. The time for the first stop commences when the diver leaves the sea bed and the time for each subsequent stop commences when the diver leaves the preceding stop.

TABLE 1   METRICATED
RN AIR DECOMPRESSION TABLES
by kind permission of the Admiralty

(1) DEPTH NOT EXCEEDING (Metres)	(2) DURATION TIME LEAVING SURFACE TO BEGINNING OF ASCENT NOT EXCEEDING (min)	(3) STOPPAGES AT DIFFERENT DEPTHS (min)					(4) TOTAL TIME FOR DECOMPRESSION (min)
		15 m	12 m	9 m	6 m	3 m	
3	No limit	—	—	—	—	—	—
12	135	—	—	—	—	—	—
	165	—	—	—	—	5	5
	195	—	—	—	—	10	10
	225	—	—	—	—	15	15
	255	—	—	—	—	20	20
	330	—	—	—	—	25	25
	390	—	—	—	—	30	30
	660	—	—	—	—	35	35
	Limiting Line over 660	—	—	—	—	40	40

(1) Depth not exceeding (Metres)	(2) Duration Time leaving surface to beginning of ascent not exceeding (min)	(3) Stoppages at different depths (min)					(4) Total time for decompression (min)
		15 m	12 m	9 m	6 m	3 m	
15	85	—	—	—	—	—	—
	105	—	—	—	—	5	5
	120	—	—	—	—	10	10
	135	—	—	—	—	15	15
	145	—	—	—	—	20	20
	160	—	—	—	—	25	25
	170	—	—	—	5	25	30
	190	—	—	—	5	30	35
	Limiting Line						
	240	—	—	—	10	40	50
	360	—	—	—	30	40	70
	450	—	—	—	35	40	75
	over 450	—	—	—	35	45	80
18	60	—	—	—	—	—	—
	70	—	—	—	—	5	5
	80	—	—	—	5	5	10
	90	—	—	—	5	10	15
	100	—	—	—	5	15	20
	110	—	—	—	5	20	25
	120	—	—	—	5	25	30
	130	—	—	—	5	30	35
	Limiting Line						
	140	—	—	—	10	30	40
	150	—	—	—	10	40	50
	160	—	—	—	15	40	55
	180	—	—	—	20	40	60
	200	—	—	5	30	40	75
	255	—	—	10	35	45	90
	325	—	—	20	40	45	105
	495	—	—	35	40	45	120
	over 495	—	—	35	40	50	125
21	40	—	—	—	—	—	—
	55	—	—	—	—	5	5
	60	—	—	—	5	5	10
	70	—	—	—	5	10	15
	75	—	—	—	5	15	20
	85	—	—	—	5	20	25
	90	—	—	—	5	25	30
	95	—	—	5	5	25	35
	Limiting Line						
	105	—	—	5	5	35	45
	120	—	—	5	10	40	55
	135	—	—	5	20	45	70
	150	—	—	5	30	45	80
	165	—	—	10	30	50	90
	180	—	—	15	35	50	100
	210	—	—	25	40	50	115
	240	—	5	30	40	50	125

489

(1) Depth not exceeding (Metres)	(2) Duration Time leaving surface to beginning of ascent not exceeding (min)	(3) Stoppages at different depths (min)					(4) Total time for Decompression (min)
		15 m	12 m	9 m	6 m	3 m	
	30	—	—	—	—	—	—
	40	—	—	—	—	5	5
	50	—	—	—	5	5	10
	55	—	—	—	5	10	15
	60	—	—	—	5	15	20
	70	—	—	—	5	20	25
	75	—	—	—	5	25	30
24	**Limiting Line**						
	80	—	—	5	5	30	40
	90	—	—	5	10	35	50
	105	—	—	5	20	40	65
	120	—	5	5	30	45	85
	140	—	5	10	35	50	100
	160	—	10	30	40	50	130
	25	—	—	—	—	—	—
	30	—	—	—	—	5	5
	40	—	—	—	5	5	10
	45	—	—	—	5	10	15
	50	—	—	—	5	15	20
	55	—	—	—	5	20	25
	60	—	—	5	5	20	30
	65	—	—	5	5	25	35
27	**Limiting Line**						
	70	—	—	5	10	30	45
	75	—	—	5	15	30	50
	80	—	—	5	20	35	60
	90	—	—	5	25	40	70
	100	—	—	5	30	45	80
	110	—	5	15	35	45	100
	120	—	5	20	35	50	110
	135	5	5	25	40	50	125
	150	5	10	35	40	50	140
	20	—	—	—	—	—	—
	25	—	—	—	—	5	5
	30	—	—	—	5	5	10
	35	—	—	—	5	10	15
	40	—	—	—	5	15	20
	45	—	—	—	5	20	25
	50	—	—	5	5	20	30
	55	—	—	5	5	25	35
30	**Limiting Line**						
	60	—	—	5	10	30	45
	70	—	—	5	20	35	60
	75	—	5	5	20	40	70
	80	—	5	5	30	40	80
	90	—	5	15	30	45	95
	105	—	5	25	35	50	115
	120	5	10	30	40	50	135

(1) Depth not exceeding (Metres)	(2) Duration Time leaving surface to beginning of ascent not exceeding (min)	(3) Stoppages at different depths (min)						(4) Total time for Decompression (min)
		18 m	15 m	12 m	9 m	6 m	3 m	
	17	—	—	—	—	—	—	—
	20	—	—	—	—	—	5	5
	25	—	—	—	—	5	5	10
	30	—	—	—	—	5	10	15
	35	—	—	—	—	5	15	20
	40	—	—	—	—	5	20	25
	45	—	—	—	5	5	20	30
	Limiting Line							
33	50	—	—	—	5	10	25	40
	55	—	—	—	5	15	30	50
	60	—	—	—	5	20	35	60
	65	—	—	5	5	20	40	70
	70	—	—	5	10	20	45	80
	75	—	—	5	15	25	45	90
	80	—	—	5	20	30	45	100
	90	—	5	5	20	40	45	115
	100	—	5	10	25	40	50	130
	110	—	5	20	30	45	50	150
	120	5	5	25	40	45	50	170
	14	—	—	—	—	—	—	—
	20	—	—	—	—	—	5	5
	25	—	—	—	—	5	5	10
	30	—	—	—	—	5	15	20
	35	—	—	—	—	5	20	25
	40	—	—	—	5	5	25	35
	Limiting Line							
36	45	—	—	—	5	10	25	40
	50	—	—	—	5	15	30	50
	55	—	—	5	5	20	35	65
	60	—	—	5	10	25	40	80
	70	—	—	5	20	30	45	100
	75	—	5	5	20	35	45	110
	80	—	5	10	25	35	45	120
	90	—	5	15	30	40	50	140
	100	5	5	20	35	45	50	160
	110	5	15	25	40	45	50	180
	120	5	20	30	40	45	50	195

Depth not exceeding (Metres)	Duration (min)	21 m	18 m	15 m	12 m	9 m	6 m	3 m	Total (min)
	11	—	—	—	—	—	—	—	—
	15	—	—	—	—	—	—	5	5
	20	—	—	—	—	—	5	5	10
	25	—	—	—	—	—	5	10	15
	30	—	—	—	—	—	5	20	25
	35	—	—	—	—	5	5	20	30
	Limiting Line								
	40	—	—	—	—	5	10	25	40
	45	—	—	—	5	5	15	30	55
39	50	—	—	—	5	5	20	35	65

(1) Depth not exceeding (Metres)	(2) Duration Time leaving surface to beginning of ascent not exceeding (min)	(3) Stoppages at different depths (min)							(4) Total time for Decompression (min)
		21m	18m	15m	12m	9 m	6 m	3 m	
	55	—	—	—	5	10	25	40	80
	60	—	—	—	5	15	30	45	95
	70	—	—	5	10	20	30	50	115
	75	—	—	5	15	25	40	50	135
	80	—	—	5	20	30	45	50	150
	90	—	5	5	25	40	45	50	170
	100	5	5	15	30	40	45	50	190
	110	5	10	25	30	45	45	50	210
	120	5	15	30	40	45	45	50	230
	9	—	—	—	—	—	—	—	—
	10	—	—	—	—	—	—	5	5
	15	—	—	—	—	—	5	5	10
	20	—	—	—	—	—	5	10	15
	25	—	—	—	—	—	5	15	20
	30	—	—	—	—	5	5	20	30
	Limiting Line								
42	35	—	—	—	—	5	10	25	40
	40	—	—	—	5	5	15	30	55
	45	—	—	—	5	10	15	35	65
	50	—	—	—	5	15	20	40	80
	55	—	—	5	5	15	25	45	95
	60	—	—	5	5	20	35	45	110
	65	—	—	5	10	25	40	45	125
	70	—	—	5	15	30	40	50	140
	75	—	5	5	20	30	45	50	155
	80	—	5	10	20	35	45	50	165
	85	—	5	15	25	40	45	50	180
	95	5	5	20	35	40	45	50	200
	105	5	15	25	35	45	45	50	220
	115	5	20	35	40	45	45	50	240
	8	—	—	—	—	—	—	—	—
	10	—	—	—	—	—	—	5	5
	15	—	—	—	—	—	5	5	10
	20	—	—	—	—	—	5	15	20
	25	—	—	—	—	5	5	20	30
	Limiting Line								
45	30	—	—	—	—	5	10	25	40
	35	—	—	—	5	5	10	30	50
	40	—	—	—	5	10	15	35	65
	45	—	—	—	5	15	20	40	80
	50	—	—	5	5	15	25	45	95
	55	—	—	5	10	20	30	50	115
	60	—	—	5	15	25	35	50	130
	65	—	5	5	15	30	40	50	145
	70	—	5	10	20	30	45	50	160
	75	—	5	15	25	35	45	50	175
	80	5	5	20	30	40	45	50	195
	85	5	10	25	35	40	45	50	210
	90	5	15	30	40	45	45	50	230

(1) Depth not exceeding (Metres)	(2) Duration Time leaving surface to beginning of ascent not exceeding (min)	(3) Stoppages at different depths (min)								(4) Total time for Decompression (min)
		24m	21m	18m	15m	12m	9 m	6 m	3 m	
	10	—	—	—	—	—	—	5	5	10
	15	—	—	—	—	—	—	5	10	15
	20	—	—	—	—	—	5	5	15	25
	25	—	—	—	—	—	5	10	20	35
	Limiting Line									
	30	—	—	—	—	5	5	10	25	45
	35	—	—	—	—	5	10	15	30	60
	40	—	—	—	—	5	10	20	40	75
	45	—	—	—	5	5	15	25	45	95
48	50	—	—	—	5	10	20	30	45	110
	55	—	—	—	5	15	25	40	45	130
	60	—	—	5	5	20	25	40	50	145
	65	—	—	5	10	20	35	45	50	165
	70	—	—	5	15	25	40	45	50	180
	75	—	5	5	20	30	40	45	50	195
	80	—	5	10	25	35	40	45	50	210
	85	—	5	15	30	40	45	45	50	230
	10	—	—	—	—	—	—	5	5	10
	15	—	—	—	—	—	—	5	10	15
	20	—	—	—	—	—	5	5	15	25
	Limiting Line									
	25	—	—	—	—	—	5	10	25	40
	30	—	—	—	—	5	5	15	30	55
	35	—	—	—	—	5	10	20	35	70
51	40	—	—	—	5	5	15	25	35	85
	45	—	—	—	5	10	20	30	40	105
	50	—	—	5	5	10	25	35	45	125
	55	—	—	5	5	15	30	40	50	145
	60	—	—	5	10	20	35	45	50	165
	65	—	5	5	15	25	35	45	50	180
	70	—	5	10	15	30	40	45	50	195
	75	—	5	15	20	35	45	45	50	215
	80	5	5	20	25	40	45	45	50	235
	10	—	—	—	—	—	—	5	5	10
	15	—	—	—	—	—	5	5	10	20
	20	—	—	—	—	—	5	10	15	30
	Limiting Line									
	25	—	—	—	—	5	5	10	25	45
	30	—	—	—	—	5	10	15	35	65
	35	—	—	—	5	5	15	20	40	85
54	40	—	—	—	5	10	20	25	45	105
	45	—	—	5	5	10	25	35	45	125
	50	—	—	5	5	15	30	40	50	145
	55	—	—	5	10	20	35	45	50	165
	60	—	5	5	15	25	40	45	50	185
	65	—	5	10	20	30	40	45	50	200
	70	—	5	15	25	35	45	45	50	220
	75	5	5	20	30	40	45	45	50	240

(1) Depth not exceeding (Metres)	(2) Duration Time leaving surface to beginning of ascent not exceeding (min)	(3) Stoppages at different depths (min)								(4) Total time for Decompression (min)
		24m	21m	18m	15m	12m	9 m	6 m	3 m	
	10	—	—	—	—	—	—	5	5	10
	15	—	—	—	—	—	5	5	15	25
	20	—	—	—	—	—	5	10	20	35
	Limiting Line									
57	25	—	—	—	—	5	5	15	25	50
	30	—	—	—	5	5	10	20	35	75
	35	—	—	—	5	5	15	30	45	100
	40	—	—	5	5	10	20	35	45	120
	45	—	—	5	5	15	25	40	50	140
	50	—	—	5	10	20	30	45	50	160
	55	—	5	5	15	25	35	45	50	180
	60	—	5	10	20	30	40	45	50	200
	65	5	5	10	25	35	45	45	50	220
	70	5	10	15	30	40	45	45	50	240
	10	—	—	—	—	—	—	5	10	15
	15	—	—	—	—	—	5	5	15	25
	Limiting Line									
60	20	—	—	—	—	5	5	10	20	40
	25	—	—	—	—	5	10	15	30	60
	30	—	—	—	5	5	15	20	40	85
	35	—	—	—	5	10	20	30	45	110
	40	—	—	5	5	15	25	40	45	135
	45	—	—	5	10	20	30	45	50	160
	50	—	5	5	15	25	35	45	50	180
	55	—	5	10	20	30	40	45	50	200
	60	5	5	10	25	35	45	45	50	220
	65	5	10	15	30	40	45	45	50	240

RN AIR DECOMPRESSION TABLES
NON-METRICATED

(1) Depth not exceeding (ft)	(2) Duration Time leaving surface to beginning of ascent not exceeding (min)	(3) Stoppages at different depths (min)					(4) Total time for Decompression (min)
		50 ft	40 ft	30 ft	20 ft	10 ft	
30	No limit	—	—	—	—	—	—
40	135	—	—	—	—	—	—
	165	—	—	—	—	5	5
	195	—	—	—	—	10	10
	225	—	—	—	—	15	15
	255	—	—	—	—	20	20
	330	—	—	—	—	25	25
	390	—	—	—	—	30	30
	660	—	—	—	—	35	35
	Limiting Line						
	over 660	—	—	—	—	40	40

(1) Depth not exceeding (ft)	(2) Duration time leaving surface to beginning of ascent not exceeding (min)	(3) Stoppages at different depths (min)					(4) Total time for decompression (min)
		50 ft	40 ft	30 ft	20 ft	10 ft	
50	85	—	—	—	—	—	—
	105	—	—	—	—	5	5
	120	—	—	—	—	10	10
	135	—	—	—	—	15	15
	145	—	—	—	—	20	20
	160	—	—	—	—	25	25
	170	—	—	—	5	25	30
	190	—	—	—	5	30	35
	Limiting Line						
	240	—	—	—	10	40	50
	360	—	—	—	30	40	70
	450	—	—	—	35	40	75
	over 450	—	—	—	35	45	80
60	60	—	—	—	—	—	—
	70	—	—	—	—	5	5
	80	—	—	—	5	5	10
	90	—	—	—	5	10	15
	100	—	—	—	5	15	20
	110	—	—	—	5	20	25
	120	—	—	—	5	25	30
	130	—	—	—	5	30	35
	Limiting Line						
	140	—	—	—	10	30	40
	150	—	—	—	10	40	50
	160	—	—	—	15	40	55
	180	—	—	—	20	40	60
	200	—	—	5	30	40	75
	255	—	—	10	35	45	90
	325	—	—	20	40	45	105
	495	—	—	35	40	45	120
	over 495	—	—	35	40	50	125
70	40	—	—	—	—	—	—
	55	—	—	—	—	5	5
	60	—	—	—	5	5	10
	70	—	—	—	5	10	15
	75	—	—	—	5	15	20
	85	—	—	—	5	20	25
	90	—	—	—	5	25	30
	95	—	—	5	5	25	35
	Limiting Line						
	105	—	—	5	5	35	45
	120	—	—	5	10	40	55
	135	—	—	5	20	45	70
	150	—	—	5	30	45	80
	165	—	—	10	30	50	90
	180	—	—	15	35	50	100
	210	—	—	25	40	50	115
	240	—	5	30	40	50	125

(1) Depth not exceeding (ft)	(2) Duration Time leaving surface to beginning of ascent not exceeding (min)	(3) Stoppages at different depths (min)					(4) Total time for decompression (min)
		50 ft	40 ft	30 ft	20 ft	10 ft	
	30	—	—	—	—	—	—
	40	—	—	—	—	5	5
	50	—	—	—	5	5	10
	55	—	—	—	5	10	15
	60	—	—	—	5	15	20
	70	—	—	—	5	20	25
	75	—	—	—	5	25	30
80	**Limiting Line**						
	80	—	—	5	5	30	40
	90	—	—	5	10	35	50
	105	—	—	5	20	40	65
	120	—	5	5	30	45	85
	140	—	5	10	35	50	100
	160	—	10	30	40	50	130
	25	—	—	—	—	—	—
	30	—	—	—	—	5	5
	40	—	—	—	5	5	10
	45	—	—	—	5	10	15
	50	—	—	—	5	15	20
	55	—	—	—	5	20	25
	60	—	—	5	5	20	30
	65	—	—	5	5	25	35
90	**Limiting Line**						
	70	—	—	5	10	30	45
	75	—	—	5	15	30	50
	80	—	—	5	20	35	60
	90	—	—	5	25	40	70
	100	—	—	5	30	45	80
	110	—	5	15	35	45	100
	120	—	5	20	35	50	110
	135	5	5	25	40	50	125
	150	5	10	35	40	50	140
	20	—	—	—	—	—	—
	25	—	—	—	—	5	5
	30	—	—	—	5	5	10
	35	—	—	—	5	10	15
	40	—	—	—	5	15	20
	45	—	—	—	5	20	25
	50	—	—	5	5	20	30
	55	—	—	5	5	25	35
100	**Limiting Line**						
	60	—	—	5	10	30	45
	70	—	—	5	20	35	60
	75	—	5	5	20	40	70
	80	—	5	5	30	40	80
	90	—	5	15	30	45	95
	105	—	5	25	35	50	115
	120	5	10	30	40	50	135

(1) Depth not exceeding (ft)	(2) Duration Time leaving surface to beginning of ascent not exceeding (min)	(3) Stoppages at different depths (min)						(4) Total time for Decompression (min)
		60 ft	50 ft	40 ft	30 ft	20 ft	10 ft	
	17	—	—	—	—	—	—	—
	20	—	—	—	—	—	5	5
	25	—	—	—	—	5	5	10
	30	—	—	—	—	5	10	15
	35	—	—	—	—	5	15	20
	40	—	—	—	—	5	20	25
	45	—	—	—	5	5	20	30
	Limiting Line							
110	50	—	—	—	5	10	25	40
	55	—	—	—	5	15	30	50
	60	—	—	—	5	20	35	60
	65	—	—	5	5	20	40	70
	70	—	—	5	10	20	45	80
	75	—	—	5	15	25	45	90
	80	—	—	5	20	30	45	100
	90	—	5	5	20	40	45	115
	100	—	5	10	25	40	50	130
	110	—	5	20	30	45	50	150
	120	5	5	25	40	45	50	170
	14	—	—	—	—	—	—	—
	20	—	—	—	—	—	5	5
	25	—	—	—	—	5	5	10
	30	—	—	—	—	5	15	20
	35	—	—	—	—	5	20	25
	40	—	—	—	5	5	25	35
	Limiting Line							
120	45	—	—	—	5	10	25	40
	50	—	—	—	5	15	30	50
	55	—	—	5	5	20	35	65
	60	—	—	5	10	25	40	80
	70	—	—	5	20	30	45	100
	75	—	5	5	20	35	45	110
	80	—	5	10	25	35	45	120
	90	—	5	15	30	40	50	140
	100	5	5	20	35	45	50	160
	110	5	15	25	40	45	50	180
	120	5	20	30	40	45	50	195

(1) Depth not exceeding (ft)	(2) Duration Time leaving surface to beginning of ascent not exceeding (min)	70 ft	60 ft	50 ft	40 ft	30 ft	20 ft	10 ft	(4) Total time for Decompression (min)
	11	—	—	—	—	—	—	—	—
	15	—	—	—	—	—	—	5	5
	20	—	—	—	—	—	5	5	10
	25	—	—	—	—	—	5	10	15
	30	—	—	—	—	—	5	20	25
130	35	—	—	—	—	5	5	20	30
	Limiting Line								
	40	—	—	—	—	5	10	25	40
	45	—	—	—	5	5	15	30	55
	50	—	—	—	5	5	20	35	65

(1) Depth not exceeding (ft)	(2) Duration Time leaving surface to beginning of ascent not exceeding (min)	(3) Stoppages at different depths (min)							(4) Total time for Decompression (min)
		70 ft	60 ft	50 ft	40 ft	30 ft	20 ft	10 ft	
130	55	—	—	—	5	10	25	40	80
	60	—	—	—	5	15	30	45	95
	70	—	—	5	10	20	30	50	115
	75	—	—	5	15	25	40	50	135
	80	—	—	5	20	30	45	50	150
	90	—	5	5	25	40	45	50	170
	100	5	5	15	30	40	45	50	190
	110	5	10	25	30	45	45	50	210
	120	5	15	30	40	45	45	50	230
140	9	—	—	—	—	—	—	—	—
	10	—	—	—	—	—	—	5	5
	15	—	—	—	—	—	5	5	10
	20	—	—	—	—	—	5	10	15
	25	—	—	—	—	—	5	15	20
	30	—	—	—	—	5	5	20	30
	Limiting Line								
	35	—	—	—	—	5	10	25	40
	40	—	—	—	5	5	15	30	55
	45	—	—	—	5	10	15	35	65
	50	—	—	—	5	15	20	40	80
	55	—	—	5	5	15	25	45	95
	60	—	—	5	5	20	35	45	110
	65	—	—	5	10	25	40	45	125
	70	—	—	5	15	30	40	50	140
	75	—	5	5	20	30	45	50	155
	80	—	5	10	20	35	45	50	165
	85	—	5	15	25	40	45	50	180
	95	5	5	20	35	40	45	50	200
	105	5	15	25	35	45	45	50	220
	115	5	20	35	40	45	45	50	240
150	8	—	—	—	—	—	—	—	—
	10	—	—	—	—	—	—	5	5
	15	—	—	—	—	—	5	5	10
	20	—	—	—	—	—	5	15	20
	25	—	—	—	—	5	5	20	30
	Limiting Line								
	30	—	—	—	—	5	10	25	40
	35	—	—	—	5	5	10	30	50
	40	—	—	—	5	10	15	35	65
	45	—	—	—	5	15	20	40	80
	50	—	—	5	5	15	25	45	95
	55	—	—	5	10	20	30	50	115
	60	—	—	5	15	25	35	50	130
	65	—	5	5	15	30	40	50	145
	70	—	5	10	20	30	45	50	160
	75	—	5	15	25	35	45	50	175
	80	5	5	20	30	40	45	50	195
	85	5	10	25	35	40	45	50	210
	90	5	15	30	40	45	45	50	230

(1) Depth not exceeding (ft)	(2) Duration Time leaving surface to beginning of ascent not exceeding (min)	(3) Stoppages at different depths (min)							(4) Total time for Decompression (min)
		70 ft	60 ft	50 ft	40 ft	30 ft	20 ft	10 ft	
	10	—	—	—	—	—	5	5	10
	15	—	—	—	—	—	5	10	15
	20	—	—	—	—	5	5	15	25
	25	—	—	—	—	5	10	20	35
	Limiting Line								
	30	—	—	—	5	5	10	25	45
	35	—	—	—	5	10	15	30	60
	40	—	—	—	5	10	20	40	75
	45	—	—	5	5	15	25	45	95
160	50	—	—	5	10	20	30	45	110
	55	—	—	5	15	25	40	45	130
	60	—	5	5	20	25	40	50	145
	65	—	5	10	20	35	45	50	165
	70	—	5	15	25	40	45	50	180
	75	5	5	20	30	40	45	50	195
	80	5	10	25	35	40	45	50	210
	85	5	15	30	40	45	45	50	230

(ft)		80 ft	70 ft	60 ft	50 ft	40 ft	30 ft	20 ft	10 ft	(min)
	10	—	—	—	—	—	—	5	5	10
	15	—	—	—	—	—	—	5	10	15
	20	—	—	—	—	—	5	5	15	25
	Limiting Line									
	25	—	—	—	—	—	5	10	25	40
	30	—	—	—	—	5	5	15	30	55
	35	—	—	—	—	5	10	20	35	70
	40	—	—	—	5	5	15	25	35	85
	45	—	—	—	5	10	20	30	40	105
	50	—	—	5	5	10	25	35	45	125
170	55	—	—	5	5	15	30	40	50	145
	60	—	—	5	10	20	35	45	50	165
	65	—	5	5	15	25	35	45	50	180
	70	—	5	10	15	30	40	45	50	195
	75	—	5	15	20	35	45	45	50	215
	80	5	5	20	25	40	45	45	50	235
	10	—	—	—	—	—	—	5	5	10
	15	—	—	—	—	—	5	5	10	20
	20	—	—	—	—	—	5	10	15	30
	Limiting Line									
	25	—	—	—	—	5	5	10	25	45
	30	—	—	—	—	5	10	15	35	65
	35	—	—	—	5	5	15	20	40	85
180	40	—	—	—	5	10	20	25	45	105
	45	—	—	5	5	10	25	35	45	125
	50	—	—	5	5	15	30	40	50	145
	55	—	—	5	10	20	35	45	50	165
	60	—	5	5	15	25	40	45	50	185
	65	—	5	10	20	30	40	45	50	200
	70	—	5	15	25	35	45	45	50	220
	75	5	5	20	30	40	45	45	50	240

(1) Depth not exceeding (ft)	(2) Duration Time leaving surface to beginning of ascent not exceeding (min)	(3) Stoppages at different depths (min)								(4) Total time for Decompression (min)
		80 ft	70 ft	60 ft	50 ft	40 ft	30 ft	20 ft	10 ft	
	10	—	—	—	—	—	—	5	5	10
	15	—	—	—	—	—	5	5	15	25
	20	—	—	—	—	—	5	10	20	35
	Limiting Line									
	25	—	—	—	—	5	5	15	25	50
	30	—	—	—	5	5	10	20	35	75
190	35	—	—	—	5	5	15	30	45	100
	40	—	—	5	5	10	20	40	45	120
	45	—	—	5	5	15	25	40	50	140
	50	—	—	5	10	20	30	45	50	160
	55	—	5	5	15	25	35	45	50	180
	60	—	5	10	20	30	40	45	50	200
	65	5	5	10	25	35	45	45	50	220
	70	5	10	15	30	40	45	45	50	240
	10	—	—	—	—	—	—	5	10	15
	15	—	—	—	—	—	5	5	15	25
	Limiting Line									
	20	—	—	—	—	5	5	10	20	40
	25	—	—	—	—	5	10	15	30	60
	30	—	—	—	5	5	15	20	40	85
200	35	—	—	—	5	10	20	30	45	110
	40	—	—	5	5	15	25	40	45	135
	45	—	—	5	10	20	30	45	50	160
	50	—	5	5	15	25	35	45	50	180
	55	—	5	10	20	30	40	45	50	200
	60	5	5	10	25	35	45	45	50	220
	65	5	10	15	30	40	45	45	50	240

APPENDIX 18—METRICATION

The decision to issue the Diving Manual in metric units was taken in view of the fact that all branches of science and technology in Britain will shortly be converted to the use of a metric system of units known as SI (System International d'Unités). In this system of units the most important fundamental units are

Unit of mass — kilogramme — kg
Unit of length — metre — m
Unit of time — second — s.

There are other basic units but the ones above are the ones of most use to the diver. All other units of measurement are derived from the basic (or defined) ones.

Eg Unit of area — square metre — m^2
Unit of volume — cubic metre — m^3
Unit of velocity — metres per second — m/s.

When quoting multiples and sub multiples of the basic or derived units the following prefixes may be used :

Factor	Prefix	Symbol
10^9	giga	G
10^6	mega	M
10^3	kilo	k
10^{-3}	milli	m
10^{-6}	micro	μ
10^{-9}	nano	n

Eg millimetres—mm or thousandths of a metre — m^{-3}.

A better understanding of the units and their use may be facilitated if we go through the types of measurements most used by divers and see how the new units differ from the traditional (or Imperial) units.

Depth

Previously depths have been measured in feet whereas they will now be measured in metres. It is convenient to bear in mind that the pressure at the surface is exactly doubled on descending 10m.

$1\ m = 3.28\ ft$ (or approx 3.3 ft)

$10\ m = 33\ ft$.

Volume

Volumes which were previously quoted in cubic feet (ft^3) should now be measured in cubic metres (m^3), but it is expected that the litre (l) which is already in common use will continue to be acceptable.

$1\ ft^3 = 0.028m^3 = 28.3\ l$ Note : $1m^3 = 1000\ l$

$1\ gal = 0.0046m^3 = 4.6\ l$

Mass

The SI system differentiates between mass and weight. Previously the pound was used for mass and the pound force was used for weight. For the confused, weight is the result of gravity acting on a mass. The unit of mass is the kilogramme (kg)

$1\ lb = 0.454\ kg$

$1\ kg = 2.21\ lb$ (or approx 2.2 lb).

Force

The unit of force is the Newton (N) which is defined as the force required to cause a unit mass (1 kg) to move with unit acceleration ($1\ m/s^2$)

$1\ lbf = 4.45N$.

$1\ kgf = 9.81N$.

Pressure

Pressure, which is the distribution of force, was previously measured in pounds-force per square inch (lbf/in^2) and should now be measured in Newtons per square metre (N/m^2). It is thought, however, that the bar

501

(b) will continue to be acceptable as a measure of gas pressure. This would be convenient since, for all practical purposes, 1 bar is almost equal to 1 atmosphere—a unit widely used up to now.

Pressure in ats = Pressure in b

$1 \text{ lbf/in}^2 = 6895\text{N/m}^2 = 6.895\text{kN/m}^2$

$14.7 \text{ lbf/in}^2 = 102\text{kN/m}^2 = 1 \text{ at} = 1.02\text{b}.$

Speed/Velocity

The former units were miles per hour (mph) or feet per second (ft/s). These should now be quoted in metres per second (m/s) but the minute and the hour will continue to be acceptable and so kilometres per hour (km/h) may be used.

1 mph = 1.61 km/h	1 km/h = 0.62 mph
1 ft/s = 0.31 m/s	1 m/s = 3.28 ft/s
1 knot = 1.85 km/h	

Flow-Rate

Flow-rate, measured up to now in cubic feet per minute (ft³/m), should be measured in cubic metres per second (m³/s) but litres per second (1/s) may be used. The minute or the hour may be used as the time interval.

$1 \text{ ft}^3/\text{m} = 0.0283\text{m}^3/\text{m} = 0.00047\text{m}^3/\text{s}$

$1 \text{ ft}^3/\text{m} = 28.31/\text{m} = 0.471/\text{s}.$

Once the new system gets under way it should lead to simplification, and ambiguities of the previous systems should be eliminated.

The main differences that will be seen are depth-gauges calibrated in metres, pressure-gauges reading bars (or megaNewtons per square metre), bottle capacities quoted in litres (or cubic metres), decompression tables reading depth in metres, Admiralty Charts (and Ordnance Survey maps) reading metres and kilometres, and mass being quoted rather than weight.

COMPARISON OF CYLINDER CAPACITIES AND MASS OF AIR CONTAINED

CAPACITY OF CYLINDER			MASS OF AIR	
Cubic Feet	Litres	Cubic Metres	Pounds	Kilogrammes
40	1132	1.132	3.1	1.40
45	1274	1.274	3.5	1.56
50	1414	1.414	3.8	1.75
55	1557	1.557	4.1	1.87
60	1698	1.698	4.6	2.10
65	1840	1.840	5.0	2.28
70	1981	1.981	5.2	2.37
75	2123	2.123	5.7	2.62
80	2264	2.264	6.1	2.78

COMPARISON OF CYLINDER PRESSURES

lbf/in^2	MN/m^2	ats	bars
1800	12.4	123	124
2000	12.8	136	138
2250	15.5	153	155
2500	17.2	170	172
2650	18.4	180	184
3000	20.8	204	208

APPENDIX 19—THE BRITISH SUB AQUA CLUB TESTS

The tests shown below and on the following pages are those in use at the time of printing. *These are changed from time to time* and the secretary and/or diving officer of your branch will be able to inform you what changes, if any, have been made. This information is also available from the Director of Coaching, 70 Brompton Road, London SW3 1HA.

Measurements have not been metricated because at the time of writing the National Diving Committee have not detailed the equivalents.

In addition, it has been agreed within the BSAC that a medical certificate be made a compulsory condition of entry. And possibly again at certain intervals. However, full details are unavailable at this time.

It must be stressed that NO BRANCH HAS THE RIGHT TO ADD, OR SUBTRACT, FROM THE PROGRAMME THAT FOLLOWS. This is to ensure a uniform standard.

SNORKEL DIVER

In the following tests the various groups must be taken in sequence, and the tests in each group taken at one time in the sequence specified (except in the case of Snorkel Diving Test—Group D). Diving suits may be worn if buoyancy correction is made before commencing the tests.

Tests in the following two groups call for the use of basic equipment, ie, fins, mask and snorkel tube. Nose clips should not be worn, and the snorkel tube should be of the single bend open end type.

SWIMMING TEST

All tests in this group to be completed without equipment.

GROUP A
1 Swim 200 yards free style (except backstroke) without a stop.
2 Swim 100 yards backstroke without a stop.
3 Swim 50 yards wearing 10 lb weightbelt.
4 Float on back for five minutes (hand and leg movement permitted).
5 Tread water with hands above head for one minute.
6 Recover six objects from deep end of training pool (one dive per object).
N.B. Item 3—weight may be reduced for junior or lady members, or those with a low buoyancy index.

PRIMARY TESTS

Before commencing training for these tests the pupil must satisfy the branch Diving Officer that he is aware of the dangers of anoxia and of eardrum rupture and is in fact able to 'clear ears' by pressure equalisation through the eustachian tubes.

GROUP B
1 Sink basic equipment in deep end of training pool. Dive for each item in turn and fit at surface.
2 Fin 200 yards, surface diving every 25 yards.
3 Tow an adult 50 yards, by BSAC method which incorporates EAR in the water. Give at least 3 effective breaths in this distance. Land body and continue EAR.
4 Perform three rolls forward, three rolls backwards (breath may be taken between rolls).
5 Fin 15 yards under water.
6 Hold breath for 30 seconds under water.

GROUP C
1 Fin 50 yards wearing a 10 lb weightbelt.
2 Release weightbelt in deep end; remove mask.
3 Fin 50 yards face submerged, using snorkel tube, no mask.
4 Complete at deep end, replace mask, surface dive, recover and refit weightbelt. Give signal—I am OK—proceeding.
5 Fin further 50 yards wearing 10 lb weightbelt.

On completion of groups A, B and C, the pupil may, at the discretion of the branch Diving Officer, progress to pool aqualung training. Concurrently with this training he should gain practical open water experience of using basic equipment by taking the Open Water Snorkel Diving Test.

OPEN WATER SNORKEL DIVING TEST

Before commencing training for this test the pupil must satisfy the branch Diving Officer that he knows and thoroughly understands the hazards of doing any form of diving when suffering from a cold, ear or sinus infection, respiratory or heart weakness. If any doubt exists a medical certificate should be obtained.

GROUP D

1 Confirm physical fitness.
2 Fin 500 yards in open water wearing basic equipment.
3 Surface dive to a depth of 20 feet wearing basic equipment.
4 Perform a rescue of a Snorkel Diver in open water and tow for 50 yards by BSAC method.
5 Attend at least three Open Water Snorkel Diving meetings, using basic equipment.

LECTURES:

Branch and training organisation; choice and use of basic equipment; ears and sinuses; circulation and respiration; hypoxia, anoxia and drowning; rescue and resuscitation; signals and surfacing drill; exhaustion and exposure; diving suits and protective clothing; ancillary equipment; snorkelling activities.

On completion of Groups A-D inclusive and on passing an appropriate examination by the branch Diving Officer, the pupil may be rated by the branch Committee as a snorkel diver.

3rd CLASS DIVER

To qualify for the rating of 3rd Class Diver, the Snorkel Diver must undertake the following training in which the qualifying tests in the various groups must be taken in sequence, and the tests in each group taken at one time in the sequence specified (except in the case of Open Water Aqualung Test—group G).

INTERMEDIATE AQUALUNG TESTS

Before commencing training for these tests the pupil must satisfy the branch Diving Officer of his knowledge of the elementary diving hazards, viz: pressure effects, burst lung and exhaustion, and of his familiarity with the diver-to-surface code of signals.

The following two groups of tests should be carried out in a training pool or in other safe water where continuous observation and control of the pupil is possible. Diving suits may be worn when taking these tests.

GROUP E

1 Fit harness and demand valve to cylinder. Test and put on aqualung.
2 Sink all equipment in the deep end of the training pool. Dive and fit without surfacing.
3 Remove mouthpiece under water, replace and clear. Repeat twice more.
4 Remove mask under water, replace and clear. Repeat twice more.
5 Demonstrate mobility in aqualung by completing three forward and three backward rolls.
6 Demonstrate buoyancy control by adjusting diving level by depth of respiration. Breathe out hard, relax and lie on bottom. Lift off bottom by controlled inspiration.
7 Remove aqualung at surface in deep end, fit snorkel tube and fin 50 yards, towing aqualung.
8 Dismantle, clean and dry aqualung, and stow away to instructor's satisfaction.

GROUP F

1 Fin 100 yards on the surface as follows:
    (a) 50 yards alternating between snorkel tube and aqualung.
    (b) 50 yards on back wearing aqualung and carrying snorkel tube, but using neither.
2 Surface drill. Dive in deep end, remove mouthpiece, fit snorkel tube and, exhaling, surface, give signal. Repeat twice more.
3 Share aqualung with companion for 25 yards at a depth not greater than 10 feet.
4 Fin 50 yards underwater with mask blacked out, lead by companion or following a rope.
5 Fin 50 yards submerged at speed. Complete in deep end where companion is simulating insensibility. Release both weightbelts, bring 'body' to the surface and tow for 25 yards by BSAC method incorporating EAR while towing.
6 Remove both sets of equipment in the water, land 'body' (assistance permitted), and carry out artificial respiration.

OPEN WATER AQUALUNG TEST

On completion of Groups E & F the pupil may, at the discretion of the branch Diving Officer, progress to open water aqualung training.

GROUP G

1 Demonstrate in open water with aqualung the surfacing drill and code of diver-to-surface-party signals.
2 Demonstrate in open water with aqualung the correct adjustment of buoyancy when wearing a diving suit.
3 Carry out at least five open water dives to a depth of not less than 20 feet, and for submerged durations of not less than 15 minutes each. A diving suit must be worn for at least one of these dives.
4 On one open water dive rescue an aqualung diver. Tow 50 yards using BSAC EAR incorporated method, another diver may assist.

LECTURES:

Physics of diving; principles of the aqualung; aqualung use and buoyancy control; the ABLJ—its use and application; burst lung and emergency ascent; air cylinders and air endurance; compressors and recharging; open water diving; diving from small boats; decompression sickness—avoidance; nitrogen narcosis, CO poisoning, oxygen poisoning, CO_2 poisoning; deep diving and its problems.

2nd CLASS DIVER

To qualify for the rating of 2nd Class Diver, the 3rd Class Diver must log a minimum of 20 additional open water dives, under the direct supervision of the Branch Diving Officer or a Diving Marshal, each of these to be of a submerged duration of not less than 15 minutes.

Of these dives, 15 may be made in lakes, rivers or similar non-tidal waters. At least five must be made in the open sea.

Five of these dives must be made to depths of not less than 60 feet. The remainder must be made to depths of not less than 20 feet.

The candidate for 2nd Class Diver should act as Dive Leader on at least four occasions and also assist as Diving Marshal on at least two open water diving expeditions under the supervision of the branch Diving Officer.

These qualifying dives are not to be regarded solely as 'experience' dives, but are part of the continuous training programme. Thus during the course of this further training the candidate should demonstrate on open water dives his ability in the following manner to the satisfaction of the branch Diving Officer:

1 At a depth of 30 feet, remove, replace and clear mouthpiece, then remove, replace and clear mask.
2 Having first established a breathing and exchange rhythm, carry out two assisted ascents from 30 ft. to the surface; first, receiving air from companion, and on the 2nd occasion, providing air to companion.
3 Demonstrate ability to find the way and navigate underwater—use of compass permitted.
4 Act as tender to a roped diver, giving and receiving satisfactory signals for a period of not less than 15 minutes.
5 Plan and execute a search using a rope at a depth of not less than 20 feet.
6 Plan and execute a search in water of very low visibility.
7 Jump into water in full equipment from a height of not less than three feet above water level in a depth of not less than six feet. Repeat twice more. Use care to ensure unobstructed water.

LECTURES:

Decompression sickness—the condition and its treatment; underwater navigation; underwater search methods; roped diver operations; low visibility and night diving; basic seamanship; charts and tide Tables; basic navigation and position fixing; expeditions: advance planning and on-site conduct; expeditions: safety and emergency actions.

On completion of the above training and on passing an appropriate examination by the branch Diving Officer, the pupil may be rated by the branch Committee as a 2nd Class Diver.

1st CLASS DIVER

This is the highest diving qualification in the BSAC. It is a national qualification which cannot be given at branch level. Despite this, it is the branch's duty to see that facilities for attaining 1st Class are available to all members. This means that provision for taking the Deep Rescue Test and Sub Aqua Medallion are just as important as the tests of lower grades, and should be provided if possible.

Apart from the personal satisfaction of attaining 1st Class, the study and work involved leading up to the examination cannot fail but to make the candidate a better diver.

The 1st Class Diver is the person the Club calls upon when representation is required in a particular area—and the National Diving Committee consists largely of 1st Class Divers.

To qualify for a 1st Class Diver's Certificate the candidate must satisfy the following conditions:

1 Be a rated 2nd Class Diver.
2 Have been continuously a member of the Club for the past three years and be in the age group 20-50.
3 Submit properly certified Diving Logbooks showing a minimum of 100 open water dives under varying conditions. A proportion of these dives should show reasonable experience of depths greater than 100 feet.
4 Submit a medical certificate of physical fitness and written proof of a satisfactory chest X-ray, both obtained during the six months prior to the examination.
5 Submit a Royal Life Saving Society Sub Aqua Medallion, or equivalent qualification, obtained not more than three years prior to the examination.
6 Submit evidence of Deep Rescue Test.
7 Submit a letter of recommendation from his branch committee.
8 Satisfactorily complete a written examination set by the National Diving Officer.
9 Pass a practical diving test as required by the National Diving Officer.

On completion of the above conditions the member may, at the discretion of the General Committee of the Club be awarded a certificate of competency as 1st Class Diver.

Up-to-date details of the examination syllabus may be obtained from the 1st Class Examination Organiser, c/o BSAC H.Q.

A list is maintained of Active 1st Class Divers. To remain on this list a 1st Class Diver has to complete a minimum of 10 dives per year. The diver concerned should submit, to H.Q., a statement signed by his branch D.O. and Chairman that he has completed at least 10 dives. The statement should be received by H.Q. not later than December 31st.

CLUB INSTRUCTOR

To attain a Club Instructor rating it is necessary to attend a week-end course/examination. Qualifications for attending courses:

1 Minimum 2nd Class Diver rating.
2 Minimum 2 years BSAC membership.
3 Minimum age 21 years.
4 Proof of medical fitness (including recent X-ray certificate).
5 Branch letter of recommendation.
6 Course fee.

ADVANCED INSTRUCTOR

This is the next grade up from Club Instructor and equates with the International 2 Star Instructor grade. The course/examination is held over a weekend and is open to Club Instructors only.

BOATHANDLING COURSES

These courses are held over one weekend and are designed to aquaint divers with basic principles of small boat handling. Successful completion of a course is endorsed in the members' log book.

DEEP RESCUE TEST

This test was not designed for a 'pass' standard, but mainly to aquaint divers with the difficulties of a deep rescue. However successful completion of the test is endorsed in the members' log book. This endorsement is an essential qualification for entry to the 1st Class Diver examination.

INDEX

INDEX

Absorption of Light 60, 99–101, 435.
Accessories, Diving 206–218.
Adjustable Buoyancy Lifejackets ('ABLJ') see Lifejackets.
Advanced Instructor 507.
Air, analysis of 162–163, 200
— cylinders 189–205.
— purity 200
— testers 162–163, 200.
Air Embolism 133–134, 140, 220, 255.
— treatment 49
Anchoring 354–355, 405–406.
Anchors 343–346.
Animals 395–396.
Anoxia 121–122.
Anxiety 62.
Aqualung Consumption 245.
— Endurance 295–296
— Maintenance 228–229.
— Principles of 176–188.
— Removal 244.
— Retrieval 244–245.
— Training 18–20.
— Use of 241–248.
Aquaplane 218.
Archaeology 423–426.
Artificial Respiration 35–44.
— Aids 41.
— Manual Methods 43–44.
— Techniques 41–42.
Ascent, Assisted 132–133, 251–254, 256.
— Buoyant 255–256.
— Free 252–255.
— Hazards 131–135.
— In Emergency 132, 249–256.
— Rate 488.
Assisted Ascent 132–133, 251–254, 256.
Asthma 108.

Bags, lifting 217–218.
Basic Equipment 167–168.
— Training 18.
Baths discipline 468–469.
Beaufort Wind Scale 486.
Bends 141. See also Decompression Sickness.
— Causes of 142–146.
Berthing 356–357.
Bibliography 152, 163, 174, 256, 376, 426, 429, 434, 478–482.
Biology 427–429.
Bites 51.
Bleeding 45–46, 48.
Block and Tackles 341–343, 410.
Boat Handling 346–361, 508.
Bone Necrosis 141–142.
'Bottles', Air 189–205.
Bottom time 284, 488.
Boyles Law 84, 94, 136.
Breathing 64–66, 89–90, 239, 247, 295.

British Sub Aqua Club, Administration 465.
— Film Library 482.
— Tests 504–508.
Broken bones, limbs 50
Bronze Medallion 455–459.
'Buddy' lines 215, 273–274, 300.
Buoyancy 87–96, 173, 238, 242, 245–248, 290.
— for lifting 90–91, 410.
— of boats 346–347.
Buoyant Ascent 255–256.
Buoys, Diver's 213, 216.
— Wreck 408.
Burns 50.
Burst lung 131–135.

Cameras 436–439.
Carbon dioxide poisoning 153.
— production 125.
Carbon monoxide poisoning 49, 147.
Cardiac arrest 38–39.
Cave Diving 304–309, 417.
Cerebrovascular system 109.
Charts 377–379.
Check, pre-dive 241, 294, 327.
Chokes 140.
Circulation 117, 137–139.
— control of 122–124.
Claustrophobia 68, 288.
'Clearing' ears 237, 239.
Club Instructor 507.
Coaches 465.
Coastguard Stations 473–474.
Code, The Diver's 465–466.
Cold 62, 174, 297.
Colour underwater 101–102, 301.
— of equipment 103–104.
Coma position 26–27.
Committee for Nautical Archaeology 423, 425.
Compass, magnetic 208, 278–280, 362, 364, 367.
— Handbearing 364, 370.
— Maintenance 229.
— Steering 365.
Compressor 197–202.
— filter 198–199.
— lubrication 199.
— operation and maintenance 199–201.
Consecutive dives 145–146, 487.
Conservation 396.
Contact lenses 59–60, 99.
Containers, specimen 217.
Contamination of air 162–163.
Contents Gauge 212–213, 241.
Control of buoyancy 245–248.
Conversions 475–477, 501–503.
Convulsions 46, 155–156.
Coronary arterial disease 109.

511

Cousteau, Jacques 176–178.
Crabs 317, 395, 397, 474.
Cramp 51.
Currents 75–77, 414–416.
Cutting, underwater 409–410.
Cylinders, air 189–205.
— buoyancy 246.
— charging 190
— maintenance 228.
— recharging 195–197.
— testing 189–190.
— threads 194–195.

Dalton's Law 85, 95–96.
Dangers 396–397, 412–420.
Dark water, fear of 67.
Decanting 201–205.
Decompression, in practice 284–286.
— stops 255–256, 285–286, 487–488.
— tables 145, 285–286, 487–500.
Decompression Sickness 136–146, 149.
— prevention of 139–141, 488.
— symptoms of 129.
— treatment of 49, 149–150.
Deep Diving 248, 289–294, 419–420, 487.
— procedure 292–293.
Deep Rescue 250, 460–462, 508.
Deep Water EAR 32.
Demand Valve 176–188.
— fitting of 240–241.
— maintenance 229.
— position of 187–188.
— types of 178–187.
Denarouze, Auguste 176.
Density 79.
Depth and exhaustion 128–129.
Depth Gauges 209–211, 280.
— maintenance 229.
Diabetes 109.
Disorientation 116.
Distress signals 473.
Dive, conduct of 325–326.
— duration 488.
— leaders 323, 327–330, 468.
— marshalls 325–327, 333–334.
— planning 295–296, 324–325.
— procedures 326–329.
— reports 381–384.
Diver's companion 328.
— Code 465–466.
— Flag 264, 469–470.
— marker buoys 213, 216, 274, 301.
Dives, Consecutive 145–146, 487.
Diving, at night 299–303.
— boat 415–416.
— expeditions 331–334.
— for pleasure 392–393.
— in caves 304–309, 417.
— in harbours 418–419, 425, 426.
— in open water 323–330.
— in rivers 450.
— inland water 416–417, 426, 448.

— organisation in a large branch 466–468.
— Operations Special Regulations 482–485.
— Sea 414–415.
— Shore 412–414.
— under ice 297–298, 417.
— wreck 418–419.
Drugs 115.
Dry Suit 170–171.
— maintenance 228.
Duck Dive 234–236.
Dumas, Frederic 176.

Ear plugs 238.
Ears 109–116, 235–238.
Echo Sounder 362, 365–366, 369, 371, 403.
Effects of Pressure 84–86, 113, 126–127, 237.
Emergency Ascent 132, 250–256.
Embolism—see Air Embolism.
Emphysema, Interstitial 134.
— treatment 49.
Entry methods 416.
Environmental stresses 61–63.
Epilepsy 108.
Equipment, maintenance of 227–229, 326.
Eustachian tube 112, 114–115, 237.
Evaporation 82.
Exercise, effects of 122–124.
Exertion 128–130.
Exhaustion 128–130.
Expedition Leaders 323, 326, 331, 333, 467.
Expeditions 331–334, 467–468.
— Scientific 385–391.
Expired Air Rescuscitation ('EAR') 26, 32, 36–38, 456, 459.
Exploration 392–397.
Explosives 409.
Exposure, film 440–441.
Extended tow 30–32.
External Cardiac Massage 38–39.
Eye, The 97.

Factories Act 418.
Fainting 51.
Fear, of dark water 67.
— of surfacing 67.
— of weed 68.
Film Library, BSAC, 482.
Filters, compressor 198–199.
Fin retainers 218.
Fins 167.
— maintenance of 227.
— use of 234–236.
First Aid 45–55.
— kit 53–55.
First Class Diver 14, 507.
First dive 19–20, 329–330.
Fish 313–316, 396–397.
— Law 474–475.
— Ring 217, 312.

Fishermen 448–450.
Fitness for diving 107, 289, 390.
Flag—see Diver's Flag.
Flares 215.
Floats, Diver's 213, 216.
Flying after Diving 286.
Fog 472.
Foul Air Poisoning 49.
Fractures 50.
Free Ascent Procedure 252–255.

Gagnan, Emile 176–178.
Gaseous exchange 120–121.
Gas Laws 94–96.
— Composition 137.
Gauges, contents 212–213.
Geology 430–434.

Hands 173–174.
Hand Signals—see Signals.
Harbour diving 418–419, 425–426.
Harness, aqualung 240–241.
Headache 51.
Hearing 61, 275.
Heart 117.
Heat loss 173–174; 290.
High tide 472–473.
Hoods, fluorescent 213–214.
Hook, crab 218.
Housings, camera 437–439.
Hulls 353.
Hydrostatic pressure 91.
Hyperventilation 239.
Hypothermia, effects of 129, 169.
— symptoms 50.
— treatment 51.
Hypoxia 121–122.

Ice diving 297–298, 417.
Inflatables 353, 356–357.
Inland water 416–417, 426, 448.
Instruction 16–18.
— techniques 20–21.
Instructor, Advanced 507.
— Club 507.
Insurance 323, 418, 446.
Internal waves 80–81.
Interstitial emphysema 134.
Itches 141.

Jellyfish 397.

Knife 206–208, 288, 298.
— maintenance 229.
Knots 270, 339–341.

Landing 358.
Launching 357–358.
Laws, Fish 474–475.
— of working underwater 482–485.
— of wreck and salvage 411.
Lectures 15–18.
Leeway 373–374.

Le Prieur, Commander 176.
Lifejackets 90, 219–226, 248, 255–256, 290.
— maintenance 229.
Lifelines 269–271, 278.
Lifesaving 25–32, 455–459.
Lifting 90, 410.
— bags 217–218.
Limiting Line 488.
Lines, safety 266–267.
— at night 302–303.
— in caves 305–307.
Lobsters 317, 395, 397, 474.
Logbooks 381–384.
Low visibility diving 287–288.
Lungs 118–121.

Maintenance of equipment 227–229.
Marine Biology 427–429.
Marker buoys 213, 216, 274, 301.
Masks 167–168.
— clearing 242.
— maintenance of 227.
— use of 233–235.
Medical certificates 107–111.
— examination 107–108.
Mental attitude 64–69.
— fatigue 129.
— illness 108.
Metrication 500–502.
Miniflares 215.
Mouthpiece, removal 242–243.
'*Mouth to mouth*' resuscitation 37.—See also Expired Air Resuscitation.
'*Mouth to nose*' resuscitation 37–38.

Nasal sprays 115.
Navigation 275–283, 362–376.
Neoprene suits 172–173.
Nervous system 108.
Night diving 299–303.
Nitrogen Absorption 148–150, 284, 291.
Nitrogen Narcosis 63, 151–152, 284.

Observation 393–394.
Open Water training 22–24.
— diving 323–330.
Orientation 61, 275–276.
Oxygen, consumption 125.
— poisoning 154–161.
— toxicity 291.

Pain 47.
Painting equipment 102–104.
Panic 23, 407.
Partial pressure 85, 95–96.
Photography 435–441.
'*Pick up*' procedure 354.
Pillar valves 191–194.
Pilotage 276–278.
Planning—see Dive Planning.
Plotting a course 372–378.
Pneumothorax, treatment 49.

INDEX

Poisoning 49.
Position, sense of—see Orientation.
Pre-dive check 241, 294, 327.
Preserving 427, 429.
Pressure 84.
— atmospheric 136.
— effects of 84–86, 113, 126–127, 148–150, 237.
— gauge 212–213, 229, 241, 296.
— hydrostatic 91.
— increase in 136.
— partial 85, 95–96.
— water 136.
Protective clothing 169–174.
Public Relations 445–451.
Pulmonary barotrauma 131.

Raising objects 398–399.
Rashes 141.
Rate of ascent 488.
Recharging 195–197.
Recompression chambers 473.
Reduction of light 100–102.
Refraction 59.
Regulator—see Demand Valve.
Relaxation 66.
Repeat Dives 145–146.
Repetitive dives 145–146.
Rescue 25–32.
— Deep 250, 460–462.
— methods 27–32.
Reserve 296.
Respiration 117–127, 137–139.
— control of 124–125.
Respiratory Arrest 35.
— Obstruction 36.
— System 108.
Resuscitation 35–44.
Rocks 430–434.
Ropes and Roping 266–274, 335–341.
Rouquayrol, Benoit 176.
Rudder 353.

Safety 412–420.
— line 266–267.
Salinity 82–83.
Salvage 408–411.
Scalds 50.
Scattering, of light 60, 90.
Scientific Expeditions 385–391.
Screw 352–353.
Sea, The 73–83, 414.
— Scale 470.
— State 353.
Seamanship 335–361.
Searches 280–283, 398, 404, 446–447.
Sea sickness 52.
Seaweed 395, 429.
Second Class Diver 14, 24, 447, 506.
Senses 59–61, 275–276.
Sextants 362, 365, 369, 374.
'Sharing' 251–254.

Shock 52–53.
Shore diving 412–414.
Signals 257–265, 267.
— Distress 473.
Silvester-Brosch method of resuscitation 43–44.
Single hose demand valve 186–187.
Sinuses 109, 113–115.
Slates 217.
Snorkel diving 233–239, 246–247.
— aqualung cover 262, 413.
— tests 504–505.
— training 18.
Snorkels 168.
— maintenance of 227.
— use of 233–236, 298.
Sound signals 264–265.
Spearfishing 310–319.
— Competition Rules 317–319.
Spearguns 310–311, 315, 475.
Spontaneous Pneumothorax 134.
Squeeze 142.
Standby diver 267, 287.
Station pointer 370–371, 375.
Stings 51.
Stops—see Decompression Stops.
Sub Aqua Bronze Medallion 455–459.
Suits, dry and wet 170–173.
Sunburn 50.
Surface Lifejacket—see Lifejackets.
Surfacing, drill 249–256, 328–329.
— fear of 67.
Swell Scale 472.
Swimming Test 15, 504.
Syncope 51.

Tables—see Decompression Tables.
Teeth 109.
Temperature 79–80, 417.
Tests, BSAC 504–508.
— Deep Rescue 460–462.
Theory lectures 15–18.
Thermocline 79–80.
Third Class Diver 13–14, 20, 24, 27, 505–506.
Tides 73–75, 379–380, 472–473.
Topography, undersea 478.
Torches 217, 280, 288, 300, 302, 406.
Touch 23, 61.
Towing 360–361.
Training organisation 13–24, 466–468.
— considerations 23–24.
— courses 20.
— in open water 22–24.
Transits 363, 367, 375, 401–402.
Turning 359–360.
Twin hose demand valve 179–185.

Unconsciousness 26, 239.
Underwater
— cameras 436–439.
— navigation 275–283.
— work 418–419, 445–447.

Valves— demand 176–188.
— pillar 191–194.
Vertigo 116.
Vision, underwater 59, 97–104, 275.
Visual Aids, 17, 21.
Volume, change of 88.

Watches 211, 280.
Waves 77, 350, 358.
— internal 80–81.
Weather 325, 348–350, 470–472.
Weed 395.
— fear of 68.

Weight, change of 88.
Weight Belt 175.
— fitting 241.
— jettison 243, 249.
— maintenance 228.
Weightlessness 61.
Wet suit 171–173.
— buoyancy of 246.
— maintenance 227–228.
Whipping 341.
Wind 350, 373, 486.
Wrecks 398–411, 418, 424–425.

X-ray 110.